D0108397

NEW YORK INSTITUTE OF FINANCE

SECURITIES OPERATIONS

SECOND EDITION

A GUIDE TO OPERATIONS
AND INFORMATION SYSTEMS
IN THE SECURITIES INDUSTRY

MICHAEL T. REDDY

NEW YORK INSTITUTE OF FINANCE

Library of Congress Cataloging-in-Publication Data

Reddy, Michael T.
    Securities operations : a guide to operations and information
systems in the securities industry / Michael T. Reddy. — 2nd ed.
        p.   cm.
    Includes index.
    ISBN 0-13-161044-9
    1. Securities industry—Data processing.   2. Information
technology.   I. Title.
HF4515.5.R44   1994   94-38882
332.63'2'0285—dc20   CIP

Printed in the United States of America

10   9   8   7   6

This publication is designed to provide accurate and authoritative information in regard to the subject matter covered. It is sold with the understanding that the publisher is not engaged in rendering legal, accounting, or other professional service. If legal advice or other expert assistance is required, the services of a competent professional person should be sought.
—*From the Declaration of Principles jointly adopted by a Committee of the American Bar Association and a Committee of Publishers and Associations*

ISBN 0-13-161044-9

 NEW YORK INSTITUTE OF FINANCE
Paramus, NJ 07652

On the World Wide Web at http://www.phdirect.com

NYIF and NEW YORK INSTITUTE OF FINANCE
are trademarks of Executive Tax Reports, Inc.
used under license by Prentice Hall Direct, Inc.

DEDICATION

To
my children,
Michael and Cathy

For
my sister, Kay,
who taught me that
persistence and determination
could make up for my woeful
lack of talent

ABOUT THE AUTHOR

Michael T. Reddy is Chairman of FCI Incorporated, a management and technology consulting firm providing services to financial institutions such as securities and commodities firms, banks, mutual funds, insurance companies, securities and commodities exchanges, securities depositories, and clearing corporations in the international marketplace.

A recognized authority on the securities industry, Mr. Reddy was previously a Senior Vice President of Merrill Lynch, Pierce, Fenner & Smith Incorporated, where he was responsible for International Operations, Systems and Telecommunications, U.S. Capital Markets Operations and Systems, and U.S. Consumer Markets Operations. He also spent nine years in the Operations Division of J.P. Morgan & Co. Mr. Reddy has served on the Board of Directors of the Options Clearing Corporation, the Intermarket Clearing Corporation, the International Securities Clearing Corporation and NASD Market Services, Inc. He was a member of the Working Committee of the Group of Thirty that recently presented recommendations to improve worldwide clearance and settlement of securities, a past Chairman of the Operations Committee of the Securities Industry Association, and has served on various other industry committees. He has lectured at the Centre d'Enselgnement et de Recherche Appliques du Management (CERAM) in Nice, France, appeared on the *Today Show*, has been quoted in the *Wall Street Journal*, and the *New York Times*, the *Los Angeles Times American Banker*, and the *Financial Times (London)*, and has testified before U.S. House and Senate committees addressing various Securities Industry matters. He is currently an Adviser to the Securities Industry Association on Clearance and Settlement issues, and is a member of the Operations Committee of the NASD.

Mr. Reddy holds a Bachelors Degree in Finance and Business Administration from Pace University and is a graduate of Harvard Business School's Advanced Management Program.

INTRODUCTION

Since the first edition of the book was published, securities processing in the U.S. has undergone major changes and will see even greater changes as the year 2000 approaches. Most of the changes are aimed at increasing safety and soundness in the U.S. marketplace, and reducing risk for investors and other market participants. This revised edition expands on the processing methods of clearing corporations and depositories, provides updates to international tax regulations, discusses changes in options processing and, most importantly, provides information on the U.S. efforts to change the settlement date for most corporate and municipal securities transactions from five days after trade date to three days after trade date. This compression of the settlement date is required by Securities and Exchange Commission Rule 15c6-1, which becomes effective on June 1, 1995.

The revised edition provides background on this rule, information on which securities transactions are included and excluded and regulatory issues to be considered. The revision also discusses mandated book-entry-only processing requirements, expected new depository eligibility requirements and changes in Institutional Delivery processing at securities depositories. In addition the revision discusses changes that are necessary for securities firms and banks to consider in preparation for T+3 processing, particularly in the areas of Operations, Information Systems, Sales, Regulatory/ Compliance and Finance/Accounting.

Other new chapters discuss implementation of a Same Day Funds Settlement System and changes that will most likely occur in the near future in the area of retail registration, an industry-wide glossary and cross-margining/cross-collateralization efforts.

This book describes the "back office" (Operations) and "data processing" (Information Systems) functions of Wall Street's securities industry. The explosion of securities trading in international markets during the 1980s, and the market crash in October of 1987, resulted in many countries examining the need to develop systems that assure the efficient and effective processing of paper and information that accompany securities trading. In recent years, a number of international organizations have focused their attention on the worldwide operations problems associated with national and international securities trading. The Federation International des Bourses de Valeurs, the International Society of Securities Administrators and the Group of Thirty, a consultative group on international economic and monetary affairs, have all recently examined the issues of clearance and settlement of securities transactions. In addition, countries like Spain, France, England, Switzerland, Italy, Japan, Hong Kong, Belgium, and others are examining their markets with the aim of modernizing their Operations and Information Systems.

Professionals in securities firms in these countries will benefit from the U.S. experience of the late 1960s when the "paperwork crunch" of that period almost brought the U.S. markets to a halt. The United States moved to ensure that would not occur by modernizing its operations and systems infrastructure—thereby reducing costs of capital, increasing liquidity and generating investor confidence. Personnel in United States firms will learn more about the basic mechanics of Wall Street's processing, as well as the unique requirements needed to support international trading.

For Operations and Systems professionals throughout the world, the book provides specific information on how to provide the back office support for cashiering, transfer, margin, branch office operations and to design the data processing systems necessary in today's "high tech" environment. Sales, Trading and Administrative professionals will learn how to support new products, manage technology, reduce operations expenses and develop reporting mechanisms for regulatory authorities. Finance and Human Resource professionals will gain firsthand knowledge on how to analyze operations and systems processing, reduce capital charges, manage the regulatory environment and determine what training needs are important for operations and systems personnel. Finally, Executive Management will learn firsthand how to manage technology in today's dynamically changing multi-currency world, how to organize for customer service and reduce costs, and how to integrate operations and systems efforts with sales and trading objectives.

HOW THIS BOOK IS ORGANIZED

The book is organized by function performed. The first chapter provides a non-technical description of the role of securities firms, products offered, the functions of stock exchanges, the roles played by Sales, Trading, Investment Banking, Finance, Administration, Operations and Information Systems. The remaining Operations chapters are presented with specifics on how to process a trade, perform Cashiering, Transfer, Dividend, Reorganization, Margin functions and work with Clearing Corporations and Depositories. Options Processing and Securities Lending and Borrowing are discussed separately because of the specialized nature of these activities. Support requirements for Branch Office Operations, Information Reporting, New Products, Customer Service, Human Resource Activities, Records Management and Managing in Emergencies are discussed in detail.

The Information Systems chapters begin with a discussion of the Evolution of Information Systems in the Securities Industry, describe what has been driving the Growth of Technology in the industry and provide specifics on how to build a Model to Manage the Information Systems resource. Specific details of the systems supporting Operations are followed by a discussion of how to go about Systems Planning, Systems Development and Data Center Management. Action steps for Organizing and Administrating the Information Systems function follow and the last chapter focuses on planning for tomorrow's Information Systems with specifics on Technology Architecture, Organizational Issues, Emerging Technologies and the Role of the Future Information Systems Executive.

In addition to the many revisions discussed above, modifications have also been made to the emerging technology section and completely new chapters have been added to this book, which discuss: Implementing T+3 Settlement in the U.S., Same Day Funds Settlement, and Future Changes to U.S. Clearance and Settlement Practices.

I have been a participant in the global efforts of the securities industry for many years and have seen the need for a basic guide to the fundamental operations of a securities firm. Whether in Europe, Hong Kong, Japan or Australia, it's evident that those responsible for providing Operations and Information Systems support will benefit from the experiences of U.S. firms during the era of automation that took place from the 1960s through the 1990s. *Securities Operations* gives a clear picture of what happens "behind the scenes" from the point after an order is received to final delivery of a product to a client's account. Many international firms are now going through similar growth phases in the development of their Operations and Information Systems areas that U.S. firms have been through in the past. *Securities Operations* shares the knowledge that has been gained in this period, the positive achievements that have been made, as well as the lessons that have been learned from the mistakes that are inevitable when change takes place.

ACKNOWLEDGMENTS

It is impossible for one person to write a book of this nature without an enormous amount of help. For their assistance in preparing this revised edition, I am deeply grateful to the following professionals and to their organizations: Toni Fibkins, Ed Adinolfi of the Options Clearing Corporation, Ron Marshall, Glen Mangold, Bruce Garland and Bill Jaenike of The Depository Trust Company, Stu Goldstein, Steve Labriola, Bob Schultz, Mike Malloy, John Vettros, Bob Woldow, Jim Ronayne and Dave Kelly of National Securities Clearing Corporation, Phyllis Cassar, Claudette Hanlan and Don Kittell of the Securities Industry Association, Fred Enriquez, Fran Maristany, Tom Tierney, Arthur Thomas and Debra Uhlfelder of Merrill Lynch and Ron Gimpel, Dawn Mastrapasqua and all my other associates at FCI Incorporated.

I also owe a debt of gratitude to a number of organizations and their staffs, particularly Merrill Lynch & Co., who granted permission to reprint a number of forms included in both editions and for the use of other resources that contributed to the final manuscript: the American Stock Exchange, Cedel, The Depository Trust Company, Euroclear, the Group of Thirty, the International Society of Securities Administrators, the National Association of Securities Dealers, the National Securities Clearing Corporation, the New York Stock Exchange, the Options Clearing Corporation, and the Securities Industry Association.

The following securities industry professionals also contributed to the first or second edition and I was extremely fortunate to have their assistance: Rudley Anthony, Michael Baker, Paul Baneky, Bill Bradley, Sheila Brody, Mary Ann Callahan, Alice Clark, Michael Clark, Sam Cohen, Kevin Davis, Chuck DeVito, Bob Dieckmann, Pat DiMattia, Gary Dolan, Fred Enriquez, John Failla, Neil Ferri, Carlos Figueroa, Joseph Fitzpatrick, Barbara Friedman, Ed Frischer, Susan Gammage, John Geelan, Julian Gibbs, John Ginelli, Ann Gofton, Al Golden, Francis Goodwin, Raymond Gottardi, Yvonne Hanna, Scott Harrison, John Hiatt, Al Howell, Al Hutwagner, Michael Keane,

David Kelly, Bill Kelvie, James Kukulski, Robert Larkin, Mel Levine, Jerry Lynch, Jay Manning, Frances Maristany, Dan Mayo, Rose Mazzo, John McCormick, Paul McHugh, Colleen McVey, Kurt Meuche, Chris Milton-Hall, Paul Morelli, Bob Moskowitz, George Mugno, Jim Murtha, Ben O'Callaghan (deceased), Pat O'Connor, Joseph Palmeri, Ed Pandolfo, Susan Perri, Ed Piscina, Salvatore Potenzano, John Puccio, Ron Readmond, Fred Rojas, Sam Romanzo, Lisa Rose, Ralph Roth, James Russo, Patricia Russo, Joe Schenk, Michael Schreier, John Scrobola, Howard Sorgen, Iggy Souto, Sam Spinello, Jan Temkiewicz, Art Thomas, Henning Tonsmann, Judith Welcom, Eric Wilkes, Hank Williams, Chuck Winters, Robert Woldow, and other friends and colleagues, particularly those at Merrill Lynch, whom I may have inadvertently not mentioned.

The technical aspects of this book have been improved enormously by the contributions of all of the above. If there are errors, they are mine alone.

CONTENTS

1
The Securities Firm

2
Order Processing

3
Cashiering

4
Transfer Services

5
Dividend/Interest Processing

6
The Reorganization Department

7
Clearing Corporations and Depositories

8
Supporting International Business

9
Options Operations

10
The Margin Department

11
Securities Lending and Borrowing

12
Branch Office Operations

13
Operations Management Information Reporting

14
New Product Support

15
Customer Service

16
Human Resource Strategies for Training and Development

17

Records Management

18

Planning for Emergencies

19

Information Systems in Securities Firms

20

Systems Supporting Securities Firms' Operations

21

Functional Responsibilities of Information Systems Departments

22

Information Systems Organization and Administration

23

Planning for Tomorrow's Information Systems

24
Implementation of T + 3 Settlement in the United States

25
Same-Day Funds Settlement System and How It Will Work

26
Future Changes in U.S. Clearance and Settlement Practices

CHAPTER 1

The Securities Firm

Before we get into the specific functions of Operations and Information Systems in securities firms, let's take a look at what the securities business is all about. While most of you are generally familiar with various departments in Operations and Information Systems, it's always helpful to step back and gain an understanding of the entire firm. So let's review the role of securities firms, describe basic products offered and discuss the most common market places (Exchanges, OTC, Money Markets). Then we'll look at the major revenue producing areas and introduce the support functions of Operations and Information Systems.

THE ROLE OF THE SECURITIES FIRM

Securities firms have three major functions in the financial market:

1. They provide a capital raising mechanism by linking people who have money (investors) to those who want to raise money (issuers, e.g. corporations, governments, partnerships).

2. They provide a pricing mechanism for the value of investments.

3. They provide a mechanism for investors to liquidate their investments.

In fulfilling these roles, securities firms are also product generators, they act as agent and/or principal in the buying and selling of listed and unlisted (OTC) securities, and they provide investment advice for individuals, corporations and governments.

CAPITAL RAISING ROLE

Most of you are familiar with the term "financial intermediary"—a public or private institution that acts as principal or agent between a lender of funds and a borrower of funds. Securities firms (as well as banks and insurance companies, et al.) are major financial intermediaries by virtue of their capital raising roles. Simply put, they serve as channels for the flow of funds from certain sectors of the economy that have money to invest to other sectors that are looking to raise money. Securities firms generally fulfill this role in their Investment Banking and brokerage activities.

PRICING MECHANISM ROLE

The securities industry, through listed exchanges and the Over-the-Counter market, provides a pricing mechanism to give an investor a realistic appraisal of the value of his/her particular investment.

The most familiar of these mechanisms are the listed exchanges. We will discuss the most well-known of these exchanges later on in this chapter and also provide an understanding of how other markets, such as those for securities which are not listed on exchanges, operate. The listed exchanges publish prices of the value of the companies listed on their exchanges on a daily basis in the financial press. In addition, the securities of many major companies that are not listed on exchanges are also published in the same financial press. The ability of the securities industry to provide this information to investors on a timely basis is one reason why the capital markets of the United States are among the finest in the world.

LIQUIDITY MECHANISM ROLE

Investors like to be able to move their cash into investments and from investments into cash in a very stable environment. The securities firms hope to move in and out of those investments for their customers without suffering a major loss on the value of investments. The firms in those markets that we know as "securities firms" provide that very important mechanism to the investor. In most investments in listed securities and over-the-counter securities today, for example, an investor can generally move in and out of those investments on a daily basis without suffering a major loss on the value of his/her investment (at least not because of the trading mechanism). In other words, there may be external factors that would affect the value of the investment, such as rumors of a financial problem in the economy, but the value generally does not shrink simply because of the market mechanism.

PROLIFERATING THE PRODUCT REVOLUTION

Securities firms are also product generators in that, by paying attention to customer needs, they provide customers with various ways to invest their money. Present day securities firms are continually developing and refining financial instruments tailored to specific customer needs. Such products would be tailored for example, for capital growth, dividend return, or tax sheltering of capital.

FINANCIAL ADVICE

The full-service securities firm not only executes orders for its clients, but also engages in various kinds of investment counseling. Full-service securities firms generally provide extensive research information to corporations and individuals.

This research is valuable because research departments spend extensive time analyzing markets, industries and particular companies. Whether the client is a corporation or individual, the counseling takes the form of:

1. Obtaining information on the customer's goals, e.g., capital gains or income generation. It is also important to understand the customer's penchant for risk-taking and his/her tax bracket.
2. Providing information on a wide range of possible investments and their long term/short term potential.

3. Providing advice on the possible trend of the securities markets in the long and short term.

4. Providing information on fiscal and monetary initiatives by governments as they relate to the investments being considered.

5. Providing recommendations that match the investment, investment climate and investor needs.

A dedicated Investment Counselor, Account Executive, Financial Consultant, etc. should be able to determine investment policies that provide for appropriate allocation of funds among a myriad of possible investment vehicles, considering the tax requirements of the client as well as the client's other financial needs, goals, objectives and requirements.

INVESTMENT PRODUCTS

Securities firms buy and sell a great variety of securities for their customers. In recent years, the types of securities have been proliferating at a rapid pace due to many factors, including greater market volume and volatility, increased consumer awareness of financial markets and marketing efforts of the securities firms. While discussions in this book will focus mainly on the support processes that securities firms use to deliver products to clients, it is important that you have an understanding of the products and markets under discussion. Each product requires processing in a unique way—processing that allows for only a small margin of error and the quality of which can be an important factor in the marketplace.

In addition to equities (common and preferred) and corporate bonds, with which most of you are somewhat familiar, securities firms now sell municipal (state and local) bonds, options, mutual funds of various types (money market funds, closed-end and open-end mutual funds, bond funds), futures, warrants, tax shelters, packaged real estate investments and various hybrid products. New or derivative products are constantly being devised as the marketplace and the economic climate change.

The following section describes the most common securities offered by securities firms and provides a general background on the markets within which these securities are offered to consumers.

TYPES OF SECURITIES

In the next few paragraphs, we'll look at the most common types of securities investments: stocks, bonds, options, mutual funds, money market investments and warrants.

STOCKS

Stock represents ownership interest in the assets and earnings of a company after allowance is made for obligations owed by the company. As most of you know, stocks are often referred to as "equities" in this sense. A firm generally issues stock to raise money to operate and expand its business and/or as a form of dividend. The maximum number of shares that a firm may issue is indicated in its charter. This maximum number of shares may be changed from time to time by action of the stockholders or "shareowners."

VARIOUS TYPES OF STOCK

The various types of stock are best described according to the rights their holders are eligible to receive. Common stock generally awards the greatest privileges in the form of ownership, voting rights and dividends, and carries the greatest risks. Since common stockholders have final claim on all earnings and assets (although dividends on preferred stock, interest payments and other debts generally must be paid off before common stockholders are eligible to receive any earnings) the value of their stock can increase far above the value of other owners, such as preferred stockholders. This privilege potentially offsets the market risks involved in holding common stock.

The other general class of stock is "preferred stock." Holders of preferred stock have priority claims on assets and earnings over common stockholders. In most cases, preferred stock is nonparticipating, which means holders of these shares have no voting privileges. Preferred stock can be cumulative, so that if management is unable to pay dividends on the shares in any given year, the dividends will accrue and be paid when sufficient funds exist. However, there is no guarantee that dividends will ever be paid. "Convertible preferred stock" allows certain preferred stock to be converted into common stock. "Callable preferred stock" generally offers the company the right to recall the issued stock at the original cost plus a premium, so that if interest rates decline, for example, the firm can reissue it at a lower interest rate.

CORPORATE AND MUNICIPAL BONDS

A bond is an instrument generally issued by a corporation or a government recognizing a debt to the bondholder. Bonds pay interest at a fixed or variable rate and generally have a fixed maturity date. Bondholders expect to receive periodic interest payments, usually semiannually, and full reimbursement on their original investment at maturity. A bond does not represent ownership in the firm and any liability is generally null and void upon repayment by the issuer. Bonds usually have maturity dates anywhere from one to thirty years. However, some bonds have an even longer term. Bonds are, therefore, classified as short, intermediate or long term. Bonds may be either registered or bearer bonds. The holder of a registered bond receives interest payments from the issuer whose name appears printed on the face of the document. On the other hand, bearer bonds place full responsibility on the holder to collect interest by redeeming coupons attached to the bond certificate.

There is an increasing trend in the securities industry toward registered rather than bearer bonds and, in fact, toward "certificate-less" stocks and bonds in which the holder is registered only on the books of the issuer and does not receive a certificate. Corporations, municipalities and the U.S. Federal government all issue bonds. Corporate bonds are traded on exchanges and in the Over-the-Counter market. Municipals bonds, issued on the local and state level to raise funds for municipalities, are traded in the Over-the-Counter market. Figures 1-1 and 1-2 will give you a listing of the most common types of corporate and municipal bonds.

Types	Description
Mortgage Bond	Property holdings are used as security for the loan. They may be close-ended whereby original creditors have senior claims or open-ended whereby all creditors enjoy equal claims.
Collateral Trust	These bonds are secured by the collateral of another corporation.
Equipment Trust	Equipment is generally pledged as a guarantee. This type of bond is commonly used by the railroad, trucking, and airline industries.
Debentures	Secured only by the good faith and name of the issuing company.
Income Bonds	These bonds only pay interest if the company shows a profit.
Floating Rates Bonds	The issuer retains the right to adjust the interest rate.
Zero Coupon Bonds	Issued at a discount from its face value with a maturity of more than one year. The holder does not receive periodic interest payments but instead receives a lump payment.

FIGURE 1-1. Most Common Types of Corporate Bonds

Types	Description
General Obligations Bonds	This type of bond is backed by the "full faith, credit, and taxing power of the issuer."
Revenue Bonds	Issued to finance projects that will generate income. The bonds are backed by this income.
Industrial Revenue Bonds or Industrial Development Bonds	Used to raise capital for building industrial plants. These bonds generate increased tax revenue and a corporation is responsible for the maturing lease.
Special Tax Bond	The bond debt is paid for by an excise tax on certain luxury items, mainly gasoline, liquor, or tobacco products.
New Housing Authority Bonds	Issued to finance housing projects and are paid by tax revenues.

FIGURE 1-2. Most Common Types of Municipal Bonds

U.S. GOVERNMENT BONDS

U.S. Government bonds, which are primarily traded on OTC with some odd lots transacted on the Exchanges, are the most secure bonds as they are backed by the guarantee of the U.S. Government. Bonds that are issued from special agencies of the government are another category and include, for example, Government National Mortgage Association bonds or "Ginnie Maes," and Federal National Mortgage Association bonds, or "Fannie Maes."

THE GROWING EMPHASIS ON OPTIONS

An option is a security that provides the owner with the right to buy or sell the underlying security at a fixed price for a specified length of time. The two basic forms of option contracts are "puts" and "calls." A put is an option giving the owner the right to sell a security at a stated price at anytime within the contracted period. A call is an option giving the owner the right to buy a security under the same conditions. The person who sells the option is called the writer of the option, and the buyer is called the owner or holder. Put and call contracts are generally written for three, six or nine months. A put or call is sold by an option writer for a cash consideration, commonly called the premium or option price. The premium is the amount the buyer pays for an option and is what the writer receives in return for granting the option.

Options are generally written or purchased to increase the rate of return on investments, to hedge against potential losses and as speculation. The vast majority of options trading today occurs on securities exchanges, although options can be traded over-the-counter. Exchange listed options are presently available on stocks, bonds, U.S. Treasury securities, securities indices and foreign currencies.

MUTUAL FUNDS

Mutual funds pool the assets of many small investors. These pooled assets are then managed by professionals who are able, as a result of the pooling, to have enough capital to buy and sell a variety of securities in a diversified portfolio, rather than just a few securities. The managers of these funds receive a fee for their work. No-load mutual funds are marketed without a commission charge; load funds charge a commission each time shares change hands.

The price of open-end funds is based directly on the net asset value of the fund. Investors can sell their shares back to the fund at the current net asset value. Closed-end funds do not stand ready to repurchase shares. When owners of closed-end funds wish to sell their shares, they may sell them in the over-the counter market or on the exchange the fund is listed with. Their price fluctuates with the supply and demand for shares of the fund.

The number of mutual funds has been rapidly proliferating in recent years. Mutual Funds with portfolios including only equities and bonds have been joined by specialized funds, such as those investing in foreign securities or technology companies.

MONEY MARKET INSTRUMENTS

Money market instruments are generally low risk, highly liquid, short-term (less than one year) debt securities. In recent years medium term notes (one to five years in maturity) have been added to this category. Other examples of money market instruments are commercial paper (unsecured short-term promissory notes, the direct obligations of their issuers), Bankers Acceptances, negotiable Certificates of Deposit and Municipal Notes.

WARRANTS

Warrants are similar to call options, since they entitle the holder to buy a fixed amount of a security at a specified price generally within a specified time limit. However, the exercise of an option involves paying the writer of the option for the stock. In the case of a warrant, the exerciser pays the issuing company. In addition, the time period over which the warrant holder has the right to buy the stock is generally substantially longer than the exercise period of a call.

Warrants, the exercise price of which is usually above the market price of the underlying common stock at the time of their issue, often are used as "sweeteners" and accompany bonds or preferred stocks as part of a package, or are issued in exchange for other securities as part of a reorganization or in a voluntary exchange. Once the warrant is issued it usually is detachable from the rest of the "package" and may be traded as a separate instrument, the value of which is derived from the security on which it is based.

PRIMARY MARKETPLACES

The most fundamental function of any market is to bring together sellers and buyers so that trading can be conducted continuously. A continuous market is swift, easy, and helps to curb heavy price fluctuations and spreads. In summary, the benefits of good securities markets are information, liquidity, low transaction cost, small adjustment of prices on the basis of new information, and the ability to absorb large volumes of securities sales. There are three basic markets that we will address in this chapter: Exchange Markets, Over-the-Counter Markets and the Money Markets.

THE FUNCTIONS OF THE EXCHANGE MARKETS

Exchange Markets provide trading facilities for stocks, bonds and/or options. These markets are generally (there are major exceptions) characterized by "auction" principles, where bids and offers are directed to central trading locations and executed by brokers and/or specialists. The specialist's main function is to provide an orderly market for the securities he/she is responsible for. "Orderly," in this sense, means a market that generally does not have large price fluctuations, and where securities can be bought and sold at any time the exchange is open for trading. Exchanges have requirements that corporations must meet before their securities will be accepted for listing. These requirements generally focus on the number of shares outstanding, the profitability of the corporation, the number of shareowners, etc. In the United States, the New York Stock Exchange is probably the best known of the securities exchanges because it is the largest in terms of equity issues offered and generally has the strictest listing requirements. Other exchanges that the reader may be familiar with, however, are the American Stock Exchange, The Midwest Stock Exchange, The Pacific Stock Exchange, The Philadelphia Stock Exchange and The Chicago Board Options Exchange. The name "Stock Exchange" in the title of the above exchanges is no longer indicative of the securities traded there because many of them trade bonds and options in addition to stocks.

WHAT IS OTC?

The Over-the-Counter ("OTC") Market takes its name from a time when listed exchanges did not exist and securities were traded "over-the-counter" of a bank or similar institution. The OTC Market consists of a network of brokers and dealers who act as agent or principal in the purchase or sale of stocks, bonds and, to a lesser extent, options. There is not any one physical location to this market. Trading departments of securities firms negotiate with customers or their agents on price over the telephone. The OTC market generally trades securities of companies smaller than those listed on the New York Stock Exchange, but there are many exceptions. According to the National Association of Securities Dealers ("NASD"), as of 12/30/88, approximately 900 NASD companies qualified for listing on the NYSE. In recent years, the NASD—the regulatory body that oversees the OTC Market—has introduced many procedures that have made more information available on the securities traded on the OTC Market, and this has led to greater liquidity for the securities that are traded there. Advances in technology, such as the National Association of Securities Dealers Automated Quotations ("NASDAQ") last sale reporting and publication of low, high and closing transaction prices, has helped this marketplace become much more accepted by the investing public.

MONEY MARKETS

The Money Market generally trades securities that have a maturity of one year or less. These securities are generally highly liquid and trade in large denominations. The most common Money Market instruments are Treasury Bills of the U.S. Government, Certificates of Deposit, Bankers Acceptances and/or Commercial Paper. Here again, there is no exchange or central place for trading. The "Market" consists of banks, securities firms and others who wish to borrow or invest large amounts for short terms.

REVENUE PRODUCING AREAS—THE SUPPORT FUNCTIONS

I never considered the terms "front office" and "back office" useful to professionals. It's more useful to use terms like "business unit" to describe those areas responsible for bringing in revenue and "support unit" to describe those areas (like Operations and Information Systems) responsible for processing activity.

The business unit functions that Operations and Informations Systems support are fairly basic: Sales/Marketing, Investment Banking, Trading and Research. Finance/Administration is another support unit which relies on Operations and Information Systems for processing related information. The business units generate revenue for the firm by listening to customer needs and generating products for those needs.

Everything that Operations and Information Systems does should be in support of the business unit. Firms that succeed in aligning the goals of the Operations and Information Systems support with the goals of the business unit will succeed in providing low cost, quality support for their customers. The chart below lists the most common business units and some of the support functions that Operations and Information Systems provides to each:

Securities Firms' Business Units

Sales/Marketing
- Prompt, Accurate Execution Reporting
- Prompt Delivery of Customers' Securities
- Accurate Dividend Processing
- Accurate Statement Processing
- Low Cost Communications
- Customer Information
- Market Information

Investment Banking
- Communications Support
- Prompt Syndicate Settlement
- New Product Processing
- Reorganization Services
- Market Information

Research
- Customer Information
- Research Data Bases
- Telecommunication Support
- Market Information

Trading	Prompt, Accurate Execution Reporting
	Prompt Delivery of Securities
	Balancing of Traders' Positions with General Ledger
	Systems Support for Trading Strategies
	Risk Management Systems
Finance/ Administration	Prompt, Accurate Bookkeeping
	General Ledger Information
	Human Resources Information
	Accurate Processing of Trades
	Compliance Reporting

INTRODUCTION TO OPERATIONS AND INFORMATION SYSTEMS

We've looked at the role of securities firms, the products they offer and the markets within which they service clients. Now let's briefly look at the major Operations and Information Systems functions that support the business units.

OPERATIONS

The Operations area of a securities firm provides a host of varied support activities to the business units and customers of a firm. Once an Account Executive receives a purchase order from a customer, the Operations area performs a myriad of tasks until the securities are delivered to the customer, or received at the firm to be held for the customer's account. The major functions that will be discussed are briefly described in the following paragraphs.

ORDER PROCESSING

The Operations processing cycle begins when a customer places an order. The Order Department is responsible for taking the customer order and routing it to the appropriate marketplace to be executed. This area generally begins the process of updating the customer's and firm's books and records.

COMPARISON

After execution, customer and firm accounts are updated and the order is passed on to comparison where this area processes, balances, and compares all transactions resulting from the trading activities of the firm and its customers.

CASHIERING

The Cashiering Department maintains the actual custody of the firm's certificates. The Cashiering Department is also responsible for receipts and deliveries of securities to and from customers and other firms.

MARGIN

The Margin Department assures that regulations concerning the extension of credit for securities are met. Margin maintains the record-keeping on each customer's deposits or withdrawals and no money or securities may be paid or delivered to a customer unless authorized by the Margin Department.

DIVIDEND

The Dividend area is responsible for collecting, disbursing, and controlling all dividends and interest with respect to the security positions of the firm and its customers.

STOCK RECORD

The Stock Record area serves as a centralized information base to show the location of securities, which securities are owned by the firm and by others, and the number of shares. This department is responsible for assuring that proper records are kept on customers' securities positions.

TRANSFER

The Transfer area is responsible for registering the customer's purchased securities into his/her name.

REORGANIZATION

The Reorganization area is responsible for updating the books and records of the firm and its customers to reflect merger and acquisition activity, stock splits, and other corporate reorganization activity.

In addition to the above departments, we will also discuss how to process work in Customer Service Departments, International Operations, Branch Office Operations, Options Operations and New Product Support. Specific chapters are provided on clearing corporations and depositories, control reporting, human resource strategies, records management, securities lending, and borrowing and planning for emergencies.

INFORMATION SYSTEMS

Ten or fifteen years ago "Data Processing" may have been an appropriate title for this area, but not today.

The systems that drive securities firms computers are as integral to the success of securities firms as any of the Operations, Sales and Trading efforts. All of us are dealing in a world where information—the type of it and the timeliness of it—determines who succeeds in the market place. Today, successful securities firms are making the technological leap from transaction processors to information processors.

In chapters 19 to 23 we'll discuss the evolution of Information Systems in securities firms, drivers of growth, and how to build a model for systems development. We'll look at specific functions that require automation in Operations, key systems in the Operations architecture and how to go about systems Planning. We'll also review Information Systems organization and administration and how to plan for tomorrow in the face of emerging technologies.

CHAPTER 2

Order Processing

Here's to the Order Processing Department! If you do everything right in the areas discussed in this chapter, all the departments in the firm's Operations group will have less overtime, fewer corrections and more satisfied customers (not to mention more profits for shareholders).

This is where it all begins. Every operations process after order entry, i.e., comparison, settlement, dividend, transfer, etc., will go more smoothly if the order processing activity goes well. This chapter provides an in-depth analysis of order processing activity. It includes definitions, flow charts, problems, solutions, and detailed summaries of the path an order takes from initial customer contact through execution of the order. More specifically the chapter discusses:

Initial customer contact

Types of orders

Order room processing

Reporting to customers

Updating the firm's records

Automated order matching

Confirmation process

Reconciling internal and external records

Problems and solutions

17

INITIAL CUSTOMER CONTACT

When a customer wants to place an order to buy or sell a security, the initial contact is usually with an Account Executive of a securities firm. The Account Executive will then find out the customer's investment objectives to assure that the transaction is appropriate for the customer. At this point, the Account Executive is ready to take the order on an order form designed to capture the necessary information. (A sample order form is shown in Figure 2-1.)

The basic information required is:

Customer name or account identifier

Buy or sell or sell short

Quantity

Security name and symbol

Price

Length of time the order is to be in force

Any specific trading instructions for the trader or exchange professional

Additional data that is also required that is not pertinent to the execution of the trade, but is necessary for proper processing, includes:

Location of the security being sold or disposition of the security being purchased

Method of payment for the purchase

Disposition of funds released on a sale

Type of account (cash or margin), if the customer has multiple accounts

Other transactions require even further information. For example, option orders require disclosure as to whether the position is a new position being opened, a liquidation, or closing of a previous position. Also, information concerning commission rates to be applied on the trade and, in some areas, additional approval of the order may be necessary, depending upon the compliance guidelines of the firm.

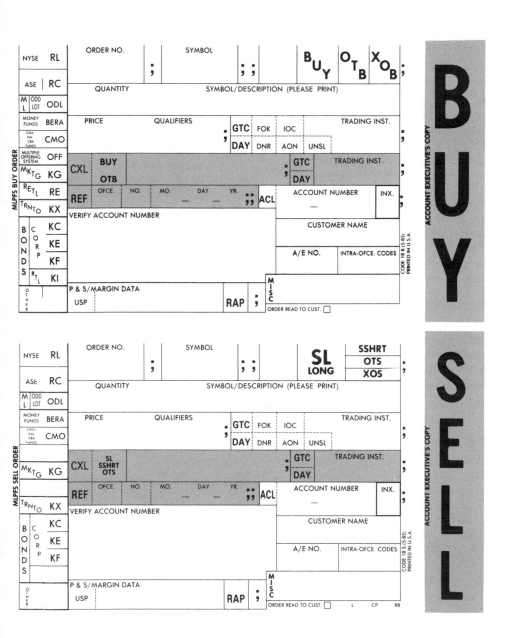

FIGURE 2-1. Sample Order Form

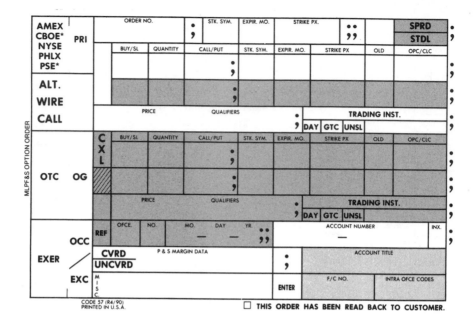

FIGURE 2-1. *(Continued)*

TYPES OF ORDERS

As mentioned above, an order represents a specific instruction from the customer, via the Account Executive, to the trading location. The particular trading strategy of the customer may suggest the type of order to be entered. For instance, if a customer wishes to purchase securities for long-range growth, then the current market price may not be a significant factor. The Account Executive could then enter a "market order." A market order is an order to buy or sell a stated amount of securities at the most advantageous price obtainable after the order is presented to the trading location.

Conversely, a customer who has short term trading goals and wants to buy or sell at a particular price will enter a "limit order." A limit order is an order to buy or sell a stated amount of securities at a specified, or better than specified price, if obtainable, after the order is presented to the trading location.

Although market and limit orders are the most common types of order instructions, there are many other instructions that allow a customer flexibility when buying or selling securities. Figure 2-2 lists order types and trading instructions with a brief definition of each. Order room personnel, as well as Account Executives, should be familiar with these terms to ensure the proper executions of orders.

There are basically four classifications of orders:

BY UNIT

This classification refers specifically to either round lot (the number of shares equal to the unit of trading for the security, usually 100 shares) or odd lot (any amount of shares less than the unit of trading).

BY TYPE

The three major types of orders are:

Market Orders

Limit Orders

Stop Orders

BY SPECIAL TYPE

The following types of orders further qualify the major types of orders:

Stop-Limit Order

Not-Held Order

Or-Better Order

Immediate or Cancel Order

Fill or Kill Order

All or None Order

BY TIME

This classification refers to the time an order is to stay active. Typical time orders are:

Day Order

Good Till Cancelled

At the Opening or Closing

All or None (AON). Market or Limit order requiring that none of an order be executed unless all of it can be executed at the specified price.

Cash Trades. Transactions which call for the simultaneous delivery and payment on the same day.

Close (CLO). Orders "on the close" may be entered any time during the day (except OTC) but will not be executed until the last trading moments of the day. The order will be executed as near to the close as trading conditions will allow.

Combination Orders. Orders that involve the purchase and/or sale of equal quantities of option puts and calls on the same underlying security, but with different strike prices and/or expiration dates.

Day Order. An order to buy or sell, which if not executed, expires at the end of the trading day on which it was entered.

Dividend On. Indicates that the buyer will receive the dividend even though the seller is entitled.

Do Not Reduce/Do Not Increase Orders (DNR/DNI). A DNR order gives instructions that the limit on the order is not to be reduced by the amount of the dividend when the security trades ex-cash dividend. A DNR applies only to ordinary cash dividends. A DNI order is defined as a limit order to buy, stop order to sell, or a stop limit order to sell which is not to be increased in shares on the ex-date as a result of a stock dividend or stock distribution.

Fill or Kill (FOK). Orders that must be executed in their entirety, immediately upon receipt, or the order shall be confirmed as cancelled.

Give Up Order. Orders that occur when a customer requests an Account Executive and office other than those who normally service the account to enter an order.

Good Till Cancelled (GTC). Orders that remain in force until they are either executed or cancelled. GTC orders will generally automatically be cancelled after 30 days.

FIGURE 2-2. Types of Order Instructions

Immediate-or-Cancel (IOC). Orders that must be filled immediately, either in their entirety or partially. The part of the order which remains unexecuted is cancelled.

Limit Order. An order to buy or sell a stated amount of a security at a specific price or at a better price, if obtainable, after the order is presented on the trading floor.

Market Orders. An order to buy or sell a stated amount of security at the most advantageous price obtainable after the order is presented on the trading floor.

Not Held Orders. An order which the floor broker can execute at his or her own discretion to try to obtain a better price than the prevailing market price. The broker is not held accountable for those orders that appear on the ticker tape after the order is received by the trading location.

Odd Lot Orders. Any number of shares less than the generally established 100 share unit or 10 share unit of trading.

Opening Order (OO). An order executed on the opening only. To guarantee the opening price, the order generally must be entered prior to 9:15 a.m. (EST).

Or Better Order. When entering orders related to the current market, the executing broker will always attempt to obtain a better price than the limit

price of the order. A limit order marked "or better" indicates that the limit price is above the market (if a buy) or below the market (if a sell).

Stop-Limit Order. An ordinary stop order becomes a market order when the stock sells at or through the stop price. The stop-limit order gives instructions for a limit order to be entered when the stop becomes effective.

Stop Order. Orders that are entered at a price above the prevailing market on a buy or below the prevailing market on a sell. When the stock sells at or through the stop price on the order, it becomes a market order.

FIGURE 2-2. *(Continued)*

ORDER ROOM PROCESSING

The flow charts (Figures 2-3 and 2-4) display the typical route an order takes (whether a buy or sell) from the customer entering the order to execution of the trade. Figure 2-5 presents a number of problems that are common to order room processing, as well as suggested solutions.

Simply put, once the order is received by the wire room operator from the Account Executive, it is wired to the proper trading location at the home office, i.e., NYSE, AMEX, OTC, etc. The trader will then notify the firm's clerk at the exchange for execution by the floor broker. A trade ticket is then prepared so that proper notification can be given to the Account Executive and ultimately the customer.

REPORTS TO CUSTOMERS

Keeping the customer abreast of activity in the account, as well as the status of current orders, is one of the most important responsibilities of the operations area. A customer is notified immediately upon execution of a trade (usually by phone), and this is followed up with a confirmation of purchase or sale which is mailed to the client.

Customers also are notified for the following:

Securities or funds due

Unexecuted GTC or open orders not executed on day of entry

Cancellations of open orders

Reductions of open orders due to a cash dividend

Increases to open orders due to a stock dividend

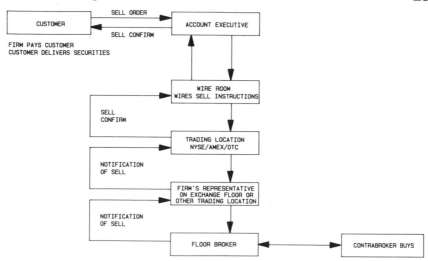

FIGURE 2-3. Customer Sells Stock

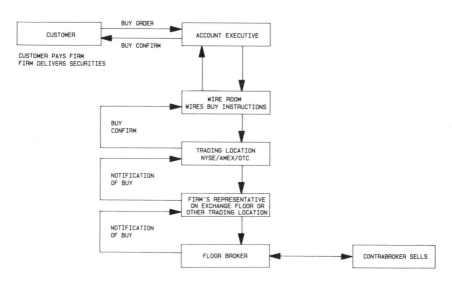

FIGURE 2-4. Customer Buys Stock

Operations Area	Operation	Description	Problems/Errors	Comments
Wire Room	Verify orders	Check order received from AE for accuracy and completeness.	Incorrect orders are returned to AE for adjustments.	Unexecuted orders require prompt action to assure customer gets best price.
	Transmit orders	Orders are wired to office via firm's communications network.	Unacceptable wire is rejected by home office. Wire clerk must determine where error is and take proper steps to adjust.	Errors can come from an AE mistake or a transmission mistake. Completed orders are alphabetically filed by Buys or Sells.
	Order match	Upon completion of trade, an execution report is wired back to branch. Wire clerk matches execution to open order file.	Incorrect matches require correction notices to be sent to home office.	Account Executive is notified on either correct matches or errors.
	Follow up	Open order file checked daily on status of unexecuted orders and correction notices.	Wire proper home office department for answers.	Wire room should keep AE informed as to status.
Order controller	Customer notification (open orders)	Customers are notified that orders that remain open for 30 days will be cancelled.	The customer may request that GTC orders remain in effect over the 30-day cancellation date.	A sample of a typical open order confirmation is shown in Figure 2-7.
	Cancel orders	Wire home office to cancel open order. Response from home office matched to original order and filed. AE and customer are notified.	Special care should be taken on cancel orders. It is possible that prior to cancellation the original order could be executed. In this case the home office would notify the branch.	Orders are cancelled by customer request or due to expiration.
	Execution errors	Corrects trade errors.	Incorrect information on an order would lead to an incorrect trade. Market action must be taken to adjust error.	Controller must be aware of status of stock on trade date, i.e., price; correct order must be entered at original price.

FIGURE 2-5. Common Order Processing Problems

Sample forms for these reports are shown in Figures 2-6 through 2-10.

We confirm the following transaction subject to the agreement
on the reverse side hereof.

SECURITY DESCRIPTION

ACCOUNT NUMBER	TRADE DATE	YOU	QUANTITY	PRICE	AMOUNT
					HANDLING/POSTAGE FEE
					SEC. EXCH. COMM. FEE
					ACCRUED INTEREST/DIVIDEND
					CHARGE OR MARK-UP/DOWN
					NET AMOUNT
					SETTLEMENT DATE

SEC. #   CUSIP #
F/C #   REF #
T.I.N.

If you have moved or plan to move, notify your Financial Consultant of your new address.

Payment for securities or other investment instruments purchased, and delivery of securities or other investment instruments sold, are due on SETTLEMENT DATE unless otherwise indicated by a DATE DUE. Delivery on or before settlement date will avoid premium charges. Please preserve this confirmation for income tax purposes.

Please write your account number shown above on the face of your check, money order or correspondence and forward to the office serving your account.

FIGURE 2-6. Securities or Funds Due Notice

OPEN ORDER CONFIRMATION

Office _____ Date _____ Account No. _____

WE CONFIRM THAT WE HAVE _____ OPEN ORDER(S) FOR YOUR ACCOUNT. PLEASE CHECK WITH YOUR RECORDS AND ADVISE US IMMEDIATELY IF THERE ARE ANY DISCREPANCIES.

IF NOT EXECUTED, THIS BUY OR SELL ORDER WILL BE CANCELLED AT THE OPENING OF THE FIRST BUSINESS DAY FOLLOWING _____.

To Buy   To Sell

ACCOUNT TITLE

FIGURE 2-7. Open Order Confirmation

Office 891   Date 10/07   Account No. 2358907

OPEN ORDER CANCELLATION

The following open order held for your account has been cancelled.

To Buy   To Sell

100 Shares XYZ @ 5

Ms. Jane Doe
123 Main Street
Anytown, USA 98743

FIGURE 2-8. Open Order Cancellation

OPEN ORDER CANCELLATION

Office 891   Date 10/07/88   Account No. 7543092

The following open order for your account has been reduced on account of ex-dividend.

To Buy   To Sell

100 General Motors Corp. @ 46
to 45 1/2 due to ex-dividend 50 cents.

ACCOUNT TITLE

Name
100 Main Street
Smithtown, New York 23987

When a security is ex-dividend for an ordinary
cash dividend the following type of open orders
will be reduced by the amount of the dividend.
1. Buy   2. Sell Stop   3. Sell Stop Limit

FIGURE 2-9. Reduction of Open Order Due to Cash Dividend

OPEN ORDER CONFIRMATION

Office 754   Date 10/06   Account No. 3876053

The following open order for your account has been increased on account of a stock dividend.

To Buy   To Sell

100 IBM @ 270 Increased to
200 IBM @ 135 due to 2 for 1
Stock Dividend

ACCOUNT TITLE

Ms. Jane Doe
609 Willow Lane
Princeton, New Jersey 32790

FIGURE 2-10. Increase to Open Orders Due to a Stock Dividend

Periodic reviews of the open order file by the Account Executive may generate client contacts to ensure that the client wishes to maintain the open order at the original entry price. If the current market price is somewhat removed from the original entry price, the Account Executive may suggest that the customer enter a new order with a price that is closer to the current environment.

UPDATING THE FIRM'S RECORDS

Recordkeeping related to the order status is generally characterized by the product indicated, the execution instructions (i.e., Buy, Sell, Sell Short, Limit, etc.) and the duration of the order's "life" (Day, GTC). Records of all these orders, based on their characteristics, must be kept. These records are generally referred to as "order files." The order files must be coordinated very closely with the execution areas such as the floor or trading room and must be kept current and accurate. The details of each order must be inspected for accuracy, and all orders that are executed must be removed from the file. The files are also adjusted to comply with the time duration or, of course, any cancellation that might be received. The files require a close coordination with the execution areas because, as the prevailing market changes, orders will become marketable and should be executed.

Once the order is executed, numerous records on the firm's security and money files must be updated and balanced.

The firm must record the purchase or sale and show that it will settle on a particular date, show who the other side of the transaction was done with, show the money due to or from the customer, show the money due to or from the party with whom the transaction took place, show regulatory fees or taxes associated with the transaction, show delivery and settlement instructions, etc. Figure 2-11 shows the various records that need to be updated and the potential problems that can occur in the process.

The "other" side of a customer transaction is usually another securities firm and is often called the "streetside" of the transaction. Exceptions to this are cross trades and transactions against the inventory of the firm. A firm executes a cross trade by matching off two customer orders that are marketable. For example, a firm receives two orders, one to buy and one to sell, one hundred shares of a particular security. Under certain conditions, these orders may be matched, thus avoiding a "street side" trade. A firm may also execute an order from its own inventory and avoid an external street side. The benefits of performing cross trades or trades through the firms inventory are twofold. It reduces paperwork and lowers costs, as everything is done "in house" as opposed to dealing with other brokers.

What is important to remember is that each trade must be recorded with all customer and "street" information. This record is generally referred to as the "Trade Blotter." Many of the home office functions such as cashiering, comparison, and vault maintenance are dependent upon accurate trade information.

Record	Problem	Solution
Settlement date	Trades entered incorrectly and not resolved during the order match process would cause an out of balance on settlement date.	Item is usually suspensed and researched and is subject to SEC Exposure regulations. May require market action or trade correction to resolve.
Purchase/sale price	Incorrect purchase or sale price would cause out of balance during the order match procedure.	A trade correction must be entered to reflect correct price.
Customer account number	Incorrect customer account number would not affect the processing of the trade, but the customer account involved must be adjusted.	A journal entry transferring the transaction from the incorrect account to the correct account must be entered.
Contraparty	An incorrect contra-party would cause an unmatched transaction during the order matching procedure.	Research in the P&S Dept. during trade date +3 (see Chapter 7 on Clearing Corporations and Depositories) may uncover problem.
Commissions, tax, and fees	Incorrect calculation of commissions, taxes, or fees would cause an incorrect billing to the customer.	Corrected billing or confirmation is sent to the customer for proper amounts.

FIGURE 2-11. Updating for Firm's Records

AUTOMATED ORDER MATCHING

The significant increase in trading activity in recent years mandated that most firms automate a procedure to match orders to executions to reduce paper work. This procedure is called "order matching." This process captures the order information in a computer after it is entered by teletype or other means. While order matching can be done for listed and OTC activity, for purpose of discussion, we will focus on listed activity.

Obviously confusion can arise when customers with similar names, in similar locations, enter orders for similar securities at similar prices. The automated order match systems eliminate many of these problems by capturing the order information on a computer file and matching it by computer to executed orders. The information that is generally captured on the computer file is:

Customer Name/Account Number

Account Executive

Security Name and Amount

Market Action (Buy/Sell)

Price

When the order is executed, a clerk enters the information on the executed order into the firm's computer system. If it is a perfect match, the computer updates the appropriate firm records. When an exception occurs, however, research begins on reconciling the exception. Some of the problems encountered and their solutions are listed on the chart shown in Figure 2-12.

CONFIRMATION TO CUSTOMERS

Although many Account Executives advise their clients by phone when trades are executed, a written report of execution is also required. Those reports which are sometimes referred to as "local bills," "confirmations" or "trade reports," must contain all the information needed by the customer for his or her records. Critical items are:

Customer account number, name and address

Trade date

Settlement date

Trade price

Principal amount

Area	Operation	Problem/Errors	Solution/Comments
Office wire room	Wires orders to central order room at home office.	Incorrect information on wire causes the trade to be entered incorrectly.	Trade correction must be entered cancelling original trade and entering new trade.
Central order room	Telephones/wires information to firm's trading area or exchange.	Transcription errors are most common.	Same as above. In a fully automated system this step is eliminated. The computer automatically sends information directly to the exchange floor.
Trading area	Receives order information and delivers to proper exchange/trading location for execution. Upon execution, details of execution are wired/phoned to central order room.	Price errors/buy for sell errors, etc.	In a fully automated system, executed reports are automatically matched by the computer and branch office is notified. Firm's records are automatically updated.
Central order room	Matches details to original order and enters execution price on order. Details are then wired to branch office.	Execution does not match open order.	Central order room researches and resolves problem with trading area or exchange floor.
Office wire room	Receives and matches details to open order. Indicates execution price and notifies Account Executive.	Execution does not match open order.	Checks to make sure original trade information was correct, then notifies central order room of problem.
Central order room	At end of day or before trading the next day all "day" orders are removed from files and checked against sale sheets to ensure no reports were missed.	If trades are missed or item is left in file an incorrect trade could be processed.	Floor is notified of orders that were entitled to execution. Answers must be received prior to opening. Branch office is notified.

Orders are always time-stamped at all locations after each operation to avoid future problems.

FIGURE 2-12. Order Matching*

Tax, interest and commissions
Postage and registration fees
Net amount

The pertinent parts of the original order are also shown on the confirmation. Items such as:

Buy or sell

Security description

Quantity

Special instruction

Various firm information may also be shown, such as:

Account Executive Number

Trade Reference Number

Security Number

Samples of confirmation forms can be seen in Figures 2-13 and 2-14.

RECONCILING THE FIRM'S RECORDS

The last phase of order processing is the balancing or reconciliation of the day's trading activity. There are two basic types of reconciliation that are necessary in the order processing area:

1. Internal balancing of customer buys and sells to other parties in the transaction, usually another firm. (This portion of the activity is known as the "street side" of the transaction.)
2. External balancing of the total street side with the individual firms who are parties in the transaction.

INTERNAL BALANCING

Internal balancing is an exception-type balancing where records are matched between the customer's transaction and other parties to the transaction. Every customer entry must have another side. The internal function involves matching the customer blotter (listing of customer trades) to the submissions to the clearing corporation, and is usually performed in the Purchase and Sales Department. Errors occur, however, and all unmatched trades must be researched and corrected. Responsibility for adjustments usually rests with the area that originally entered the information. Some of the problems and suggested solutions associated with this activity are shown in Figure 2-15.

BROKER BROS.
ONE WALL STREET
NEW YORK, NEW YORK 10004

MEMBER
NEW YORK
STOCK EXCHANGE

WE CONFIRM THE
FOLLOWING TRANSACTION
SUBJECT TO THE AGREEMENT
ON THE REVERSE SIDE HEREOF

ACCOUNT NO.	TRADE DATE	SETTLEMENT DATE	MARKET TYPE	SALES PERSON
35289176	06/18	06/25	OTC	350

ACCOUNT TITLE

MS. JANE DOE
TWO MAIN STREET
ANYTOWN, USA

TRANSACTION	QUANTITY	SECURITY DESCRIPTION		NET AMOUNT
BOT	2,000	UP AND COMING IND.		10,216.46
5	10	25.00	.23	191.23
PRICE	PRINCIPAL	INT OR STATE TAX	REG. FEE	COMMISSION

FIGURE 2-13. Buy Confirmation

BROKER BROS.	MEMBER
ONE WALL STREET	NEW YORK
NEW YORK, NEW YORK 10004	STOCK EXCHANGE

WE CONFIRM THE
FOLLOWING TRANSACTION
SUBJECT TO THE AGREEMENT
ON THE REVERSE SIDE HEREOF

ACCOUNT NO.	TRADE DATE	SETTLEMENT DATE	MARKET TYPE	SALES PERSON
1035278	11/05	11/12	NYSE	245

ACCOUNT TITLE

JOHN X. CUSTOMER
12 ANY STREET
OSHKOSH, ILL 13268

TRANSACTION	QUANTITY	SECURITY DESCRIPTION		NET AMOUN'
SLD	1,000	FLY BY NIGHT AIRLINES		8,787.37
9	9,000	25.00	.18	187.45
PRICE	PRINCIPAL	INT OR STATE TAX	REG. FEE	COMMISSIOI

FIGURE 2-14. Sell Confirmation

Problems	Solutions
Street entered with no customer side	Customer side is added by the order originator
Customer entered with no streetside	Streetside is added by the floor
Incorrect number of shares or price	Incorrect trade is deleted and correct trade is added
Incorrect security (i.e., ABC Com. entered instead of ABC Pfd.)	Incorrect security is deleted and correct security is added
Trade executed as buy should be sell (vice-versa)	Incorrect trade is deleted and reentered properly

FIGURE 2-15. Internal Balancing

EXTERNAL BALANCING

The firm's records identifying the contraparty to customer transactions must agree with the records of the contraparty. Price errors, wrong contra-party, and so forth are reconciled with individual brokers or through clearing corporations. Unmatched trades are adjusted during the comparison cycle in the Purchase and Sales Department. Because of the internal balance, the customer should always be in balance during the external balancing function. Some of the problems and solutions associated with this activity are shown in Figure 2-16.

The flow chart in Figure 2-17 shows the roles which both internal and external balancing play in the order cycle.

Problems	Solutions*
Incorrect CUSIP number	Researched by Data Entry
Suspended securities	Researched by Data Entry and Floor
Incorrect symbol	Researched by Data Entry and Floor
Invalid broker	Researched by Data Entry and Floor

*All corrections and adjustments are made in the Purchase and Sales Department.

FIGURE 2-16. External Balancing

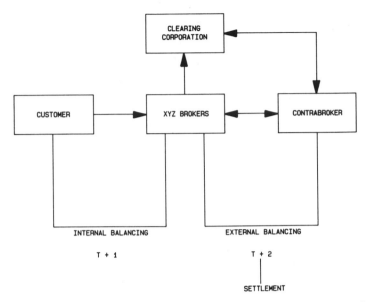

FIGURE 2-17. The Internal and External Balancing Cycle

CHAPTER 3

Cashiering

The Cashiering Department is the focal point of all receipt and delivery of securities and money. Operations Managers know that even if all other steps in the operations process go well, the cashiering process must be performed efficiently or the firm could incur unnecessary interest expense, overtime and other costs, simply trying to receive and deliver securities promptly and accurately.

This chapter will discuss the structure and organization of the Cashiering Department and provide detailed information on receive and deliver, control, audit, and stock record functions. The major SEC and NYSE rules and regulations governing operations of a Cashiering Department will also be discussed.

STRUCTURE AND ORGANIZATION

There are two major securities processing functions of Cashiering Departments: a) receiving and delivering securities, and b) monitoring control records on the receive and deliver activities. Large firms may break these functions into two departments as depicted in Figures 3-1 and 3-2, while smaller firms will simply break out the control and processing function into sections of one department such as in Figure 3-3.

A description of the responsibilities of the various sections is shown in Figure 3-4.

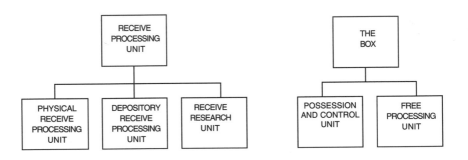

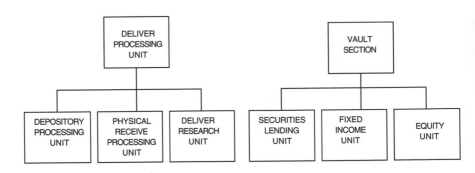

FIGURE 3-1. Cashiering Department—Large Firm Receive
and Deliver

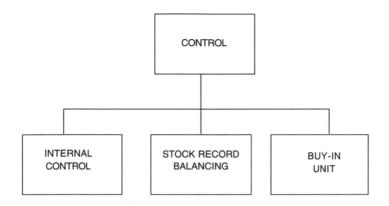

FIGURE 3-2. Cashiering Department—Large Firm Control

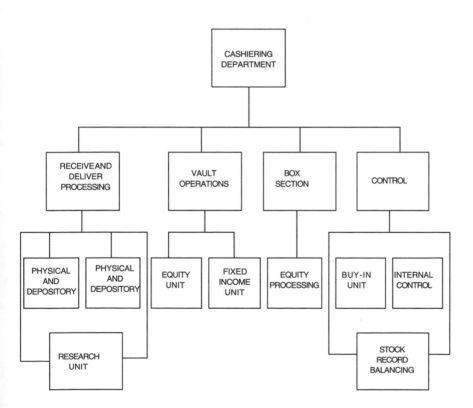

FIGURE 3-3. Cashiering Department—Small Firm

Section	Responsibilities
Receive processing	Processes all incoming securities
	Microfilms securities and distributes to appropriate areas for processing
	Processes all depository activity
	Responsible for physical certificate receives coming in-house
	Follows up on fail to receive problems
Deliver processing section	Responsible for processing delivery of securities by either physical certificates or book-entry adjustments to firm's depository position
	Follows up on problems related to customer deliveries
	Monitors and balances stock loan accounts
Box section	Responsible for satisfying firm's securities delivery commitments
	Allocates firm's inventory to each delivery requirement
	Initiates stock borrow requests
	Maintains inventory of firm's segregation position
	Responsible for assuring avoidance of delivery fails
Vault section	Maintains custody of securities that are in possession of firm
	Maintains inventory for daily segregation purposes
Control	Responsible for daily monitoring and balancing of both branch and home office security positions
Fail control	Controls and monitors fails and fail accounts
	Insures firm's compliance with regulations
	Processes receipt and issuance of buy-in orders
Stock record	Assures that firm's security records are in balance

FIGURE 3-4. Cashiering Major Securities Processing Functions

CASHIERING OPERATIONS FUNCTIONS

Now let's get into more detail on the work of each of the areas. We'll focus on what's done, how it's done, the problems encountered and potential solutions. We'll start with the processing areas of Receive, Deliver, Box and Vault, and then cover the control areas of Stock Record and Fail Control.

RECEIVE AND DELIVER

PHYSICAL RECEIVE PROCESSING

All incoming physical deliveries are taken in (received) by the Receive Section. They can be delivered in by the Clearing House or "over the window" (e.g., by messenger from another firm). The following steps are taken when processing a physical receive:

The certificate is received and microfilmed for control purposes.

It is checked against the firm's pending receive records for name of security, number of shares, identification of customer or firm from whom received, money and settlement date.

It is checked to see if it is in good deliverable form (negotiable).

Certificate numbers are recorded.

The firm's records are updated to reflect receipt of securities. They are then matched to pending receive file.

A check may be issued to the delivering broker.

The security is routed to the Box Section.

This scenario charts the steps taken for a physical receive that matches perfectly with the firm's records. If discrepancies are uncovered during this process, an attempt is made to reconcile them. However, if the discrepancy cannot be resolved, the certificate is returned to the delivering party.

PHYSICAL DELIVERY PROCESSING

The Deliver Section receives certificates from the box section for delivery to the customer, contra broker/dealer or depository/clearing corporation. The following steps are taken by the deliver clerk upon receipt of securities:

Verify that certificates are in good delivery form.

Microfilm certificates.

Process entry to firm's records showing certificates leaving the firm.

Make delivery of certificate as per instruction. Certificates can be delivered as follows:

> Over the window to an institution or broker;
>
> Through the Clearinghouse;
>
> To a branch office to be redelivered;
>
> To an agent to be redelivered;
>
> Directly mailed to a customer if fully paid.

DEPOSITORY RECEIVE AND DELIVER

The advent of depositories and clearing corporations has made a great difference in the processing of receives and delivers. Instead of the cumbersome processing of physical certificates as detailed above, simple book entries are made between member firms' accounts at the depository. Payments are made by the securities firm to the depository, and the transaction settles without the physical movement of certificates.

The procedure followed by the Cashiering Department is to match the pending receive file against the depository's listing of certificates received and booked into the firm's depository account. A small firm may perform this operation manually, although this process is becoming more and more automated.

In a fully automated system a computer matches the firm's records to the depositories. This greatly reduces and simplifies the work of the Receive Section, as the clerk will only have to deal with those items that are unmatched.

Figure 3-5 shows the information provided by DTC for receives and deliveries. After this information is received from the depository, the firm's books and records are updated to reflect the changes in the firm's account at the depository and the fail files of the firm.

Receiving Party	CUSIP Number	Security Description	Share Quantity	Dollar Amount
0005	833102GY6	ABC Corp.	500	$498,008.54
Contra 0005 totals		1 item		$498,008.54
2301	341420YH4	XYZ Corp.	100	$101,384.72
Contra 2301 totals		1 item		$101,384.72
Grand totals		2 items		$599,473.26

Participant: Broker Bros.
10/31

DTC Deliveries Delivered and Credited

Receiving Party	CUSIP Number	Security Description	Share Quantity	Dollar Amount
0006	833102GY6	ABC Corp.	500	$497,713.54
Contra 0006 totals		1 item		$497,713.54
0161	341420YH4	XYZ Corp.	100	$101,309.72
Contra 0161 totals		1 item		$101,309.72
Grand totals		2 items		$599,023.26

FIGURE 3-5. The Depository Trust Company DTC Deliveries Delivered and Credited

PROBLEMS ENCOUNTERED IN RECEIVE AND DELIVER PROCESSING

There are many problems that could come up with certificates received or delivered, either as physical certificates, or as a book entry from/to the depository, that do not match the firm's records. The procedure works in the following manner: The Purchase and Sales Department sends a daily pending receive/deliver file to the Cashiering Department. Those certificates received/delivered by physical delivery, or through the depository by the Cashiering Department, are matched to the pending receive/deliver files. On the receive side, if there is a major discrepancy, such as security description or major variances in price or share quantity, the clerk may place the certificate into a "suspense account" (a record maintained for money or security balance differences until such time as they are reconciled). If the discrepancy cannot be reconciled, it is sent back to the contrabroker or the depository as a DK (Don't Know) trade.

Exception processing was mainly a manual procedure in the past. However, with the advent of more sophisticated computer systems, automatic matches can be made against the firm's records. If the information concurs, there is an automatic match and the pending receive/deliver file is updated. Anything not matched is shown as an exception.

Figure 3-6 illustrates some of the most common types of problems encountered and the steps that may be taken to effect their resolution.

Problem	Solution
Wrong price, amount, or security description	Contact originating area (Margin, Institutional Sales, Purchase & Sale Dept.) to verify trade.
No record as a pending receive	Contact originating area of trade to see if trade was omitted; if so add trade.
No record or customer account number (items being transferred to a customer's account from another broker)	Contact Margin Department to see if there is a pending receive of which Cashiering was not notified.
No CUSIP number exists for the security	Check to see if security has had a name change; if so add new CUSIP number.
Security/quantity discrepancy between firm's record and depository or contraparty	Verify original firm record or contact contraparty.
DK'd by contraparty	Verify entry trade with originating party (trader/salesperson). Ask trader/salesperson to contact customer/broker and get them to agree to accept new delivery.

FIGURE 3-6. Receive/Deliver Processing

FAIL CONTROL

One of the most important functions of the Cashiering Department is the handling and control of fails. If a security is not received or delivered on settlement date it is considered a fail. If a securities firm sells a stock and does not make delivery, the item is listed on the firm's books as an open "fail to deliver." This is considered a receivable as the firm will not receive payment until delivery is made. The reverse is true on "fails to receive."

Because of various rules, regulations (discussed later in the chapter) and financing costs, it is important that you constantly attempt to reduce the number of outstanding fails. For instance, if you fail to deliver securities to another firm, you do not get paid by that firm and will have to finance the position overnight. Many firms judge how well a Cashiering Department is operating by how they control the fails to deliver. Fails to receive also require special attention. In this case, however, it is the responsibility of the delivering broker to make delivery.

The controlling of fails is basically a simple procedure, and in most firms it is a computerized process. Even though most procedures are performed within a computer, let's take a look at what happens if the processing were manual. On the day prior to settlement, a listing is prepared for both the Receive and Deliver Sections of all securities settling the next day. Each section will respectively mark off those items that are delivered or received. The remaining items are considered fails. A new listing is prepared of open fails to receive or deliver. The listing is checked daily, on the deliver side for securities that become available for delivery, and on the receive side for securities coming into the firm or for buy-in purposes. Once a fail is cleared up, it is removed from this listing and an entry is made to the firm's records removing the item from a fail account.

Because of the large volume of trades executed by securities firms, fail control records must be balanced daily. The firm's subsidiary records for security and money should match the general ledger and the records of clearing corporations.

BOX AND VAULT PROCESSING

The responsibility for custody of all securities in the possession of a securities firm lies within the "Vault" and "Box" Sections of the Cashiering Department.

These terms emanate from years ago when securities firms used to keep their securities in actual boxes stored in vaults. It was common to keep securities that were not fully paid for by customers and/or owned by the firm in boxes separate from securities that were fully paid for by customers and had to be segregated from all other securities.

Actually all physical securities are kept in a vault, segregation of fully paid and non-fully paid securities is always maintained, and those non-fully paid are placed in areas where they can be accessed easily (this area may be an actual box, separate vault, etc.).

Box Section

All securities that may be used for deliveries, loans, or collateral are kept alphabetically in what is known as an "active box." After checking for negotiability and matching to appropriate instructions the Receive and Deliver Section forwards the securities received in to the Box Section. The box clerk enters the securities received on the box record and files them in the "active box."

The procedure is reversed when the box clerk receives instructions from the Deliver Section. Entries are made to the box record, the security is removed from the "active box" and forwarded to the Deliver Section. Transfer tickets, segregation instructions, or fail tickets will also generate the removal of certificates from the "active box."

Vault Section

Vault clerks perform basically the same functions as the box clerks but they are usually working with nonactive securities. These securities are commonly referred to as "segregated" securities or securities in "safekeeping." SEC Rule 15c3-3 prohibits firms from utilizing securities fully-paid for by customers. Additionally, securities in margin accounts in excess of the amount required as collateral are also placed in segregation.

Figure 3-7 lists the various forms and instructions that a box or vault clerk deals with on a day-to-day basis. Although these forms vary from firm to firm, the information is basically the same. We have included sample copies of these forms (see Figures 3-8, 3-9 and 3-10) along with information as to how the departments handle the forms and how they are used to enter the information on the firm's records.

STOCK RECORD SECTION

The Stock Record Section is responsible for assuring that the firm's securities positions are always in balance. For this reason, the Stock Record Section becomes the focal point for all security movements within the firm. The Stock Record Section maintains a record showing the location of all securities on hand, those due or held for the firm by others, and those due from or held by the firm for others.

For any security movement within the firm, an instruction must be given to Stock Record so that the firm's records can be kept up-to-date. These records operate on a double entry principle. In other words, for every long position there must be a short position.

The following simple example illustrates this accounting entry:

A customer buys 100 shares of XYZ Corp.

Customer Account	**Firm Account (e.g., vault position)**
(1) 100 XYZ Purchase (Long)	(1) 100 XYZ (Short)

Form	Definition and Purpose	Comments
Segregation ticket	Instructions from the Margin Department to the vault to segregate or place in safekeeping certain securities; also used as a record and means of identifying ownership.	A daily computer-generated listing originated in the Margin Department
Transfer instructions	Instructions to the vault by the Margin Department to remove securities from the vault and send to the Transfer Department for delivery to the transfer agent.	See Figure 3-4
Receive ticket	Accompanies securities received by the firm from the customer. Acts as a record for recording the entry to the firm records. Receive tickets are prepared by the branch office or the Receive Section.	See Figure 3-5
Deliver ticket	Prepared by the Deliver Section on instructions from the Margin Department. Vault clerk attaches ticket to the certificate and forwards to the Deliver Section. Instructions are also prepared in the Margin & Transfer Department and the branch office.	See Figure 3-6
Box sheet or ticket	The box or vault clerk prepares a ticket whenever securities are received in or delivered out. This not only functions as a control of the movement of securities but is used by the Stock Record Section for balancing purposes.	Most brokerage firms have automated this procedure. Vault/Box clerks input directly into a system which generates a listing for the various users.

FIGURE 3-7. Forms and Instructions

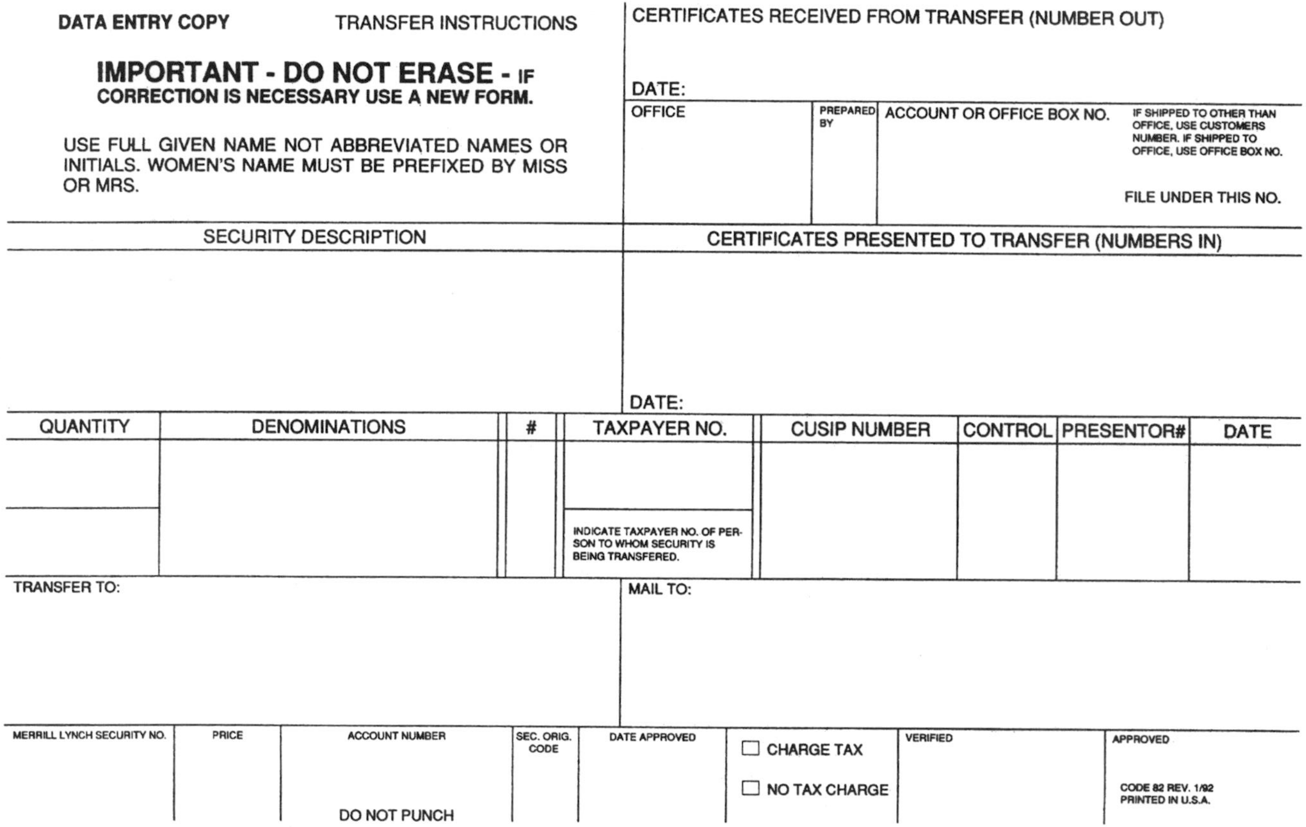

DATA ENTRY COPY TRANSFER INSTRUCTIONS

IMPORTANT - DO NOT ERASE - IF CORRECTION IS NECESSARY USE A NEW FORM.

USE FULL GIVEN NAME NOT ABBREVIATED NAMES OR INITIALS. WOMEN'S NAME MUST BE PREFIXED BY MISS OR MRS.

CERTIFICATES RECEIVED FROM TRANSFER (NUMBER OUT)

DATE:

OFFICE	PREPARED BY	ACCOUNT OR OFFICE BOX NO.	IF SHIPPED TO OTHER THAN OFFICE, USE CUSTOMERS NUMBER. IF SHIPPED TO OFFICE, USE OFFICE BOX NO. FILE UNDER THIS NO.

SECURITY DESCRIPTION

CERTIFICATES PRESENTED TO TRANSFER (NUMBERS IN)

DATE:

QUANTITY	DENOMINATIONS	#	TAXPAYER NO.	CUSIP NUMBER	CONTROL	PRESENTOR#	DATE
			INDICATE TAXPAYER NO. OF PERSON TO WHOM SECURITY IS BEING TRANSFERED.				

TRANSFER TO:

MAIL TO:

MERRILL LYNCH SECURITY NO.	PRICE	ACCOUNT NUMBER	SEC. ORIG. CODE	DATE APPROVED		VERIFIED	APPROVED
		DO NOT PUNCH			☐ CHARGE TAX ☐ NO TAX CHARGE		CODE 82 REV. 1/92 PRINTED IN U.S.A.

FIGURE 3-8. Transfer Instructions*

SECURITIES DELIVERED TO NEW YORK AND CUSTOMER RECEIPT

MICROFILM NUMBER

DATE RECEIVED	OFFICE BOX	A/E NUMBER	RECEIVING OFFICE	DO NOT PUNCH-CUSTOMER ACCOUNT NUMBER

RECEIVED FROM

SAME DAY SHIPMENT, USE FULL 8 DIGIT NUMBER. IF CHARGED TO BOX, USE OFFICE PREFIX ONLY.

FILE UNDER THIS NUMBER

SECURITY NUMBER	SECURITY QUANTITY	SEC. DESC. (INCLUDING CLASS AND PAR VALUE OR PURPOSE OF ISSUE)	PUNCH THIS OFFICE BOX/ CUSTOMER ACCOUNT NO.

DATE SHIPPED	REFERENCE NO.	REGISTERED OWNER CODE	OVERRIDE CODE	COUPON/INTEREST STATUS & SCA	TYPE OF BONDS
		1☐ 2☐ 3☐ 4☐			☐ REGISTERED ☐ COUPON

DOCUMENTS ATTACHED

☐ CODE 82 ☐ CODE 47 ☐ CODE 116 ☐ STOCK/BOND POWER ☐ RESOLUTION ☐ AFFIDAVIT OF DOMICILE/ DEBT ☐ INHERITANCE TAX WAIVER ☐ DEATH CERTIFICATE ☐ COURT APPOINTMENT DATED

☐ LIST OTHERS:

(STATE)

REGISTERED OWNER(S), CERTIFICATE NUMBER(S) AND DENOMINATION(S)

EAS - LEGAL TRANSFERS	MISCELLANEOUS				FOR N/N SECURITIES
☐ CHARGE FEE (ES) ☐ FEE WAIVED (EW) ☐ CHARGE OFFICE (EB)	☐ SECURITIES SOLD	☐ HOLD AT ML	☐ EXPIRING SECURITIES	☐ REDEMPTION FOR ACCT.	☐ PAY ☐ DO NOT PAY

SPECIAL INSTRUCTIONS

	BOX POSTED	PREPARED BY	VERIFIED BY

*Copies of the Receive Instructions are given to: 1) The customer as a receipt; 2) The Margin Department for updating of the customer ledger; 3) The Vault/Box area along with the certificate; 4) The Stock Record or Data Processing area; 5) Receive Section files (if the Receive Instructions are prepared at a branch office, one copy is kept on file at the branch).

FIGURE 3-9. Receive Instructions*

DELIVERY TICKET							HEADRUNNER OR INSURANCE		

THE ATTACHED SECURITIES ARE DELIVERED AGAINST PAYMENT

IF SHIPPED DIRECT TO CUSTOMER, USE CUSTOMER'S NUMBER.
IF SHIPPED TO OFFICE, USE OFFICE BOX NUMBER.
▼ FILE UNDER THIS NUMBER.

DELIVER ORDER OUT INSTRUCTIONS

THE SECURITIES ATTACHED HERETO OR DELIVERED HEREWITH ARE LEFT IN YOUR CUSTODY FOR INSPECTION AND VERIFICATION ONLY. TITLE THERETO NOT TO PASS FROM US OR OUR PRINCIPAL UNTIL WE RECEIVE FINAL PAYMENT THEREFOR. PAYMENT BY CHECK SHALL NOT BE DEEMED FINAL UNTIL COLLECTED FROM THE DRAWEE BANK.

ORIGINATOR NO.	DELIVERED VIA	ACCOUNT NUMBER				TRADE DATE	SETTLEMENT DATE	DELIVERY DATE
161	DTC							

IDENTIFICATION NO.	DELIVER OR SHIP TO:		C.H. NUMBER	ADDITIONAL CERTIFICATE NUMBERS
13-5674085				

QUANTITY	CUSIP NUMBER	SECURITY DESCRIPTION	NET AMOUNT
			PRICE

26

MERRILL LYNCH SECURITY NUMBER	SEC. ORIG. CODE	ACCOUNT NUMBER		PAID	OFFICE	DATE	N.Y. MONEY

NOTE: IF CHECKED BELOW:
CERTIFICATE NUMBERS
☐ DUE BILL ATTACHED

*1. Two copies are sent to the customer along with certificates; the customer keeps one for his or her records and signs the other and returns it to the firm.

2. One copy is given to the Margin Department.

3. One copy is retained by the Cashiering Department.

4. One copy is given to the Stock Record Department or Data Processing area.

FIGURE 3-10. Deliver Instructions*

The firm shows a purchase in the customer's account of 100 shares while showing a delivery (usually from another broker) in a firm account of 100 shares.

Customer	**Firm Account**
(1) Purchase 100 XYZ	(2) Deliver 100 XYZ
(2) Receives 100 XYZ or delivery to customer	(1) Receive 100 XYZ to customer or receive out of firm account

Once delivery has been made to the customer all positions on the firm's books are balanced. A long position indicates one of the following:

Ownership of securities

Claim to securities

A short position indicates:

Segregation

Fail to Receive

Transfer

All transactions result in a long and short entry to the firm's books (stock record). However, these entries usually originate in different areas of the firm. For instance, in the original example, the purchase of 100 shares by the customer could have originated in a trading area with a copy of the instructions delivered to Stock Record. The receipt of the security from the opposing broker would have originated in the Receive and Deliver Section.

All activity is balanced every day and differences generally known as "breaks" are resolved immediately.

"TAKE-OFF BREAKS"

Out of balances result from a trade or security processing input error. In other words, a trade or security movement (receive or deliver) may be erroneously entered or omitted from the firm's records. That is, the number of shares or the security description may be incorrect, or a long may be entered as a short or vice versa. Naturally, this would cause an out-of-balance or a "break" in the firm's records.

Information to the stock record is posted or entered on a daily basis. As mentioned earlier, the information for posting is received from various areas of the firm such as:

Purchase and Sales Department—customer confirmations.

Transfer Department—items sent to or received from the transfer agent.

Receive and Deliver—items sent to or received from customer, other firms and depositories.

Stock Loan Department—items loaned to or borrowed from other firms.

Dividend Department—security positions that may be affected by stock dividend or stock splits.

Reorganization Department—Security positions affected by company reorganizations.

This information generates a daily summary of activity known as a "take-off." Any out of balances (longs do not equal shorts) on the take-off are considered take-off breaks. Breaks must be acted upon immediately so that the stock record will be kept in balance.

For a better understanding of the take-off and stock record refer to Figure 3-11. This displays a fictional stock record position on 4/1. On 4/2, various transactions generate a balanced take-off which ultimately creates a new stock record position.

Using the same stock record position of 4/1, and the same transactions of 4/2, refer to Figure 3-12. In this case, the delivery of 50 shares to offset the purchase by customer "C" is posted to ABC PFD in error. Research will show that the ABC PFD position is out of balance and Stock Record Section will adjust the position the next day.

RULES AND REGULATIONS

This section discusses those regulations that have a major impact on Cashiering departments. Each rule will be discussed individually, giving a definition of the rule, why it was established, and how it applies to the various Cashiering functions.

SEC RULE 15C3-3

This rule is commonly known as the "customer protection rule." It deals with custody of customer fully-paid and excess margin securities, as well as calculation and establishment of a reserve bank account for the exclusive benefit of customers. The rule was adopted in January of 1973, under the Securities and Exchange Act of 1934.

ABC CORP.

Stock Record 4/1

Customer "A"	Long 100 SHS	
Customer "B"	Long 200 SHS	
Segregation		Short 200 SHS
Box account		Short 100 SHS

Stock record in balance

Total longs or debits = 300 Shares
Total shorts or credits = 300 Shares

Transactions of 4/2

Customer "A"   has 100 shares delivered to
Customer "B" sells 100 shares
Customer "C"   buys 50 shares

Daily Take-Off of 4/2	*Longs*	*Shorts*
Customer "A"		100 SHS (Reduces long position)
Customer "B"		100 SHS (Reduces long position)
Customer "C"	50 SHS	(Adds to long position)
Segregation	100 SHS	(Reduces short position)
Box account	50 SHS	(Net of del. & purchase
		(Reduces short position)
	200 Shares =	200 Shares

Stock Record 4/2

Customer "B" LONG 100 SHS		
Customer "C" LONG 50 SHS		
Segregation	Short 100 SHS	
Box account	Short 50 SHS	

Stock record in balance

Total longs are debits = 150 Shares
Total shorts or credits = 150 Shares

FIGURE 3-11. Fictional Stock Record Position on 4/1

Daily Take-Off of 4/2	*Longs*	*Shorts*
Customer "A"		100 SHS
Customer "B"		100 SHS
Customer "C"	50 SHS	
Segregation	100 SHS	
Box account	100 SHS	
	250 SHS =	200 SHS - Take-off out of balance

ABC PFD.

Box account	50 SHS - Take-off out of balance

The stock record clerk makes a simple adjustment to balance the take-off and stock record positions.

Debit the box account for ABC PFD. - 50 SHS
Credit the box account for ABC CORP. - 50 SHS

FIGURE 3-12. Fictional Stock Record Position on 4/2

Two pertinent sections of the rule deal with custody of securities and reserve formula calculations, which are discussed separately.

CUSTODY OF SECURITIES

A securities firm must promptly obtain and maintain the physical possession or control of all customer fully-paid securities and excess margin securities. This will ensure that customer's securities are not utilized in the business to finance transactions of the firm or other customers, or for speculative or unsafe purpose.

These securities are either segregated (kept on hand but physically apart from other securities), or located in another control location and subject to the segregation instructions of the firm. In either instance they are free from any liens or encumbrances. Securities located in another control location must be obtainable with reasonable notice and such receipt may not be incumbent upon the payment of funds.

RESERVE FORMULA CALCULATION

A securities firm must maintain with a bank, cash or qualifying securities, in an account entitled "For the Exclusive Benefit of Customers," sufficient to meet the needs of its customers. The amount required is determined by a formula which compares customer related credits to customer related debits. The excess of the credits over debits is the reserve requirement.

This calculation is generally made weekly and the necessary deposits must be made one hour after opening of banks on the second business day after the computation date.

SEC RULE 17A-13

This rule is often called the "quarterly security count rule." It mandates that at least once each calendar quarter all securities held by the firm be subject to count and verification to the firm's books and records. In effect, an inventory process must take place. This count should be conducted or supervised by personnel other than those directly responsible for maintaining the securities. Many firms have an internal auditing staff to control these security counts.

A complement to this rule is NYSE Regulation 440.21, which further directs that specific security locations such as security depositories and certain security types (such as U.S. Treasuries), be counted or confirmed at least monthly, or more often as good business practice dictates.

The rule also requires the recording of all security differences which remain unresolved seven business days following their discovery in an account on the firm's books and records.

NYSE RULE 387

This rule states the conditions under which Cash on Delivery (COD) privileges may be given to a customer. The NYSE revised this rule in January of 1983, to include mandatory comparison and automated settlement through a depository. Although there are exemptions, the rule specifically requires that any client trading in a depository eligible security, using an agent who is a member of the depository, must affirm trades prior to settlement date and settle the trade through the depository.

COD privileges can be extended only if the following conditions are met:

Customers must supply the broker with the name and address of their agent, and the name and account number on file with the agent.

Each order placed by the customer must be made as a COD transaction.

The customer must receive a trade confirmation by the next business day after execution.

Customers must supply their agent with instructions for settlement no later than trade date plus four business days on a purchase, and on trade date plus three business days on a sale.

Customers or their agent should utilize the facilities of a securities depository for the confirmation, acknowledgment, and book entry settlement of all depository eligible transactions.

SEC RULE 17a-4

This is called the "records retention rule" and it establishes the time periods that records must be retained by securities firm relative to, among others, the net capital, customer protection and security count rules. It states that the records relative to, and in support of these computations, must be preserved for at least six years.

SEC RULE 17a-5

This rule states that every member of a national securities exchange doing any business with the public, or any securities firm transacting business through any member of a national securities exchange, shall file answers to the SEC's financial questionnaire containing the information required by form X-17a-5.

CHAPTER 4

Transfer Services

Transfer services is an area that most Operations Managers never get very excited about except when something goes wrong. When the transfer process is handled properly it is, well, boring! When it is handled improperly it can cause control problems, cost hundreds of thousands of dollars in interest losses, and upset Account Executives and customers.

In this chapter, we'll review the basic transfer process and the legal transfer process. We provide checklists to show how the transfer process works and negotiability requirements for many types of legal transfers. We'll also look at the recent involvement of depositories in the transfer process, and discuss common problems and suggested solutions.

REGISTRATION OF SECURITIES

Operations Managers know that bearer securities do not require registration, and therefore, do not require the services of transfer agents. Registered securities require transfer services to protect the owner in whose name the securities are registered, and to protect the corporation who issued only a specific quantity of securities. There are two types of transfer services: Regular Transfer and Legal Transfer.

REGULAR TRANSFER

When a client of a securities firm purchases registered securities, the client has the option of allowing the shares to remain in the account with the securities firm for safekeeping or to take delivery of them.

Generally, if the securities firm retains the customer's certificates, they are stored in the firm's vault, or at a depository, and registered in the firm's name. This is commonly referred to as being registered in "street name." If the client wishes to receive the shares, registration and delivery instructions must be given by the client to the securities firm at the time of the trade or when delivery is desired.

To consummate a transfer, the securities firm must advise the transfer agent in writing, normally in the form of a transfer instruction (see Figure 4-1 for a typical transfer instruction), which will indicate how the shares are to be registered. The transfer agent's responsibility is to act upon the transfer instruction, if it is in acceptable format.

PREPARING SECURITIES FOR TRANSFER

The checklist, shown in Figure 4-2, is designed to show how to prepare a security for transfer. Please note that the Transfer Department can receive securities for transfer from the branch office as shown, another home office department, or another firm, to satisfy a trade or transfer of an account. The basic procedures will be the same regardless of the origination of the securities and instructions.

LEGAL TRANSFERS

The general rule for transferring securities out of a holder's name is: The certificate must be endorsed on the reverse side exactly as it appears on the face or front of the certificate. In many instances, however, it is not possible for the registered owner to perform this function. To compensate for this situation, documentation must be provided by the endorser of the certificate, which could authorize the acceptance of a signature by both the securities firm and the transfer agent. Many of these transfers are in satisfaction of legal requirements such as in the case of estates.

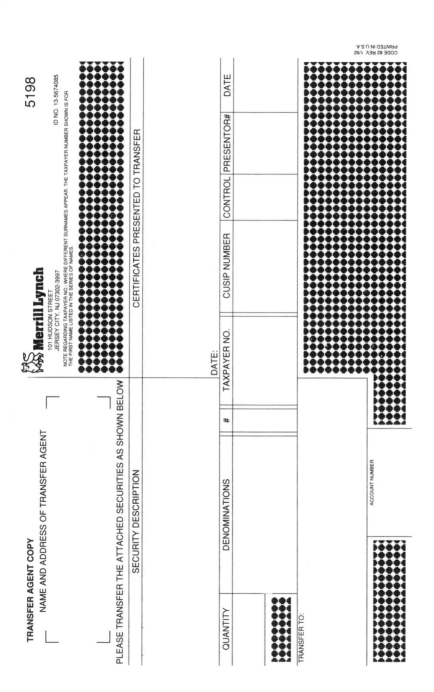

FIGURE 4-1. Transfer Instructions

Branch Office

Account Executive (AE)

Prepares transfer instruction.

Bookkeeper

Checks transfer instruction for legibility and completeness.

If securities are being delivered, matches security to transfer instruction for accuracy. Instructions must match exactly with the security description, security number, and customer name or return to AE.

Checks account to verify that securities have been fully paid for and have a long (debit) position.

Determines if any short position in the account will affect the transfer.

Ensures that no similar transfer has been approved previously.

Checks pending file to ensure that no correction is pending against the securities in question.

Verifies that proper approval has been received.

Prepares and sends package to home office.

Home Office

Transfer Department

Receives package and compares contents to package summary sheet.

Microfilms entire contents of package.

Checks certificates for negotiability.

Makes bookkeeping entries into firm's system.

Sends securities and instructions to transfer agent.

FIGURE 4-2. Steps Involved in Preparation of a Security
for Transfer

The charts displayed in Figures 4-3 to 4-6 show some of the more common types of legal transfers, their definitions and the documents required for negotiability. As you can see, there are many specifications, and it would be a good idea to keep a reference tool of this nature readily available.

Type of Estate	Negotiability Requirements*										Definition of Estate
	1	2	3	4	5	6	7	8	9	10	
Name of decedent	X	X	X	X							Securities registered in the name of an individual now deceased
Property of deceased		X	X	X							Securities held in "street name" in the account of the decedent at the time of death
Joint tenants with right of survivorship (one deceased)			X	X	X	X					Securities registered in the name of two or more people, one of whom is deceased
Joint tenants with right of survivorship (all deceased)	X	X	X	X	X						Securities registered in the name of two or more people who are all deceased
Community property			X	X	X		X	X	X		A form of property ownership between husband and wife, one deceased
Named executor or administrator (deceased, resigned, or discharged)	X	X									Executor or administrator named is deceased, resigned, or discharged
Named executor or administrator	X								X		Securities registered in the name of the executor under the will or administrator for the estate of the deceased

*Negotiability requirements:

1. Endorsement by the legal representative of the estate (of the last decedent).

2. Court certified certificate of appointment of the estate representative (of the last decedent), dated within 60 days of submission to the transfer agent.

3. Notarized affidavit of domicile (for both decedents), covering two-year period.

4. Inheritance tax waiver, if required under residency laws covering state of domicile or statutes regarding state of security incorporation (for both estates).

5. Original certified copy of the death certificate (of the first decedent).

6. Endorsement by the surviving tenants.

7. Copy of the community property agreement certified by the county auditor.

8. Endorsement by the surviving spouse.

9. Notarized affidavit by the surviving spouse that: securities were held as community property at the time of death; no proceedings have been instituted for the purpose of having a will admitted to probate; all claims of creditors have been paid or provided for.

10. Certified corporate resolution, if the legal estate representative is a corporate fiduciary.

FIGURE 4-3. Legal Transfer Estates

Type of Custodianships	Negotiability Requirements*											Custodianship Definitions
	1	2	3	4	5	6	7	8	9	10	11	
Name of minor (not UGMA)†	X	X										Securities registered in the name of a minor
Name of custodian (Minor of age)			X	X	X							Securities registered in the name of a custodian for a minor who has attained legal age under UGMA
Custodian deceased:												Securities registered in the name of a custodian for a minor under UGMA where the custodian is deceased
Appointment by court order						X	X					
Appointment by deceased custodian						X		X	X			
Appointment by minor over 14 years old					X	X		X				
Appointment by virtue of being minor's custodian	X	X										
Deceased minor		X				X				X	X	Securities registered in the name of a custodian for a minor under UGMA where the minor is deceased
Deceased ward		X				X				X	X	Upon death of the ward, the securities held under tutor, guardian, committee, or conservator constitute part of the estate

*Negotiability requirements:

1. Endorsement by the guardian of the minor (as successor custodian).
2. Court certified certificate of appointment of the legal guardian (estate representative), dated within 60 days of submission to the transfer agent.
3. Endorsement by the former minor.
4. Endorsement by the former custodian as final act of discharge.
5. Certified copy of the birth certificate of the former minor.
6. Endorsement by successor custodian appointed by order (legal representative of the estate).
7. Court order appointing the successor custodian or a court certified certificate of appointment dated within 60 days of submission to the transfer agent.
8. Appointment of successor by deceased custodian (by minor).
9. Original certified copy of death certificate of the deceased custodian.
10. Notarized affidavit of domicile.
11. Inheritance tax waiver, if required under residency laws covering state of domicile.

†Uniform Gifts to Minor Act

FIGURE 4-4. Legal Transfer Custodianships

Type of Corporation	Negotiability Requirements*										Definition of Corporation
	1	2	3	4	5	6	7	8	9	10	
Name of corporation	X	X	X								Securities registered in the name of a corporation
Transfer to an officer or a third party	X		X	X							
Change of corporation name	X	X			X						
Merger/consolidation/ reorganization	X	X	X			X					
Dissolution or distribution	X	X	X		X		X	X			
Name of unincorporated association (with governing body)	X							X	X		Securities registered in the name of unincorporated associations, such as clubs, societies, or similar bodies, which have a governing body
Name of partnership	X										Securities registered in the name of a partnership
Trade name (sole owner)	X									X	Securities registered in the name of a company where the owner is sole proprietor

*Negotiability requirements:

1. Endorsement by authorized officer of the corporation, other than the officer endorsing the resolution or any general partner in a partnership or sole owner of a sole proprietorship.

2. Corporate resolution empowering the officer, endorsing the securities, to sign, sell, and transfer securities on behalf of the corporation; dated within 30 days of submission to the transfer account executed under the corporate seal and endorsed by another officer of the corporation.

3. Evidence of election, if officers are not specifically named in the resolution, one of the following will be required: corporate authorization to sell and endorse securities; certification by secretary of the corporation; certificate of incumbency.

4. Corporate resolution specifically authorizing transfer of securities to an officer or third party as an individual, dated within 30 days of submission to transfer agent.

5. Proper state or federal certificates evidencing change of corporate name or dissolution.

6. Evidence must be provided indicating the nature of changes.

7. Affidavit indicating all debts and liabilities have been paid or provided for.

8. Evidence of the authorized officer's authority to act (i.e., bylaws, charter).

9. Evidence of authorized officer's incumbency.

10. Certification that the registered holder is a sole proprietorship.

FIGURE 4-5. Legal Transfer Corporations

Types	Negotiability Requirements*										Definitions
	1	2	3	4	5	6	7	8	9	10	
Name of husband and wife	X	X									Securities registered in the name of husband and wife, where husband and wife are divorced
Power of Attorney			X	X							Securities registered in the name of a stockholder with an attorney appointed to act on his or her behalf
Trustee in bankruptcy or receivership					X	X					Securities registered in the name of a bankrupt individual or company
Name of tenant							X	X			Life tenant registrations are established under a will or agreement. It names a life tenant and a naked owner
Upon death of life tenant							X		X	X	(remainderman) defining their responsibilities. The life tenant is the person who derives the benefit during his or her lifetime, while the naked owner has ultimate control according to the terms of the will. The naked owner becomes sole owner upon death of life tenant
Power of attorney			X	X							Securities registered in the name of a stockholder with an attorney appointed to act in his or her behalf

*Negotiability requirements:

1. Endorsement by transferee.
2. Court-certified final decree of divorce clearly assigning securities to the husband and wife.
3. Endorsement by attorney-in-fact.
4. Copy of the power of attorney specifically authorizing the transaction requested. It must state that the attorney in fact has the authority to sell, transfer, and assign securities.
5. Endorsement by the trustee or receiver.
6. Court-certified certificate or appointment of receivership dated within 60 days of submission to the Transfer Agent.
7. Endorsement by life tenant (naked owner).
8. Court-certified copy of the document where the power to sell is granted.
9. Original certified copy of death certificate of the life tenant.
10. Certified copy of the court document which first established the registration.

FIGURE 4-6. Legal Transfer Miscellaneous

THE ROLE OF THE TRANSFER AGENT

The primary function of the transfer agent is to control the issuance and cancellation of certificates of a particular corporation.

This is done by using blank certificates designed by the company, which are maintained and controlled on the agent's premise. The agent acts upon the written instructions presented to them by the securities firm. In addition to retaining the cancelled certificates and instructions presented for transfer, the agent is responsible for maintaining a current record of all owners of the company's securities.

All transfer agents must conform to established legal guidelines when transferring securities into or out of a holder's name. These rules not only spell out what is a bonafide registration, but also the language that the registration must follow. Furthermore, the transfer agent must adhere to all local, state, and federal regulations imposed upon a particular issue or a given industry. It is the responsibility of the agent to refuse to transfer a certificate if the instructions or legal documents presented are not in proper order.

Transfer agents often perform other functions for the companies they service beyond the physical issuance and cancellation of certificates. These services include:

The preparation and processing of dividend payments to stockholders.

The placement of stop transfers, and the replacement of outstanding certificates when a stockholder reports a certificate lost or stolen.

The distribution of various financial statements and publications.

DEPOSITORY INVOLVEMENT

In recent years, securities firms have been trying to reduce flows of physical securities from clients to securities firms, from transfer agents to securities firms, and so on. A major advance in this area has been the use of depositories.

Depositories "immobilize" certificates, crediting and debiting member firms by bookkeeping entry as transactions occur. If securities to be transferred are held in a depository, the Transfer Department will issue instructions to the depository to transfer the securities.

During the past few years, the securities industry has begun using the depositories for the processing of both transfer instructions and securities for transmission to the transfer agent. The depositories perform a significant transfer function for participating firms. They serve as a centralized processing area for the submission of securities firms' transfer instructions to corresponding transfer agents. Instructions from various firms are collated by issue and submitted to the agents using the certificates stored in the depository. The depository receives back from the transfer agent the re-registered securities or rejected transfer instructions.

An additional automated procedure is now common in the major firms in conjunction with depositories. These member firms are submitting their transfer instructions to depositories via magnetic computer tape. The depository, in turn, submits a tape to the transfer agents, who register and issue new certificates under a fully automated system.

NEGOTIABILITY

A certificate is negotiable if it meets all the requirements necessary to be transferred to a new owner. These requirements are as follows:

The registered owner signs the back of the certificate exactly as the name appears on the front. All parties must sign if there is more than one individual owner.

The certificate requires a stamp, applied beneath the signature by a bank or securities firm, guaranteeing that the endorser and the registered owner are one and the same. This can be done manually or by a mechanically applied "plate."

Authorized signatures must be on file with the transfer agent.

Stock/bond powers can also be signed in lieu of the certificate. This document is a replica of the reverse side of a "standard" stock or bond certificate.

In certain instances, the certificate cannot be signed by the registered owner, and legal documentation must be submitted as discussed under Legal Transfers.

CONTROL PROBLEMS

Because of the enormous amount of movement of certificates involved in the transfer process, tight controls must be maintained to avoid errors and loss of certificates. Proper controls will also allow the firm to:

Follow-up on aged transfers

Research errors

Balance positions

Keep track of the locations of customers' securities

The most common way to control securities flowing in and out of the firm is to microfilm them as they arrive and assign a control number and position on the firm's security records. As the securities move from department to department or out to a transfer agent or depository, they should again be microfilmed and balanced to position records.

Table 4-1 lists some of the more common problems that could develop during transfer processing and solutions to avoid these problems.

The flow charts shown in Figures 4-7 and 4-8 display the typical trail that a certificate follows during the transfer process. Figure 4-7 shows a regular transfer with a night processing unit preparing securities for next day processing.

Figure 4-8 shows the steps taken to process a legal transfer.

Problem	Solution
Lost securities	Microfilm securities upon arrival and departure
Wrong number of securities transferred	Quality control checks at receive and deliver areas
Improper documents accompanying transfer instructions	Quality control checks at local office and at transfer receive area
Aged transfer backlog	Daily follow-up review for all open transfers; constant communication with transfer agent
Improper endorsement of certificates	Publication of transfer instruction guide to all offices and areas responsible for transfer processing

TABLE 4-1. Transfer Processing

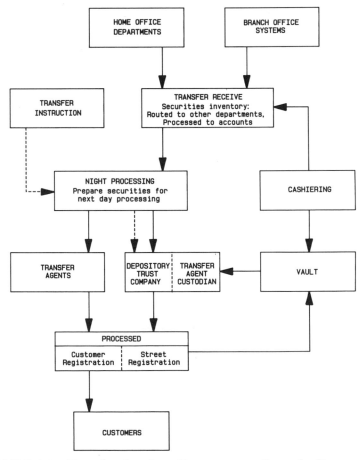

FIGURE 4-7. Transfer Services Department: Steps in Processing a Certificate

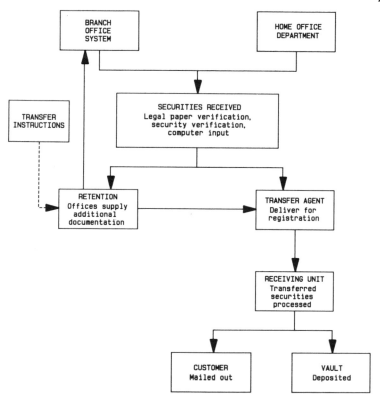

FIGURE 4-8. Transfer Services Department: Steps in Processing a Legal Transfer

CHAPTER 5

Dividend/Interest Processing

The expected receipt of dividends from stock ownership and interest from bond ownership is one of the major reasons why investors purchase securities. It is understandable, therefore, that the processing of information relative to dividends and interest is a major factor of customer service. This chapter will discuss the complex activity that takes place in a typical Dividend Department of a multi-branch securities firm. In order to give you a good working knowledge of dividend and interest processing in today's complex environment, we will include information on:

The Nature of Dividends and Interest Payments

Due Bills

Ex-Date, Record Date and Payable Date

Interest

The Structure of the Dividend Department

Proxy Department Processing

Processing Problems and Solutions.

*EXAMINING THE FUNDAMENTALS OF STOCK DIVIDENDS
AND BOND INTEREST*

DIVIDENDS

Individuals who buy stock in a corporation essentially become "owners" of that corporation. As owners, they are entitled to a share of the profits. Dividends are the distributions of a company's profits to its shareholders. These payments are designated by the Board of Directors of a corporation and distributed proportionately to the customers' holdings. Although corporations are not required to pay dividends to stockholders, most companies will make every effort to do so. Whether or not a firm issues a dividend is generally contingent upon the financial health of the company, the cash needs of the corporation, and the general expectations of the investors.

Because the issuance of dividends is a complex activity and, depending upon the corporation, can be a highly voluminous undertaking, most public companies generally contract with a Dividend Disbursing Agent ("DDA") to process dividend payments. These agents are usually commercial banks or, in rare cases, securities firms, which house the capabilities to maintain the records of stockholders and efficiently process and disburse large amounts of payments. Stock dividends are paid in either cash or stock, both of which undergo similar processing procedures, which will be discussed in more detail later in the chapter.

INTEREST

While stockholders reap the benefits of dividends from their investments, bondholders receive a somewhat similar compensation in the form of interest. Bonds are issued by corporations as well as federal, state and local governments in order to raise capital. A person who buys a bond essentially lends money to the issuer with the bond certificate as proof of the loan. The issuer then agrees to pay the bondholder a predetermined amount of money each year for the use of the bondholder's money—this incremental payment is referred to as interest. In most cases, interest payments are made semi-annually and are paid out as cash at a fixed rate.

Bonds are issued in either "registered" form with the name of the bondholder written on the face of the certificate, or in "bearer" form, which has no imprinted name and belongs to whomever legally holds the bond. Payment of interest on registered bonds is directed to the holder designated on the certificate.

In order to pay the interest to the owner of a bearer bond, the issuer includes a coupon sheet as part of the bond certificate. As coupons reach their "payable date," they are presented to a designated coupon collection agent, usually a bank, who then pays the interest to the bearer.

DIVIDEND ANNOUNCEMENTS

As we stated previously, it is a corporation's Board of Directors that decide to issue a portion of the firm's net earnings to the shareholders in the form of dividends. Dividends are generally announced in newspapers, company letters, and/or financial services publications. The Dividend Department of a securities firm will usually subscribe to as many sources of dividend announcements as possible in an effort to assure that the firm knows when to credit client accounts with dividends proceeds. The major sources of dividend announcements are: general systems services, such as Telestat Information Service, that provide users with daily computer tapes of dividend information; specialized financial services publications such as *Standard & Poor's Dividend Record* and *Moody's Dividend Record* (see Figure 5-1) which supply daily, weekly and quarterly dividend listings alphabetically by paying corporations; and lastly, regional and national newspapers which carry corporate dividend announcements either as bona fide news items or as ads placed by the company (see Figure 5-2). In some cases, particularly with Over-The-Counter securities, companies may inform stockholders by personal letter.

Standard & Poor's
Dividend Record

of

Dividend Payments made in 19

and Declared in 19   for Payment in 19

FIGURE 5-1. Standard & Poor's Dividend of Record of Dividend Payments

Reprinted by permission of Standard & Poor's.
Copyright McGraw-Hill Book Company.

CORPORATE DIVIDEND NEWS

Dividends Reported December 30

Company	Period Amount	Payable date	Record date
REGULAR			
Cadema Corp pfA .... S	.20	1–27–89	1–13
Nalco Chemical Co .... Q	.33	3–10–89	2–20
New Jersey Steel Corp ..... Q	.15	2– 1–89	1–16
Production Operators .... Q	.04	2–15–89	1–13
Republic Capital Group ... Q	.30	1–30–89	1–16
IRREGULAR			
Pegasus Gold Inc .... –	.10	1–31–89	1–13

FUNDS · REITS · INVESTMENT COS · LPS

Company	Period Amount	Payable date	Record date
American Realty Trust .... Q	p.18	1–27–89	1–13
p-Amount increased from previously declared 15 cents.			
Axe-Houghton Fund B ...... Q	h.12	1– 9–89	12–30
Axe-Houghton Inco Fd ...... Q	h.12½	1– 9–89	12–30
Axe Houghton Stock Fund –	h.05	1– 9–89	12–30
Drexel Burnham Fund ..... Q	vv.93	1–10–89	12–30
vv-Payment consists of 50 cents from capital gains and 43 cents from income.			
Drexel Ser Tr Bond Deb .. M	h.06¼	1–10–89	12–30
Drexel Series Tr Convert . Q	h.10	1–10–89	12–30
Drexel Ser Tr Govt .... M	h.05¾	1–10–89	12–30
Drexel Series Tr Growth .. Q	ww.35	1–10–89	12–30
ww-Payment consists of 32 cents from capital gains and three cents from income.			
Drexel SeriesLtd Govt ...... M	h.05½	1–10–89	12–30
Drexel Ser Tr Opt Inco .... Q	h.03	1–10–89	12–30
Drexel Series Tr Priority . M	rr.30	1–10–89	12–30
rr-Payment consists of 24 cents from capital gains and six cents from income.			
Franklin Corporate Cash .. M	nn.16	1–13–89	1– 3
nn-Corrected by fund.			
Franklin Rising Dividends Q	m.09	1–13–89	1– 3
m-Corrected by fund.			
Genesis Fund .... –	r.01	12–30–88	12–30.
r-Initial income dividend distribution.			
Loomis Sayles Capital Fd A	h.61	12–30–88	12–30
Loomis Sayles Mutual ..... Q	h.50	12–30–88	12–30
MFS Managed Sectors Tr –	h.09	1– 3–89	12–30
Manhattan Fund .... A	w.20	12–30–88	12–30
w-Payment consists of four cents from capital gains and 16 cents from income.			
Mass Capital Dev Fd .... S	h.09½	1– 3–89	12–30
Mass Capital Dev Fd .... A	k.63½	1– 3–89	12–30
Mass Fincl Devel Fund ... Q	h.08½	1– 3–89	12–30
Mass Fincl Devel Fund ... A	k.021	1– 3–89	12–30

Company	Period Amount	Payable date	Record date
Mass Fincl Special Fd ..... S	pp.486	1– 3–89	12–30
pp-Payment consists of 38.6 cents from capital gains and 10 cents from income.			
Mass Investors Trust .... Q	h.10	1– 3–89	12–30
Mass Investors Trust .... A	k.8080	1– 3–89	12–30
Lifetime Capital Growth ... S	h.06	1– 3–89	12–30
Lifetime Dividends Plus ... Q	h.149	1– 3–89	12–30
United Kingdom Fund ...... –	y.09½	1–12–89	12–30
y-Final amount; the declaration on December 22 was an estimate; payment consists of 4 1/2 cents from capital gains and five cents from income.			

INCREASED

	–Amounts––––			
Company		New	Old	
Cornerstone Fincl .... Q	.25	.09	2–15–89	1–30

SPECIAL

Company		Amount	Payable	Record
Cornerstone Financial ...... –		1.00	2–15–89	1–30
New Process Co .... –	n1.70	2– 1–89	1–13	
n-Reported incorrectly in an earlier edition.				

A-Annual; Ac-Accumulation; b-Payable in Canadian funds; F-Final; G-Interim; h-From Income; k-From capital gains; M-Monthly; Q-Quarterly; S-Semi-annual.

* * *

Stocks Ex-Dividend January 4

Company	Amount	Company	Amount
Augat Inc	.10	IllinoisPwr8.52%pf	1.06½
BellSouth Corp	.59	Ill Power 8.94%pf	1.11¾
Boston Edison Co	.45½	Ill Pwr 11.75%pf	1.46⅞
Boston Ed 8.88%pf	2.22	Ill Pwr adj pfA	.75
Carolina Pwr & Lt	.71	Illinois PwradipfB	.95
Centrl Maine Power	.38	Inland Steel pfC	.90¾
Du Pont $3.50pf	.87½		
Du Pont $4.50pf	1.12½	JerseyCnPL4%pf	1.00
General Mills Inc	.47	JerseyCnPL8%pf	2.00
HMG CourtlandProps	1.00	JerseyCnPL8.12%pf	2.03
Illinois Power Co	.66	JerseyCnPLpfE	1.97
Ill Power 4.08%pf	.51	JerseyCnPLpfH	.546⅞
Ill Power 4.20%pf	.52½	Lincoln National	.62
Ill Power 4.26%pf	.53¼	Medtronic Inc	.30
Ill Power 4.42%pf	.55¼	Montana Power Co	.69
Ill Power 4.70%pf	.58¾	Oklahoma Gas & El	.59½
Ill Power 7.56%pf	.94½	Penney (JC) Co	.50
Ill Power 8%pf	1.00	Technitrol Inc	.21
IllinoisPwr8%pf'86	2.00	Unocal Corp	.25
Ill Power 8.24%pf	1.03	Wash Gas Light	.47

FIGURE 5-2. Dividend Information Announced in Financial Newspapers

CATEGORIES OF DIVIDENDS

The payments which appear in these various publications are referred to as "regular announced dividends." "Late announced dividends" are those which are declared too late to be included on the Dividend Disbursing Agent's ("DDA") records. Due to a very limited stockholder base, some smaller corporations issue dividends unannounced. This means there is a very limited notification of the dividend payment, appearing only in regional newspapers. Unannounced dividends pose a particular problem for the Dividend Department, which may be totally unaware that a dividend has been declared until checks need to be issued. The special processing problems involved will be discussed later in the chapter.

CRITICAL DIVIDEND DATES

Both the issuing and processing activities related to dividends are anchored to specific dates which must be considered throughout the payment cycle. The following seven benchmark dates are critical in determining the schedule of dividend announcements and payments:

Declared Date	Date on which a corporation's Board of Directors votes and approves payment of stockholders dividends.
Record Date	Date on which stockholders must be listed on Dividend Disbursing Agent (DDA) records to receive declared dividend.
Payable Date	Date on which corporations actually pay the declared dividend.
Trade Date	Date on which customer buys or sells a security.
Settlement Date	Date on which customer pays for purchase or receives payment for sale of a security.
Ex-Date	Date that stock is traded on the market less (ex) the price of the dividend.

The ex-dividend date or ex-date sometimes causes confusion. Very simply, it is the first day the stock trades without the dividend (ex = without). This is also the day that the price of the stock is reduced by the amount of the dividend. This means that the purchaser will not receive the dividend already declared but not yet paid. Instead the purchaser will benefit from the lower price. Ex-date is established by the executing market and is usually four business days before record date.

To understand the concept of ex-date, let's look in closer detail at its relation to trade and settlement date. The following examples will serve to clarify the ex-date concept.

EXAMPLES

Let's assume that ABC stock is purchased on September 16. ABC Corp. stock is selling for $50 per share on Monday, September 15, and the company is going to pay a $1 dividend. Other things being equal, the price of the stock will be $49 when trading begins on ex-date.

Mon	Tues	Wed	Thurs	Fri	Sat	Sun	Mon	Tues	Wed
9-15 Stock at $50 per Share	9-16 Trade Date (stock at $49 per share)	9-17 Ex-Date	9-18	9-19	9-20	9-21	9-22	9-23 Record Date Settlement Date	9-24

In the above case, the buyer would be entitled to the dividend because the stock would be registered in the buyer's name on record date.

If the stock was purchased on September 17, the purchaser would not be entitled to the dividend.

Mon	Tues	Wed	Thurs	Fri	Sat	Sun	Mon	Tues	Wed
9-15	9-16	9-17 Trade Date Ex-Date	9-18	9-19	9-20	9-21	9-22	9-23 Record Date	9-24 Settlement Date

The ex-date system was set up because stock bought between ex-date and record date would not have to be delivered to the buyer until after record date. The buyer would not receive the stock in time to have it registered in the buyer's name on record date, and therefore would not receive the dividend from the DDA.

Since the trade settles after record date, the buyer does not receive the dividend from the DDA. The buyer receives the value of the dividend from the seller in the price paid by the buyer as it is reduced by the amount of the dividend. In order for the buyer of the stock to be entitled to receive the dividend payment, the stock must be bought before ex-date.

The following quick reference guide shows who is entitled to the dividend.

Entitled to Dividend	**Not Entitled to Dividend**
Buys *BEFORE* ex-date	Buys *ON* or *AFTER* ex-date
Sell *ON* or *AFTER* ex-date	Sells *BEFORE* ex-date

DUE BILLS

The ex-dividend date takes on particular significance when a large or valuable stock split (usually 25% or more) is declared. In this instance, it is the policy of the listing agents to postpone the "ex-dividend" date until the split has been paid. This process often leads to the issuance of "Due Bills."

A Due Bill is a promissory note (I.O.U.), issued by a securities firm or a bank, promising the bearer of the Bill the amount of the stock or cash distribution on or after a specific date. See Figure 5-3 for a sample of a Due Bill.

A Due Bill is physically attached to those securities sold with a dividend, interest, or other distribution, but where delivery occurred too late to denote the buyer the holder of record. The purpose of the Due Bill is to confirm the holder as rightful owner, even though there was a failure to deliver the agreed upon securities within a designated time. Because the Due Bill concept itself and its subsequent processing requirements can be somewhat complicated, we'll take a more in-depth look at the application of Due Bills.

As we discussed, exchanges postpone the "ex-dividend" date until a stock split has been made if the split is of significant value. With this postponement, the particular stock is not quoted at the

No. M   2453

FOR VALUE RECEIVED, the undersigned,
holder of record at the close of business on _____ , of
_____ (_____) shares of _____ Stock
of _____ , represented,
by Certificate No. _____ hereby assigns, transfers and sets over
unto _____
_____

the _____ (_____) and
the _____ (_____) share of _____ Stock of
entitled as a stock distribution, and hereby irrevocably constitutes and appoints _____
attorney to transfer the shares representing said stock distribution on the books of said corporation
with full powers of substitution in the premises.

Dated _____

              BY _____
                                          Authorized Signature*
                                          Authorizing resolutions filed
In presence of: with the New York Stock Exchange

_____

    *A Due Bill must be signed by the party in whose name the certificate to which it is
attached stands and must state the number of shares and the serial number of the certificate. A
Due Bill signed by a non-member must be guaranteed by a member or a member's firm in the
same manner as required in the case of an assignment of stock and must be redeemed by the
member or firm having an office in the vicinity of the exchange.

FIGURE 5-3. Due Bill for Stock

substantially lower "ex-dividend" price prior to the payable date,
when the distribution is received by the shareholder.

    If the stock were reduced prior to the date that the stockhold-
ers receive their distribution, it would reduce the collateral value of
the stock prior to the payable date, and the stockholders would not
be able to supplement such collateral with the split stock received
from the company.

As a result of the postponement of the "ex-dividend" date, purchasers of the stock continue to pay the "old" (pre-split) price until the ex-date. Since it is not possible for them to become stockholders of record, they will not receive the stock distribution from the company. In such cases, the ruling of the exchange provides that the sellers in such transactions, having received the "old" price against their sale, are required to give the purchasers Due Bills covering the amount of the split.

> *Example* ABC is paying a 2 for 1 stock split dividend. The old price of ABC stock prior to the ex-date was $600 per share. On the ex-date, each share is now worth $300 due to the 2 for 1 split which gives the customer one additional share for every old share, reducing the value of each share by half.

Let's assume that the customer is using the ABC security as a loan collateral. The bank has one single share in its possession which was originally worth $600, and is now worth $300.

The value of the share after the record date would be $300, if the stock went ex-dividend in the usual method with delivery of the other share made directly to the customer in whose name the value of the stock is no longer sufficient to cover the loan. If the loan was for 100% of the face value of the original share ($600), the bank could call the loan for the difference in value since the old share is now worth only $300.

In order to protect the customer on outstanding collateral loans, the ex-date for stock dividends which carry Due Bills is usually one business day after payable date. The stock dividend is either mailed out by the DDA prior to the payable date, so that it can be received by stockholders of record on the payable date or, if the stock dividend is mailed out by the DDA on the date to be received by the shareholders after the payable date, the ex-date would be the day after the payable date.

As the ex-date is usually the day after the payable date, all stock in movement from the day after the record date to four business days after the ex-date (Due Bill Period), must be considered for the dividend. All shipment of the stock between banks and brokers during a Due Bill period must be accompanied by the Due Bill. This is a promise to pay the stock dividend on presentation of the Due Bill on or after the "Due Bill Off" date. This insures that even though the customer had stock transferred to or from another firm, the dividend accompanied the shipment in the form of a Due Bill.

As with dividend payments, there are specific dates which are critical to Due Bill processing:

Record Date	Date on which the stockholder must be listed as registered holder on DDA records to be eligible for declared dividend.
Due Bill on Date	Day after record date when all physical securities receives/delivers must be accompanied by Due Bill.
Payable Date	Date on which registered holder should receive the dividend distribution of stock cash, rights or warrants from the company or DDA.
Ex-Date	The ex-date on *cash* dividends "carrying" Due Bills is usually the *same* as the payable date. *Stock, rights, and warrants* distributions "carrying" due bills usually have an ex-date one day after the payable date.
Due Bill Period	The period from the day after the record date (Due Bill on date) up to and including the Due Bill off date.
Due Bill off Date	Four business days after the Ex-Date with trades settling on this date with dividend; trades settling after the Due Bill off date are without dividend. This is also the last day that Due Bills will be required on physical receives and deliveries of securities carrying Due Bills.

CHARACTERISTICS OF BOND INTEREST

The issuance and processing of bond interest is similar to that of stock dividends. We have divided the discussion of these two for the purpose of clarity, but the operational procedures are basically the same in most securities firms.

The payment and processing of bond interest is less complicated than that of stock dividends in two respects—generally, bonds do not "split" and interest is almost always paid out as cash only.

The annual rate of interest, which is indicated on the face of the certificate, is expressed as a percentage of the "face value" or "maturity amount" of the bond. The annual interest to the holder can be determined by simply multiplying the annual interest rate by the face value. Since most bonds pay interest semiannually, divide this annual interest by two for the semiannual payment per bond.

> *Example* On a bond with a face value of $1,000 and an annual interest rate of 8%, the annual payment of interest will be $80 and the semiannual payment is $40 per bond.
>
> $1,000 × .08 = $80 annual interest payment
>
> $ 80/2 = $40 semiannual interest payment

As with dividends, the processing of bond interest closely correlates with specific dates. Holders of bonds in their own name (registered bonds) on record date are paid interest on payable date. Similar to dividends, registered bonds have an ex-interest date, which is five business days prior to payable date.

As a result, all bond purchases, which settle up to and including the business day preceding the payable date, are transacted with the semiannual interest payment for that same payable date.

From this perspective, we can see the registered bonds are processed much in the same manner as stock dividends, except that bond movement must be "picked up" from the day after record date up to and including the business day preceding the payable date. This is, in effect, the Due Bill period for registered bonds, although it is referred to as an "interim accounting period."

Bearer bonds are not as firmly tied to designated dates and require only that coupon be "clipped" and presented to a coupon collection agent for redemption after the payable date noted on the bond.

THE DIVIDEND DEPARTMENT

Since we are now familiar with the concept underlying the receipt of a dividend, let's focus on how a typical Dividend Department functions in a large multi-branch securities firm. Keep in mind as we discuss the various sections and processing functions that we are speaking in generic terms. Our general intent is to provide a guide which describes all or most of the responsibilities in the department.

ORGANIZATION

The organization chart in Figure 5-4 is a schematic representation of the main sections of a typical Dividend Department. Because the functions of processing dividends arc governed by rules promulgated by the exchanges and the SEC, they will be similar in nature throughout the industry. While the names of the sections may differ from firm to firm, the basic duties and responsibilities will remain the same.

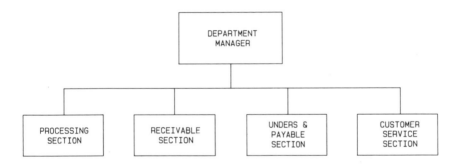

FIGURE 5-4. A Typical Dividend Department

DIVIDEND PROCESSING SECTION

The Dividend Processing Section is responsible for all facets of dividend and interest processing for "the street" and customers, for both stocks and bonds. Some of the basic responsibilities of the section are:

1. Receiving and analyzing information from such varied sources as Telestat Services, Standard and Poors, Moodys, and various newspapers to assure that the announcements of dividends and interest are noted by the firm.

2. Inputting, deleting, and modifying information to the firm's Master Dividend File, which lists all record date positions.

3. Effecting the necessary corrections to previously processed dividend/interest payments such as trade corrections, rate adjustments, IRS reportability, cancellations of positions, etc.

4. Reconciling the department's various processing accounts.

RECEIVABLE SECTION

Major responsibilities of the Receivable Section are:

1. The collection of all dividend or interest owed to the firm as a result of fails, loans, or record date dividend and interest claims.

2. The collection and proper application of all physical checks and securities received by the department.

3. Receipt and issuance of Due Bills as necessary during Due Bill period.

UNDER AND PAYABLE SECTION

The Under and Payable Section performs functions that include:

1. Researching underpayments and overpayments from DDA's and corporations.

2. Paying out cash or stock on record date claims made by other banks or securities firms.

3. Collecting and reconciling all dividend and interest payments from the depositories.

CUSTOMER SERVICE SECTION

The Customer Service Section serves as a liaison between the customer and the firm regarding dividend and interest problems. Usually, it receives inquiries directly from branch offices regarding problems relating to incorrect dividend allocations to their clients. Any necessary corrections are then processed by the customer service area to solve the problem. Please keep in mind that a separate section devoted to customer service is usually a feature of a large securities firm. Smaller firms will usually have inquiries and complaints from their branches or sales offices directed to the Dividend Section directly responsible for the questioned action, without the intermediary of a Customer Service Section.

THE DIVIDEND PROCESSING CYCLE

Now that we have a broad idea of what each section of the Dividend Department does, let's look in more detail at the dividend processing cycle itself. Your firm receives payment from Dividend Disbursing Agents for those clients for whom you are holding securities. It is the responsibility of the Dividend Department to properly distribute these payments to your clients. In order to complete this task, the firm must obtain an accurate listing of all holders of record. To clarify the procedure for you, we will separate the process into pre-record date, record date, payable date, and post-payable date processing.

PRE-RECORD DATE PROCESSING

The dividend processing cycle begins with pre-record date processing. The Dividend Department obtains announcement details from a variety of different internal and external sources such as Standard and Poor's, Moody's, and Telestat. All of these vendors provide details of equity dividends and bond distributions. This information is analyzed and applied to a master file, which stores all announcement detail information on securities which your firm is holding for its clients.

RECORD DATE PROCESSING

The next step in the process is to obtain an accurate listing of record date positions for the security. To do this, the current record date positions are extracted from the stock and bond record for each dividend or interest announcement that was recorded on the Dividend Master File. This file is known as the pending file, which will be the basis for all corrections and adjustments made between record and payable date (see Figure 5-5).

Date 11/16			*Summary Record Date Position—Dividends*		
SEC Number	NY Record Date	Paydate	Description 1	CUSIP Number	Rate
50356	881116	881212	XYZ Pub Service	60624910010	.3000000000
50356	881116	881212	XYZ Pub Service	60624910010	.0200000000

FIGURE 5-5. Dividend Pending File

POST-RECORD DATE—PRE-PAYABLE DATE

The pending file, created as a result of the comparison of announcement detail to the record date position, is the basis for the potential dividend payment between record date and payable date. During this time a considerable amount of adjustments are made to the pending positions prior to the payable date. Because securities are held in various locations throughout the firm, accurate information regarding the registration of these securities must be obtained in order to properly credit the dividend. The major sources of adjustments are branch office box and home office location reporting. (A box, you recall, is the place where securities are stored.) Each home office department (such as the Transfer Department) or branch office must submit a box report (Figure 5-6) to the Dividend Department on the securities they are holding. This report lets the Dividend Department know in whose name the security is registered. The reports are then balanced to assure that all securities are accounted for. If these reports are not submitted, the charge (debit) is calculated and passed on to the appropriate suspense account for that particular box or location, since the Dividend Department was not informed of the proper registration. Location reporting in essence creates other receivable accounts for the potential charge or debit. The transfer of the charge would be dependent on the following conditions:

1. Shares reported to be registered in the name of a customer will result in the transfer of the debit to that customer because the customer will be paid directly by the transfer agent.

2. Shares that are reported as registered in the name of the securities firm will result in the transfer of the debit to a Dividend and Interest receivable account. There it will await the receipt

of the dividend on payable date from the Dividend Disbursing Agent.

3. Shares reported to be registered in the name of a financial institution or individual who is not a client of the firm will result in the transfer of the debit to a Dividend and Interest claims receivable account. This then becomes a claim item which must be obtained from the other institution.

Location Box Number	CUSIP Number	NY Record Date	Pay Date	Description	Position

	Short Adjustments		Long Adjustments	Certificate Numbers Registration	Certificate Numbers Out
Date	Shares	Account No.	Shares	Account No.	

FIGURE 5-6. Sample Box Report

Payable Date

On the day prior to payable date, positions on the pending file are updated to identify non-resident aliens, TEFRA tax codes, and the method of payment (whether a client wishes a check or a credit to the account). The payment is calculated based on the adjusted record date position and payment is made.

POST-PAYABLE DATE PROCESSING

Post-payable date activity generally involves late location box reporting, the processing of late or unannounced dividends and interest payments, and customer adjustments due to erroneous rate and record date applications.

As previously stated, a charge or debit will be made to most location box suspense accounts on payable date if that location did not submit a location box report detailing the proper registration. Late location box reporting occurs as a result of that location "working off" the suspense debit that was charged on the payable date. These adjustments are performed by Dividend Department personnel.

Post-payable date processing also includes late or unannounced dividend and interest applications. These occur when the announcement of the dividend is not received by the record date. In some instances, the Dividend Department is not aware of the dividend until the actual payment is received. Upon notification of the dividend, the announcement detail must be entered into the system, and a record date position must be reconstructed from the stock or bond record to create a pending file. The local boxes must be notified of the positions they reflected on record date and a box report must be requested from each. As soon as all processing details are completed, payments to customers are made.

In addition, post-payable date processing also includes adjustments relating to dividend and interest payments that were previously paid to clients. Generally, this involves a customer inquiry which is forwarded from a branch or sales office to the Dividend Department. The inquiry could be about a bad rate, a dividend the client did not receive, a late dividend, etc. The inquiry is researched and if an adjustment is needed, one is made by journal entry.

OTHER FUNCTIONS OF THE DIVIDEND DEPARTMENT

There are other aspects of the Dividend Department's functions which need to be discussed in more detail if you are to be fully aware of the complexities involved in maintaining a smoothly functioning department. The areas which we will cover in the following discussion are: fails, stock loans, under and over payments, and claims.

FAILS

The Dividend Department must collect all dividends and interest which are the result of fails to receive. As you are aware, a fail exists when a securities firm sells stock to another firm and fails to deliver the shares or bonds on or before the settlement date. Any fail which is outstanding on record date must be settled with the dividend or interest included. The claim process is usually done in two ways:

1. If the failing firm is a member of the Dividend Settlement Service (a claim service sponsored by the National Securities Clearing Corporation and used by its members) they can be billed through DSS (see Figure 5-7).

2. If the failing firm is not a member of DSS, a formal claim notice must be sent. Claim forms (see Figure 5-8) must be maintained, controlled, and tracked in order to ensure that payment is received. It is important for the manager to constantly review the collection of the dividend due on fails to avoid undue exposure to the firm.

DIVIDEND SETTLEMENT SERVICE

National Securities Clearing Corporation

FOR RETURNED NOTICES OF INTENT. COMPLETE REVERSE SIDE

DIVIDEND CLAIM ☐

INTEREST CLAIM ☐

	CLEARING MEMBER	CLEARING NUMBER	DATE OF CLAIM/INTENT	CHARGE DATE
TO:				

WE HEREWITH MAKE CLAIM FOR THE DIVIDEND/INTEREST ACCRUING ON THE FOLLOWING SECURITY

QUANTITY	SECURITY DESCRIPTION	RECORD DATE	PAYABLE DATE	RATE	AMOUNT DUE

REASON FOR CLAIM:

☐ A YOU WERE FAILING TO DELIVER TO US OVER THE RECORD DATE — DATE OF FAIL (SETTLEMENT DATE) ________ CLEAN UP DATE (DELIVERY DATE) ________

☐ B ACCOUNT OF STOCK LOAN OVER RECORD DATE

*☐ C ACCOUNT OF CLAIM WE HELD THE SECURITIES DESCRIBED BELOW REGISTERED IN YOUR NAME OVER THE RECORD DATE

LIST ALL CERTIFICATE NUMBERS PERTAINING TO THIS CLAIM

☐ IN HOUSE PROOF ATTACHED ________ NATURE OF PROOF

IN CONSIDERATION FOR YOUR ACCEPTANCE OF THIS CLAIM, WE GUARANTEE TO HOLD YOU FREE FROM ANY LOSS OR DAMAGE THAT MAY ARISE FROM FUTURE CLAIMS ON THIS DIVIDEND/INTEREST PAYMENT. IN THE EVENT THIS CLAIM IS FOUND TO BE ERRONEOUS WE AGREE TO ACCEPT A RECLAMATION FROM YOU IN THE AMOUNT INDICATED ABOVE. ***A PENALTY CHARGE OF FIFTY DOLLARS ($50.00) MAY BE ASSESSED FOR ERRONEOUS CLAIMS IN THIS CATEGORY (C).**

SUBJECT TO THE BY-LAWS AND THE RULES OF NSCC.

	CLEARING MEMBER	CLEARING NUMBER
FROM		

________ OFFICIAL SIGNATURE

PREPARED BY ________ FIRST PRINTED NAME

TELEPHONE NO. ________

FIGURE 5-7. Dividend Settlement Services Form

Reprinted by permission of the National Securities Clearing Corporation.

Stock Loans

A Stock Loan involves the borrowing of securities from another firm, using cash as collateral. Again, if a stock loan is outstanding on record date the dividend or interest must be included when the loan is settled. The procedures for collection of dividends due on stock loans are similar to those for collection of fail claims.

Date _____

Re: _____

The certificate for the securities, registered as shown, had not been transferred out of the name of the registered holder, when the books of the Company closed for the record date.

Amount	Descriptions	Certificate Number & Registered Holder	Interest or Dividend Rate	Record Date	Payable Date

Amount Being Claimed _____

The registered holder of these securities on the books of the Company will receive, or has received, payment which belongs to the actual owner of the securities on the record date.

Therefore, to settle the claim for this amount made on us by the actual owner of these securities, on the record date, may we ask that you send us the amount indicated.

By: _____
Dividend Department

FIGURE 5-8. Record Date Claim Form

UNDER- AND OVERPAYMENTS

"Unders" and "Overs" are underpayments or overpayments received by the securities firm from the Dividend Disbursing Agents.

These payments result from either a DDA processing error or incorrect reporting of securities by a location box. In order to verify an underpayment, dividend personnel must research the accuracy of all location box reports that were previously submitted. The procedure for solution is:

1. For situations where location box research determines that securities were registered in the name of a customer, the customer account is charged and a credit is applied to the dividend receivable account.

2. For situations where securities were reported as registered in the name of an individual who is not a client, the debit is transferred to a claim receivable account and the item will be treated as a claim. A claim letter or DSS charge is prepared and delivered to collect the underpayment.

3. If the research indicates that all location box reports are corrects, then the DDA's payment is challenged. A listing of all certificates registered in the firm's name and held on record date must be prepared and forwarded to the DDA for verification of the payment.

Overpayment results when securities are registered in your firm's name but are being held by another financial institution over the record date. The credit for the dividend remains in an overpayment account, pending future claims or box reports. If a claim from another institution or client is valid, the account claimed is disbursed from the overpayment account.

CLAIMS

A claim is the result of your firm having in its possession securities registered in other names on record date. Because these securities are registered in other names, the DDA will pay the dividend or interest to the registered owners of the securities only. Since your firm is the new owner of the securities, the dividend must be claimed from the securities firms, banks, institutions, or individuals that received the unentitled payment from the DDA or paying company. Some of the reasons why securities may be held on record dates registered in another name are:

1. Securities were brought in too late to transfer.

2. Securities may be in transit to the Transfer Agent and not received by them in time. Although these securities may not be on the premises, your firm is the owner.

3. Securities which cannot be transferred due to lack of, or incorrect legal documents.

4. Unsigned securities.

These claims must be collected, usually through the DSS, or by phone, mail or research to the other parties.

COMMON PROBLEMS AND THEIR SOLUTIONS

It is obvious from the discussion of the dividend/interest processing cycle, the complexity and variety of functions performed by a typical department creates an environment where problems can occur.

Figure 5-9 gives a brief description of the most common problems encountered by the Dividend/Interest Department. These do not cover every problem that you'll encounter, but, there are certain categories of problems that seem to reoccur frequently. The chart will give you an idea of what they are and some solutions.

INTERNATIONAL EQUITIES

Dividends for international equities create some special processing situations. Although the processing procedures are basically the same, the issue of currency conversion poses an additional step. In many cases, the Dividend Department must manually convert an exchange rate into U.S. dollars or calculate the tax rate based on whether the rate was stated as a net or gross. The calculation of the tax rate can also leave the firm open for a market risk situation because of currency fluctuations.

In addition, some firms allow clients to be paid in the currency of the international security. This may be a time consuming process as the amount must be manually converted. With the growing trend towards a global marketplace, it is becoming increasingly common to have these types of transactions totally automated, which will alleviate the work load of the department.

Type of Problem	*Potential Solution*
Receipt of Checks	
1. Receipt of dividend check with no breakdown.	1. Call agent to determine what securities are being paid.
2. Receipt of dividend check by other departments or branches.	2. Call DDA to determine where check was sent.
Unannounced Dividends/Interest	
Dividend/interest payment is never announced, receipt of check is only notification.	1. Call DDA to verify record date, rate.
	2. Manually create a record date position.
	3. Do processing and box reports.
Late Announced Dividend/Interest	
Dividend/interest payment is not announced until after record date, but before payable date.	1. Manually create a record date position.
	2. Make processing adjustments.
Due Bills	
Proper Due Bill is not attached to security when it is received in.	Contact delivering firm to obtain Due Bill.
Trade Corrections	
1. "As Of" trade adjustments made after settlement date.	1. New position will not appear as part of record date position.
	2. Manually make adjustment to pending file.
2. Dividend Department is never notified of trade adjustments.	1. Client claims dividend after payable date.
	2. Must research to see if client was entitled to dividend.
	3. If entitled, client must be credited.
Transfer Problems	
1. Items are not transferred by record date.	1. Client claims dividend.
	2. Must challenge Transfer Department to determine whose name the certificate was registered in.
	3. If client is entitled to dividend, must reverse entry and credit client.
2. Client or contrabroker were paid dividend to which they were not entitled.	1. Dividend Department will reflect in underpayment.
	2. Must research Location Box Reports to determine in whose name the certificate was registered.
	3. Must claim dividend from contrabroker or charge customer.

FIGURE 5-9. Common Dividend Problems and Their Solutions

REGULATIONS

Each regulatory agency develops rules which must be adhered to by those companies listed on exchanges and NASDAQ. A thorough working knowledge of these regulations is critical to not only the issuing companies, but to the Dividend Department Manager as well, because the dividend processing cycles are contingent upon the established practices of the regulatory agencies. For example, dividend ex-dates are mandated by the regulatory agencies and therefore dividend processing units are bound to adhere to these assignments. The chart in Figure 5-10 lists the most noteworthy regulations with which the Dividend Manager should be familiar.

THE PROXY DEPARTMENT

The Proxy Department is responsible for forwarding all written material that is issued by a corporation to those clients for whom they are holding that security. When securities are held for clients, but registered in a firm's name, the issuing corporation does not know the name of that client. Their records only indicate one shareholder: the securities firm. Therefore, all materials such as annual reports, newsletters, dividend information, proxies etc., are sent directly to the securities firm who must, in turn, forward the material to the beneficial owners.

Because the proxy area is sometimes part of the Dividend Department it is included in this chapter. However, keep in mind that in a large firm the Proxy Department is usually a stand-alone department, due to the volume of material that passes through the area on a daily basis.

PROXIES

One of the rights that a stockholder who is holding shares with voting privileges has is participation in deciding certain matters of that corporation. This is done by voting on the election of officers and directors, amendments to company policy and approval of company objectives. Because most of these issues are voted on at the company's annual meeting, which most stockholders are unable to attend, they exercise their voting privilege by proxies.

New York Stock Exchange	
Announcement	Seven days in advance of the record date to allow time for publication by Standard & Poor's.
Delivery system	Five day delivery system trades must settle five business days after trade date.
Ex-date	On regular announced dividends, ex-date is four business days prior to the New York record date. (All securities listed on the NYSE must have a transfer agent in New York City. Therefore, only one record date, the New York record date, will be applied.)
Transfer agent	The transfer agent must be located in New York City.
American Stock Exchange	
Announcement	Seven days in advance of the record date.
Delivery system	Five day delivery system.
Ex-date	On regular announced dividend, four days prior to record date. Securities listed on the AMEX are not required to name a transfer agent in New York City. If the security trades on the exchange but transfers outside of NYC, the Dividend Department creates a New York equivalent record date to ensure that ex-date will still by four business days prior to the New York record date.
Transfer agent	The transfer agent is not required to be in New York City.
Over-the-Counter	
Announcement	Companies are not required to publicly announce the dividend before record date.
Ex-date	
Regular announced dividends	Four business days prior to the listed record date regardless of where the stock transfers.
Late announced dividends	Ex-date is the first business date after the first official announcement.
Unannounced dividends	Ex-date is the first business day after the payable date.
Transfer agent	The transfer agent is not required to be in New York City.

FIGURE 5-10. Stock Exchange Rules Which Apply to Dividends

PROXY VOTING INSTRUCTIONS	Broker Bros. will vote its proxy in accordance with the indicated
11/14/88 ANNUAL MEETING	instructions. However if no instructions are given, its proxy
100 SHARES	will be voted as recommended by the board of directors.

Yes   No

DIRECTORS RECOMMEND:

SELECTION OF
BOARD
OF DIRECTORS

1. Vote for Items 1, 2, 3

For all
Nominees _____

2. Ratify Selection of Independent Accountants

Withhold
all
Nominees _____

3. Continue Investment Advisory Agreement

Others   _____

List of Nominees _____

John Q. Stockholder
100 Main Street
Anytown, USA
99754

FIGURE 5-11. Sample Proxy Card

PROXY DEPARTMENT PROCEDURES

When the Proxy Department receives a communication from a corporation, the first step is to check the Stock Record for the number of accounts involved. Proxy will then request the additional number of copies from the corporation. The same procedure is followed for proxies. Each customer receives a proxy card indicating voting instructions and actions to be taken by the customer. See Figure 5-11 for an example of a proxy card. Two sets of labels are generated. One contains the customer's name, address, and account number which will be placed on the mailing envelope. The other label contains the same information, but in addition, it will also reflect the number of shares owned. This label is attached to the proxy and mailed to the client. Proxies must be received by a cut-off-date, which will allow enough time for the counting and forwarding of proxy cards to the corporation. When the cards are returned, the Proxy Department tabulates the proxy votes and forwards the results back to the corporation.

CHAPTER 6

The Reorganization Department

Most readers who have had any involvement with corporate reorganizations know that it is a complicated process. During the past few years corporate reorganization activity has increased dramatically as company after company buys another, retires debt, splits its stock, refinances its capital, or "calls" its debt securities. Securities firms, acting as agents for their clients, generally set up separate departments to process the activity associated with reorganizations and this chapter will focus on that activity.

We'll look at types of reorganization activity, the major sections of a Reorganization Department, how to process related activity, and common processing problems and their solutions.

TYPES OF REORGANIZATION

For discussion purposes, let's define "Reorganization" as a change in a corporation's outstanding debt or equity securities. The basic types of reorganization activities that impact securities firms are:

Tender/Purchase Offers.	An offer to purchase outstanding shares of a security at a specified price. The offer can be made by the company itself, a subsidiary of the company, or another company. (See Figure 6-1.)

Notice of Offer to Purchase for Cash
All Outstanding Shares of Common Stock
(Including the Associated Common Share Purchase Rights)

of

Insilco Corporation

at

$31.75 Per Share Net

by

INR Acquisition Corp.

a corporation owned by an affiliate

of

Wagner & Brown

INR Acquisition Corp., a Connecticut corporation (the "Purchaser") wholly owned by INR Partners, a general partnership organized under the Texas Uniform Partnership Act ("INR Partners"), is offering to purchase all outstanding shares of Common Stock, par value $1.00 per share (the "Shares"), of Insilco Corporation, a Connecticut corporation (the "Company"), and the associated Common Share Purchase Rights (the "Rights") at $31.75 per Share, net to the seller in cash, upon the terms and subject to the conditions set forth in the Offer to Purchase dated August 31, 19   (the "Offer to Purchase") and in the related Letter of Transmittal (which together constitute the "Offer"). All references to Shares shall include the associated Rights. The Company has agreed in the Merger Agreement (as defined below) to redeem all outstanding Rights immediately prior to consummation of the Offer if requested to do so by the Purchaser. Tendering shareholders will not be obligated to pay brokerage commissions or, except as set forth in Instruction 6 of the Letter of Transmittal, transfer taxes on the purchase of Shares by the Purchaser pursuant to the Offer.

THE OFFER AND WITHDRAWAL RIGHTS WILL EXPIRE AT 12:00 MIDNIGHT, NEW YORK CITY TIME, ON WEDNESDAY, SEPTEMBER 28, 19   , UNLESS THE OFFER IS EXTENDED.

The Company's Board of Directors has unanimously determined, in accordance with the recommendation of a Special Committee of the Board, that each of the Offer and the Merger (as defined below) is fair to, and in the best interests of, the Company and its shareholders, employees, customers, creditors and suppliers and other affected constituencies, and recommends that shareholders accept the Offer and tender their Shares in the Offer.

The Offer is conditioned upon, among other things, (1) a minimum of 16,700,000 Shares being validly tendered and not withdrawn prior to the expiration of the Offer (the "Minimum Condition") and (2) the funds necessary to consummate the Offer and pay all related fees and expenses being made available to the Purchaser.

The Offer to Purchase and the related Letter of Transmittal contain important information which should be read carefully before any decision is made with respect to the Offer.

Requests for copies of the Offer to Purchase and the related Letter of Transmittal and other tender offer materials may be directed to the Information Agent or the Dealer Manager at their respective telephone numbers and addresses set forth below and will be furnished promptly at the Purchaser's expense. The Purchaser will not pay any fees or commissions to any broker or dealer or any other person (other than the Dealer Manager) for soliciting tenders of Shares pursuant to the Offer.

The Information Agent for the Offer is:

MORROW & CO., INC.
Call Toll-Free 1-800-634-4458

Signature Place	345 Hudson Street	39 South LaSalle Street
14785 Preston Road – Suite 550	New York, New York 10014	Chicago, Illinois 60603
Dallas, Texas 75240	(212) 741-5511	(312) 444-1150
(214) 788-0977	(Call Collect)	(Call Collect)
(Call Collect)		

The Dealer Manager for the Offer is:

Merrill Lynch Capital Markets
Merrill Lynch World Headquarters
North Tower
World Financial Center
New York, New York 10281-1201
(212) 449-4280
(Call Collect)

August 31, 19

FIGURE 6-1. Offer to Purchase Outstanding Shares
Reprinted by permission of Merrill Lynch, Pierce, Fenner & Smith Incorporated.

Redemptions.

The liquidation of a debt issue on or before the maturity date. Redemptions may be called in part or in their entirety (see Figure 6-2).

Conversions.

The exchange of equity or debt for a different class of equity or debt. Conversion privileges generally have an expiration date after which the shareholder still retains ownership in the original security.

Stock Split.

The division of the outstanding shares of a corporation into a larger number of shares. A shareholder affected by a two for one split would be entitled to one additional share for each share held at the time of the split. Such decisions generally must be voted by the directors and approved by the stockholders (see Figure 6-3).

Reverse Stock Split.

The opposite of a stock split whereby the total number of shares outstanding is decreased. Shareholders involved in a one for two split would decrease their holdings by one share for each two shares held. As with stock splits, the board of directors and stockholders generally must give their approval (see Figure 6-4).

Mergers.

A plan initiated when two or more companies elect to combine their assets and liabilities to form one company. A merger agreement generally must be approved by both the board of directors and shareholders of each company involved (Figure 6-5).

NOTICE OF REDEMPTION

Bearings, Inc.

has called for redemption all of its
8½% Convertible Subordinated Debentures Due 20

Bearings, Inc. (the "Company") has called for redemption and will redeem, on October 26, 19 , all of its 8½% Convertible Subordinated Debentures Due 20 (the "Debentures") outstanding on that date at a redemption price of 105.95% of their principal amount, plus accrued interest to that date. The aggregate redemption price per $1,000 principal amount of Debentures will be $1,079.57, including $20.07 in accrued interest (the "Redemption Price"). *On October 26, 19 , the Redemption Price will become due and payable on each Debenture and interest thereon will cease to accrue on and after said date.* Debentures may be presented for payment at the office of AmeriTrust Company National Association, Corporate Trust Division, 2073 East Ninth Street, Second Floor, P.O. Box 6477, Cleveland, Ohio 44101 or AmeriTrust Company of New York, Corporate Trust Division, 5 Hanover Square, 10th Floor, New York, New York 10005.

The Debentures are convertible into the Company's Common Stock at a conversion price of $41.54 per share prior to the close of business on October 26, 19 , when the conversion privilege expires. *Debentureholders should take note that in order to effect conversion, the Debentures must actually be in the possession of AmeriTrust Company National Association or Ameri-Trust Company of New York not later than the close of business on October 26, 19 .* The conversion privilege may be exercised by delivering the Debentures to be converted, together with appropriate documentation, to either AmeriTrust Company National Association at its above address or AmeriTrust Company of New York at its above address.

On September 24, 19 , the last reported sale price of the Company's Common Stock on the New York Stock Exchange was $40.75 per share. Debentureholders should take note that unless the market price of the Common Stock rises to $44.85 per share or more, cash to be received upon redemption would exceed the market value of Common Stock into which the Debentures are convertible.

A formal Notice of Redemption and form of Letter of Transmittal will be sent to all holders of record of Debentures, who should read such documents for a full description of the terms of the redemption and the available alternatives to redemption. Additional copies of such documents may be obtained by mail from AmeriTrust Company National Association.

September 29, 19

FIGURE 6-2. Notice of Redemption

Reprinted by permission of Merrill Lynch, Pierce, Fenner & Smith Incorporated.

Johnson & Johnson Declares Stock Split, 16% Rise in Dividend

By a WALL STREET JOURNAL *Staff Reporter*

...NEW BRUNSWICK, N.J.—Johnson & Johnson declared a 2-for-1 stock split and a 16% quarterly dividend increase, after posting a 13% increase in fourth-quarter earnings.

The split, the first since a 3-for-1 in 1981, is intended to increase the number of Johnson & Johnson shareholders by making the stock price more affordable, a company spokesman said. It is payable May 10 to shares of record April 26 and is subject to shareholder approval at the company's annual meeting April 26.

The dividend boost, to 29 cents a share after the split, is payable June 6 to shares of record May 26. The current quarterly dividend is 50 cents a share.

In New York Stock Exchange composite trading yesterday, Johnson & Johnson closed at $89 a share, up 50 cents.

Net income in the latest quarter was $184 million, or $1.11 a share, compared with $163 million, or 95 cents a share, a year earlier.

The biggest sales jump took place in the company's international pharmaceutical division, where sales in the quarter rose 14% to $341 million from $298 million a year earlier. Total sales rose to $2.2 billion from $2.03 billion.

FIGURE 6-3. Notice of Stock Split

* * *

National Realty Plans 1-for-5 Reverse Split

By a WALL STREET JOURNAL *Staff Reporter*

DALLAS—National Realty L.P. said it plans a one-for-five reverse split of the company's units on Jan. 20.

The real-estate investment partnership said the reverse split is intended to decrease the transaction costs of trading in the units and to increase the price enough to allow buyers to purchase the shares on margin.

In American Stock Exchange trading yesterday, National Realty closed at $2.125, unchanged.

National Realty, which has about 45 million units outstanding, was formed in 1987 when Southmark Corp. rolled 35 real estate partnerships into one public partnership. Southmark, a Dallas real estate and financial services concern that has been struggling with a huge debt load, owns about 8% of National Realty. A Southmark unit is the managing general partner of National.

* * *

FIGURE 6-4. Notice of Reverse Stock Split

Triangle Industries, Inc.

has been acquired by

Pechiney S.A.

We acted as financial advisor to
Triangle Industries, Inc.
in this transaction.

Merrill Lynch Capital Markets

FIGURE 6-5. Acquisition Notice

Liquidation.

Cash distributions made to the stockholders in proportion to and in order of preference of ownership after the remaining assets of the corporation have been converted to cash and its creditors paid. These distributions may be made by a first and final payment or by a series of payments over a number of years.

Rights Offering.

The opportunity offered to stockholders to buy an additional interest (common or preferred stock, bonds, notes etc.) in the company in proportion to the number of shares owned. Rights have a market value of their own and can be actively traded. Rights usually must be exercised within a short period of time and are generally offered to current shareholders before being offered to the public. Holders of rights have three options: 1) selling the rights; 2) exercising the rights (taking advantage of the new purchase price); or 3) letting the rights expire (see Figure 6-6).

50,000 Units

ENERCO, INC.

$25.00 per Unit

Each Unit Consists of
One Share of $3.00 Convertible Preferred Stock and
25 Common Stock Purchase Warrants

The Company is offering to the holders of its outstanding Common Stock of record on January 16, 19   (the "Record Date") the right to subscribe, pursuant to transferable subscription certificates (the "Rights"), for up to 50,000 Units consisting of 50,000 shares of the Company's $3.00 Convertible Preferred Stock (the "Preferred Stock") and 1,250,000 Common Stock Purchase Warrants (the "Warrants"). Holders of the Company's Common Stock, $.01 par value (the "Common Stock") will receive one Right for each 1,000 or fewer shares of Common Stock owned on the Record Date. Each Right will entitle the holder to purchase 10 Units at $25.00 per Unit (the "Subscription Price"). Each Unit consists of one share of Preferred Stock and 25 Warrants. **Rights may not be exercised for fewer than 10 Units.**

The Preferred Stock will be convertible at the option of the holder at any time, unless earlier redeemed, into shares of the Company's Common Stock at a conversion price of $.40 (equivalent to 62.5 shares of Common Stock for each share of Preferred Stock). The Preferred Stock will be redeemable at the option of the Company, in whole or in part, at $26.50 per share if redeemed prior to October 1, 19   and thereafter at prices declining to $25.00 per share on orafter October 1, 19   , plus accrued and unpaid dividends to the redemption date. Dividends on the Preferred Stock are cumulative from the date of original issuance and are payable quarterly commencing on the last day of the quarter following the quarter in which this offering is completed. See "Description of Company Securities - Preferred Stock."

Each share of Preferred Stock will be accompanied by 25 Warrants. Each Warrant entitles the holder to purchase one share of Common Stock at an exercise price of $.30 per share until June 30, 19   , at an exercise price of $.40 per share from July 1, 19   until June 30, 19   , and at an exercise price of $.50 per share from July 1, 19   until June 30, 19   . The Warrants expire on June 30, 19   unless extended by the Company. The Warrants will become detachable for separate transfer and will become exercisable, in whole or in part, upon issuance. See "Description of Company Securities - Warrants."

The offer to stockholders expires at 5:00 P.M., Mountain Standard Time, on February 28, 19   . Any Units not purchased upon the exercise of the Rights will be offered to the public at the Subscription Price on a best efforts basis (1) by the President of the Company, who will receive no additional compensation for making such sales, and (2) by member firms of the National Association of Securities Dealers, Inc. at a selling commission of 10 percent of the price to the public. Such member firms may be deemed to be underwriters within the meaning of the Securities Act of 1933. Units may also be offered on a non-commission basis by the President of the Company to suppliers of goods and services in cancellation of debt owed to such suppliers by the Company.

On January 16, 19   , the Company's Common Stock was quoted in the over-the-counter market at $.10 bid, $.18 asked. Prior to this offering, there has been no market for the Rights, Units, Preferred Stock or Warrants of the Company. Although there can be no assurance that a public market will develop, it is anticipated that prior to completion of the offering the Rights may be traded in the over-the-counter market and, if and when the offering is completed, that the Units, Preferred Stock and Warrants will be traded in the over-the-counter market. The public offering prices of the Units, the exercise prices of the Warrants and the conversion price of the Preferred Stock into Common Stock have been arbitrarily determined by the Company. See "Risk Factors."

THE SECURITIES OFFERED BY THIS PROSPECTUS ARE SPECULATIVE AND
INCLUDE A HIGH DEGREE OF RISK. SEE "RISK FACTORS".

THESE SECURITIES HAVE NOT BEEN APPROVED OR DISAPPROVED BY THE SECURITIES
AND EXCHANGE COMMISSION NOR HAS THE COMMISSION PASSED UPON THE
ACCURACY OR ADEQUACY OF THIS PROSPECTUS. ANY REPRESENTATION
TO THE CONTRARY IS A CRIMINAL OFFENSE.

	Subscription Price and Price to Public	Selling Commission		Proceeds to Company (3)	
Per Unit	$ 25.00	Minimum $ -0- Maximum $ 2.50 (2)		Maximum $ 25.00 Minimum $ 22.50	
Total Minimum Offering 20,000 Units (1)	$ 500,000	Minimum $ -0- Maximum $ 50,000 (2)		Maximum $ 500,000 Minimum $ 450,000	
Total Maximum Offering 50,000 Units (1)	$1,250,000	Minimum $ -0- Maximum $ 125,000 (2)		Maximum $1,250,000 Minimum $1,125,000	

(1) The Units are being offered on a best efforts mini-maxi basis. All cash proceeds from the sale of the first 20,000 Units will be transmitted by noon of the next business day after receipt to a non-interest bearing escrow account with Union Bank & Trust (the "Escrow Agent") until 20,000 Units have been sold for cash (or in exchange for the cancellation of debt) and collected and cleared funds for all cash sales are on deposit with the Escrow Agent. Unless 20,000 Units are sold for cash (or in exchange for the cancellation of debt) within 90 days from the date of this Prospectus (which period may be extended for an additional 30 days by the Company), the offering will be withdrawn and all cash funds promptly returned to subscribers by the Escrow Agent without deduction therefrom or interest thereon. Subscribers have no right to the return of their funds during the term of the escrow. If the minimum is reached, the remaining 30,000 Units will be offered on a best efforts basis until the first to occur of the following: (i) all of the Units being offered hereby are sold, (ii) 120 days after the date of this Prospectus or (iii) the Company determines to earlier terminate the offering.

(2) Maximum selling commission assumes that all Units are sold by member firms of the National Association of Securities Dealers, Inc. at a selling commission of 10 percent.

(3) Before deducting expenses of the Company estimated at $50,000.

Any unsubscribed Units offered by the Company or member firms of the National Association of Securities Dealers, Inc. will be offered subject to receipt and acceptance by them and subject to the right to reject any order in whole or in part and to certain other conditions.

The date of this Prospectus is January 17, 19

FIGURE 6-6. Rights Offering

Exchange/Acquisition Offer.

An offer made by a corporation to exchange one issue of its securities for another, (e.g., equity shares for a debt issue). It could also be an attempt by one company to gain control of another company by obtaining a percentage of issued and outstanding shares. The acquiring company will offer shares of its own company in exchange for shares of the other firm.

Warrants.

A Warrant entitles the owner to subscribe to additional shares of a security issue at a set price during a specified time period. Warrants differ from Rights in that Warrants are generally issued for longer terms. They are offered as a part of a unit to make a stock or bond offering more attractive to the investor.

Units.

A unit is a combination of at least two types of securities, (i.e. bonds and warrants, or common stock and warrants). Clients may elect to either split or combine the component securities. It should be noted that the splitting and combining of unit positions does not require the physical presentation of securities to any external agency.

Invitation to Tender.

A purchase offer whereby shareholders will specify the offering price at which they elect to tender (exchange) their assets.

Put Bonds.   Allows the holder to have the securi-
                                    ty redeemed by the corporation at
                                    specified time intervals. The time
                                    intervals are listed in the bond's
                                    indenture statement. However, the
                                    holder may decide to retain the bond
                                    and not redeem it. This differs from a
                                    Call Bond where only the corporation
                                    can elect to redeem the issue before
                                    the maturity date.

All these changes can be grouped under two broad categories—"Expiring" and "Perpetual" Offers. Expiring offers are voluntary and have set deadlines while perpetual offers are involuntary.
The following lists the various examples of expiring and perpetual
offers:

Expiring	**Perpetual**
Tender Offers	Splits
Exchanges Offers	Stock Mergers
Conversions	Cash Mergers
Rights Offerings	Name Changes
Subscriptions	Redemptions
Warrants	Call Bonds
Put Bonds	
Invitations to Tender	

MAJOR SECTIONS OF A REORGANIZATION DEPARTMENT

The Reorganization Department has to support customer needs,
branch office needs and other operating departments needs. To do
so the department should have the following units:

Plans Section
Securities Processing

Redemption Section

Perpetual Exchange Section

Expirations Section

Let's first review the responsibility and operation of the Plans Section, since all reorganization activity begins here.

PLANS SECTION

The Plans Section is responsible for gathering key information on actual or proposed changes in the capital structure of corporations. The section performs this function by researching, interpreting and analyzing various financial publications. The information can be found in a variety of industry publications including general circulation publications such as the *Wall Street Journal,* and specialized services such as the J.J. Kenny Bond Service, or the Financial Information Card Service. Information will also be received from paying agents, depositories, custodian banks, or directly from the corporation initiating the change. Once the necessary information is obtained, it is summarized and transmitted to the affected clients, branch offices, and home office locations.

The Plans Section plays a key role in ensuring that reorganizations are carried out properly to reduce client or firm exposure, and to maximize opportunities for the firm and its clients. A failure to learn of a change, or a failure to properly understand or communicate the terms of a reorganization, can be very expensive for the firm and its clients. The receipt and interpretation of capital change information by the Plans Section is the mechanism which drives the brokerage firm's reorganization process.

PLANS SECTION PROCESSING

Once the reorganization or capital change information is received or identified, it is reviewed and analyzed to determine the type and degree of complexity. Time frames are then established to determine the operational method and manner in which to process the change. The following lists the steps which should be covered in order to process the capital change.

1. The stock record is reviewed to determine the number of customer accounts affected by the change.

2. A Plan Analyst will contact the information agent, designated by the corporation, and order a sufficient quantity of offering circulars or prospectuses to be disseminated based on customer holdings. The analyst will usually order extra copies to be maintained on file in the section.

3. A sample of a "Letter of Transmittal" is also requested from the information agent. Copies of these documents will accompany the physical certificates when they are submitted to the transfer or paying agent.

4. Upon receipt of the offering circular or prospectus a client letter is developed. These are usually called "To Clients for Whom We Hold" letters. The letter basically summarizes the information contained in the offering circular or prospectus and gives the expiration dates, final date to enter instructions to the brokerage firm, and advises what actions, if any, the client may have to take. Since most capital changes are repetitious in nature, the section most likely will have past copies of similar letters on file. The analyst can merely select the appropriate letter, update the necessary information, and have the document retyped. These letters generally must be approved by a firm's Legal Department before dissemination. Figure 6-7 is an example of a client letter.

5. The client letter is then forwarded to the affected clients. If a prospectus or offering letter is required, it will be included with the client letter. This could be done by the section personnel or through the firm's Mail Department. The names and addresses of the clients are obtained through the firm's master name and address file. Mailing labels could be generated, or the names and addresses could be applied to the letters themselves.

6. A memorandum is sent to the branch offices and the appropriate home office departments advising them of the capital change. In cases where no action is required on the part of the

DECEMBER 15, 19
SEC # A1234

PROCESSED DATE DEC 15, 19

TO CLIENTS FOR WHOM WE HOLD:

ABC UTILITY
SERIES 19   REVENUE BOND
11% DUE JANUARY 10, 20
ABC POWER PLANT COMPANY PROJECT

WE HAVE BEEN ADVISED THAT IN ACCORDANCE WITH THE TERMS AND
PROVISIONS OF THE INDENTURE GOVERNING THE ABOVE ISSUE, THE ENTIRE
OUTSTANDING ISSUE HAS BEEN CALLED FOR REDEMPTION AS OUTLINED
BELOW:

REDEMPTION DATE   JANUARY 10, 19

FOR EACH $1,000 PRINCIPAL AMOUNT OF BONDS REDEEMED, YOU WILL
RECEIVE:

PRINCIPAL $1,000.00
PREMIUM $ 20.00
TOTAL AMOUNT $1,020.00

IN CASES WHERE THE SECURITIES ARE CALLED ON A REGULAR
INTEREST PAYMENT DATE THE ACCRUED INTEREST WILL BE PAID IN
THE USUAL MANNER BY THE BOND INTEREST DEPARTMENT.

AT THE TIME OF REDEMPTION AN ENTRY WILL APPEAR ON THE
MONTHLY STATEMENT INDICATING A DELIVERY OF THE SECURITY
VERSUS A CREDIT OF THE APPLICABLE PROCEEDS.

XYX SECURITY FIRM
INCORPORATED

FIGURE 6-7. Client Letter—Notice of Redemption

client, this memorandum merely serves as an information vehicle. Figure 6-8 is an example of a memorandum advising of a
bond redemption. This notification would be for information
purposes only, since the redemption would be processed automatically.

JAN 25, 19
PLAN #F1234

RURAL COMMUNITY SCHOOL DISTRICT
BUILDING AND SITE BOND
7.20% DUE FEBRUARY 1, 20

CASHIERS-ALL OFFICES   ENTIRE REDEMPTION

REASON   IN ACCORDANCE WITH THE TERMS AND PROVISIONS OF THE
            INDENTURE GOVERNING THE ABOVE ISSUE, THE ENTIRE
            OUTSTANDING ISSUE HAS BEEN CALLED FOR REDEMPTION AS
            OUTLINED BELOW:

REDEMPTION DATE   FEBRUARY 01, 19
LAST COUPON DATE   NOVEMBER 01, 19

FOR EACH $1,000 PRINCIPAL AMOUNT OF BOND REDEEMED, CLIENT WILL
RECEIVE:

PRINCIPAL $1,000.00
PREMIUM $ 30.00
TOTAL AMOUNT $1,030.00

REDEMPTION AGENT: BANK AND TRUST COMPANY
                         MAIN STREET
                         ANYTOWN, USA 55555

NOTE #1   NO INSTRUCTIONS ARE NECESSARY. REDEMPTION WILL BE
             PROCESSED AUTOMATICALLY.

NOTE #2   IN CASES WHERE THE SECURITIES ARE CALLED ON A REGULAR
             INTEREST PAYMENT DATE THE ACCRUED INTEREST WILL BE
             PAID IN THE USUAL MANNER BY THE BOND INTEREST
             DEPARTMENT.

NOTE #3   THE ABOVE COUPON AND ALL SUBSEQUENT COUPONS MUST
             BE ATTACHED TO BONDS PRESENTED FOR REDEMPTION.

NOTE #4   AT THE TIME OF REDEMPTION AN ENTRY WILL APPEAR ON
             THE MONTHLY STATEMENT INDICATING A DELIVERY OF THE
             SECURITY VERSUS A CREDIT OF THE APPLICABLE PROCEEDS.

NOTE #5   ANY INQUIRIES REGARDING THE ENTIRE REDEMPTION SHOULD
             BE DIRECTED TO THE HOME OFFICE REORGANIZATION
             DEPARTMENT.

FIGURE 6-8. Internal Notice of Bond Redemption
Used by permission of Merrill Lynch, Pierce, Fenner & Smith
Incorporated.

7. A memorandum, or "Cashier's Memo" as it is sometimes called, is also given to the appropriate area within Reorganization that will be responsible for processing the capital change.

Once the capital change information is communicated to the firm's clients, sales network and home office areas, the processing function is then undertaken by the specific operating unit responsible for the change. This may be the "Redemption Section," the "Expiration Section" or the "Perpetual Exchange Section." Let's first look at how to process securities and cash during a corporate reorganization.

HOW TO PROCESS SECURITIES AND CASH DURING A REORGANIZATION

The securities processing function focuses on the management and control of security inventory by Reorganization personnel to substitute the original holdings for those outlined by the offer. Once a capital change is announced, the Reorganization Department assumes control of all cashiering functions, (i.e., fails, deliveries, etc.) for the affected security. The following describes the processing steps involved:

1. Instructions are generated to all inventory holding locations within the firm to request that the affected securities be directed to the Transfer Department for routing to a depository prior to the established cutoff date. However, if the affected security is a "valuable conversion," the certificates would be sent to the Reorganization area. A "valuable conversion" is one where the market value of the convertible security is worth more than the redemption proceeds. The Reorganization processing area responsible for the offering would control the conversion and deal directly with the agent and bypass the depository. A valuable conversion notation should be highlighted on a Cashier's Memo in order to alert the Account Executives of the advantages in converting the shares.

2. If securities are held at a depository, the Reorganization area will advise the depository to make deposits directly with the paying or transfer agent. This is done by issuing a Depository Instruction Form (see Figure 6-9). The firm will also send a Letter of Transmittal to the depository.

	PARTICIPANT NAME		SERIAL NUMBER	
D			**T 621810**	
VOLUNTARY OFFERING INSTRUCTIONS	PARTICIPANT NUMBER	DATE	REORG. ACCOUNT **4444**	

SURRENDERED SECURITY IDENTIFICATION			
QUANTITY	CUSIP NUMBER		SECURITY DESCRIPTION
	ISSUER	ISSUE	CK	

The DTC Participant indicated above hereby certifies that the securities described above are credited to its DTC Free account and authorizes DTC to deduct such securities from its account and to surrender such securities to the appropriate agent on its behalf for the purpose indicated below in accordance with the DTC Rules, Voluntary Offerings Procedures and other applicable procedures.

PURPOSE
(Check Boxes as
Required)

A. ☐ **EXCHANGE OR TENDER**
Two copies of Letters of Transmittal (L/T's) attached. L/T to be submitted to Agent by DTC on behalf of Participant.
☐ **CONDITIONAL TENDER—MINIMUM QUANTITY** _____
☐ **ODD LOT TENDER**

B. ☐ **EXCHANGE OR TENDER—GUARANTEE OF DELIVERY PREVIOUSLY**
SUBMITTED TO AGENT BANK BY PARTICIPANT ON_____
                                                                    DATE
To fulfill Guarantee of Delivery provided for under the offer, two copies of L/T, copies of Guarantee of Delivery, Counter Receipt (and/or Due Bill) are attached.
☐ **CONDITIONAL TENDER—MINIMUM QUANTITY** _____
☐ **ODD LOT TENDER**

C. ☐ **OPEN INVITATION TO TENDER**
BID PRICE _ _ _ _ _ . _ _ _ _ _ (UNSEALED BID)
Two copies of Letters of Transmittal (L/T's) attached. L/T to be submitted to Agent by DTC on behalf of Participant.
☐ **CONDITIONAL TENDER—MINIMUM QUANTITY**_____
☐ **ODD LOT TENDER**

D. ☐ **OPEN INVITATION TO TENDER—GUARANTEE OF DELIVERY PREVIOUSLY**
SUBMITTED TO AGENT BANK BY PARTICIPANT ON _____
                                                                        DATE
BID PRICE _ _ _ _ . _ _ _ _ (UNSEALED BID)
To fulfill Guarantee of Delivery provided for under the offer, two copies of L/T, copies of Guarantee of Delivery, Counter Receipt (and /or Due Bill) are attached.
☐ **CONDITIONAL TENDER—MINIMUM QUANTITY**_____
☐ **ODD LOT TENDER**

E. ☐ **REPAYMENT**
F. ☐ **ROLL-OVER**
G. ☐ **CD EARLY REDEMPTION**
H. ☐ **RETAINMENT**
I. ☐ **RELINQUISHMENT**

CONTRA SECURITY IDENTIFICATION			
CUSIP NUMBER			CONTRA SECURITY DESCRIPTION
ISSUER	ISSUE	CK	

PARTICIPANT COORDINATORS:	
NAMES	TELEPHONE NUMBERS

IMPORTANT NOTE: Participants must deliver this instruction to the DTC Reorganization Section, 23rd Floor, 7 Hanover Square, New York, New York 10004. Participants located outside New York City, who are unable to deliver this instruction to the DTC Reorganization Section can facsimile transmit the instruction by calling (212) 709-1094. Participants must confirm immediately with DTC that their facsimile transmission has been received. The original copy marked "Confirmation Only," is to be forwarded to the Reorganization Section, immediately after transmission along with any additional required documentation.
7443 (3/90)

FIGURE 6-9. Depository Instruction Form

3. All incoming securities from the other holding locations are prepared for presentation to the designated paying agent. The securities are made negotiable and the Letter of Transmittal is also completed.

4. Any inquiries from the sales network pertaining to an offer are answered.

5. Securities which were physically held by the firm are forwarded to the agent. The agent will verify receipt of the certificates and return a receipt, usually called a "Window Ticket," to the Reorganization area. Figure 6-10 is an example of a "Window Ticket."

6. All exchange information should be recorded and maintained in an "agent" file which serves as a control mechanism for the physical inventories presented to the agent until the offer expires.

7. Upon receipt of the newly issued securities or cash proceeds from the paying agent, the "agent" file is closed and entries are created to reflect the reorganization into the records of the firm.

8. The old security position is removed from the firm's records, and new securities are routed to the proper box locations. At this point, the firm's and the customer's records are updated to reflect the new positions.

9. All cashiering functions revert back to their normal areas of responsibility.

The Reorganization area may, on occasion, not be able to submit all of the firm's certificates to the paying agent by the expiration date. If this occurs, they will prepare a Notice of Guaranteed Delivery which allows for an extension after the expiration date.

At times, a firm's client may deposit securities that were affected by a prior capital change, such as a bond with a past due redemption or a perpetual exchange. When these securities are received by the firm, they are routed to the Reorganization area and subsequently forwarded to the agent on an individual basis. The client's assets will be substituted when Reorganization receives the new capitalization and/or cash from the paying agent.

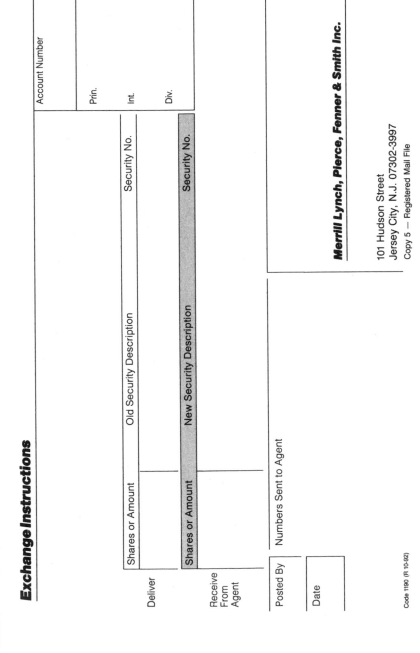

FIGURE 6-10. Exchange Instructions

CLIENT PAYMENT PROCESSING

Shortly after the capital change expires, the Reorganization area will call the paying agent to ascertain if the funds and/or securities are available. Upon receipt, the check and/or securities are then deposited into a Reorganization "House Processing Account."

Client entries are processed crediting the customer with the substitutions. It should be noted that a capital change is effected once these entries are processed.

Now let's look at the different functions performed in the Redemption, Expiration and Perpetual Exchange sections.

REDEMPTION SECTION PROCESSING

The Redemption Section is primarily accountable for obtaining the funds in exchange for debt instruments held by a securities firm for its customers when they become due. These issues may be "maturing" or "called bonds." A called bond may be retired (redeemed) in full or in part by the issuer corporation prior to the maturity date.

REDEMPTIONS OF SECURITIES FOR THE UNDERLYING CASH PROCEEDS

The volume of redemptions can increase due to declining interest rates. As such, corporations may elect to redeem an issue with a high interest payment either partially or in its entirety.

The cash rate to be paid is determined by the terms of the indenture governing a bond issue, and the articles or certificates of incorporation governing a stock issue. In addition to this specific cash rate, supplemental funds may be available reflecting interest accrued to the date of redemption on a bond issue, or accrued and unpaid dividends on a stock issue to the date of retirement.

Redemptions take different forms based on the type of issue involved. The two most common forms are Maturing Bonds and Called Securities.

MATURING BOND/NOTES (NONCONVERTIBLE)

When the due date for a redemption is approaching, it is the responsibility of the bond redemption processing area to ensure all bonds are deposited with a collection agent prior to payment date.

The collection agent generally is a bank contracted by the securities firm to process the securities and interface with the paying agent.

The Bond Redemption Section will perform the following:

1. Request physical securities from all holding locations.

2. Prepare securities for shipment to the paying agent, (i.e., make negotiable and fill out Letters of Transmittal). Securities may also be deposited for redemption on behalf of a firm by depositories and regional offices.

3. Process inquiries pertaining to redemptions.

4. Follow procedures to ensure prompt collection of funds from paying agents and/or depositories.

5. Make bookkeeping entries into client accounts indicating the delivery of the issue being redeemed and credit for the appropriate funds on the redemption date.

CALLED SECURITIES

Equity and debt securities may be called for redemption either in their entirety or in part. This is not done arbitrarily; it is stated in the company's articles of incorporation whereby each year (or whatever time period is specified), the issuer may call a certain number of shares/bonds. The company will select, by lot, certificates representing the number of shares/bonds being called.

In processing a partial call, the involved Reorganization area must determine if any securities the firm holds appear on the list of called certificates provided by the issuer.

The processing area takes the following action steps:

1. All holding locations are instructed to check their inventories for called certificates and route them to Reorganization.

2. Procedures are followed to ensure that depositories advise Reorganization of the number of called certificates they will redeem on behalf of the firm.

3. Physical called certificates are prepared and submitted to the redemption agent.

4. An impartial lottery is conducted to determine which of the firm's customers will be selected to participate. Their holdings may be called in part or in entirety. The results of the lottery are reflected by bookkeeping entries which remove the old position in the customer's account and replace it with a "called" one. The impartial lottery has to be approved in advance by the Securities and Exchange Commission.

5. Procedures are followed to ensure prompt collection of funds from redemption agents and/or depositories.

6. Bookkeeping entries are made into clients' accounts that indicate a delivery of the called security and a credit of the appropriate funds on the redemption date.

PERPETUAL EXCHANGE SECTION PROCESSING

The Perpetual Exchange Section is responsible for processing of current changes wherein the customer *must* participate. The offers are involuntary from the client's perspective, and as stockholders, they receive substitutions (cash and/or new securities) for their assets. As opposed to expiring offers, these changes are considered "open-ended." In most cases, the client does not have to initiate the exchange process.

Although most perpetual offers do not require a client response to initiate processing, expiring offers, on the other hand, need client instructions or orders within a specified time frame. As an example of a perpetual exchange, let's look at the processing of stock splits.

STOCK SPLITS

Stock splits are used to adjust the number of outstanding shares of a corporation's stock. A split-up increases the aggregated number of shares outstanding, while a reverse split decreases the number of shares outstanding.

A corporation may elect to split-up its stock (usually its common stock issue) for a variety of reasons. Some reasons are as follows:

To effect a wider distribution of the shares in the hands of the public. The split-up will generally lower the market price of the stock, thereby increasing the issue's marketability.

The corporation may be required to show a greater number of shares outstanding in order to be listed on a stock exchange.

As part of the company's planned growth, or as a forerunner to a proposed merger or acquisition, or another company.

A reverse split is the exact opposite of a split-up. Under a reverse split, the stockholder receives fewer shares in exchange for their original holdings.

Upon confirmation that a split is in effect, a letter outlining the details is sent to the firm's clients holding the involved security by the Plans Section. The branch office network is also advised via a similar document (see Figure 6-11).

At this point, Reorganization assumes all cashiering functions for the "old" security, (i.e., fails, deliveries, etc.).

The Perpetual Exchange area is responsible for this type of reorganization and will perform the following:

1. Request physical securities from all holding areas of the firm.

2. Prepare securities for shipment to the exchange agent, (i.e. make negotiable and fill out Letters of Transmittal). Securities may also be deposited for exchange on behalf of the firm by depositories.

3. Process inquiries pertaining to the split.

4. Follow procedures to ensure prompt collection of the underlying shares from the agent.

5. Suspend aged deposits at agents (40 days) in compliance with SEC rule 15c3-3.

6. Make bookkeeping entries into client's accounts indicating a delivery of the old securities and a receive of the new securities.

The terms of the split are ongoing. The Reorganization area keeps an open working file of the issue until all physical securities

JANUARY 18, 19
SEC # A6789

XYZ STATE BANK
Common Stock Par Value $5.00

CASHIERS-ALL OFFICES

SPLIT-UP AND CHANGE IN PAR VALUE

SECURITY RECEIVED   XYZ State Bank
Common Stock Par Value $.50

RATIO   10 shares of XYZ State Bank Common Stock Par Value
$.50 for each share of XYZ State Bank Common Stock
Par Value $5.00 held

AGENT   XYZ State Bank
1000 Main Street
Anytown, New Jersey 55555
Attention: John Q. Smith, Chief
Executive Officer

NOTE # 1   No instructions are necessary. Exchange will be processed automatically.

NOTE # 2   A letter has been sent to clients on our records advising of this change. At the time of exchange, an entry will appear on clients' statements indicating a delivery (EXCHANGE) of the old security and a receive (EXCHANGE) of the new security.

HOW TO RECORD: ALL CERTIFICATES DATES PRIOR TO JANUARY 1, 19
SHOULD BE RECORDED AS COMMON STOCK PAR VALUE
$5.00 AND ALL CERTIFICATES DATES JANUARY 1, 19
AND SUBSEQUENT TO SHOULD BE RECORDED AS PAR
VALUE $.50.

FIGURE 6-11. Internal Notice of Stock Split

on the record have been exchanged and all accounts on the firm's records have been changed to reflect the new security. Any shares received by the firm on any future date will be routed to the Reorganization area and subsequently be automatically exchanged on an individual account basis.

EXPIRATION SECTION PROCESSING

The main function of the Expiration Section is to process changes in the capital structure of corporations where a firm's customer must elect to participate within a stated period of time. These changes are considered "closed-ended," due to the specific time frame mandated by the offer. Therefore, inaccurate or untimely execution processing may cause undue exposure and substantial monetary loss to the firm or its customers.

EXPIRATION ORDERS

As noted previously, a client can elect to participate in an expiration capital change within a specific time frame. As such, the client should receive notification which highlights the capital change and if necessary, a prospectus or offering circular detailing the offer. If the client decides to participate, instructions must be given to the Account Executives prior to the expiration date. Therefore, firms will usually establish a deadline of the business day prior to the expiration date for accepting orders from the branch office.

Upon receipt of the customer's order or instruction, the processing units can then advise the depository to exchange, tender, convert, etc., the securities being held on behalf of the client.

COMMON PROCESSING PROBLEMS

The Reorganization Department can encounter any number of problems in processing a capital change. The most common problems are as follows:

Problem	**Solution**
Failure to receive detailed information (prospectus) on time or insufficient number of copies received.	Duplicate materials in-house with Legal Department approval.
Late notification of capital change.	Distribute letter to clients containing information regarding change and advising that the prospectus will be mailed separately. Notify branch offices and other internal areas of actions taken.

Problem	**Solution** *(cont'd)*
Receipt of ambiguous capital change information.	Contact Legal Department before disseminating information.
Inability to submit all physical certificates to the paying agent by the expiration date.	Submit Notice of Guaranteed Delivery to paying agent.
Unable to contact client by expiration date.	Contact Legal Department and Executive.

CHAPTER 7

Clearing Corporations and Depositories

The execution of a trade is only the first step in the process, which generally culminates three days later in settlement.[1] One of the most important aspects in the operation of the securities business is the comparison of trades which involves the matching between counterparties of details of a securities trade as preparation for final settlement. Because trades executed between brokers and traders on the exchanges and the over-the-counter market are verbal agreements between the participants, trade matching must be performed later in the operations cycle. Obviously, matching of a trade is only complete when both sides of the trade agree on every detail—price, quantity and security. The matching of trades between securities firms is known as comparison. The clearance process determines what counterparties owe and what they are due to receive on settlement date.

Because of the immense trade volume involved, it is very difficult for securities firms to compare and clear trades among themselves. Therefore, most transactions are compared, cleared, and settled through clearing corporations and depositories. In this chapter, we will look at the functions of clearing corporations and deposito-

---

[1] Discussions herein on settlement date refer to settlement as occurring on T+3 which the industry is expected to initiate on June 1, 1995. Prior to that time, settlement data for purposes of this chapter is T+5.

127

ries and how they help securities firms in the comparison, clearance and settlement process.[2]

CLEARING CORPORATIONS

In the securities industry, a clearing corporation simplifies the process of comparison, clearance and settlement between member firms after a trade is executed. An organization is qualified to become a member of a clearing corporation if it satisfies at least one of the following criteria:[3]

1. It is a broker/dealer registered under the Securities Exchange Act of 1934, as amended.

2. It is a bank or trust company, including a trust company having limited power, which is a member of the Federal Reserve System or is supervised and examined by state or federal authorities having supervision over banks.

3. It is a registered clearing agency with the SEC.

The participants submit their trade data to one central location—the clearing corporation—which in turn matches buyers with their stated sellers and sellers with their stated buyers. In addition, the clearing corporation eventually puts itself "between" the member firms and a depository, thereby facilitating the actual delivery of the securities and payment of funds. The participants in the trade are freed from the cumbersome details of physical delivery and are presented with net security and money positions for settlement.

The National Securities Clearing Corporation (NSCC) is the nation's leading provider of centralized clearance and settlement, and handles 97% of equity and bond transactions in the U.S. NSCC

---

[2] This chapter discusses processes and services provided by the National Securities Clearing Corporation (NSCC) and The Depository Trust Company (DTC). NSCC, DTC and the other depositories and clearing corporations mentioned herein provide excellent facilities and are constantly upgrading these facilities and their services. These organizations should be contacted directly for an in-depth discussion of services offered.

[3] National Securities Clearing Corporation, *Rules and Procedures,* October, 1978, revised February, 1987.

is owned equally by the New York Stock Exchange (NYSE), the American Stock Exchange (AMEX), and the National Association of Securities Dealers (NASD). Clearing in the U.S. is also done through the Stock Clearing Corporation of Philadelphia (SCCP) and the Midwest Clearing Corporation (MCC). There are also specialized clearing corporations dealing with specific products, such as the Options Clearing Corporation, the Government Securities Clearing Corporation and the Mortgage Backed Securities Clearing Corporation. Because the functions and operations of most clearing corporations are similar, let's take a look at the largest, the National Securities Clearing Corporation (NSCC).

CLEARING CORPORATION PROCEDURES

To understand how a clearing corporation functions, the following sections describe clearing corporation procedures. We will use the largest, the National Securities Clearing Corporation (NSCC) as an example, keeping in mind that the functions and operations of other clearing corporations are similar.

WHAT IS COMPARISON?

Comparison is the process whereby two parties to a trade agree on the details of a previously executed trade. Comparison is sometimes referred to as "trade matching." In theory, all securities firms' Purchase and Sales Departments[4] could contact each other, one by one, to account for each trade and confirm the details of their trading commitments. However, the sheer size of the industry and its high level of activity make this approach impractical. Instead, most securities firms participate in NSCC's Comparison Systems, achieving greater efficiency.

The logic behind comparison is straightforward: When the same detailed information about a transaction is reported to NSCC by both the buy-side participant and sell-side participant, they have acknowledged the contractual terms of their trade.

Comparison is fitted to the unique aspects of the various marketplaces and the securities traded in them. Separate comparison

---

[4] Most departments in securities firms that process the comparison activity are called "Purchase and Sales" Departments or "P&S" Departments.

systems are operated for trades in equities listed on the New York and American Stock Exchanges; for transactions in corporate and municipal bonds and unit investment trusts; for equities traded over-the-counter; and for securities traded on a when-issued basis.

While each system varies somewhat, the comparison technique is similar in all of them. Buyers and sellers submit trade information to NSCC in standardized formats. Normally, trade information is submitted directly to NSCC in New York via direct data transmission. In addition to the normal input deadline, which is midnight of Trade Date (or "T"), each system provides methods for adding or correcting trade data on subsequent days.

Throughout the comparison and clearance cycle, an attempt is made to provide as much flexibility and as wide a variety of error-resolution techniques as participants find useful. In addition, efforts are made to maximize the use of automated capabilities. Currently, the majority of the trades received by NSCC are "locked-in" trades, that is, trades received directly from the various markets through their automated systems.[5]

Future trends indicate that more trades will be locked-in, thereby reducing the work of the member firms' Purchase and Sales Departments in submitting trades to NSCC.

THE CLEARANCE PROCESS

The first step in the clearance process is trade comparison: assuring that the buy and sell side components of a trade agree. Currently the Listed Comparison System processes by far and away the majority of NSCC's activity—600,000 plus sides each day (each trade, of course, has two sides). NSCC's OTC Comparison System, which processes equity and debt transactions in the over-the-counter market, currently handles some 300,000 sides per day, or about 80% of total OTC activity. The vast majority of NSCC transactional volume, however, does not require matching. These trades arrive at NSCC effectively matched and are known as "locked-in" trades.

Buy and sell orders routed and executed through automated systems at each marketplace are reported to NSCC via a computer-to-computer linkage. NSCC receives more than 90% of equity input

---

⁵   National Securities Clearing Corporation Annual Report, 1993.

via locked-in trades. Each marketplace has its own automated order entry and matching systems.

The New York Stock Exchange systems are:

Designated Order Turnaround (DOT)—routes market orders up to 2,099 shares and keeps track of limit orders up to 30,099 shares to assist the specialist in executing and reporting orders.

Opening Automated Report System (OARS)—stores certain orders received by the NYSE to facilitate a more efficient and accurate stock opening and trade reporting.

The American Stock Exchange systems are:

Post Execution Reporting (PER)—similar to the NYSE DOT system.

Opening Automated Report System (OARS)—similar to the NYSE OARS system.

Automated systems serving the over-the-counter market are:

Small Order Execution System (SOES)—automatically executes agency orders as large as 1,000 shares at the best available price.

Computer Assisted Execution Service (CAES)—allows submitter acting as principal to lock-in a trade up to 20,000 shares.

Automated Confirmation Transaction (ACT)—reports to clearing agency on evening of trade date on previously negotiated (via telephone) two party trades of OTC securities.

Order Confirmation Transaction (OCT)—enables firms or marketmakers to initiate and execute buy and sell orders of any size automatically, without telephone contact through NASDAQ terminals. Firms transmit orders to selected marketmakers who then respond electronically, either confirming or rejecting the transaction.

Intermarket Trading System (ITS)—enables a broker or market maker in any participating marketplace to reach electronically a counterparty in a competing marketplace whenever the

Consolidated Quotation System indicates a better execution may be available elsewhere.

Qualified Special Representative—Through his/her own in-house trading system, a market maker acting as a qualified special representative can lock-in a trade for submission to clearing.

TRADE COMPARISON

NSCC's Listed Comparison System processes non-locked-in equity trades on the New York and American Stock Exchanges. Each trade executed on the floors of the New York and American Stock Exchanges and in the over-the-counter marketplace that is not locked-in requires a formal confirmation as a binding contract with the counterparty. NSCC comparison sheets eliminate separate paper confirmation requirements for interdealer or broker-to-broker trades.

The following is a day-by-day account of the comparison system, beginning with the evening of Trade Date—known in clearing jargon as "T".

TRADE DATE (T)

Typically, both firms enter details of the trade to NSCC via computer-to-computer (CPU-CPU) linkages. Trade match criteria are based on the market in which the trade was executed, trade date, CUSIP (the industry's numerical identification code given to each class and issue of security), quantity, price and contra-side. Although not part of the match criteria, exchanges also require participants to submit audit trail data to assist market surveillance departments in trade reconstruction. Audit trail data includes all match data as well as executing broker badge number, contra-executing broker badge number, time of trade execution and coding to indicate the nature of the trade. Once a trade is entered into the system, NSCC assigns a unique 11-digit control number that remains with the trade throughout its duration in the system.

TRADE DATE + 1 (T+1)

On the day after trade date (T+1), NSCC issues Regular Way contract sheets, which indicate the status of its attempts to match trades, as follows:

Compared Trades—confirmed transactions that need no further action prior to settlement. If necessary, however, trade cancellation procedures may be used, which require the consent of both parties.

Uncompared Trades—transactions in which the details submitted by both parties (buyer and seller) to the trade do not match.

Advisory Trades—transactions in which trade data submitted by a counterparty does not match data submitted by the participant. If the latter has not submitted any trade data, this Regular Way contract sheet entry advises the participant of all other contra input. (See Figure 7-1.)

In order for settlement to occur, action must be taken on uncompared and advisory trades. NSCC accepts trade correction data on T+1 and T+2 in many formats: CPU-CPU, PC to CPU, tape or paper. Primary source for listed equities is the On-Line Correction System (OCS) run by the NYSE.

TRADE DATE + 2 (T+2)

T+2 is the last day to reconcile trades for T+3 settlement. T+2 begins with the distribution of new counterparty reports, which recap trades compared the previous day.[6] Reconciliation efforts continue for any trades remaining unmatched.

At the end of T+2, NSCC compiles another series of contracts for distribution on T+3. These contracts itemize transactions that have been added as a result of T+2 reconciliation procedures. Figure 7-2 is an example of an Added Trades Contract.

Any trade still uncompared after its advisory cycle expires is dropped from the comparison system. However, participants can continue to process these uncompared trades through NSCC. For any of these trades compared after T+3, NSCC will settle with the participants two days later. For dividend and interest purposes, a record of the original Trade Date is shown on the contracts and forwarded to NSCC's accounting system for processing.

---

[6] NSCC also provides the ability for firms to settle T+2 and older input on a next-day basis using their one-day settlement capability. Such late trades are submitted to NSCC no later than 9 P.M. on T+2. These trades are included in the CNS system for next-day settlement.

```
··· ·'? GRUITY-SYSTEM T-DATE          ADVISORIES         08/29/94    12·05
                                            USER-NAME  M/161   003
MAJOR-FIRM·        M     TRADE-DATE  08 29 94    BUY/SELL· B
SYMBOL: ----------       PRICE· --- --- ---     CONTRA-FIRM· ----

     LN S Q    B                                  CNTR CNTR MAJR S CA EXEC
     NO C I DK S QUANTITY      SYMBOL      PRICE   FIRM BDGE BDGE P ND TIME
     **   *    #  TRD-DATE· 08/29/94    **** TOP  OF DATA **** ****
ADV 02         B        500 ALL          26    5 8   M    X    000X        1002 ADV
ADV 03         B       4000 AZA          23    5 8   MAB  1168 0222        1036 ADV
ADV 04         B      15800 BHI          19    1 2   CJD  1242 0512        1028 ADV
ADV 05         B      10000 BS           22          M    0507 0507        1051 ADV
ADV 06         B       7100 CCL          44    5 8   LB   000X 0058        1058 ADV
ADV 07         B       5000 CCL          44    3 4   LB   000X 0058        1000 ADV
ADV 08         B       5000 CCL          44    3 4   LB   000X 0058        1001 ADV
ADV 09         B       2000 DOW          73    3 4   GS   0026 0555        1134 ADV
ADV 10         B      15000 DOW          74    3 8   M    0077 0077        1043 ADV
ADV 11         B      10000 ENC          18    1 8   FSC  0018 000X        1041 ADV
ADV 12         B       7900 MAR          30    3 8   M    1718 000X        1117 ADV
ADV 13         B      10300 HO           58    1 2   SWB  0802 0827        1027 ADV
ADV 14         B      14000 MSX          14    5 8   GS   X    X           0941 ADV

SEL COD:  S=STAMP-ADV  K=DK-ADV   N=KNOWS                     ENTER-EDIT
PF-KEYS: PF1-UPDATE PF2-SCROLL PF7-BKWD PF8-FWD PF12-MENU CLEAR-CANCEL/REFRESH
   NYSE EQUITY-SYSTEM T-DATE  UNCOMPARED / ADVISORIES    08/29/94    12:05
                                            USER-NAME: M/161   003
MAJOR-FIRM:        M     TRADE-DATE: 08 29 94    BUY/SELL: -
SYMBOL: ----------       PRICE: --- --- ---     CONTRA-FIRM: ----

     LN S Q    B                                  CNTR CNTR MAJR S CA EXEC
     NO C I DK S QUANTITY      SYMBOL      PRICE   FIRM BDGE BDGE P ND TIME ___

SEL COD: C=CHG D=DEL I=INHB R=RVRS S=STMP K=DK-ADV N=KNOWS     ENTER-EDIT
PF-KEYS: PF1-UPDATE PF2-SCROLL PF7-BKWD PF8-FWD PF12-MENU CLEAR-CANCEL/REFRESH
   NYSE EQUITY-SYSTEM T-DATE  UNCOMPARED / ADVISORIES    08/29/94    12:0
                                            USER-NAME: M/161   003
MAJOR-FIRM:        M     TRADE-DATE: 08 29 94    BUY/SELL: B
SYMBOL: ----------       PRICE: --- --- ---     CONTRA-FIRM: ----

     LN S Q    B                                  CNTR CNTR MAJR S CA EXEC
     NO C I DK S QUANTITY      SYMBOL      PRICE   FIRM BDGE BDGE P ND TIME
     **   *    #  TRD-DATE: 08/29/94    **** *** ***  **** **** ****
ADV 02         B       7100 CCL          44    5 8   LB   000X 0058        1058 ADV
ADV 03         B       5000 CCL          44    3 4   LB   000X 0059        1000 ADV
ADV 04         B       5000 CCL          44    3 4   LB   000X 0058        1001 ADV
    05         B      10000 CCL          44    3 4   LB   000X 0058        1001
    06         B      10000 CCL          44    3 4   P    0740 0058        1001
    07         B       3000 CCP          24    1 8   D    0978 X           0942
    08         B      11000 CFL          29    1 8   BS   0933 0840        1038
    09         B      15900 CFL          29    1 8   LB   000X 0840        1038
ADV 10         B      23600 CHW           7    7 8   SB   0810 X           1120 ADV
    11         B       4000 CNS          15    1 2   P    0030 X           1038
    12         B      15400 CNS          15    1 2   P    0030 X           1038
    13         B        700 CUM          41    1 2   ITSN 000X 0433        1104
    14        'B      10000 DOW          72    7 8   EC   0903 0877        0956

SEL COD: C=CHG D=DEL I=INHB R=RVRS S=STMP K=DK-ADV N=KNOWS     ENTER-EDIT
PF-KEYS: PF1-UPDATE PF2-SCROLL PF7-BKWD PF8-FWD PF12-MENU CLEAR-CANCEL/REFRESH
   NYSE    EQUITY-SYSTEM  UNCOMPARED / ADVISORIES     08/29/94    12:04
                                            USER-NAME: M/161   003
MAJOR-FIRM:        M     TRADE-DATE: -- -- --    BUY/SELL: -
SYMBOL: ----------       PRICE: --- --- ---     CONTRA-FIRM: ----

     LN S Q    B                                  CNTR CNTR MAJR S CA EXEC
```

FIGURE 7-1. National Securities Clearing Corporation Advisory Form
Used by permission of the National Securities Clearing Corporation.

```
      NO C I DK S QUANTITY    SYMBOL      PRICE     FIRM BDGE  BDGE P ND TIME
      **   *    * TRD-DATE: 08/26/94   **** *** ***  **** **** ****
          02       S      200 TCI       47  1 2  WS   X     X     ND
          03       S     3700 ABF       28  7 8  DOT  X     X        1117
  ADV     04       S     3400 ABF       28  7 8  M    X     000X     1203 ADV
          05       S      100 ADM       24  7 8  DOT  X     X        1117
          06       S       67 ADM       24  7 8  LAB  X     X        1117
  ADV     07       S      100 AIG       96  1 4  MGS  X     X        1255 ADV
          08       S      100 AIG       96  3 8  DOT  X     X        1117
          09       S     7000 AL        26       BF   0473  0326     1226
  ADV     10       S     7000 AL        26  1 8  BF   0473  0326          ADV
          11       S       83 ARD       12       PGA  X     X        1117
          12       S       50 BLS       59  3 8  ERN  X     X        1117
  ADV     13       S      100 CLX       51  5 8  ITSN SPEC           1539 ADV
          14    DK S      600 CNF       22  1 4  SBH  000X  X        1021

  SEL COD: C=CHG D=DEL I=INHB R=RVRS S=STMP K=DK-ADV N=KNOWS      ENTER-EDIT
  PF-KEYS: PF1-UPDATE PF2-SCROLL PF7-BKWD PF8-FWD PF12-MENU CLEAR-CANCEL/REFRESH
  NYSE     EQUITY-SYSTEM       ADVISORIES       TRADES        08/29/94   12:07
                                                 USER-NAME: M/161    003
  MAJOR-FIRM:    M      TRADE-DATE: -- -- --     BUY/SELL: -
  SYMBOL: ------------  PRICE: ---- --- ---      CONTRA-FIRM: ----

      LN S Q  B                            CNTR CNTR MAJR S CA EXEC
      NO C I DK S QUANTITY    SYMBOL      PRICE  FIRM BDGE BDGE P ND TIME
      **   *    * TRD-DATE: 08/26/94   **** TOP  OF DATA **** ****
  ADV 02      B      200 CRD       38  3 8  JPM  0111  05B5     0951 ADV
  ADV 03      B      200 HPH       23       NFS  0130  0001          ADV
  ADV 04      B     5000 MD        58  3 8  RJ   0634  0827     1513 ADV
  ADV 05      S     3400 ABF       28  7 8  M    X     000X     1203 ADV
  ADV 06      S      100 AIG       96  1 4  MGS  X     000X     1255 ADV
  ADV 07      S     7000 AL        26  1 8  BF   0473  0326          ADV
  ADV 08      S      100 CLX       51  5 8  ITSN SPEC           1539 ADV
  ADV 09      S     2000 DS        16       P    X     X        1251 ADV
  ADV 10      S     3300 EC        27  3 8  NSI  0719  000X     1233 ADV
  ADV 11      S     8000 EMC       18       AC   8164  X        0949 ADV
  ADV 12      S    10000 ENE       30  1 4  P    X     0527          ADV
  ADV 13      S    12600 FD        20  3 4  D    0001  X        1124 ADV
  ADV 14      S      300 FDA       36  1 8  ITSN SPEC           1144 ADV

  SEL COD: S=STAMP-ADV  K=DK-ADV  N=KNOWS                       ENTER-EDIT
  PF-KEYS: PF1-UPDATE PF2-SCROLL PF7-BKWD PF8-FWD PF12-MENU CLEAR-CANCEL/REFRESH
```

FIGURE 7-1. *(Continued)*

T+2/Continuous Net Settlement

Preparing for settlement through NSCC's Continuous Net Settlement (CNS) and Balance Order Systems is the principal focus of T+2. CNS is an automated clearance accounting system, which arrives at a net figure per participant due for settlement in a particular security. CNS provides for automatic book-entry delivery or receipt of the securities versus net money settlement.

To simplify the actual exchange of securities, the CNS system summarizes and nets together each participant's daily transactions in each issue with any previous day's open positions to create a single

National Securities Clearing Corporation   OTC Purchase Contract - Added Trades   Page 1 P
Member No. 0995 Member Name ABC & Co.   Settlement Date 08/25

COMPARED PURCHASES

QUANTITY	CONTRACT MONEY	SUMM DIFF	PRICE	BUY EXEC SELL	SELLER	SELL EXEC BRKR	ID CODE	STATUS	QUANTITY	MONEY	DATE	NUMBER
2	900	27,000.00				CNS TOTAL CARRIED FORWARD						
1	300	600.00				NON-CNS TOTALS CARRIED FORWARD						
3	1,200	27,600.00				GRAND TOTALS CARRIED FORWARD						

CNS * BRITISH TEL PLC ADR 2ND ITM
         CUSIP 111021 30 9 0 0 2

| BYT | 300 | 7,500.00 | ABCC | | 25.00000 | BCDE | 0003 | A1 | | | | 0036352268 |
| | 300 | 5,500.00 TOTAL | | | | | | | | | | |

1	300	7,000.00			CNS A/T TOTAL
0	0	0			NON-CNS A/T TOTAL
1	300	7,500.00			TOTALS SUBMITTED TODAY
2	1,200	34,500.00			CNS FINAL CONTRACT TOTAL
1	300	600.00			NON-CNS FINAL CONTRACT TOTAL

Subject to the By-Laws and the Rules of NSCC.

FIGURE 7-2. OTC Purchase Contract

Used by permission of the National Securities Clearing Corporation.

long position (securities due to participants), or a single short position (securities due from participants). CNS requires participants to deliver and receive net security positions by book-entry movements at a depository, rather than by physical delivery of certificates. As the positions are matched, NSCC becomes the contra-side to each participant's requirements and guarantees the settlement obligation. Because deliveries and receipts are made through a depository, CNS applies only to depository eligible securities (those securities which can be processed by a depository system).

The first step of the CNS process involves the summarization of transactions due to settle on T+3. The CNS Consolidated Trade Summary (See Figure 7-3), issued early on T+2, lists trades in CNS-eligible issues that have been accounted for and are ready for settlement on T+3.

TRADE DATE + 3 (T+3)

T+3 is Settlement Day, the day when NSCC facilitates the orderly and controlled exchange of securities and money for all of its participants through interaction with their Cashiering Departments. The principal securities processing system on T+3 is CNS. First, CNS obligations are passed against the participant's securities account at the depository. CNS short positions, except those exempted by the participant, are satisfied by debiting the participant's account (to the degree that sufficient shares or bonds are on deposit) and crediting NSCC's account at the depository. Then the total shares or bonds are credited to the depository accounts of participants with CNS long positions.

During the late afternoon of T+3, NSCC produces an Accounting Summary (see Figure 7-4), which provides a comprehensive review of each participant's CNS activity for that day's settlement. Included in the report is information regarding net trades reaching settlement, deliveries and receipts, interest and dividend totals reaching payable date, open security positions and money balances. DTC also produces a report to participants indicating all movements into or out of the participant's DTC account.

MONEY SETTLEMENT

Money settlement is the final stage of NSCC's transaction processing. On T+3, each participant's debit and credit obligations are

National Securities Clearing Corporation   CNS Compared Trade Summary

Member No. 0995   Member Name ABC & Co.   Settlement Date 08/25   Page 1

MKT	SEC SYMBOL	CUSIP	SECURITY DESCRIPTION	CNTA BRKER	PURCHASED	SOLD	PRICE	CONTRACT DEBIT	MONEY CREDIT	TRADE DATE
OC	BUD	035229103000	ANHEUSER BUSH COS INC	001	400		30.0000	12,000.00		08 18
OC	BUD	035229103000	ANHEUSER BUSH COS INC	002	500		30.0000	15,000.00		08 18
PC	BUD	035229103000	ANHEUSER BUSH COS INC	003		50	30.0000		1,500.00	08 18
			TOTALS		900	50		27,000.00	1,500.00	
			NET		850			25,500.00		
OC	BTY	111021309000	BRITISH TEL PLC ADR 2ND ITM 103		300		25.0000	7,500.00	1,500.00	08 18
CR	BTY	111021309000	BRITISH TEL PLC ADR 2ND ITM 161		1,000		25.0000	25,500.00	1,500.00	08 18
			TOTALS		1,300		32,500.00			
			NET		1,300		32,500.00			
			STOCK TOTALS		2,200	50		59,500.00	1,500.00	
			NET		2,150	50		58,000.00		
			TOTAL TRADES		2,200	50		59,500.00	1,500.00	
			NET TRADES		2,150	50		58,000.00		

Subject to the By-Laws and the Rules of NSCC.

FIGURE 7-3. CNS Compared Trades Summary

Used by permission of the National Securities Clearing Corporation.

National Securities Clearing Corporation
Member No. 0995   Member Name ABC & Co.

CNS Accounting Summary
Settlement Date 08/25   Page 1

CUSIP	SECURITY DESCRIPTION	OPENING POSITION LONG/SHORT(-)	SETTLING TRADES BUY/SELL(-)	STOCK DIV MISC ACTIV REC/DEL(-)	RECEIPTS & DELIVERIES REC/DEL(-)	CLOSING POSITION L/S(-)	CURRENT MARKET PRICE	CURRENT MARKET VALUE LMV/SMV(-)
035229103	ANHEUSER BUSCH COS INC		850	10	860-		30.00	
111021309	BRITISH TEL PLC ADR 2ND ITM		1,350		650-	650	25.00	16,250.00

National Securities Clearing Corporation
Member No. 0995   Member Name ABC & Co.

CNS Accounting Summary
Settlement Date 08/20   Page 1

MONEY SUMMARY

YESTERDAY'S CLOSING BALANCE	100,000.00
YESTERDAY'S CNS SETTLEMENT	100,000.00-
TODAY'S OPENING BALANCE	-0-
SETTLING TRADES	58,000.00
CASH DIVIDENDS AND INTEREST	
MISCELLANEOUS ACTIVITY	
TODAY'S CLOSING BALANCE	58,000.00

MARKET VALUE SUMMARY

LONG MARKET VALUE	16,250.00
SHORT MARKET VALUE	
NET MARKET VALUE	16,250.00

CNS SETTLEMENT

TODAY'S CLOSING BALANCE	
LESS MARKET VALUE	
TODAY'S CNS SETTLEMENT	41,750.00

Subject to the By-Laws and the Rules of NSCC.

FIGURE 7-4. CNS Accounting Summary
Used by permission of the National Securities Clearing Corporation.

accumulated in their individual accounts within the Money Settlement System. CNS passes to settlement the value of the firm's contract money, adjusted for the change in the market value of open positions, and the value of dividend and interest obligations that have reached pay date.

On the night of T+3, the Final Settlement Statement (see Figure 7-5) is processed reflecting money received or paid against net obligations. The statement also reflects any adjustments to net monies that were made after the production of the Preliminary Settlement Statement.

CNS is an invaluable tool for the participant. It takes the immense volume of trades submitted by each participant and nets them down to one security and money position for each security.

The flow chart illustrated in Figure 7-6 gives a summary of the interrelationships between the participants, the clearing corporation and the depository. As you can see, the services provided by NSCC's comparison and clearance function are a vital part of the trading process. The functions performed by the clearing corporation, allied with the depository, have been instrumental in allowing the marketplace to process the increasing trade volume of the last decade in an automated and efficient manner.

SPECIAL SERVICES

In addition to the functions discussed above, NSCC provides certain special services for its member firms. These services aid in smoothing the processing in special situations where the normal functions do not apply. Some of these services are described in the following sections.

BALANCE ORDER AND TRADE FOR TRADE ACCOUNTING

The Continuous Net Settlement System provides for an orderly and efficient system, in conjunction with most DTC eligible issues for the settlement of trades by book-entry procedures. However, there are certain trades involving non-CNS eligible securities which also must be settled. One system to settle these trades, Balance Order Accounting, nets deliveries when securities are not eligible for CNS processing.

National Securities Clearing Corporation	Final Settlement Statement		
Member No. 0995 Member Name ABC & Co.	Settlement Date 08/25 Reporting Time 23.12 Page 1		
SETTLEMENT TRANSACTIONS	DEBIT	CREDIT	ADJUSTMENTS
82 CNS MONEY SETTLEMENT	41,750.00		
98 SETTLEMENT CHECK——CERTIFIED		41,750.00	
98 SETTLEMENT CHECKS——TOTAL	41,750.00		
TOTALS	41,750.00	41,750.00	
BALANCE		.00	
Subject to the By-Laws and the Rules of NSCC.			

FIGURE 7-5. Final Settlement Statement.
Used by permission of the National Securities Clearing Corporation.

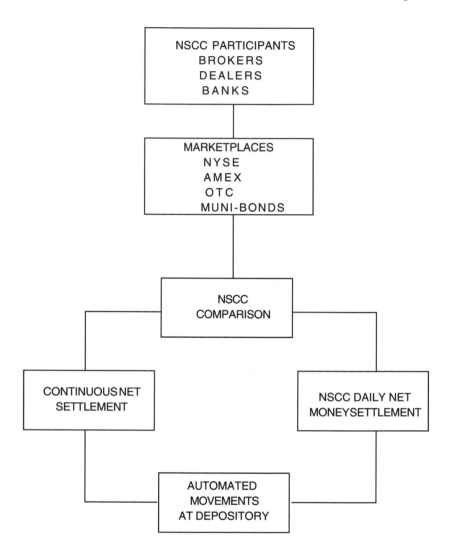

FIGURE 7-6. The Clearing Corporation as Part of the Trading Process

The system nets these trades into a simple buy or sell position, or positions per security and assigns a deliverer or receiver based on net positions. Balance Order tickets are generated and distributed to participants, informing them to exchange securities versus payment with other participants in order to settle their net purchases and sales.

TRADE-FOR-TRADE AND SPECIAL TRADE TRANSACTIONS

Trade-for-Trade and Special Trade Transactions are settled on an individual basis and are not netted with other trades. Therefore, when these trades settle, they maintain the details that were reported originally to NSCC, including price. Trade-for-Trade accounting is a special service for participants of NSCC's municipal bond program.

Special Trade accounting is available for all processing systems to account for those transactions which both parties have designated as Special Trades on comparison input.

THE DIVIDEND SETTLEMENT SERVICE

NSCC also provides a service for the orderly processing of dividend and interest claims between participants. The Dividend Settlement Service (DSS) allows for claims to be denied or satisfied within a specified time period.

THE NATIONAL TRANSFER SERVICE

The National Transfer Service (NTS) moves securities within a network of transfer agents located in 50 cities throughout the United States and Canada. NTS permits firms to forward most transfers to NSCC, rather than interfacing directly within the more than 200 transfer agents processing registered securities.

INDIRECT EXECUTING BROKER INPUT BY CLEARING BROKERS

A broker who executes trades, but is not a member of NSCC, can clear its trades through an NSCC Clearing Broker. The Executing Broker's trades are submitted for comparison processing through a Clearing Broker who is a member of NSCC, under the Clearing Broker's own clearing number. The procedure varies by market:

> For NYSE and AMEX trades, only the number of the Clearing Broker is identified in comparison. These trades settle through the Clearing Broker's account. The Clearing Broker in turn settles with the Executing Broker.

> In the OTC, Municipal and UIT Comparison Systems, the Clearing Broker similarly processes all of the transactions under its own clearing number, but also identifies each Executing Broker by a four-digit alpha code known as the

Executing Broker symbol, which is assigned by NSCC and the NASD. The alpha symbols enable Clearing Brokers to keep track of their Executing Broker's activity, but the responsibility for ultimately settling a compared trade remains with the Clearing Broker.

NEW YORK WINDOW

BACKGROUND

In recent years the financial community has become increasingly aware of the underlying risks and high expenses associated with post-trade processing. Several steps have been taken to address these concerns including:

reduction in the number of physical securities

automation of manual processes

consolidation of functions

relocation of financial institutions from downtown New York City

NSCC responded to the changing environment by approaching several broker/dealers about creating a facility that could consolidate various functions across multiple firms. Through centralization, the firms would realize additional cost reductions, improvements in operating efficiencies, and transform themselves from being securities processors into becoming information processors.

In 1992, NSCC and several firms embraced the concept of developing a centralized processing facility that would act as an extension of participants' back offices for certain functions associated with processing of physical certificates, and called it the "New York Window." Together it was determined that the services should be phased in, thereby allowing the industry to achieve benefits in the short term. Also, NSCC and the firms decided that the New York Window should act as an extension of the firms' own operations by receiving information directly from participating firms in an instruction driven manner. The initial phase of the New York Window was the development of a processing center for physical certificates. These services provide significant benefits to the securities industry, while the depositories work to make all securities eligible for depository processing. Subsequent phases of the New York Window services will include centralizing other redundant operational functions.

In April, 1993, NSCC implemented its first customer on the New York Window's facility for the processing of physical securities. The clearance of physical securities creates the platform for all future New York Window services. As the most basic processing function, physical "receives" and "deliveries" represent the first logical step in NSCC assuming broader functions for participating firms.

NSCC and the pilot organizations decided it was necessary to first develop a processing center for physical securities in an effort to address the skyrocketing unit costs. Although the number of certificates is declining at record pace, each firm is required to maintain the infrastructures necessary to process these physical securities.

With the creation of a shared common facility, it is assumed that cost savings will be realized across the industry and individually to each firm. Specifically through the centralization process, participating firms will see cost reductions as it relates to personnel and premises.

The Window Platform

The New York Window, as an extension of the firm's own operation, acts on its user's instructions. The information can be electronically transmitted through the firm's existing communications links to NSCC. The decision to have a seamless interface between the New York Window and its participants was a major priority for NSCC during the development stages. Broker/dealers and banking institutions are able to access the New York Window system in a batch, or interactive mode through computer-to-computer links, or on-line via remote terminals.

Firms who batch information to the New York Window can utilize the current NSCC Broker Network, which connects firms to NSCC's mainframe systems at SIAC's Shared Data Center. Data will automatically be routed from the Shared Data Center to the New York Window's system. The Broker Network performs pre-edit checks on all data it receives from any communication device. The input facility within the Broker Network is known as DATATRAK, and the output facility is AUTOROUTE.

With the current advances in communication and technology, NSCC believes that it is only a matter of time until the entire financial community becomes real-time trade processors. To meet these

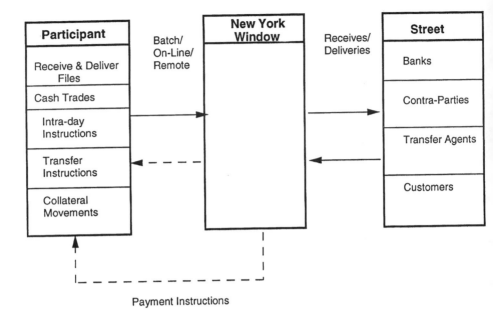

Figure 7-7. The Window Platform

changes in the industry, NSCC has established interactive computer-to-computer access for its firms to interface with NSCC services, including the New York Window. Through an interactive link, the New York Window can receive transaction messages on-line, immediately process those instructions, and submit actual results back to the firm in a real-time environment.

NSCC will also install an on-line, real-time interface into the New York Window system accessible through remote terminals at the firm's location. The data entry functions can be used by any participating organization through remote terminals. Some firms may use it as a contingency back-up for their computer-to-computer transmissions, or as their only means for submitting instructions real-time (if they are configured for batch processing only). The firms will also use remote terminals to submit and receive administrative messages interactively to support daily processing.

The New York Window system will electronically transmit information on clean-up activity directly to the firm's internal systems, thereby providing its participants with the opportunity to automatically update their organization's internal records. Other file updates will include unmatched receives, payment instructions, delivery DK updates, daily reconciliation summaries, and inventory statements.

THE SERVICES DEFINED

The first phase of the New York Window can accommodate the processing of all physical securities including, but not limited to, government securities, mortgage-backed securities, money market instruments (such as medium term notes, CDs and commercial paper), and more traditional instruments (including equities, corporate and municipal bonds). The Window is capable of handling sizable transaction value and significant trade volumes.

The initial services include receipt and delivery of securities over-the-window or through NSCC's envelope services, processing of transfers of physical securities, facilitating the movements of physical securities for reorganizations, coordinating the distribution of underwriting, processing of DTC withdrawals and deposits, end-of-day settlement and messenger services. Custodial services are also currently offered to complement the expediting process.

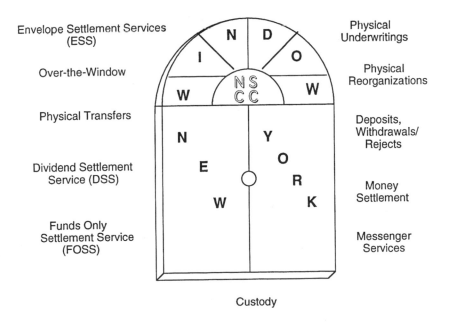

FIGURE 7-8. The New York Window

Over-the-Window Transactions: NSCC receives securities over-the-window, verifies them for correctness and makes appropriate turnaround deliveries. Deliveries are made according to turnaround instructions or from inventory.

Envelope Settlement Services (ESS) Transactions: All envelope settlement receives and deliveries are processed through the Window for the firms and their correspondents. The Window retrieves envelopes, verifies securities' negotiability and correctness, processes receive and deliver entries, packages securities, and prepares credit lists and processes all reclamations.

Funds Only Settlement Service (FOSS) Transactions: FOSS related activities include retrieving and delivering envelopes, preparing credit lists, verifying charges, and processing reclamations per the firm's instructions.

Dividend Settlement Service (DSS) Transactions: The New York Window will retrieve dividend settlement envelopes, accept notices of intent, and verify daily dividend settlement charges against participant instructions.

Physical Transfers: The Window accepts prepackaged items from its participating clients or prepares inventory items, delivers securities to transfer agents, furnishes participants with all window ticket information and retrieves completed transfers from agents.

Physical Reorganizations: The broker/dealers and banks will inform the New York Window of the corporate actions, and NSCC will deliver securities from inventory to agents, retrieve securities or proceeds, and implement the instructions for completed reorganizations.

Physical Underwriting: The Window supports the broker/dealers during the closing process including counting certificates, verifying for correctness and preparing certificates for delivery or pickup. In addition, securities are tracked to help the lead manager identify flipping activity.

DTC Deposits and Withdrawal/Rejects: With the Window, NSCC accepts pre-packaged items or packages depository-eligible inventory items, and delivers them to DTC for deposit. Withdrawn or rejected items are retrieved from DTC and delivered based on the participant instructions. When possible, rejections are corrected and re-deposited.

Money Settlement Services: At the end of each business day, the New York Window transmits a report with a balanced recap of all activity. Bank certification of checks is also coordinated, and checks are delivered to meet settlement obligations (or drafts are retrieved and processed according to the firm's instructions).

Messengers: The Window will provide messenger services to accomplish clearance activities, as well as to accommodate individual requests by participating firms.

Custody: To round off the physical securities processing functions, the Window offers a limited custody service. Custody accounts are provided for securities received and not yet needed for turnaround. The Box Account maintains securities in street name pending further instructions. The Custody Account maintains securities registered in firm name or bearer form.

BENEFITS OF USING THE NEW YORK WINDOW'S SERVICES TO PROCESS PHYSICAL CERTIFICATES

With the market moving toward book-entry only settlement, broker/dealers and banking institutions have seen a significant decline in the number of securities that settle via physical delivery. Because physical operations involve high fixed-costs, more firms are looking to achieve economies of scale through the centralization of processing physicals.

The initial services of the New York Window gives these organizations the opportunity to reduce costs associated with processing and maintaining physical certificates. The Window provides a range of services and is able to offer a variable cost structure. In addition to the current platform of services, NSCC expects to develop new products and services as the Window responds to the industry's requirements for centralizing other operational functions.

FUTURE TRENDS

The clearing corporation responds quickly to marketplace trends. As transactions become increasingly automated, so too does the clearing corporation's processing. As previously mentioned, the majority of the trades are received as locked-in trades directly from the various markets. Future developments will see this percentage steadily increasing. Computer-to-computer links between the clearing corporation and its participants will also witness significant growth. These include CPU-to-CPU links as well as the increasing use of personal computers to transmit data.

Another major development is the increasing emphasis on the international marketplace. As securities firms increase their involvement in the global financial arena, the problems of comparing and clearing international trades will have greater significance to the domestic manager. A mechanism is needed to coordinate domestic clearing with international clearing systems. To represent their domestic members, the International Securities Clearing Corporation (ISCC) was formed as a wholly-owned subsidiary of NSCC. ISCC's flagship service, Global Clearing Network, provides centralized clearance and settlement for U.S. brokers, dealers, and banks that trade in overseas markets. In addition, ISCC offers direct linkages with central clearing and depository organizations in other countries. This is the first step in smoothing the way for their members' increasing presence in the international arena.

REGULATORY REQUIREMENTS

Clearing corporations are subject to the rules of the various regulatory bodies and agencies that govern the securities industry. There are a number of regulations that are germane to securities firms' interactions with the clearing corporation. Figure 7-9 illustrates some of the more common regulations affecting comparison and clearance.

DEPOSITORIES

For the U.S. investor, the stock certificate has always represented ownership of a security. However, because of the existence of the physical certificate, the capability of the industry to handle large volume transactions is hampered. The inherent problems in the delivery and receipt of physical certificates makes for cumbersome processing. Some in the industry would like to eliminate the stock certificate entirely, especially since virtually all institutions and more retail investors are comfortable leaving their securities with a bank or broker-dealer, as opposed to holding them directly. However, it does not seem that this will be happening for quite a while and thus increased emphasis has been placed on "immobilizing" the stock certificate.[7] Immobilization of securities means reducing the number of physical certificates that pass between securities

New York Stock Exchange Regulations

Rule	Requirement
Rule 132	This rule stipulates that each party to a trade contract shall submit data regarding its side of the contract to a clearing agency except in previously agreed cases. Includes the definition of a qualified clearing agency.
Rule 134	This rule governs the resolution of "questioned trades." Questioned trades are those trades reported by the clearing agency which are questioned by a member organization. Rule 134 stipulates the process by which questioned trades should be investigated and resolved by the participants.

Municipal Securities Rulemaking Board

Rule	Requirement
G-12 amendments effective August 1, 1984 and February 1, 1985	These amendments require all interdealer trades after February 1, 1985 to be cleared through a clearing corporation's automated facilities.
G-15 amendments effective August 1, 1984 February 1, 1985	These amendments require broker/dealers to use a securities depository's automated confirmation and settlement service for deliver versus payment and receive versus payment customer transactions.

Securities and Exchange Commission

Rule	Requirement
17A	This rule provided for the establishment of a national system for clearance and settlement. It also established qualifications for registration of a clearing agency with the SEC.

FIGURE 7-9. Regulatory Requirements Affecting Clearing Corporations

---

[7] However, there is an increasing acceptance by investors of certain securities, principally municipal securities, being issued in Book-Entry-Only (BEO) form. With BEO issue, a global certificate representing the full face value of the issue is deposited with a depository. No certificates are available to investors, and transfer of ownership is recorded on the depository's books and is also reflected on the books of the bank for the account of the beneficial owner(s).

firms and customers by leaving the actual certificate in a central depository. Thus, instead of constantly processing stock certificates, the securities firm handles only the transfer of the interest from one owner to another through bookkeeping entries.

After many efforts to change the statutes, the New York Stock Exchange established a central certificate service in 1968 (now known as The Depository Trust Company), a securities depository established to service NYSE member firms. A depository retains large denominational form stock certificates for each of its participants. The selling firm advises the depository to debit its account and credit the buying firm's account, without the necessity of moving the certificates. By this simple book-entry procedure, the problems of complex certificate delivery are bypassed.

At the present time, there are three stock and bond securities depositories in the United States. These are the Depository Trust Company, the Midwest Securities Trust Company, and the Philadelphia Depository Trust Company. In addition, Participants Trust Company is the depository for securities of the Government National Mortgage Association. However, as with NSCC, our discussion will focus on the largest, the Depository Trust Company.

HISTORY AND MISSION

In 1966 the New York Stock Exchange established a Central Certificate Service (CCS), a securities depository created to provide service to NYSE member firms under the auspices of the exchange's then Clearing Corporation. CCS was superseded in 1973 by the Depository Trust Company (DTC). DTC is now independent from the exchange, therefore facilitating the participation of banks and institutions in DTC activities along with securities firms. By 1976, banks and securities firms were permitted to own DTC stock directly.

DTC's primary mission is to reduce the cost of securities processing by financial intermediaries serving the public. It does so through its automated systems, its telecommunications linkages with its participants and others, and its relationships with thousands of firms that serve as transfer agents, paying agents, exchanges agents, and redemption agents for securities issuers.

The depository can best be understood as an agency with three functions:

1. A custodian for the securities of participants: $7.5 trillion at year-end 1993.

2. An accounting system whose books record activity affecting the securities in DTC's custody: $27.8 trillion in book-entry deliveries were made between users in 1993.

3. A communications system for post-trade processing used by participants to connect with DTC and through it to other depository users, transfer agents, and other agents acting for securities issuers.

In order to maximize its usefulness to participants, DTC has continually sought to make more securities issues, and more types of securities, eligible for its services. Having begun with New York Stock Exchange listed stocks, the depository added stocks listed on the American Stock Exchange, then over-the-counter and other equity issues, and then listed and unlisted corporate debt. In 1981, the depository began to make bearer municipal bonds eligible for its services, followed by registered municipal bonds. A number of types of securities that settle only in same-day funds were added, beginning in 1987. That process is continuing, with commercial paper becoming eligible in October, 1990. More than 1.1 million securities issues (CUSIPs) are now eligible for DTC services. According to DTC's 1993 annual report, the depository has in custody for participants approximately:

78% of the shares of companies represented in the Dow Jones Industrial Average;

70% of the shares of all NYSE-listed U.S. companies;

57% of the shares of issues included in NASDAQ and 50% of American Stock Exchange-listed U.S. companies;

86% of the principal amount of outstanding corporate debt listed on the NYSE; and

95% of the principal amount of outstanding municipal bonds.

OWNERSHIP

Each year, the amount of stock in DTC that each participant is permitted to buy is recalculated to reflect yearly variations in usage.

Participants are generally allowed to purchase any, all, or none of the stock which they are allotted, at their discretion. The yearly stock reallocation takes place prior to the annual stockholder's meeting, so that stockholders will be able to vote newly acquired shares in the election of the Board of Directors, which occurs at the meeting.

SERVICES

The Depository Trust Company provides a wide range of services for its participants to further promote its mission of reducing costs for its bank and broker-dealer users. This section discusses the following seven services:

1. Accepting deposits of securities for custody
2. Making computerized book-entry deliveries of securities which are immobilized in its custody
3. Creating computerized book-entry pledges of securities in its custody
4. Providing for withdrawals of securities on a routine or "urgent" basis
5. Underwriting distributions
6. Dividends and interest
7. Redemptions

These services permit a participant to leave securities with DTC for safekeeping while facilitating their delivery to another party on the books of the depository. Securities are held in a central location. The services allow for collection of payment from the receiving party for the securities delivered, and the withdrawal of certificates desired by any of DTC's customers.

The widespread use of these services by participants permits timely, secure, accurate, and low-cost processing. Let's look at each of these services in more detail.

CERTIFICATE DEPOSITS

Deposits of certificates may be made in any eligible security issue at DTC's main office, or at various bank and clearing corporation offices nationwide which act as DTC depository facilities.

Eligibility is determined according to criteria specified by DTC. The number of eligible securities is constantly expanding, with the total at the end of 1993 rising to over 1,200,000.[8] Securities are held in the depository's vaults, separated by issue. The participants' accounts are maintained on the depository's books and changes in the accounts can be made without physical security movement. Figure 7-10 gives a simplified version of the depository's vault and the breakdown of securities between participants.

ABC	CO.	100	SHARES
GHI	CO.	500	SHARES
LMN	CO.	50	SHARES
PQR	CO.	1000	SHARES
STU	CO.	300	SHARES
XYZ	CO.	100	SHARES

THE DEPOSITORY'S BOOKS

	FIRM A	FIRM B	FIRM C	FIRM D
ABC CO.	30 SHARES	30 SHARES	20 SHARES	20 SHARES
GHI CO.	100 SHARES	200 SHARES	100 SHARES	100 SHARES
LMN CO.	20 SHARES	5 SHARES	10 SHARES	15 SHARES
PQR CO.	500 SHARES	200 SHARES	100 SHARES	200 SHARES
STU CO.	100 SHARES	50 SHARES	50 SHARES	100 SHARES
XYZ CO.	70 SHARES	10 SHARES	10 SHARES	10 SHARES

FIGURE 7-10. The Depository's Vault

---

[8] The Depository Trust Company Annual Report, 1993.

DELIVERIES

Deliveries in the settlement of securities transactions may be with or without the condition of money payment, depending upon the participant's instructions. DTC provides for the settlement of all deliveries when payment is requested, as well as other payments such as cash dividends and interest payments allotted to participants, through its daily settlement system. The foundation of this system is a DTC settlement statement, which portrays each participant's entire financial settlement activity by type of transaction, and summarizes all transactions into a net dollar amount owed to DTC, or to the participant, and paid daily.

PLEDGES

This service is a computerized book-entry method for effecting collateral loans between a securities firm and a bank by pledging as collateral securities held within the depository. Securities to be used as collateral are entered into a pledged position, until the collateral is released. The securities generally never leave the depository and all movements are made by book-entry.

CERTIFICATE WITHDRAWALS

There are two major types of certificate withdrawals from DTC:

1. *Withdrawal-by-Transfer (WT),* in which securities are transferred daily to the name of a participant's customer. Ordinarily, the newly registered certificates requested by participants are available to them one week after DTC receives the withdrawal instructions.

2. *Urgent Withdrawals or Certificate-On-Demand (COD),* in which certificates are released to the requesting participant the same day.

UNDERWRITING DISTRIBUTION

Underwriters of new and secondary issues distribute them by book-entry against payment, whether or not certificates are available to investors. In 1993, lead managers used DTC to distribute 21,572 new corporate and municipal underwritings valued at $988 billion.

DIVIDENDS AND INTEREST

DTC collects dividend and interest payments for securities in its custody. In 1993, DTC received more than 2.1 million payments for participants from 4,395 paying agents, with a monetary value in excess of $400 billion. Upon receipt of these dividend and interest monies (almost 100% received on payable date), DTC allocates these monies to its participants based on their holdings in DTC's custody.

REDEMPTIONS

When a security in the depository's custody matures or is called by the issuer, DTC presents it for redemption to one of over 6,000 agents and pays the proceeds to affected participants. In 1993, DTC processed redemptions in over 175,000 issues for a total dollar value exceeding $469 billion.

CLEARING AND SETTLEMENT INTERFACE

In addition to the services described above, Depository Trust maintains an interface with the National Securities Clearing Corporation (NSCC) and other clearing corporations. Securities firm participants in DTC can utilize their positions at DTC to settle with other firms whose transactions are cleared by NSCC.

Depository Trust's interfaces with the other clearing agencies constitute a major element in the national system for the clearance and settlement of securities transactions. These interfaces enable participants in various clearing agencies to use their securities positions in one location to settle transactions in other clearing corporations by book-entry deliveries. This arrangement eliminates the interregional movement of securities certificates, thereby further contributing to immobilization.

INSTITUTIONAL DELIVERY SYSTEM

The Institutional Delivery (ID) system is a process for reporting, affirming, and settling trades between broker/dealers and institutions. The main function of the system is to present a single method to coordinate comparison and settlement activity among securities firms, institutions, and custodian banks. In conjunction with this, the ID system provides efficient, automated methods to accomplish its goal.

The primary objective of the ID system is to avoid most of the errors and delays associated with traditional comparison and settlement methods, as well as to decrease the manual efforts for this function. In addition, the ID system enables institutions and custodian banks to better manage their cash balances, providing early notice of fund needs and availability. The mechanics of the ID system are as follows:

1. A securities firm executing an institutional trade furnishes DTC with the trade data (price, quantity, date, etc.), which the depository then passes on to the firm's institutional customer, the customer's agent and other interested parties, in a form that is recognized as a legal confirmation.

2. If the ID confirmation accurately reflects the institution's order, the institution sends an acknowledgment to DTC (called an "affirmation"). If the confirmation does not agree with the institution's records of its order, the institution can act early enough in the settlement cycle so that the securities firm can enter the proper corrections into the ID system.

3. When affirmation of the trade confirmation is received, DTC forwards settlement instructions to the customer's agent and submitting firm.

4. If the deliverer has enough securities in its DTC account, the depository will automatically complete the delivery by book-entry on the morning of settlement date, and process the related money settlement as directed.

5. If the deliverer does not have enough securities in its DTC account, it will be notified by DTC early in the morning of settlement date. The deliverer still has the opportunity to provide securities for delivery later on in the same day.

6. If the security is not DTC eligible, the deliverer and receiver may use specially prepared DTC instructions to settle the transaction outside DTC.

Until June of 1994, DTC's ID system operated in a batch, overnight process. With the pending implementation of a T+3 settlement cycle in 1995 for securities, however, a more rapid interchange of trade data and subsequent affirmation is needed. Therefore, DTC has now converted its ID system to an interactive mode, whereby securities firms can now enter trade data multiple times throughout the day, and confirmations can be immediately generated. Institutions, or their agent banks acting on their behalf, can send affirmations to DTC also on an interactive basis. It is expected that all parties to an institutional trade will utilize the optional interactive features of the ID system by the time T+3 is implemented.

INTERACTIVE ID SYSTEM

The following section briefly describes the new, interactive ID system. All new service features are optional.

The new system provides for a Standing Instruction Database (SID) that will act as a central repository for all customer/account and settlement information. SID will allow institutions to enter customer/account related data (including interested parties, the agent internal account number of the customer and the agent number). It will also allow broker/dealers to "link" their broker internal account numbers to the specific customers/accounts established by the institution. It will also allow agents, clearing agents, executing broker/dealers and clearing brokers to enter settlement information for a depository or country and security type. As appropriate, the broker/dealer would be notified of the establishment of this information and any subsequent changes or deletions.

Since DTC will maintain the database and append the necessary information to broker/dealer trade input, SID will enable broker/dealers to eliminate internal processing of customer account information. SID will also ensure the most timely updating of this information: once entered, updates will apply to all trades received thereafter, eliminating any time lags due to broker/dealer processing of the data. Once an account has been established on SID, normal daily processing activities, described below, can take full advantage of this information.

The first activity to take place is the broker/dealer's execution of a trade on behalf of the institution. The broker/dealer will be able to communicate the details of the execution via the Notification of Order Execution (NOE) function. The broker/dealer can provide the notification: 1) for each execution of a trade; 2) once the block order has been filled; and/or 3) at the end of the day, if the block has not been completely executed. The exact use of Notification of Order Execution will be flexible, thereby allowing it to be tailored to the requirements of both broker/dealer and institution.

The institution would generally use the Notification of Order Execution to prime the allocation process. The system will also allow the institution to reject the NOE. The reason for rejection of the NOE would be included in the rejection message (e.g., Don't Know, etc.).

Assuming acceptance of the Notification of Order Execution, the institution could then prepare Institution Instructions. These instructions contain individual trades, account allocations of block trades, and step-out broker information. Allocations and step-out information are needed by the executing broker/dealer prior to entering trade input to DTC. The Institution Instructions would be forwarded to the broker/dealer and, if the institution and broker/dealer have elected to match, the data would be retained by DTC for that purpose. The Institution Instructions provided to the broker/dealer would be augmented by the broker internal account number, if resident on SID.

Upon receipt of the Institution Instructions, the executing broker/dealer (or broker/dealers if this were a step-out trade) would ensure their accuracy. If the information did not agree with the execution, the broker/dealer would submit an Institution Instruction Cancel/Correction including the reason for rejection (e.g., wrong CUSIP, over-allocated, etc.).

Assuming the Institution Instructions are accurate, the broker/dealer could then allocate the trade, and provide DTC with broker trade input—one per account. If the broker internal account number for the account is resident on SID, there will be no need for the broker/dealer to enter customer, interested party, agent, and clearing agent information. Further, if the broker/dealer entered clearing broker information into SID, this information could also be eliminated from the input.

Since the new system will merge the existing ID and International ID systems, broker trade input can be submitted to DTC in one of three formats: 1) existing domestic; 2) international; or 3) a unified enhanced format. The enhanced format, besides unifying the domestic and international formats, allows for cancellation and correction via broker confirmation number, in lieu of cancellation by DTC control number or the administrative cancellation procedure. It also allows for matching of DTC ineligible issues by codifying settlement related information. All three formats may be submitted interactively throughout the day, or once daily at the broker/dealer's choosing. Broker/dealers can either submit trade input (exclusive of customer and settlement information) by linking their broker internal account number to the customer/account established on SID, or retrieve the information from their internal customer databases, and include this information on each trade submitted.

For broker/dealers and institutions electing to match, DTC would compare broker trade input to Institution Instructions. If a match is found, and the institution has affirmation authority, a matched affirmed confirmation is generated; otherwise, a matched confirmation is produced. The matched affirmed confirmation takes the place of both the confirmation and eligible/ineligible/CNS eligible trade report, and can be provided to all parties named on the confirmation. The matched confirmation would be used to notify the affirming party that the institution agrees with the details of the trade. The affirming party could then affirm the trade, and a matched affirmed confirmation would be produced.

If a match is not found, but all details other than the money fields required to calculate settlement amount match, then a Potential Match Report would be generated, and forwarded to the broker/dealer and institution immediately. If a Potential Match cannot be ascertained, an Unmatched Report would be generated to institutions and broker/dealers at the end of the day. The report would list all unmatched broker trade input and Institution Instructions, inclusive of those items previously reported on the Potential Match Report. In addition, Unmatched Confirmation and Unmatched Institution Instructions would be made available to all named parties.

Trades could be unmatched because either the institution or broker/dealer failed to submit their input, or because one or both of the submissions are incorrect. Incorrectly submitted broker/dealer trade input or Institution Instructions can be canceled and resubmitted, as required. The new cancellation procedure facilitates the process by allowing broker/dealers to cancel trade input by use of the broker confirmation number, and institutions to cancel Institutional Instructions by the institution reference number (both of which are assigned by the submitting party).

For traditional confirmation/affirmation processing, if the affirming party agrees with the confirmation, an affirmation is submitted and an affirmed confirmation (the equivalent of the current Eligible/Ineligible/CNS Eligible Trade Reports) is generated to the deliverer, receiver, and any other party to the trade that requests it. All confirms not affirmed by end of day will be listed on the T+2/T+3/T+4 Unaffirmed Report[9] which will be available to the broker/dealer, affirming party, and other parties named on the confirmation.

If the institution disagrees with the confirmation, an Institution Request for Cancellation/Correction (IRFCC) can be submitted. The IRFCC indicates the reason(s) the institution is requesting the broker/dealer to cancel/correct the confirm. The IRFCC is forwarded to the broker/dealer who, if in agreement with the institution, can use the previously described cancellation procedure to cancel the existing trade and resubmit the corrected trade.

In addition to the cancellation and resubmission procedure described previously, a new correction procedure will be made available. The correction procedure allows broker/dealers to process corrections to fields that do not affect net amount, settlement information, or the parties to the trade. These corrections will produce corrected confirmations, or corrected affirmed confirmations, depending on whether the trade was previously affirmed. Since these changes are "non-material," re-affirmation of these corrections will not be required. Non-material fields include: account type, market, role, special instructions, and data elements in the security description.

Whether matching or confirmation/affirmation is being used, a Cumulative Eligible Trade Report (CETR) will be produced at the end of day T+3 (approximately 4:00 a.m.). The CETR will be available to deliverer and receiver, and other parties named on the confirmation. The report lists all previously affirmed confirmations.

---

[9]   Dates and timeframes discussed herein will change upon implementation of SEC Rule 15c6-1, which mandates T+3 settlement on June 1, 1995. Readers should contact DTC for more detailed information.

DTC eligible issues may be settled using improved Authorization/Exception procedures. These procedures will allow for the authorization of unaffirmed/unmatched trades, and the authorization of trades on settlement date and beyond. Global authorization, with or without exception, can be utilized for trades affirmed, or trades submitted (and unaffirmed) prior to close of business two days prior to settlement (S-2). These trades appear on the Cumulative Eligible Trade Report, or the T+4 Unaffirmed Report, and provide a stable base for Global authorization. Global Authorization/Exception of affirmed trades will be available on the day prior to settlement (S-1) and until 11:00 a.m. on settlement date (S). Global authorization on settlement date is being added as a "fail safe" should a participant be unable to globally authorize trades by evening of S-1. Trades affirmed or submitted on S-1 or beyond will require trade-for-trade authorization. Trade authorization on S-1, or after original Deliver Order (DO) cutoff on settlement date, (or days thereafter) will be submitted to DTC's night cycle. The T+5 reports will be modified to reflect unaffirmed/unmatched trades, trades for various settlement days, and will list all trades processed by the night cycle. Trades authorized prior to the original DO cutoff will be submitted immediately to DTC's dayside processor. Dayside trades will be reported on current deliver order outputs (e.g., Deliver/Receive, Dropped Delivery Reports).

AUTOMATION OF DEPOSITORY SERVICES

To lower the operating costs of the depository and its users, DTC continues to increase the automation of its operations and communications with its participants, transfer agents and others. The depository has four principal vehicles for automated communication with users:

1. Computer-to-Computer Facility (CCF and CCF II): CCF is used for direct computer-to-computer communication between DTC and user IBM mainframes. CCF II serves the same purpose as CCF, but can also communicate with non-IBM user computer mainframes and personal computers.

2. Mainframe Dual Host (MDH): A computer-to-computer telecommunications system, MDH lets users send and receive

time-critical data in a real-time environment. Data submitted through MDH is processed immediately, and notification of the activity is instantaneous and continuous.

3. Participant Terminal System (PTS): Linked directly to DTC's computers, PTS is a network of almost 2,000 computer terminals located in participant offices in the U.S. and Canada. Participants use PTS to send instructions, inquiries, and other messages to DTC, and to receive messages and reports.

4. PTS Jr: This is a dial-in network for low-volume users, which contains all of the functionality of PTS at a reduced cost, although at reduced speed.

Supporting International Business

In 1986, the total volume of turnover on the world's sixteen major stock exchanges grew tenfold to 2.9 trillion U.S. dollars. In 1987, cross border equity trading by itself totaled 1.3 trillion U.S. dollars.[1] Almost all firms are aware of the increased volume of international transactions, and most have been struggling to set up Operations Departments to process this trading efficiently. Operations personnel in U.S. firms are very comfortable with the types of institutions in place today in the U.S. that serve as centralized securities depositories or clearing corporations: e.g., the Depository Trust Company, the National Securities Clearing Corporation, the Midwest Securities Trust Company and the Philadelphia Depository Trust Company. These institutions arrange for timely and effective comparison and settlement of trades. On the international side, however, there is no "central" or "global" depository/clearance system to compare and settle all types of securities. While Euroclear and Cedel serve the fixed income market need for efficient and cost effective settlement of international trades, these organizations are not yet in a position to process the vast majority of international equity transactions.

As the international markets continue to expand, it's important that Operations Managers have a basic understanding of the differ-

---

[1] Global Equity Analysis Report, SIA, 1988.

165

ences in processing in countries outside of the U.S.. Figure 8-1 offers a brief compendium of some different products traded in various countries. Processing this business can be complicated and usually requires a dedicated unit with expertise specific to the international marketplace. Each country often has its own trading and settlement practices, time zone differences, and regulatory environment.

This chapter, then, focuses on those aspects of international operations that managers should know about because they are so different from domestic U.S. operations. We will look at the use of custodian banks, Euroclear and Cedel, areas of risk and exposure, international cash management, tax regulations, international communications, common problems, and what the future operations environment will need to look like to have effective and efficient cross border transaction processing.

INTERNATIONAL OPERATIONS PROCESSING

TRADING ENVIRONMENT

In many countries, foreign broker/dealers are not allowed to become members of local domestic exchanges. In addition, in countries where local exchange memberships are permitted, the cost of building an execution and clearing capability is very expensive. Therefore, many U.S. securities firms use international brokers to execute and clear their trades. Similarly, many firms use international banks for custodial, settlement, and paying agent services, because of the expertise of local custodian banks and the expense necessary to duplicate that expertise.

As with domestic securities, a typical transaction begins when a customer calls an Account Executive and places an order. The order will be sent to the firm's trading desk and, for purposes of our discussion, let's assume the trading desk goes to a broker/dealer in the country where the security is traded for execution.

Figure 8-2 depicts the trading process involved in this international securities transaction.

The Operations Manager should be looking for timely execution reports, trade date or trade date plus one confirmations, acceptance of firm settlement, and payment procedures and responsiveness to audit and reconciliation requirements.

SECURITIES

	Australia	Belgium	Canada	Denmark	Fed. Rep. Germany	France	Hong Kong	Italy	Japan	Luxembourg	Mexico	Netherlands	Norway	Singapore	South Africa	Spain	Sweden	Switzerland	United Kingdom	United States
Common Share	●	●	●	●	●	●	●	●	●	●	●	●	●	●	●	●	●	●	●	●
Preferred Share	●	●	●	●	●	●	●	●	●	●	●	●	●	●	●	●	●	●	●	●
Convertible Share	●		●	●	●	●		●	●	●	●	●		●				●	●	●
Investment Certificate	●			●	●			●	●					●	●			●		●
Global/Jumbo Certificate	●	●			●	●		●		●	●	●		●		●		●		●

DEBT

	Australia	Belgium	Canada	Denmark	Fed. Rep. Germany	France	Hong Kong	Italy	Japan	Luxembourg	Mexico	Netherlands	Norway	Singapore	South Africa	Spain	Sweden	Switzerland	United Kingdom	United States
Corporate Bond	●	●	●	●	●	●	●	●	●	●	●	●	●	●	●	●	●	●	●	●
Government/State Bond	●	●	●	●	●	●	●	●	●	●	●	●	●	●	●	●	●	●	●	●
Convertible Bond	●	●	●	●	●	●		●	●	●		●		●	●	●	●	●	●	●
Floating Rate Bond	●		●	●	●	●	●	●	●	●		●		●	●		●	●	●	●
Zero Coupon Bond	●		●		●	●			●	●		●		●	●	●			●	●
Public Authority Bond			●	●	●	●	●		●	●		●	●	●	●	●	●	●	●	●
Bank Issued Bond		●	●	●	●		●		●	●	●	●	●	●	●		●	●		●
Mortgage-backed Bond			●	●	●				●					●	●					●
Bond with Warrant	●				●	●		●	●			●		●	●		●	●		●

MONEY MARKET

	Australia	Belgium	Canada	Denmark	Fed. Rep. Germany	France	Hong Kong	Italy	Japan	Luxembourg	Mexico	Netherlands	Norway	Singapore	South Africa	Spain	Sweden	Switzerland	United Kingdom	United States
Certificate of Deposit	●	●	●	●	●	●	●	●	●	●	●	●	●	●	●	●	●	●	●	●
Commercial Paper	●	●	●	●	●	●	●	●	●	●	●	●	●	●	●	●	●	●	●	●
Treasury Bill	●	●	●	●	●			●	●	●	●	●		●	●	●			●	●
Bankers Acceptance	●		●		●	●	●		●	●	●	●		●	●				●	●
Time Deposit	●		●	●	●				●	○	●	●		●			●	●	●	●
Call Money	●		●	●	●			●	●	●	●	●		●	●	●	●	●		●

OPTIONS & FUTURES

	Australia	Belgium	Canada	Denmark	Fed. Rep. Germany	France	Hong Kong	Italy	Japan	Luxembourg	Mexico	Netherlands	Norway	Singapore	South Africa	Spain	Sweden	Switzerland	United Kingdom	United States
Options Based on Equities	●			●	●									●	●	●	●	●	●	●
Options Based on Bonds	●		●	●	●									●			●		●	●
Options Based on Indices	●		●	●	●							●					●			
Futures	●		●	●	●				●		●			●	●	●	●	●	●	●

FIGURE 8-1. Major Products by Country*

*Source: ISSA Folders, International Society of Securities Administration (ISSA), Switzerland.

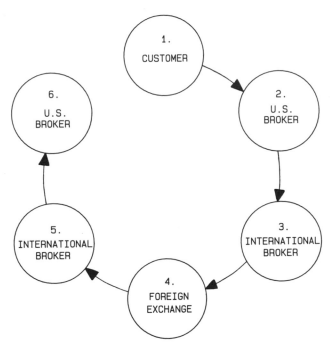

FIGURE 8-2. International Securities Transaction Participants

CUSTODIAN SERVICES

Just as the trading area often uses international institutions to execute the trade, Operations Departments often use international custodian banks to perform the settlement function. Here again, the reasons are cost and knowledge of the local marketplace. On trade date the Operations Departments will issue receive or deliver instructions to the custodian bank. In some countries, it's vital that instructions get issued on trade date because settlement can be in as short a timeframe as one day. On settlement date the custodian bank will receive/deliver the securities and pay/receive monies.

This process is far more complicated than described in the above paragraph. Let's look at the services a custodian bank will usually perform:

1. Work with the executing international brokers to coordinate receipt and delivery of securities based on instructions provided by their depositors (your firm).

2. Keep securities collectively by category rather than individually. The depositor is entitled to the same number of securities as deposited, but not to the identical securities. Generally, securities deposited with custodians may be registered in the custodian's name, or in the name of a nominee company, but always for the benefit of the depositor. Securities are generally registered this way, unless the depositor asks the custodian to register the securities in the names of the depositors' customers.

3. Collect all dividends, interest and other payments of income or capital relating to all securities deposited, except for securities registered in individual names, or directly payable to the depositor or to the registered holder. Such cash dividends or other cash payments are generally converted into U.S. currency and forwarded to the depositor's correspondent bank, unless otherwise instructed. In the case of dividends or interest paid to a broker or dealer which are the property of the depositor or the registered owner, custodians will make claims against other brokers for dividends/interest on behalf of their depositor.

4. Submit maturing securities for payment as they are called for redemption. Notification of any rights, offerings, exchange offers, tender offers, consolidations, and any other corporate action proposed by issuers of securities held in custody, is the responsibility of the custodian.

5. Forward proxies in accordance with the instructions given by the depositor.

6. Deliver or transfer the securities in accordance with depositor instructions and process the purchase of securities as the depositor instructs. Instructions given to the custodian by the depositor include those transmitted by telex, or cable, or telegram with appropriate control codes.

7. Provide monthly statements in whatever order required showing the delivery of all securities to and from the custodian.

NEGOTIATING POINTS FOR OPENING CUSTODIAN ACCOUNTS

Let's look at some negotiating points a U.S. Operations Manager should keep in mind when opening an international custodian account:

1. Discuss the applicable laws and national jurisdiction that may apply to disputes between bank and depositor. Most banks will prefer the laws of the custodian country, but some banks negotiate this point. SEC rules will generally provide superior protection for the depositing firms.

2. Negotiate for an "overdraft" settlement account or credit line. This will enable settlement of transactions even if the cash is not on deposit at the bank to settle trades. It is almost impossible to anticipate how much will be needed in various currencies at each bank on any one day because of irregular settlement conventions. The bank can grant a line of credit so settlements can take place without a credit balance in the account. The bank will charge interest on the overdrawn amount for the time it stays overdrawn.

3. Negotiate the lowest rate possible over the LIBOR rate. Don't be shy about this because banks earn enormous sums from the inefficiencies of the settlement process.

4. Insist on interest (LIBOR rate or above) on any credit balances in the accounts.

5. Insist on same day notification on any corporate actions in your firm's portfolio, and assurance that the bank will do whatever is beneficial for your firm and its customers on rights offerings and other corporate actions in cases of miscommunication.

6. Insist on a monthly list of holdings with the custody bank, both securities and cash.

7. Ask the bank to provide a monthly list of all security movements they have made. This will help balance any discrepancies you might have at month end.

8. Insist on daily activity lists of cash and securities movements.

9. Insist that the bank collect dividends and interest. Also insist that the bank advise of any certificates held that are not in nominee name. All securities should be held in nominee name so dividends will be easily collected by the bank. The bank then distributes the monies or stock to the accounts for which they hold securities. In some instances, the custodian will hold certificates in street name or client name, due to the length of time it takes to re-register the certificates.

10. Insist that a security code, specific to your firm, be set up with the bank to reduce the possibility of fraud in the telexing of instructions.

11. Insist that the bank accept liability in case of their error or neglect, such as cases where the bank does not act on instructions, does not convert funds, or does not protect customers on right offerings or corporate actions.

12. Ensure that the bank keeps an updated list of authorized signatures from the firm. All written correspondence should have the signatures verified by the bank.

Communications regarding settlement with custodian banks are probably the most important aspect of your relationship with them. Daily transmissions of receive and deliver activity and funds movements are essential, and must be matched to pending instructions transmitted to custodian banks. In the case of incorrect comparisons, the custodian bank must be responsive to inquiries to resolve discrepancies. When pending instructions are matched, the necessary entries to firm records should be processed to reflect this activity. Fails on international transactions must be resolved immediately with custodian banks, or customers selling securities, because buy-in regulations in some countries are strictly enforced.

Figure 8-3 provides information on guidelines relative to settlement dates for equities.

Country	Iso* Code	Alternative† Code	Currency	Usual Settlement Date (Days after Trade Date)
Australia	AUD	AUS$	Australian dollar	As agreed, but usually 10 business days
Belgium	BEF	BFA	Belgium franc	1 business day
Canada	CAD	CAN$	Canadian dollar	5 business days
Denmark	DKK	DKA	Danish kroner	3 business days
Fed. Rep. of Germany	DEM	DMK	Deutchemark	2 business days
France	FRF	FFR	French franc	Varies with account period
Hong Kong	HKD	HD$	Hong Kong dollar	1 business day
Italy	ITL	LIT	Lira	Varies with stock exchange calendar
Japan	JPY	Y	Yen	3 business days
Luxembourg	LFR	LUXFR	Luxembourg franc	5 business days
Mexico	MP	MP	Mexican peso	2 business days
Netherlands	NLG	HLF	Netherlands guilder (Holland florin)	2–12 business days
Norway	NOK	NKR	Norwegian krone	3–6 business days, 1 business day for physical delivery
Singapore	SGD	PP	Singapore dollar	1 business day
South Africa	ZAR	S$	Rand	Every Tuesday for trades made prior to preceding Friday
Spain	ESP	SP	Spanish peseta	Friday following week of trade
Sweden	SEK	SKR	Swedish krona	5 business days
Switzerland	CHF	SFR	Swiss franc	3 business days
United Kingdom	CBP	L	Pound sterling	Varies with account period
United States	USA	US$	U.S. dollar	5 business days

*International Organization for Standardization.
†Used by most financial services organizations.

FIGURE 8-3. Settlement Dates by Country

INTERNATIONAL "CLEARING SYSTEMS"

EUROCLEAR AND CEDEL

In countries outside the United States, the costs of securities transfer and registration are significantly higher than in the United States. In some cases, laws and regulations preclude movement of securities outside the country of issue. It's very important, therefore, that you have a strategy to effectively settle non- U.S. securities transactions. The use of international depositories, like Euroclear and Cedel, can provide great efficiencies for settlement of securities eligible to be processed through those depositories.

The creation of Euroclear and Cedel (Centrale de Livraison de Valeurs Mobilieres) was a progressive response to the needs of international market participants (see Figure 8-4, Euroclear/Cedel Fact Chart). Initially created to meet the growing market demand for an efficient settlement procedure for Eurobond trades, Euroclear and Cedel have broadened their scope to encompass other internationally traded securities such as equities.

SERVICES PROVIDED

Let's review some of the services provided by Euroclear and Cedel. Each international participant is provided with a single bank account in which settlement transactions can occur in a variety of currencies and security issues (see Figure 8-5, Euroclear/Cedel Participant Bank Account). These organizations offer an international network of custodian banks located in major financial centers to provide payment facilities. The banks permit participants to deposit securities for safekeeping and servicing, withdraw securities as needed or, on request, transfer monies of Euro-currency.

At Cedel, securities deposited at these banks can be held in fungible or non-fungible form at the request of the participant. Daily statements are provided to participants detailing transactions, quantity of securities held, currency transactions and debit/credit balances.

	Euro-clear	*Cedel*
Established	1968	1971
Location	Brussels, Belgium	Luxembourg
Address	Euro-clear Operations Centre Rue de la Regence 4, B-1000 Brussels Belgium Telephone: (322) 529 1211 Telex: 61025 MGTEC B	Centrale de Livraison Valeurs Mobilieres S.A. 67, Bd. Grande-Duchesse Charlotte, P.O. Box 1006, L-1010 Luxembourg Telephone: (352) 44 99 21 Telex: 2791
		London Representative Office 77, London Wall London EC2N 1BU Telephone: (01) 588 41 42 Telex: 894628
		New York Representative Office One World Trade Center, 8351 New York, New York 10048 Telephone: (212) 775-1900 Telex: 324172
Number of participants	Over 2,250	2,100
Value of securities deposited	U.S. $527 billion	U.S. $208 billion
Service offered	Clearance Custody Securities lending and borrowing Cash clearing	Clearance Custody Security lending and borrowing Cash clearing
Communications system	EUCLID	CEDCOM
Account type	Fungible	Fungible/nonfungible
Securities accepted	Eurobonds, foreign bonds (e.g., Yankees, Samurais), international equities, certificates of deposit, commercial paper, and others	Eurobonds, foreign bonds (e.g., Yankees, Samurais), international equities, certificates of deposit, commercial paper, and others
Method of clearing	Book-entry	Book-entry
Foreign currencies handled	27	27

*Facts and figures listed are based on 1987 Annual Reports published by Euro-clear and Cedel. These organizations may have added other products and made changes to their processes as shown in Figures 8-5 and 8-6 since that time. They should be contacted directly for a more in-depth description of services and settlement procedures.

FIGURE 8-4. Euroclear/Cedel Fact Chart*

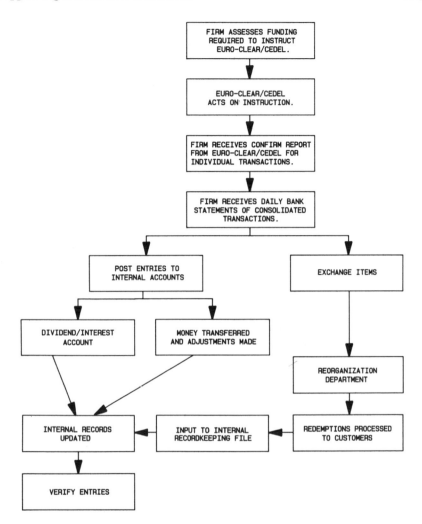

FIGURE 8-5. Euroclear/Cedel Participant Bank Account

Securities borrowing and lending services are also provided by these organizations. Participants may borrow securities to ensure delivery on a timely basis, thereby reducing their financing costs. Additionally, participants may lend all or part of their holdings to other participants. Lenders receive interest on the principal value of securities loaned and thereby gain an additional yield on their investments.

Euroclear and Cedel will collect coupon proceeds on behalf of participants and credit their accounts on payment date. Redemption proceeds are processed in a similar manner. Euroclear and Cedel will advise participants previous to, or on redemption date, of any partial call/full redemption, and credit the proceeds and remove the position from the participant's account.

SETTLEMENT PROCEDURES

Euroclear and Cedel provide participants with highly efficient methods of settling transactions (see Figure 8-6). Upon receipt of instructions, Euroclear/Cedel will simultaneously deliver/receive securities against a receipt/payment of money. This is accomplished by means of a book-entry transfer and, therefore, the need for physical movement of securities is reduced. Additionally, a computer link is maintained between both organizations to effect those settlements requiring inter-organizational transfers.

Euroclear participants can prepare settlement instructions with a variety of priority designations. These instructions are settled according to their assigned order of priority. Cedel, however, prioritizes settlements by internally assigning a sequential reference number to each instruction received.

To initiate a book-entry transfer via either organization, the settlement instructions input to a computer terminal or telex system must contain the following information:

Date

Trade price

Name of participant

Nominee security amount

Currency value

Name of issue

Interest rate

Maturity date

Settlement date (value date)

Issue's custodian security number

On settlement date, the instruction activity will appear on the participant's daily telex or computer interface media.

Due to the five-hour or six-hour time difference between New York and the depositories, all instructions settling the next business day must be validated by 10:45 a.m. Eastern Standard Time. Once an instruction is entered, certain situations such as unmatched instructions on the processing file, insufficient securities, or lack of funds will prevent settlement.

Unmatched instructions on the processing file will occur if one participant on a transaction is lacking instructions, or there is a difference in a critical field between participants' instructions. Critical information includes custodian security number, nominal amount of securities, settlement date, or money value. Money value discrepancies of $25 or less will be matched using the money value as indicated by the seller.

Resolution in these cases will require verifying internally the correctness of the instructions. If incorrect, the instructions must be canceled. If correct, the counterbroker must be contacted and instructed to either enter their receive instructions, or rectify any critical field differences.

Insufficient securities will occur when a participant has instructions to make a delivery, but lacks the sufficient inventory at Euroclear or Cedel. In the event of this occurrence, participants can settle transactions by utilizing the automatic bond borrow service or the opportunity bond borrow program offered by each organization.

The automatic bond borrow service allows a participant to borrow securities from another participant in order to satisfy a delivery instruction. A nominal fee is charged for each outstanding borrow based on the current market value of the securities. The automatic bond borrow program can be utilized only upon receipt of instructions from a participant. In the event a participant does not elect to be an automatic borrower, or does not request that Euroclear/Cedel borrow securities via the opportunity bond borrower program, a transaction will settle only upon the custodian's receipt of the necessary securities. Euroclear and Cedel produce daily listings indicating all unsettled transactions resulting from insufficient inventory.

Interest payments on securities are based on the inventory position as of the day prior to payable date with certain exceptions.

Interest payments on non-U.S. dollar denominated bonds are processed automatically. Once payments are received, instructions can be directed to the custodian bank requesting that the funds be converted into U.S. dollars. Upon conversion, the U.S. dollars are transferred from the bank account into the corresponding interest account. Interest payments on U.S. dollar denominated bonds are, however, processed by the participant.

Dividend payments are paid in the currency of issue and can be converted to U.S. dollars on request. These funds are applied to the depositories' account in the same manner as interest payments on non-U.S. dollar denominated bonds. In addition, dividend payments do not have to be made in the form of a cash disbursement. Equity securities may declare stock dividends or warrants may be issued.[2]

AREAS OF RISK AND EXPOSURE AND WHAT TO DO ABOUT THEM

Risks related to clearance and settlement of international securities and cross border transactions are different than the risks associated with domestic securities transactions. Time zone differences, currency fluctuations, restrictions on removal of securities from the country of issue, use of custodian banks, and differences in general business practices all contribute to increasing risk and exposure to securities firms and their customers. The following sections review some of the major areas of risk.

CURRENCY FLUCTUATIONS

International trading is generally done in the currency of the local country. As a result, trades done in other than U.S. dollars generate two transactions—security trade and a currency trade. As an example, let's say you buy a pound sterling security for 1 million

---

[2] Euroclear and Cedel are constantly upgrading their settlement processes and services and may have made changes to those described above. These organizations should be contacted directly for a more in-depth description of services and settlement procedures.

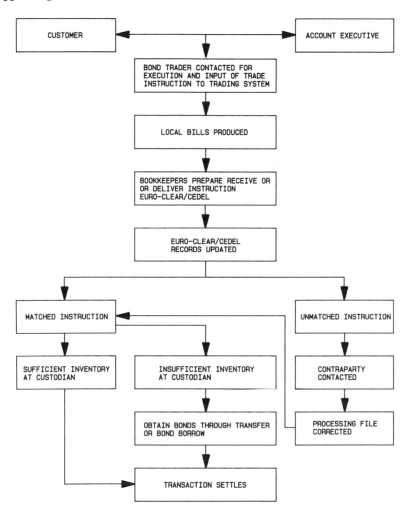

FIGURE 8-6. Euroclear/Cedel Transaction Flow

pound sterling on Monday and the U.S. dollar-to-pound sterling ratio is $1 = .56 pounds. The amount you owe the selling firm is 1 million pounds or $1.790.000 U.S. Let's also assume you don't own any pound sterling—you have to buy some (i.e., convert your dollars to pound sterling). Since you are working in a U.S. firm your books and records are in U.S. dollars. Your firm's books and records reflect the fact that you own a security and owe $1.790.000 U.S. If you don't buy the pound sterling immediately, e.g., you wait two weeks for settlement, and the pound sterling/U.S. dollar ratio fluctuates, you could lose money just on the currency fluctuation, without any change in the value of the security. On settlement date you buy the pounds sterling, but the U.S. dollar-to-pounds ratio is $1 = .53 pounds. To obtain the million pounds you owe the selling broker you have to put up $1.890.000 U.S.—*a $100.000 U.S. loss*—all because the ratio between the U.S. dollar and pound sterling changed!

The currency risks are the same for dividends and interest earned in non-U.S. dollars. The danger here is that many companies in foreign countries will pay dividends and interest, but announcements of their payouts are not as well known as announcements of U.S. exchange listed companies. Long time delays can occur and subject the firm to currency risks.

To avoid these problems, Operations Managers need to develop a currency conversion system that includes hedging capability to mitigate the risks. The system should include the following accounts:

Customer Accounts

Trading Accounts

Broker/Dealer Accounts

Custodian Accounts

Production Credit Accounts

Receivables and Payables Accounts

Tax accounts

Fail Accounts

In addition, all fail accounts should be "marked to the market" for currency changes on a daily basis, and the Trading Department should receive daily listings of exposure by currency.

REGISTRATION AND TRANSFER OF INTERNATIONAL SECURITIES

The United States has a fairly sophisticated system for the transfer and registration of securities. It has, however, taken many years and significant regulation to develop this system. Many other countries do not have well-developed systems and many transfer agents are not regulated at all. As a result, registering securities in customer name often produces lengthy delays in obtaining proceeds of sales when customers want to sell securities registered in the customer's name.

As previously discussed, international securities are generally held by a custodian for the securities firm and its customers. Sales orders should not be executed until the Operations Department has confirmation that the custodian has possession of the security. If customers request that their securities be transferred to their name and sent to them, customers should be made aware that they will be unable to sell their securities until the securities have cleared transfer.

In the event that an account is long an international security, and the customer requests that it be registered and shipped, operations must verify that the security in question can be delivered. Certain issues cannot be registered and others require supporting documentation before any transmittal can take place.

As a general rule, transfer of deliverable international securities requires 8-12 weeks. As with domestic transfers, a fee is usually required. Certificates must not be earmarked, written upon, or stapled together, as these actions may cause them to be treated as mutilated certificates which must be replaced. The replacement process is costly and time consuming. Because of the time and cost involved in registering and shipping international securities, customers should be advised to leave the certificates in nominee name whenever possible. If securities are in transfer and then sold, the sales will result in fails to deliver. These fails can take a very long time to resolve, and firms can incur regulatory capital charges and interest expenses. For this reason, registration of international securities should be restricted to those countries or situations where the Operations Manager knows that the firm and its customers will not be adversely affected.

TIME ZONE DIFFERENCES

Unless your firm has extensive communications facilities, twenty-four hour processing, and sophisticated computer support, time zone differences can present real problems. For international processing operations, this means that a normal (9-5) day does not allow efficient communications with the rest of the world, and shift operations must be planned in order to resolve problems and reconcile differences. For international operations staff in local offices, the time zone difference causes a "compression" of processing.

For example, in Zurich, transatlantic order activity might be compressed between the hours of 3 p.m. and 4 p.m. because of the five- or six-hour time difference. Instructions to custodian banks in the Far East should receive priority because those countries are already a day ahead in terms of business hours.

Time zone differences, if not managed, can result in poor communications with custodian banks, as well as late notification of receive and deliver activity. International traders often do their business outside of U.S. hours, at home or away from office facilities. This involves their keeping records of activity more or less on their own, without standardized procedures. Orders for this kind of trading must be entered the following day, and effective means of handling "as of" types trades must be in place. Even when orders are processed during normal business hours, trading practice often calls for orders to be executed first, and customer account numbers assigned afterwards. Obviously internal record breaks result and exception systems must be in place to segregate these trades for late delivery instructions. Figure 8-7 depicts the magnitude of international time differences.

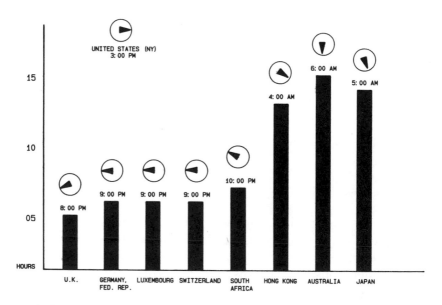

FIGURE 8-7. Magnitude of International Time Differences

PHYSICAL SECURITIES HELD OVERSEAS

Custodian banks assume responsibility for safekeeping securities held for depositors. Auditing standards vary significantly and it is important to use a custodian bank that meets U.S. regulatory standards. Security counts should take place at least monthly with audit statements submitted for depositor review. Under SEC Rule 15c3-3, U.S. regulators must approve custodians before securities held at those custodians will be considered as good control locations.

FREE SHIPMENTS OF SECURITIES

In countries outside the United States, many firms permit delivery of securities to be made without getting simultaneous receipt of money. In the United States, the practice of "delivery versus payment" is the usual procedure and the risk of not receiving value for value is eliminated.

The credit risk involved with free shipments is obvious. If your firm does allow this practice in the international marketplace, the following safeguards should be put in place:

Do not allow free shipments without prior Credit Department approval.

Establish credit lines for all concerned firms and/or customers.

Obtain "omnibus" agreements for the transactions with counterparties with whom the position is permitted.

Obtain detailed, daily status reports from custodians on all free shipments outstanding.

Provide trading/sales management with daily lists of outstanding free shipments.

Mark-to-the-market all outstanding free shipments on a daily basis.

Free shipments should be vigorously discouraged. Arrangements should be made for a "deliver versus payment" process, whereby the customer provides payment with a certified or bank guaranteed check at the same time securities are delivered.

CUSTODIAN SERVICES

While custodian services are covered in another section of this chapter, it's mentioned under "Risk and Exposure" because the choice of an inefficient custodian can cause service delays in shipments of securities to customers, significant interest expense, regulatory problems, and customer dissatisfaction. When markets in individual countries get very active in a short time span, the country's processing infrastructure may not be able to cope with the increased volume. The choice of an appropriate custodian will help the Operations's Department better serve customers and maintain appropriate controls.

TRADING INTERFACE

Although operations cannot initiate trading to hedge currency fluctuation on settlement activity, they have direct access to the flow of information, which can be the basis for such trading decisions. Risk can be reduced or minimized if traders are aware of pending settlement in foreign currencies, fail situations, and funds requirements by using the forward market to hedge these situations. Every effort should be made to develop projections in these areas and advise traders accordingly.

COMMON PROBLEMS AND SOLUTIONS

Trading and settlement of international securities presents the Operations Manager with many unique problems because business practices differ country-by-country. Figure 8-8 presents some common processing problems, their probable causes and suggested solutions.

Problem	Result	Possible Causes	Potential Solutions
Discrepancies in custodian bank positions versus firm.	Firm cannot accurately process deliveries, interest cost, delays in dividends, rights, and/or exchanges.	1. Nonuniform monthly statements/positions from banks.	1. Telex banks for proper reconciliation of balances, review procedures for monthly statements.
		2. Untimely confirmation of telexes from bank.	2. Establish confirmation due dates from bank. Telex custodian banks instructing them as to your need for timely telex information regarding trades and dividend activity.
		3. Misdirected telexes to firm from bank and within firm.	3. Isolate problem bank/department. Improve communications procedures by defining firm recipient to the bank.
		4. Standard reference is not carried throughout life cycle of trade to identify the trade.	4. Implement a standard single reference number system throughout the life cycle of trades for tracking, research, and definition.
		5. Banks reference trade date, but U.S. firms reference settlement date.	5. Define trade dates and settlement dates as they apply to international trades and how they affect ownership, dividend entitlement, and fail criteria for each country.
		6. Nonstandard internal research/filing/balancing procedures; lack of job task definition/procedures.	6. Write and implement standard job task definition/procedures training guides and train personnel accordingly.
		7. Custodian bank systems operating beyond capacity.	7. Examine efficiency and capabilities of the custodian bank facilities on a quarterly basis. Maintain potential exposure data.

FIGURE 8-8. Common Types of Processing Problems

Problem	Result	Possible Causes	Potential Solutions
Discrepancies in international broker's records versus firm's.	Firm cannot effect timely deliveries; results in customer dissatisfaction, adverse regulatory capital charge impact, and market exposure.	1. International brokers do not issue uniform statements on a timely basis.	1. Renegotiate custodial contract or change custodians.
		2. No standard reference number throughout life cycle of trade to identify trade.	2. Assign reference number on all new telexes to avoid incomplete record files.
		3. Brokers deliver a high volume of "partials."	3. Use same reference number for partials and complete deliveries.
		4. Brokers reference trade date but firm references settlement date.	4. Implement a standard single reference number system throughout the life cycle of trades for tracking, research, and definition.
		5. Non-uniform confirm/telex definition of required fields by broker and by firm impedes communication.	5. Develop standard telex format to be utilized for mutual benefit.
		6. Misdirected telexes to firm and from firm.	6. Redefine the routing procedure internally and externally.
Missing rights.	Firm has financial exposure if customer wishes to exercise or sell rights that expire.	1. Not informed of international rights offering.	1. Request to be on the mailing list of major New York banks for rights information. Subscribe to financial publications for international rights offerings.
		2. Inaccurate stock record, not updated to "as of" entries, not inputted due to telex delays.	2. Alert custodian banks of need for expeditious handling and communication to minimize impact of "as of" adjustment situations.
		3. Inventory discrepancies with custodians.	3. Reconcile inventory positions on a daily basis.

FIGURE 8-8. *(Continued)*

Problem	Result	Possible Causes	Potential Solutions
		4. Internal conflict of priorities over exchange offerings versus delivery orders.	4. Establish procedures with firm's exchange area to expedite exchange transactions.
		5. No indications on trades by traders, (when trading on or about ex-date) whether trade was done with rights or ex-rights.	5. Establish procedures whereby trades must indicate whether trade was done with rights or ex-rights.
Untimely payments/ receipts of monies associated with trade.	Funds used lost due to financing of customer trades being absorbed by firm. Firm loses use of funds; results in possible interest exposure and customer dissatisfaction.	1. International trades are two trades: security and currency. Payment made separately from security.	1. Establish separate foreign currency accounts and U.S. currency accounts for each international account to maintain well-defined records and balances.
		2. No automated currency conversion capability.	2. Establish automated currency conversion capability to avoid manually intensive operations.
		3. No procedural definition to internally compare brokers "delivery/ receipt" telex to bank confirms/statements.	3. Establish procedures to coordinate telex instructions to actual receipt/payment of monies.
International fails to receive.	Firm may be unable to deliver other settled transactions; could cause rights/ dividend exchange problems; market exposures.	*External Causes* Local country settlement rules, transfer problems, custodian errors, wrong instructions.	*External Solutions* Maintain close liaison with custodians and brokers and implement detailed procedures to be followed in each country to effect settlement.
		Internal Causes 1. Stock record updated at time of confirming telex entries with inaccurate "as of" entries causes incorrect stock record.	*Internal Solutions* 1. Reconcile "as of" records on a daily basis.

FIGURE 8-8. (*Continued*)

Problem	Result	Possible Causes	Potential Solutions
		2. Telex delays in confirming positions to firm from custodian.	2. Match all trades to confirming telex; establish acceptable fail to receive standards for each country/custodian.
		3. Nonstandard internal procedures/time frames for follow-up versus settlement date.	3. Standardize internal procedures by country to assure timely follow-up versus settlement date.
		4. Lack of standing instructions at custodian or at firm.	4. Develop procedures to maintain accurate standing instructions.
		5. Discrepancies in settlement date instructions.	5. Confirm settlement date on trade date.
		External Causes	*External Solutions*
International fail to deliver.	Firm incurs interest loss; regulatory capital impact; market exposure.	Local country settlement rules; transfer problems; custodian errors; wrong instructions.	Maintain close liaison with custodians and brokers and implement detailed procedures to be followed in each country to effect settlement.
		Internal Causes	*Internal Solutions*
		1. Incorrect stock record; resulting in firm inaccurate "as of" trades.	1. Reconcile "as of" trades on a daily basis.
		2. Telex delays between firm and custodian.	2. Match all trades to confirming telexes on a daily basis.
		3. Fail to receive, security in transfer, or otherwise unavailable.	3. Expedite fails to receive, establish security borrowing program.
		4. Nonstandard internal procedures/time frames for follow-up versus settlement date.	4. Standardize internal procedures/time frames for deliveries on a country-by-country basis.
		5. Lack of standing instructions at custodian banks or firm.	5. Develop procedures with customers, brokers, and custodians to maintain accurate standard file instruction.

FIGURE 8-8. *(Continued)*

Problem	Result	Possible Causes	Potential Solutions
Delayed exchanges or conversion of securities to ADRs or ADRs to securities.	Firm may be unable to deliver; could cause problems in dividends, rights offerings, etc.	1. Lack of procedures to follow-up on exchanges.	1. Monitor issuing bank ADR procedures with custodian to ensure that the ADR and the underlying shares are exchanged on the same day to maintain continuity of ownership.
		2. Inaccurate stock record due to "as of" entries.	2. "As of" entries must be administered and assessed for dividend implications and trade entry discrepancies, as many "as of" adjustments involve previous incorrect entries which are being adjusted.
Traders change standing instructions.	Firm could lose control over records.	Lack of communications between Trading and Operations, lack of specific trading and operational duties.	Define responsibilities of Trading and Operations personnel regarding delivery instructions, establish specific procedures for new delivery instructions.

FIGURE 8-8. (*Continued*)

INTERNATIONAL CASH MANAGEMENT

The magnitude and diversity of cash flows in the securities industry, taken in conjunction with interest rate fluctuations and currency exposure, accentuates the importance of efficient cash management and control systems. Securities firms operating in the international arena must recognize local market conditions and, more specifically, the structural and procedural differences of the banking environment in different countries. An international cash management program must encompass not only the collection and disbursement of funds, but liquidity management and exposure/risk management as well.

A securities firm with branch offices in many countries must address the specific needs of each office and its customer base to develop a uniform approach to facilitate the flow of funds on a global basis. In examining customer cash activity within the local banking system of a given country, and the banking and credit needs of the office to accommodate this activity in the most efficient manner, the following checklist can be used:

Does the office need a local account to accommodate customer cash activity?

Is there a need for a local banking arrangement to clear locally drawn customer checks?

Is it necessary to maintain a foreign currency account or a U.S. dollar account or both?

If local accounts are necessary, how could the firm most efficiently minimize cash-on-hand?

Are local credit facilities needed?

Must separate accounts be maintained for expense and payroll disbursements?

How are excess cash balances resulting from local office business utilized?

Do customer relations necessitate special foreign exchange requirements?

How can the local office assist in clearing international currency checks and maintaining relationships with correspondent banks?

Because securities firms vary in size and the number of branch offices maintained, there are numerous methods used to develop efficient cash management. The most important however, is to have a policy with appropriate procedures spelling out how the firm wants to process cash receipts and disbursements. If procedures are not developed, the firm can lose the availability of cash for days and incur the associated interest costs, reducing or eliminating profits from the firm's normal business.

The preferred method of collecting funds is by direct wire transfer from the local country to a U.S. bank in U.S. dollars. If the firm permits payments in international currencies, procedures should be set up so that the funds are directed to one bank, converted to U.S. dollars (unless the firm has a need for an international currency) and forwarded to a U.S. account as rapidly as possible.

If the firm has numerous receipts coming in on a daily basis, one method to review is an international lock box arrangement. A global or international cash letter service is used by international banks who need to clear U.S. dollar checks in the most efficient manner, or by multinationals who have subsidiary offices acting as central collection points for their check remittances. In the latter case, this service would be used to direct deposits of non-local currencies through the company's correspondent bank network. An international lock box, however, is the most common method used to accelerate the availability of funds on check remittances. The longer the collection and conversion period of international currency checks, the greater the risk of foreign exchange loss. The longer the delay on receipt of good funds, the greater the interest loss. Collection procedures constitute an integral part of international cash management. Using an international lock box provides reduced credit risk, minimized foreign exchange exposure, and maximized interest revenue.

TAX REGULATIONS

U.S. INVESTORS

United States residents are normally subject to non-U.S. withholding tax on dividends or interest received from another country. Customer statements should reflect a credit for the gross dividend or interest, and a debit for the tax withheld. Computation of tax withheld for foreign dividends and interest can thus easily be accomplished by extracting the tax details from the customers' monthly statements.

Figure 8-9 gives a country-by-country summary of the percentage of dividend and withholding tax for U.S. residents. It should be noted however, that rules and laws of other countries are constantly changing and may affect the amount of withholding. More detailed withholding data may be obtained through the U.S. Internal Revenue Service.

For a U.S. Resident Receiving Dividends or Interest from Sources In: **	Percent of Dividend Withheld	Interest
Australia	15	10-90
Austria	10	0-100
Belgium	15	15-85
Canada	15	15-85
Denmark	15	0-100
Finland	15	0-100
France	15	10-90
Fed. Rep. of Germany	15	0-100
Ireland	0	0-100
Israel	25	25-75
Italy	15	30-70
Japan	15	10-90
Luxembourg	7.5	0-100
Mexico	55	21-79
Netherlands	15	0-100
Sweden	15	0-100
Switzerland	15	5-95
Rep. of South Africa	15	10-90
United Kingdom	15	0-100

* These rates often fluctuate and are estimated to be current as of June 1994. The author assumes no liability for the accuracy or completeness of information contained herein.

**1. The rates represent favorable tax treatment for a U.S. resident. In some situations U.S. residents may be paid at the unfavorable withholding rate and a reclaim form must be prepared and forwarded to the local tax authorities to secure a refund and thus achieve a favorable tax status.

2. Correct withholding depends on two levels of criteria: domicile of client, and type of account. For example, in the Netherlands, the following U.S. Domiciled accounts would be subject to different withholding rates:

Account Type	Appropriate Rate of Withholding
U.S. Resident Individual	15%
Non-Profit Organizations	0%
IRA Account	25%

3. Withholding rates may vary by issue. For example, a multi-national corporation may derive income from various sources and multiple withholding rates may apply.

FIGURE 8-9. Taxes Withheld*

Non-U.S. Investors

Nonresident aliens and foreign corporations are taxed by the United States, for the most part, only on income from U.S. sources. Under U.S. law, securities firms are obligated to withhold a tax on dividends and interest paid to all nonresident aliens and foreign corporations. Withholding is at the statutory rate of 30%, unless such income is directly connected with a U.S. trade or business, or unless otherwise specified by tax treaties. Figure 8-10 lists the countries with the applicable rates that should be used in coding new accounts. In certain instances, the withholding rate for an account may be other than rates for the indicated country of residence, as noted in the list of exceptions.

INTERNATIONAL COMMUNICATIONS

Regional Considerations

The international environment can be divided into three different categories, based on the quality of the local communications and regulatory constraints. In Europe, there is high-quality communications and data processing support with single satellite coverage (i.e., a single satellite's broadcast area "footprint" can cover most offices in the region). In the Asia/Pacific and Middle East regions, there are high-quality support infrastructures, few restrictions on data flows and multiple satellite coverage. In Latin America, the quality of data processing and communications support is generally very low, satellite coverage nonexistent, and regulatory trends becoming restrictive, e.g., Brazil, where transborder data flows may eventually be defined as "real exports."

Since many firms have significant operations in these three regions, the Operations Manager is faced with a variety of options for the design of business support and the location of processing facilities. For example, the Operations Manager can (see page 199):

	Rate (%)	
Country	*Dividend*	*Interest*
Algeria	30	30
Andorra Principality	30	30
Angola	30	30
Anguilla	30	30
Antigua	30	30
Argentina	30	30
Australia	15	10
Austria	15	0
Azores	30	30
Bahamas	30	30
Bahrain	30	30
Bangladesh	30	30
Barbados	15	12.5
Belgium	15	15
Belize (British Honduras)	30	30
Bermuda	30	30
Bolivia	30	30
Borneo	30	30
Brazil	30	30
Brunei	30	30
Burma	30	30
Burundi	30	30
Cambodia	30	30
Cameroon	30	30
Canada	15	15
Canary Islands	15	10
Cayman Islands	30	30
Channel Islands	30	30
Chile	30	30
China, Peoples Republic of	10	10
Colombia	30	30
Congo	30	30
Cook Island	30	30
Costa Rica	30	30
Cuba	30	30
Cyprus	15	10
Czechoslovakia	30	30
Denmark	15	0
Dominica	30	30

FIGURE 8-10. Withholding Rates for Non-U.S. Residents*

Country	Rate (%) Dividend	Interest
Dominican Republic	30	30
Ecuador	30	30
Egypt	15	15
El Salvador	30	30
Ethiopia	30	30
Falkland Island	30	30
Fiji	30	30
Finland	15	0
France	15	0
French Republic of Africa	30	30
French Somaliland	30	30
Gabon	30	30
Gambia	30	30
Germany, Federal Republic of	15	0
Ghana	30	30
Gibraltar	30	30
Godella Valencia	30	30
Greece	30	0
Grenada	30	30
Guam**	30	30
Guatemala	30	30
Guyana	30	30
Haiti	30	30
Honduras	30	30
Hong Kong	30	30
Hungary	15	0
Iceland	15	0
India	25	15
Indonesia	15	15
Iran	30	30
Iraq	30	30
Ireland	15	0
Isle of Man	30	30
Israel	30	30
Italy	15	15
Ivory Coast	30	30
Jamaica	15	12.5
Japan	15	10

FIGURE 8-10. (*Continued*)

Country	Rate (%)	
	Dividend	*Interest*
Jordan	30	30
Kenya	30	30
Korea	15	12
Kuwait	30	30
Laos	30	30
Lebanon	30	30
Liberia	30	30
Libya	30	30
Lithunia	30	30
Liechtenstein	30	30
Luxembourg	15	0
Macao	30	30
Madagascar	30	30
Malawi	30	30
Malaysia	30	30
Malta	15	12.2
Mauritius	30	30
Mexico	30	30
Monaco	30	30
Montserrat	30	30
Morocco	15	15
Mozambique	30	30
Nepal	30	30
Netherlands	15	0
Netherlands Antilles	30	0
Nevis	30	30
New Caledonia	30	30
New Guinea	30	30
New Zealand	15	10
Nicaragua	30	30
Niger	30	30
Nigeria	30	30
Norway	15	0
Pakistan	30	30
Panama	30	30
Paraguay	30	30
Peru	30	30
Philippines	25	15
Poland	15	0

FIGURE 8-10. (*Continued*)

Country	Rate (%)	
	Dividend	Interest
Portugal	30	30
Puerto Rico**	30	30
Qatar	30	30
Rumania	10	10
Russia (Union of Soviet Socialist Republics)	30	30
Rwanda	30	30
St. Christopher	30	30
St. Lucia	30	30
St. Vincent	30	30
Saudi Arabia	30	30
Senegal	30	30
Seychelles	30	30
Sierra Leone	30	30
Singapore	30	30
Somalia	30	30
South Africa, Republic of	30	30
Spain	15	10
Sudan	30	30
Surinam	30	30
Swaziland	30	30
Sweden**	15	0
Switzerland	15	5
Syria	30	30
Tahiti	30	30
Taiwan	30	30
Tanzania	30	30
Thailand	30	30
Tobago	30	30
Trinidad	30	30
Tunisia	20	15
Turks & Caicos Islands	30	30
Turkey	30	30
Uganda	30	30
United Arab Emirates	30	30
United Kingdom+	15	0
Uruguay	30	30
Venezuela	30	30
Vietnam	30	30
Virgin Islands (British)	30	30

FIGURE 8-10. (*Continued*)

Country	Rate (%) Dividend	Interest
Western Samoa	30	30
Yemen	30	30
Yugoslavia	30	30
Zaire	30	30
Zambia	30	30

* These rates often fluctuate and are estimated to be current as of June 1994. The author assumes no liability for the accuracy or completeness of information contained herein.

+ The United Kingdom includes England, North Ireland, Scotland, and Wales. It does not include the Channel Islands or the Isle of Man, both of which are listed separately.

**Exceptions to the Withholding Rate Table:

Exception 1 (Guam only): All individuals who can verify resident status within Guam and Guam corporations incorporated herein are exempt from withholding of NRA tax on dividend/interest payments. These accounts should be placed on a nonresident alien file, but at a withholding rate of 0%.

Exception 2 (Puerto Rico only): Since citizens of Puerto Rico have the same status as citizens of the U.S., no tax is withheld from them, with the following limited exceptions where a 30% tax withholding rate on dividend/interest payments applies: 1)individuals who resided on Puerto Rico on April 11, 1899 and elected to become Puerto Rican citizens but not U.S. citizens under the Organic Act of 1917; 2)individuals born in Puerto Rico of alien parents prior to January 17, 1941 who failed to take advantage of the U.S. naturalization laws upon taking up residence in Puerto Rico; 3)businesses incorporated in Puerto Rico are subject to a 30% tax withholding rate on dividend/interest payments.

Exception 3 (Sweden only): Nonresident aliens who are Swedish citizens are entitled to the benefits under the U.S.-Swedish tax treaty wherever they reside. However, if the treaty rates between U.S. and the country of residence are lower than those under the U.S.-Swedish tax treaty, the lower rate prevails.

Other Exceptions:

A nonresident alien who has diplomatic or consular status will have tax withheld on the basis of the rates applicable to the country of citizenship and not to the country of residence.

FIGURE 8-10. (*Continued*)

Foreign private foundations are subject to a special tax rate of 4% on both dividend and interest payments derived from sources within the United States. However, no tax on investment income will be levied on private foundations which are subject to a treaty providing that such income will be exempt from income tax.

If the Internal Revenue Service determines that a foundation is a foreign tax-exempt charitable foundation (and not a private foundation), no tax should be withheld.

A joint account where only one party is a U.S. citizen must be placed on a Nonresident Alien File, but at the rate of the country where the NRA half resides. Only half of the dividend/interest payments of the account will be taxed at the country's rate.

FIGURE 8-10. (*Continued*)

1. Develop a unique set of processing systems for each region, taking maximum advantage of the communications infrastructure of each of the individual regions. Areas with poor communications will most likely have lower quality operating support than those with good communications. A plan for increased participation in local markets may be best supported by regional telecommunications capabilities.

2. Develop a single set of processing systems which will operate in all regions at the lowest common denominator of communications infrastructure. This might degrade the communications capabilities of one region as compared with the regionally specialized system option above. However, the total development costs will probably be much lower.

3. Centralize processing as much as possible in one location (e.g., London), putting only remote terminal equipment in each of the other regions.

4. Decentralize processing, putting microcomputers and telecommunications support in each office, storing as much data and doing as much processing as possible locally.

Centralize processing, regionalize processing, decentralize processing—all are viable options depending on your firm's objectives. But the cost of having to change approaches once a system is in place is likely to be high. Therefore, it is important to choose the alternatives that best accommodate the firm's objectives and the requirements of future regulation and local business practice. The decision should be made in the context of the firm's business. Whichever path is chosen, the system should be built so as not to constrain future business direction.

REGULATORY TRENDS/LOCAL BUSINESS PRACTICES

One of the key concerns of many international clients is the confidentiality of their financial dealings. Some clients consider this an important aspect of their business relationship and would react negatively to having their accounts "carried" or "processed" in their home country, thereby being possibly subject to greater scrutiny and control by local authorities.

In addition to increased access to customer records, an expansion of local processing capability might violate agreements with tax and regulatory authorities, and present a challenge to the legal status of international offices.

If the extent of processing done by a local office implies that it is "carrying accounts" of its own, or executing trades at the branch office level, local regulators may argue that the firm is conducting unlicensed business. Tax authorities may also demand that the office be set up as a profit center, with local commission accounting and substantial restrictions on the costs which can be transferred from the home office to the account of a local office.

Before determining the "optimal" network design, the firm's legal and financial staff should be asked to review local government regulatory and financial implications of the potential network.

CHARACTERISTICS OF AN EFFECTIVE INTERNATIONAL SYSTEM

Let's look at some very specific issues that need to be addressed when you have to develop an international communications system:

The system should provide each international office with a full set of operating capabilities during local business hours. Messages, orders, or research data should be able to be sent at any time to any location or market, with immediate updates of appropriate records as soon as a transaction is completed.

Although an individual location on the international network may be closed at any given time (e.g., due to a central system holiday, business hour schedules or operating problems), this should not affect the ability of other locations to communicate with each other. Open locations should be able to transmit messages (e.g., telexes, orders, confirms) on a store-and-forward basis to closed locations. Major database facilities (e.g., customer information, research data) should be available at all times throughout the network.

The development of intelligent distributed switched networks can provide alternative access and control. Instead of running the switching center from one central computer, the control can be at the functional level within a region. Each regional block of lines or trunks can have its own processor, so a problem in one place will not impact all users. By contrast, in a centralized environment, a single problem could disrupt the whole system.

The system must be able to accept and convey a wide variety of data formats from a wide variety of sources. The system should be able to intermix voice, telex, graphics, electronic mail, sales support data and quotes, freely and easily, with no degradation of transmission quality or response time, and at a lower cost than doing each one separately.

Ideally, operations should be able to add new equipment to the network and delete old equipment, change basic circuit routings, bypassing damaged or embargoed circuits, use satellites or packet switched networks with relatives ease. A flexible architecture leads to more effective return on investment, and provides access to rapidly emerging technologies.

Support resources must be "mobile," ensuring that systems are portable and interchangeable within different departments and across functions. Especially important is the compatibility of disparate systems, software packages, and peripheral devices in the various business units that may have to be linked from time to time. Uncoordinated diffusion of technology could result in a technologically fragmented environment, an "Electronic Tower of Babel," with many groups and functions virtually isolated by incompatible machines.

FUTURE CHANGES IN INTERNATIONAL CLEARANCE AND SETTLEMENT

The events of October, 1987 certainly highlighted the major risks of trading in securities markets. Problems associated with clearance and settlement of securities transactions during that period also became severe enough that securities firms chairmen and regulatory bodies now understand that present settlement mechanisms throughout the world are not sufficient to sustain continued explosive growth. Prompt clearing and settlement of securities transactions no longer just "helps" the marketplace, it is a must for any country's market to develop and sustain a capital raising mechanism.

Country and industry leaders throughout the world are now focusing on how to improve settlement systems employed in their markets and how to establish appropriate links between markets. In March 1988, the Group of Thirty, an independent international consultative group convened a symposium in London on clearance and settlement issues in the global securities markets. This group focused on a number of issues after drawing on the expertise of certain practitioners chosen for their knowledge of settlement techniques. Recommendations were formulated to improve global processing, and these recommendations will dramatically affect the ways in which global securities markets develop new systems to increase efficiency and reduce risk through facilitating cross-border securities trading.

The following eight areas are those changes that could dramatically impact securities firms throughout the world.[3] Operations Managers need to begin to plan now for these changes, to develop the systems and procedures necessary to accommodate these potential changes. The dates mentioned below are very aggressive and may not be achievable. The recommendations are directional, need more practioner review (for the United States particularly recommendations 5 and 6), but clearly indicate where the industry is heading.

---

[3] The following paragraphs are excerpted from working paper documents prepared by a Working Committee of the Group of Thirty. The dates specified in the following pages were projections made in 1988. The author was a member of the Working Committee.

1. *The industry will aim to have, by 1990, all comparisons of trades between direct market participants (i.e., brokers, broker/dealers and other exchange members) accomplished by T+1.*

The lack of timely, efficient, and disciplined matching systems is considered by practitioners to be the most risk-prone component of the securities processing cycle. Considering the logistics associated with different types of markets, trade matching should occur no later than trade date plus one (T+1).

There are primarily two types of comparison systems: two-sided and one-sided. The two-sided system is typically operated by a market or an exchange and is restricted to that organization's members, usually brokers and broker/dealers. Both parties to the trade input data directly into a central matching system, which then compares the trade. The parties are notified if there is a discrepancy. In many of these systems, the trade may be carried through to settlement and members may assume a liability for the group as a whole. This ensures that a cleared trade will settle regardless of any individual default by a member. A comparison system will also ensure that all non-matching trades will be returned for adjustment on a timely basis. This gives the trading parties opportunity to correct the discrepancy/conflict in time for settlement.

To accomplish these objectives will require an automated system with the following major functions:

Trade detail reporting to counterparties

Trade matching capability

Trade error resolution capability

Ability to "lock in" trades that match

In order to ensure that the T+1 standard is met, the system must be designed so that trade reporting to participants is accomplished prior to the evening of T+1 and, if possible, on trade date.

Comparison systems will monitor the performance of their members. Non-compliance may engender severe penalties. If a member does not respond by deadline, then it will have to accept the trade as entered by the counterparty and/or receive a financial penalty.

The T+1 comparison standard will allow for the acceleration of the settlement cycle, thereby reducing the market and counterparty risk associated with outstanding trades.

2. *The industry will attempt to have indirect market participants (such as institutional investors, or any trading counterparties which are not broker/dealers) be members of a trade comparison system which achieves positive affirmation of trade details by 1992.*

The lack of a uniform and disciplined trade confirmation/affirmation capability among institutional investors introduces another significant element of risk into the securities processing cycle. Failure to compare trades in a timely manner can increase the rate of failure of settlement, which amplifies market risk.

One-sided comparison systems exist for institutional investors who may not wish to join a two-sided comparison system associated with an exchange or marketplace. These investors may be unwilling or unable to participate in a risk sharing scheme, such as that typically found in a two-sided system. They require access to a comparison system which links them, their broker and their operational agent (such as a custodian bank). In this case, the institutional investor receives a list of trades to which he/she is the counterparty. He/she must then affirm or deny the trades within an established time frame.

One-side comparison systems link indirect members to a central clearing system or securities depository. These systems require some communication systems capability, either in place or in development. Of course, the most efficient system will require a high degree of automation, with participants having on-line, real time access to information, such as clearing and settlement data (to manage positions) and accounts (to manage cash).

3. *By 1992 most countries will have an effective and fully developed central securities depository, organized and managed to encourage the broadest possible industry participation.*

A Central Securities Depository (CSD) provides participants with an efficient low-risk method for achieving early and secure transaction settlement. The CSD will have the capability for trade clearance, safe custody and settlement/post-settlement processing of securities and information, such as corporate actions and dividend/interest processing.

The depository's principal function is to immobilize or dematerialize securities, thereby assuring that the bulk of securities transactions are processed in "book entry" form.

The most important feature of the book-entry method is that a transfer of a given quantity of an issue from one account to another can be effected by a simple debit or credit on the books of the CSD. The only condition to this transfer is that a sufficient credit balance must exist in the securities and cash positions of the appropriate members' accounts.

CSDs will be structured to include a payment system, maintaining cash accounts for their members, or this may be linked to a separate payments system. In the former case, the CSD processes a payment transaction by crediting or debiting the cash account of the member financial institution simultaneous to processing the securities side of the transaction. This two-sided process assures that each security transaction is, in fact, a delivery versus payment, a key ingredient in limiting risk in the settlement process.

Settlement of securities transactions within the Central Securities Depository will be effected either on a trade-for-trade basis, or after the employment of a trade netting system, depending on the particular volume characteristics of each market and its participants.

Ideally, the Central Securities Depository will contain all fungible issues in its markets. Practically, the CSD will accept as many domestically traded securities issues as possible, in bearer or registered form; be they equities, debt instruments, warrants, money markets, or other types of instruments.

The ultimate objective of each country's Central Securities Depository will be either to immobilize or dematerialize the issues that it obtains. While dematerialization offers particular advantages with regard to efficiency and flexibility, the laws and practices of some countries and their markets do not permit dematerialization. In these situations, the major goals of the depository will be accomplished by immobilizing certificates, provided a system is in place that permits settlement without transfer and re-registration.

4. *In environments where it is currently not the practice, delivery versus payment (DVP) will be employed as the method for settling all securities transactions between direct and indirect market participants by 1992.*

An area of substantial risk in the settlement of securities transactions occurs when securities are delivered without the simultaneous receipt of value by the delivering party. Simultaneous exchange of value is important to eliminate the risks of price change and failure to perform according to contract. DVP effectively eliminates any exposure due to delay of delivery from a counterparty.

Either a CSD which combines clearance and depository functions, or separate clearing and depository systems, can be used to facilitate the simultaneous exchange of securities and cash value (or credit) that minimizes this type of risk. In fact, DVP can be accomplished through linkage to a final payment system, a system of bank guarantees, or a clearance and depository agency's financial guarantees.

However, even without the existence of a CSD with access or linkage to a final payment system, steps will be taken to minimize the risk associated with securities deliveries. That is, systems will exist which ensure that 1) securities are delivered only against a certified check; or 2) the mechanism for securities deliveries is linked to a payments system so that payment is made simultaneously, although through separate systems. Either of these methods and others that will be designed, minimize the risk of delivery of securities without the receipt of good value.

5. *A "Rolling Settlement" system will be adopted by all markets. Final settlement will occur on T+3 by 1992.*

In a "rolling settlement" environment, trades settle on all business days of the week. This process limits the number of outstanding trades, thereby reducing market exposure.

Final settlement on trade date plus five (T+5) by 1990 and T+3 by 1992 will be a minimum standard to contain risk, while setting a realistic target that all countries should be able to achieve. Markets which are currently operating on a time frame of T+5 or shorter will examine moving to the final standard of T+3 by 1990. The primary objective here is to shorten the delay between trade date and settlement date; the secondary objective is to standardize settlement time frames throughout international markets.

Global trade settlement will ultimately be standardized across markets. This will allow all parties to a trade to work within the same framework.

In order to minimize counterparty risk and market exposure associated with securities transactions, same day settlement should be the ultimate goal. But in an environment which is neither totally centralized or automated, same day settlement is not feasible. The diversity and complexity of international markets preclude this possibility in the near term.

Even assuming the existence of centralized clearing agencies and depositories in each major market, with trade comparison systems, for both direct and indirect market participants, same day settlement is not a realistic standard for the near future. If trade comparison by T+1 is accomplished in the majority of cases, institutional investors will still need to allow sufficient time to ensure that their agents can make either cash or securities available in time for settlement, particularly for the increasing number of cross border transactions. Various regulations, laws, practices, etc. will have to be changed to facilitate timely payments by retail customers.

One approach to achieving compliance with the T+5 standard among a maximum number of participants includes encouraging institutional investors to leave standing instructions with their custodians, setting reasonable limits. These instructions would permit custodians to settle the majority of trades without immediate reference to their clients.

Author's Note: In the United States a change from T + 5 settlement to a shorter settlement date could significantly impact retail investors if current practices (e.g., mailing of confirmations, paying by check, etc.) and regulations are not changed. In my opinion, one of the most important impediments to compressing settlement dates is the physical certificate commonly used to represent ownership of securities like equities and corporate or municipal bonds. If the United States were to gradually eliminate the use of physical certificates in the above categories of securities (as is done in options and most U.S. Treasury issues), there is a far better chance that settlement dates could be compressed more easily. Under any circum-

stances, however, the task of changing investors' behavior in this
area, without adversely impacting the marketplace, is formidable.

6. *All securities settlement systems will move to a "Same Day
   Funds" environment, with payment for securities transactions
   among financial firms processed in an immediately available
   form by 1992.*

Inconsistent methods of final payment for the settlement
(delivery) of securities transactions exist today. In many markets,
next day funds are the standard; in others, some securities types are
paid for in delayed funds and some in immediate funds. These situations create an environment where the finality of payment for
securities is not always assured and inject a needless element of
uncertainty into the system.

The advent of electronic funds transfer systems has enabled
the use of wire transfer payments for securities transactions. Use of
these systems for final payments for securities transactions results in
the electronic transfer of cash in available or "good" funds on the
same day, with a cash clearing system (usually the central bank)
standing in the middle. A consistent method of payment for securities transactions will eliminate differences between instruments settling in same day funds and others, thus making for simpler
accounting and payment systems, and reducing counterparty risks
in these transactions.

This type of payment system will permit final, simultaneous
and irrevocable payment for all types of securities transactions.
Eliminating check drawing will promote greater efficiency and
reduce risk, while incurring the additional benefit of reducing "float"
in the world's payment system. In an ideal environment, all payments would be simultaneous with the movement of securities and
irrevocable. However, if this cannot be achieved, final payment at
the end of the day based on netted transactions would be satisfactory, assuming risks are identified and it is clear who bears them.

7. *Countries with sophisticated markets will adopt the standard
   for securities messages developed by the International
   Organization for Standardization (ISO Standard 7775) and
   will adopt the ISIN numbering system for securities issues as*

defined in the ISO Standard 6166, at least for cross-border transactions. These standards should be operational by 1992.

No worldwide securities numbering system exists at this time. A great number of countries with highly developed securities business identify issues by code numbers, but these numbers have no significance outside the country concerned. Securities of the same issue are identified by different numbers in different countries where they may be physically held and/or recorded. As a result, the national numbers are not satisfactory for cross-border transactions. The rapid expansion of international securities business has created an urgent need for a universally acceptable International Securities Identification Number.

ISO (the International Organization for Standardization) is a worldwide federation of national standards bodies (ISO member organizations), whose charter states:

"Because of its strong rationalization effect, the introduction of an internationally applicable numbering system would substantially facilitate and support international securities business".[4]

The ISO is mandated to develop and promulgate standards for communications, including various numbering systems associated with international commerce.

Various standards for numbering securities exist today, including CUSIP, SEDOL and others. In order for trade information to be communicated in a consistent format and handled by computers, a single numbering standard and message system would be ideal. Such a system is provided by the international standard known as ISIN (International Securities Identification Number). The ISIN number consists of a country code, a security's domestic code number, and a check digit to validate the code.

The reality today is that substantial investments have already been made in the infrastructure of various systems that use their own numbering and message systems. Options thus include either a conversion to the ISIN numbering system immediately, or the construc-

---

[4]   Source: ISO 6166, International Organization for Standardization, 1986.

tion of tables that uniquely translate from an existing number-ing/message system to the ISIN numbering system and ISO message format.

A security's domestic identification number should supersede any other number, so foreign countries dealing in an international-ly traded security should adapt their codes to conform with the security's domestic number. In addition, if the security is identified by several different codes within its country of origin, these codes must be consolidated so that one identification number remains.

8. *Clearing corporations and depositories in each market will establish information sharing programs for cross-market cred-it standards and monitoring systems for participants who deal in multiple markets.*

The rapid increase and proliferation of derivative products has added a new dimension of risk to the clearing process. To the extent possible and practical, entities clearing these instruments should be closely coordinated and supervised. In many countries where derivative products are being formulated, common informa-tion sharing with other related clearing organizations will be insti-tuted at the outset.

The sharing of information will allow the clearing entity to focus on participant exposure to the system in a more informed and intelligent manner. Such concerns as credit limits, position monitor-ing and system exposure are more controlled in a coordinated clear-ing environment. Information sharing among separate clearing agencies will be designed to provide the same level of risk aware-ness and security that would be achieved through a common clear-ing entity. In addition, sharing of information between internation-al clearing and depository organizations will be encouraged.

CHAPTER 9

Options Operations

Since the inception of listed options trading in 1973 (see Figure 9-1), the securities industry has experienced enormous growth in options trading volumes. The standardization of option terms and the formation of a liquid secondary market provided a new investment vehicle that, if used properly, can complement virtually any investment philosophy ranging from the speculative to the conservative. The growth of options trading volume, the next day settlement characteristics, and the complexity of the product have caused most securities firms to set up Options Operations Departments separate and distinct from other security processing areas.

In this chapter we'll look at the characteristics of listed options, the role of the Options Clearing Corporation ("OCC"), and the structure and functions of an Options Operations Department in a securities firm. We'll cover in detail the functions of order entry, exchange floor operations, exercise and assignments, what goes on over expiration weekend, balancing with OCC, settlement of funds and securities, and the impact of dividends and stock splits.

AVERAGE DAILY VOLUME
(1984 – 1993)

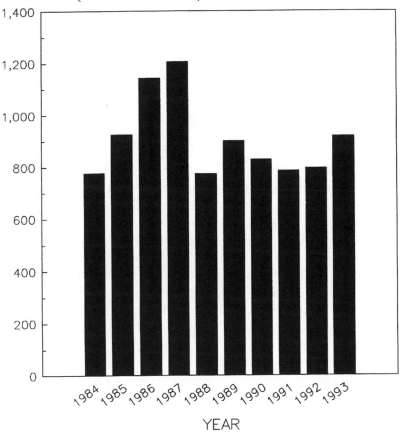

CONTRACTS(IN THOUSANDS)

Used by permission of the Options Clearing Corporation.

FIGURE 9-1. OCC Average Daily Volume

CHARACTERISTICS OF LISTED OPTIONS

CERTIFICATELESS SECURITIES

In contrast to equities and most debt instruments, listed options truly are a "certificateless security," since all trading activity settles in book-entry form and the sole record of ownership is a position on the books of the Options Clearing Corporation. An option is effectively a legal contract granting the holder the right to buy, in the case of a call, or sell, in the case of a put, a specified quantity of the underlying asset at a fixed price upon exercise during the life of the option. An option which can be exercised at any time prior to its expiration is an "American style option," while an option which can be exercised only at its expiration is a "European style option."

Since listed options are "certificateless" securities, the only records of ownership are the bookkeeping entries maintained by OCC and its clearing members. Consequently, investors look to the confirmations and statements they receive from their securities firms to confirm their positions as holders or writers. (A writer of an option is the person who sold the option, and a holder of an option is the person who purchased the option. See the Appendix for a glossary of terms.) Securities firms look to the reports distributed by OCC to confirm positions.

UNDERLYING ASSETS

Listed put and call options are generally available on three types of underlying assets: common stocks, stock indices, and foreign currencies. Options on common stocks are typically referred to as "equity options," while options on government debt, indices, and foreign currencies are referred to as "non-equity options" or "NEO options." The principal difference between equity and NEO options is the settlement terms for exercise and assignment activity.

STANDARDIZED TERMS

Listed options have standardized terms, including the expiration date, the exercise (or strike) price, and the quantity of the underlying asset covered by the option. An option's expiration date is the day on which that option contract expires. After the expiration date, the option buyer no longer has any rights, and the option seller no longer has any obligations under the contract. As a result, if an option is not exercised prior to expiration, it no longer has any value.

Equity options, government debt options, and index options currently expire on the Saturday following the third Friday of their expiration month. Foreign currency options expire on the Friday preceding the third Wednesday of the month (mid-month options), or on the last Friday of the month (in the case of end-of-month currency options).

The exercise price of an option is the price at which the underlying asset will be exchanged in the event the holder exercises rights under the contract. Therefore, the exercise price, in the case of a call, is the price at which the buyer of the option may purchase the underlying asset.

The value of an option is referred to as its premium, and represents the amount paid by the buyer to the seller (or writer) in exchange for the legal rights granted with the option. An option premium typically consists of two components: intrinsic value and time value. Intrinsic value is the amount, if any, by which the option is "in-the-money." A call option is "in-the- money" if the strike price is below the current market price for the underlying asset. Time value, on the other hand, is whatever value the option has in addition to its intrinsic value. It reflects interest rates and what a buyer is willing to pay for the option, with the expectation that its value will increase prior to the option's expiration. The fundamental determinants of an option's time value are: 1) the probability that the option will expire in the money (the volatility of the underlying security; 2) the risk free rate of return; and 3) the time remaining to expiration.

Options are often referred to by "type," i.e., puts and calls are types of options. The same type of option on the same underlying security is called a "class." All of the puts on a security constitute one class, while all of the calls on the same security constitute another class.

An options "series" constitutes that group of options of the same class that have the same exercise price, expiration month, and cover the same number of shares of the underlying stock.

Listed options are generally traded on the following national securities exchanges:

The Chicago Board Options Exchange (CBOE)

The American Stock Exchange (AMEX)

The Philadelphia Stock Exchange (PHLX)

The Pacific Stock Exchange (PSE)

The New York Stock Exchange (NYSE)

The exchanges, the National Association of Securities Dealers (NASD) and the Options Clearing Corporation, have established standards that an underlying security must meet before options on that security will be listed.

As a given option series expires, new series will be listed for expiration in the furthest month permissible. Strike prices are set at specified intervals by the exchanges and OCC. Generally, the strike prices fit the following guidelines:

For stocks over $100 per share, strike prices are set at $10 intervals (e.g. 100, 110, and 120);

For stocks over $50 but less than $100 per share, strike prices are set at $5 intervals;

For stocks under $50 per share, strike prices are set at $2.50 intervals.

Strike prices for index options are set at 2 1/2 point and 5 point intervals, while strike prices for foreign currency options have intervals which are unique to each currency. During the time period when options having a specific expiration month are outstanding, the exchanges will add new series with different strikes any time the price of the underlying asset moves through the mid-point of the interval. For example, if ABC is trading at 69 there will be options listed with strike prices of 65 and 70. However, if ABC was subsequently trading at 72 1/2, the options would be listed at a strike price of 75.

ROLE OF THE OPTIONS CLEARING CORPORATION (OCC)[1]

Now let's look at the role Options Clearing Corporation plays in listed options. The OCC is jointly owned by the option exchanges discussed previously. However, OCC's Board of Directors is comprised of nine Clearing Member Directors, one management director and representatives of the exchanges and NASD. Consequently, OCC's Clearing Members, through their board representatives, exercise effective control over the Corporation. OCC has, from its inception, operated as a not-for-profit corporation, and it is regulated by the Securities and Exchange Commission. OCC's purpose is threefold: 1) it is the guarantor for all listed option contracts; 2) it is the issuer of all listed option contracts; and 3) it is the processor of all listed option contracts that are traded, serving as agent for clearing and recordkeeping.

OCC AS GUARANTOR

In its role as guarantor, OCC facilitates an active secondary market in listed options. As the guarantor, OCC effectively places itself between the buyer and the seller in each option trade guaranteeing that premium monies, or monies due upon exercise/assignment, will in fact be paid when due; and that securities, cash, or currencies deliverable as a result of exercise/assignment, will in fact be delivered when due. In this way, OCC divorces the original buyer (or holder) of the option from the original seller (or writer).

Conversely, every option writer is obligated to OCC for performance under the contract. Therefore, OCC may assign the exercise notice submitted by any holder to any writer in the same options series. The obligation of each writer to OCC is guaranteed by the securities firm, or clearing member, who maintains the writer's account.

This clearing member guarantee is the first line of defense in a system of safeguards, called the "back-up system," designed to provide substance to OCC's guarantee. However, within this context OCC effectively assumes some credit risk with respect to each clearing member. This risk is similar to the risk assumed by a bank when

---

[1] OCC is constantly upgrading its systems and procedures and should be contacted directly for more detail regarding processing.

it issues a standby letter of credit to guarantee a commercial paper issue: the guarantee is, in effect, a contingent liability and the probability it will be called on is remote. In fact, during the 14 years prior to 1987, there were few occasions where OCC was called on to fulfill its guarantee as the result of a clearing member bankruptcy. Nevertheless, just as any prudent creditor would do, OCC manages this credit risk by:

> Subjecting each clearing member applicant to a thorough initial credit review requiring that they meet defined standards of financial responsibility;
>
> Securing and maintaining complete credit documentation; and,
>
> Conducting routine rigorous assessments of each clearing member's creditworthiness.

At the same time, OCC's exposure differs from that of a bank in an important way. Specifically, the dollar value of OCC's exposure can, and frequently does, fluctuate dramatically from one day to the next. Consequently, OCC has developed additional safeguards to effectively manage this risk. First, each business day, OCC quantifies its potential exposure by marking updated options positions to their current market price. This exposure is then subjected to a rigorous analysis designed to quantify the price risk inherent in each position (i.e., the reasonable, potential change in each position's value over the next business day). The combination of these activities results in a margin requirement for each clearing member.

Second, prior to the market's opening each business day, OCC settles all trades from the preceding business day, and collects collateral deposits equal to each clearing member's margin requirement. Each night, all collateral deposit balances are updated, marked to market and, where appropriate, discounted to cover the price risk inherent to the collateral.

Third, OCC continuously monitors general market conditions, especially with respect to the positions of those clearing members subject to closer than normal surveillance, identifying those situations where its exposure may be under-collateralized. If OCC determines that additional collateral is appropriate, it issues a "variation margin call," which must be met within one hour of the time a member firm is notified.

Finally, OCC maintains a second line of defense in the form of a clearing fund whose purpose is to "back-up" the margin deposits of clearing members in the event that such deposits are not immediately realizable, or prove to be inadequate. All clearing members are required to contribute to this fund, and each member is contractually obligated for a second tranche in the unlikely event the fund is ever exhausted. After meeting this second tranche requirement, a member could legally withdraw from membership. However, if the firm remains a clearing member, it is obligated for further contributions if the need arises.

OCC AS ISSUER

Since OCC is the issuer of listed options, the terms and conditions of each contract are defined by OCC's By-Laws and Rules. In the event of a corporate reorganization, stock split, merger, or similar event, it is OCC who adjusts the terms of each contract. In response to such events, OCC issues "Information Memos" to its clearing members regarding these adjustments. Such events may significantly impact existing option positions, alter the profitability of option trading strategies and/or impose unique operational requirements. Consequently, the contents of such memos should be broadly disseminated to Account Executives, Registered Options Principals, the Trading Desk, and all appropriate Operations Departments.

Additionally, since listed options are securities, OCC, as the issuer, registers these securities with the Securities and Exchange Commission, each of the 50 states (Blue Sky Registrations), and Securities Commissions in the provinces of Canada. This registration process entails the annual filing of a Form S-20 Prospectus (a copy of which is available from OCC upon request) with the Securities and Exchange Commission under the Securities Act of 1933. OCC and its participants also publish and broadly distribute to investors an options disclosure document. The document's title is *"Characteristics and Risks of Standardized Options."* Since options trading requires investor sophistication and may entail a high degree of risk, securities firms' clients must receive a copy of this document prior to, or at the time they open an options account.

OCC as Processor

OCC's role as processor is more comprehensive than just settling trades. This is due to the certificateless environment in which options are traded and OCC's role as guarantor.

Essentially, OCC's role as processor encompasses:

Receiving matched trade input from participant exchanges.

Receiving post trade input (e.g., adjustments, exercises, and transfers of account) from clearing members.

Receiving and processing margin deposit/withdrawal activity from clearing members.

Updating clearing members' prior position balances with each day's activity.

Randomly assigning exercise notices to clearing members who have open short positions.

Communicating the appropriate results of this process to clearing members, banks, depositories, correspondent clearing corporations, and exchanges.

The flow chart in Figure 9-2 provides a high level representation of this process, while the following paragraphs provide a brief description of each component in the process.

Each participant exchange is responsible for providing OCC with trade input. For example, after an order has been executed on a participant exchange, that exchange will provide to OCC the buy and sell side of each transaction. One of the benefits associated with OCC is the standardization of trade records for input to OCC. This standardization in trade record formats allows OCC to provide clearing members with machine readable output listing both matched and unmatched trades for all option exchanges, a service which offers member firms significant efficiencies in reconciliations of option trades.

Clearing members provide OCC with post-trade transactions. This activity is supported by a variety of input media including: forms submitted to OCC, an on-line computer system whereby clearing member personnel key transactions directly into OCC's systems; machine readable media (e.g., magnetic tapes, etc.); and CPU to CPU transmissions. Figure 9-3 summarizes the daily time frames for this process for non-equity products.

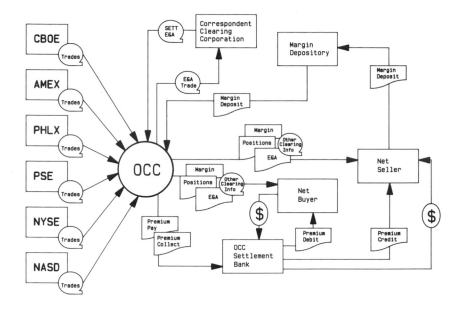

FIGURE 9-2. OCC as Processor*

*Used by permission of the Options Clearing Corporation.

By 6:00 a.m.	C/MACS Available for input of Exercise Notices, Position Adjustments, Transfer of Account and CMTA Transfers on Expiration Day C/MACS Report Inquiry Availabliity
Prior to 8:00 a.m.	Distribution of the Following Output: Data Service Tape Contract Control Report Daily Margin Report (No Report on Expiration Date) Daily Margin Report Settlement Summary (No Report on Expiration Date) Daily Position Reports (Activity and Summary) Matched Transfer Report Unmatched Transfer Report Clearing Member Reject/Modification Report Clearing Member Trade Assignment Report Exercise/Assignment Activity Report Exercise Settlement Report Exercise/Assignment Netting Report Exercise Settlement Response Report Settled Fails Report Preliminary Exercise Report (Expiration Day Only) Advisory In-The-Money Report†

FIGURE 9-3. The Options Clearing Corporation Non-Equity Operational Time Table*

*Used by permission of the Options Clearing Corporation.

	Clearing Fund Status Report (Monthly)
	Daily Depository Activity Report
	Depository Record Report (Weekly)
	Pending Escrow Report
	Escrow Settlement Report
	Listing of Expired Escrows/Assigned Escrows Response Report (First Business Day after Expiration Date)
	Final Listing of Expired Escrows Report (Second Business Day after Expiration Date)
	Foreign Currency Margins Report
	FX Currency Exercise/Assignment Report
	FX Selective Gross-Up Activity Report
	Clearing Member Netted Foreign Currency Report
	Clearing Member FX Exercise Settlement Report
	Foreign Currency Settled Items Report
	Pledge Loan Reports (Pledgee)
	Pledge Loan Reports (Pledgor)
10:00 a.m.	Drafts Guaranteed by Bank** (Funds due OCC)
	Foreign Currency Drafts Guaranteed by Bank** (Funds due OCC)
	Market Maker Over-Pledge Draft Guaranteed by Bank** (Funds due OCC)
	Last Input (Hard Copy) of Position Adjustments, Transfers of Account, and CMTA Transfers to OCC on Expiration Day
	Preliminary Exercise Report Responses due to OCC on Expiration Day
11:00 a.m.	Last Input of (Machine Readable) Position Adjustments, Transfers of Account, and CMTA Transfers to OCC on Expiration Day
	Checks Guaranteed by Bank** (Funds due Clearing Member)
11:30 a.m.	Margin Withdrawal Requests to OCC
1:00 p.m.	DVP Authorization Form to OCC on Business Day Following Exercise
2:00 p.m.	Last Input of (Hard Copy) Spread Instructions to OCC
	Last Input of (Hard Copy) Position Adjustments to OCC
	Last Input of (Hard Copy) Transfers of Account to OCC
	Last Input of (Hard Copy) CMTA Transfers to OCC
	Last Input of Unmatched Transfer Report Tear-Offs to OCC
	ERD Deposits to OCC
	ERD Withdrawals to OCC
	ERD Rollovers to OCC
	ERD Cash Only Entries to OCC
	ERD Pending Responses to OCC
	ERD Assigned Escrow Responses to OCC
	Option Pledge Instructions to OCC
	Option Pledge Release Instructions to OCC
	Letter of Credit Deposits or Amendments to Outstanding Letters of Credit ‡

FIGURE 9-3. *(Continued)*

	Depository Receipts to DTC
	Depository Releases to OCC
	Depository Transfers to OCC
	Margin Depository Receipts to DTC
	Margin Depository Releases to OCC
	Clearing Fund Depository Receipts to DTC
	Clearing Fund Depository Releases to OCC
Prior to 3:00 p.m.	Cash Margin Withdrawals are Transferred to Clearing Member's Bank Account**
	Foreign Currency Credits are Transferred to Clearing Member's Bank Account**
	Final Exercise Report Distributed (Expiration Day Only)
4:30 p.m.	Last Input of (Machine Readable) Spread Instructions to OCC
	Last Input of (Machine Readable) Position Adjustments to OCC
	Last Input of (Machine Readable) Transfers of Account to OCC
	Last Input of (Machine Readable) CMTA Transfers to OCC
	Last Input of Exercise Notices for OCC Validation
5:00 p.m.	Last Input of Exercise/Assignment Response Report Tear-Offs to OCC
	Final Exercise Responses Due to OCC on Expiration Day
	Position Adjustments Input Due to OCC on Expiration Day
8:00 p.m.	Last Input of (Hard Copy) Exercise Notices to OCC
	Last Input of (Hard Copy) Exercise Deletion Notices to OCC
	Last Input of (C/MACS) Spread Instructions to OCC
	Last Input of (C/MACS) Position Adjustments to OCC
	Last Input of (C/MACS) Transfer of Account to OCC
	Last Input of (C/MACS) CMTA Transfer to OCC
	Last Input of (C/MACS) Exercise Notices to OCC

Table is in chronological order and times refer to Eastern Time.
†Distribution starts two weeks prior to expiration day.
**All amounts settled in immediately available funds.
‡When letters of credit are being substituted for cash, member firms should deposit the letters of credit to OCC by 1:00 p.m. Eastern Time. The resulting delivery of credits representing excess margin will be deposited into clearing member bank accounts by 2:00 p.m. Eastern Time.

FIGURE 9-3. (*Continued*)

TYPES OF POSITION INFORMATION

OCC maintains position information for each clearing member by Option Series. This information is further broken down into three account types: 1) a customer account; 2) a market maker account, which is further broken down into market maker subaccounts (one for each individual market maker/specialist clearing through that member); and 3) a firm account for the proprietary positions of that clearing member. Each business day OCC produces a "Daily Position Summary Report" (see Figure 9-4) delineating a clearing member's positions in each account type by Options Class and Series. This information is available in SAR, machine readable media (CPU to CPU transmission or magnetic tape), or microfiche. Additionally, OCC reports are available in multiple locations (e.g., New York, Philadelphia, Chicago, San Francisco, and Los Angeles) and OCC provides a remote report print capability.

In addition to a Daily Position Summary Report, OCC provides other reports, the most important of which are:

A Daily Position Activity Report of all trades compared and cleared on the preceding business day, plus exercises, and post trade transactions which affect ending positions;

Exercise and Assignment Activity Reports;

Margin Reports reflecting a clearing member's margin requirement, net premium pay/collect and margin deposits by asset type in each OCC account (see Figure 9-5).

OCC's margin requirements can be met by:

Deposits of the underlying security as "cover" via an escrow receipt or depository pledge;

Deposits of approved stocks for value via a Depository Pledge;

Deposits of Treasury Securities for value;

Letters of Credit;

Cash.

THE OPTIONS CLEARING CORPORATION

D   DAILY POSITION SUMMARY REPORT

A FIRM #   FIRM NAME   E   PRODUCT KIND

B ACCOUNT TYPE   C OPTION TYPE
                  F ACTIVITY DATE

CONTRACT DESCRIPTION			LAST	BEGINNING POSITION			****** ENDING POSITION ******				E/A ACTIVITY		****** PREMIUM ******	
SYMBOL	MO	YR	STRIKE	ACT	LONG	SHORT	UNSEG	LONG	SHORT	EXER	ASGN	PAY	COLLECT
		G		H				I			J		K
1	2	3		1	2	3	1	2	3				

L Premium Total in USD for Account – within product kind – Calls

M Net Pay/Collect for Account – within product kind – Calls

N Premium Total in USD for Account – within product kind – Puts

O Net Pay/Collect for Account – within product kind – Puts

P Premium Total in USD for Account – within product kind – Calls and Puts combined

Q Net Pay/Collect for Account – within product kind – Calls and Puts combined

R Origin Summary in USD

1 Net Call Premium – for Account – all product kinds combined

2 Net Put Premium – for Account – all product kinds combined

3 Premium Settlement for Account – all product kinds combined

4 Variation Settlement for Account – all product kinds combined

FIGURE 9-4. OCC Daily Position Report
Used by permission of the Options Clearing Corporation.

THE OPTIONS CLEARING CORPORATION

NON-EQUITY OPTIONS
C DAILY MARGIN REPORT

PAGE 1 V.066

DATE 06/08
PROGRAM-ID UMG050

TIME 03:15:46
D ACTIVITY DATE 06/08***

FIRM NO. FIRM NAME
A 917 SMITH SECURITIES
B CUSTOMER

OPTION SERIES	SETTLEMENT DATE	LONG (EXERCISE)	UNSEG	SHORT (ASSIGN)	DEPOSIT	SERIES NET	MARKING PRICE		PREMIUM MARGIN
AMEX MAJOR MARKET INDEX F			H	CLASS GROUP J		K			M
E 1 XMI AMEX MAJOR MARKET INDEX									
2 CALLS							L		
3 06 -- 530		G 2		2		2S	43.625000		8,725.00DR
2 PUTS									
3 06 570		2					3.125000		0.00
N AMEX MAJOR MARKET INDEX				CLASS GROUP TOTALS					
PREMIUM MARGIN									8,725.00DR
ADDITIONAL MARGIN									
UPSIDE/DOWNSIDE								4,748.22DR	0.00
MULT FACTORS								0.00	0.00
NET UPSIDE/DOWNSIDE								4,748.22DR	0.00
O BROAD-BASED INDEXES				PRODUCT GROUP TOTALS					
PREMIUM MARGIN									8,725.00DR
ADDITIONAL MARGIN									
UPSIDE/DOWNSIDE								4,748.22DR	
NET ADDITIONAL MARGIN								0.00	4,748.22DR
TOTAL MARGIN REQUIREMENT									13,473.22DR
P ACCOUNT TOTAL									
TOTAL REQUIREMENT									13,473.22DR
TOTAL MARGIN									13,473.22DR

FIGURE 9-5. OCC Daily Margin Report
Used by permission of the Options Clearing Corporation.

OCC Exercise Procedure

The exercise of options can be complex; let's look at how the exercise program works before we discuss the option operations area of securities firms. In order to accomplish an early exercise (i.e., prior to expiration) the clearing member, in whose account the option is held long, must submit an exercise notice to OCC. Such early exercise notices may be submitted via OCC's on-line system, but in either event, it must be submitted no later than 8:00 p.m. However, OCC will not accept exercise notices for expiring options on the last trading day for those options. Expiring options can be exercised on Expiration Saturday utilizing OCC's "Exercise by Exception" System.

Exercise Notices tendered to OCC are randomly assigned to clearing members with an open short position in that Option Series. Essentially, this computerized process entails: reading all exercise notices for a given option series; totalling the short contracts that are open; calculating a "skip interval" (a given number of positions are skipped or passed over); and, generating a random number as the starting point. Then, based on this starting point, exercises are assigned to the clearing member whose position corresponds to that starting number in a predetermined quantity (e.g., 25 contracts), and then the skip interval is counted off and the next "block" of exercise notices is assigned. This process is repeated until all contracts exercised in that Series have been assigned. Those clearing members who have been assigned are notified of this activity via OCC's Delivery Advice Report, or the Exercise and Assignment Activity Report in the case of certain NEO contracts, prior to 8:00 a.m.. These reports will notify the clearing member as to the Series, contract quantity and account type (i.e., customer, market maker subaccount or firm) assigned. Assignments in the customer account must be reallocated by the clearing member to specific customers, in accordance with the clearing member's established procedures. These procedures for reallocating exercise notices must be fixed, disclosed to the customer, and approved by an exchange. Most firms utilize a random allocation method. However, some firms utilize a "first-in/first-out" method.

STRUCTURE AND FUNCTIONS OF A SECURITIES FIRM'S OPTIONS OPERATIONS DEPARTMENT

The organizational structure of an Options Operations Department normally depends upon the size of the securities firm, the amount of options trading volume processed, and the sophistication of the information systems. For example, the clearing function may be located within the Options Operations Department, or be handled by a firm's Purchase and Sales Department. Option order traffic may be directly transmitted to the Department by the branch office network, or sent to a central wire and order processing facility for handling and routing to the exchanges.

An Options Operations Department may have an internal coordination unit responsible for the development and implementation of option trading systems, or this area might be part of a firm's central system development area. The department may designate a section or unit to specifically handle OTC options and index options. These units may, however, bc incorporated within a Control area.

Due to the physical location of the CBOE and the trading volume handled on that exchange, firms may also have personnel in Chicago to process, clear, and balance transactions executed there. Thus, the configuration of the Options Operations Department is determined by a firm's own needs, internal and external efficiencies, and system capabilities.

No matter how the department is structured, it must be systemically linked to the option exchanges and the OCC. This is necessary due to the next day settlement feature of options, market volatility, and the internal and external balancing process inherent in all option transactions.

Figure 9-6 provides a sample organization structure for an Options Operations Department. Let's now look at the department's basic functions and responsibilities.

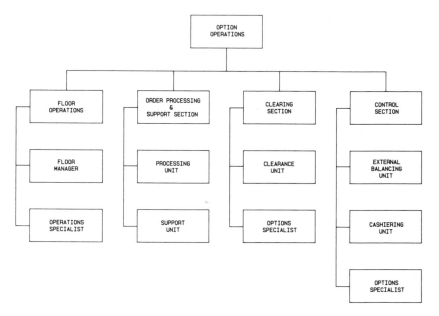

FIGURE 9-6. Options Operations Organization

FLOOR OPERATIONS

Floor Operations, while usually part of the department structure, is physically located on the floor of the various exchanges. It is responsible for the timely and accurate processing of option orders, reports, messages and quotes directed to the floor. It represents the member firm in all phases of floor activities.

ORDER PROCESSING AND SUPPORT

The Order Processing and Support area is responsible for answering sales office inquiries regarding the status of an order, reviewing "day orders" for missed reports, and handling "challenge" wires received from a branch office, if the office disputes the price at which an option trade was executed. Fail and DK problems are also handled in this area.

CLEARING

Clearing may be part of a firm's P&S Department. The area is basically responsible for the accurate internal balancing of option transactions. It may also handle inter-firm transfer of accounts and reconcile stock record differences in the latter, if not under the responsibility of a firm's Stock Record Department. Clearance units may be assigned the added responsibility of performing "post-settlement" account number changes and commission adjustments.

CONTROL

The two primary functions of the Control area are the balancing of the firm's internal option positions to the records of the OCC, and the processing and control of exercises and assignments. Other responsibilities can include position adjustments, regulatory reporting, trade corrections, and control of collateral documents. In some firms, the control of collateral documents is proof that deposits of the securities of the institutional customers, not being held by the member firm, are in fact maintained with banks, trust companies or other depositories (i.e., escrow or depository receipts). For puts, the documents are proofs that institutional customers have funds available to purchase the securities if assigned. When these customers write an option against any of these securities, government regulations require that the clearing member keep the collateral document on file as if it were the actual stock certificate.

Option Specialists in the Clearing and Control sections act as a liaison with the sales offices on complex option problems. These can include market errors, problems on profitable expiring option positions, commission calculations and assignments.

FUNCTIONS OF OPTIONS DEPARTMENTS

ORDER ENTRY PROCEDURES

Each new options account must be approved for trading by a Registered Options Principal (ROP), who is responsible for supervising the trading activities of the account. The customer will also have to provide more financial information and investment objective information than required for the opening of a regular cash or margin account. Figure 9-7 is an example of a typical Option Information Form utilized by securities firms.

Merrill Lynch OPTION INFORMATION - INDIVIDUAL & JOINT ACCOUNT

PERSONAL AND FINANCIAL DATA FURNISHED BY CLIENT

ACCOUNT NUMBER	FC#	NO. OF DEPENDENTS	HOME PHONE NUMBER	

ACCOUNT TITLE		DATE OF BIRTH	MARITAL STATUS

ACCOUNT TITLE (2ND PARTY)		DATE OF BIRTH	MARITAL STATUS

STREET ADDRESS

CITY	STATE	ZIP CODE

EMPLOYER'S NAME CHECK ☐ IF RETIRED, PREVIOUS EMPLOYER'S NAME	POSITION	BUSINESS PHONE NUMBER

SPOUSE'S NAME/2ND PARTY CHECK ☐ NOT EMPLOYED ☐ IF EMPLOYED, EMPLOYER'S NAME	POSITION	BUSINESS PHONE NUMBER

CLIENT'S APPROXIMATE ANNUAL EARNINGS
☐ BELOW $25,000-STATE AMOUNT _____
☐ $25,000-$50,000   ☐ $50,000-$100,000   ☐ OVER $100,000

SPOUSE'S APPROXIMATE INCOME (IF APPLICABLE)
$

COMBINED TOTAL ANNUAL INCOME FROM ALL SOURCES
$

INVESTMENT OBJECTIVES
☐ INCOME   ☐ HEDGING   ☐ SPECULATION

DOES CLIENT HAVE RESTRICTED STOCK?   IS CUSTOMER A CONTROL PERSON?
☐ YES   ☐ NO   ☐ YES   ☐ NO

(IF YES, SHARES OF RESTRICTED STOCK OR STOCK HELD BY A CONTROL PERSON, EXCEPT TO THE EXTENT SALABLE UNDER RULE 144, MAY NOT BE USED TO COVER A SHORT POSITION IN CALL OPTION CONTRACTS, SATISFY MARGIN REQUIREMENTS OR BE DELIVERED AGAINST EXERCISE OF A PUT OR CALL OPTION.)

	CASH/CASH EQUIVALENTS $

CLIENT'S LIQUID ASSETS

MARKETABLE SECURITIES $

1) TOTAL LIQUID ASSETS $

(OMIT EQUITY IN HOME)
2) OTHER ASSETS $

TOTAL OF 1 + 2 MINUS TOTAL LIABILITIES
NET WORTH $

TYPE OF OPTION TRADING DESIRED - ☐ EQUITY   ☐ INDEX

☐ BUY CALLS	☐ BUY PUTS	☐ SPREADS
☐ WRITE CALLS	☐ WRITE PUTS	☐ COMBINATIONS (STRADDLES, ETC.)
☐ COVERED	☐ COVERED	
☐ UNCOVERED	☐ UNCOVERED	

LIST PREVIOUS ACCOUNTS WITH OTHER FIRMS
1.
2.

REQUIRED DOCUMENTS

☐ "CHARACTERISTICS AND RISKS OF STANDARDIZED OPTIONS" PROVIDED TO CLIENT   DATE

POWER OF ATTORNEY   NAME OF AGENT
☐ LTD.   ☐ GENERAL

☐ CMA/CBA MARGIN ACCOUNT   ☐ CODE 108 HYPOTHECATION CONSENT FORM SIGNED BY CLIENT

CHECK ALL INVESTMENT EXPERIENCES THAT APPLY

☐ EQUITY OPTIONS _____ YRS.   ☐ STOCK INDICES _____ YRS.   ☐ STOCK _____ YRS.

☐ COMMODITIES _____ YRS.   ☐ BONDS _____ YRS.   ☐ OTHER (SPECIFY) _____ YRS.

PRIOR TRADING ACTIVITY
☐ SELDOM   ☐ MODERATE   ☐ ACTIVE

DECLARATIONS   APPROVALS

TO BE COMPLETED BY RESIDENT VICE PRESIDENT / RESIDENT MANAGER PRIOR TO OPTION TRADING

APPROVED FOR OPTION TRADING AS FOLLOWS:	EQUITY	INDEX
1 - BUY CALLS	☐	☐
2 - BUY PUTS	☐	☐
3 - WRITE COVERED CALLS	☐	☐
4 - WRITE UNCOVERED CALLS	☐	☐
5 - WRITE COVERED PUTS	☐	☐
6 - WRITE UNCOVERED PUTS	☐	☐
7 - SPREADS	☐	☐
8 - COMBINATIONS, STRADDLES	☐	☐

FINANCIAL CONSULTANT SIGNATURE   DATE

RESIDENT VICE PRESIDENT/RESIDENT MANAGER SIGNATURE (MUST BE R.O.P.)   DATE

REGISTERED OPTION PRINCIPAL'S SIGNATURE (IF OTHER THAN RESIDENT VICE PRESIDENT/RESIDENT MANAGER)   DATE

CODE 1014 (REV 11/93)   **BRANCH OFFICE COPY**

FIGURE 9-7. Option Information Form
Reprinted by permission of Merrill Lynch, Pierce, Fenner & Smith Incorporated.

The customer is also required to sign a standard option agreement attesting that he/she has received and read the Disclosure Document (*"Characteristics and Risks of Standardized Options"*), understands the high risk involved, will not violate position or exercise limits, is financially able to sustain any losses from the writing or purchase of options, and understands the member firm's exercise assignment allocation method. Once approved, the client can commence trading.

When a customer wishes to place an order to buy or sell an option, the Account Executive (AE) forwards the request to the office wire operator who transmits the order to the "home office" or, if a firm has the systems capability, the order is sent directly by the branch office to the appropriate exchange where the option is traded. The order is given to the firm's representative who then acts to execute the order or it may be executed through an exchange's auto execution system.

An order consists of several parts:

Buy or Sell

Type—call or put

Open or Close

Quantity—number of contracts

Description of Option (i.e., stock symbol, strike price, and expiration month)

Price—either a market or a limit order

Customer Account Number

Account Type—Customer, Firm, or Market Maker.

Figure 9-8 is a copy of an Option Order Ticket utilized by one clearing member.

COMMON ERRORS MADE IN ENTERING OPTION ORDERS

The additional elements necessary to enter an option order, (as opposed to other orders), can lead to a high incidence of description errors. They can also result in clearing problems, which we will examine later in the chapter.

Now, let's look at an option order and the problems that may arise if it is not processed properly.

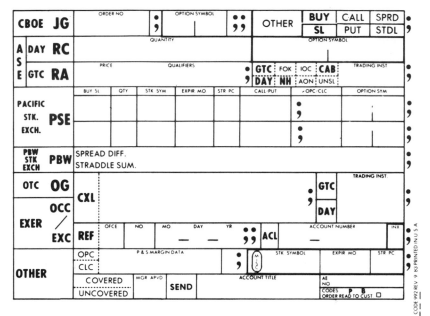

FIGURE 9-8. Option Order Ticket

Suppose a customer wants to buy a call option of XYZ "at the market" with a strike price of 130, expiring in October, and currently does not have a position in the option. The order should be entered as BUY 1 CALL XYZ OCT 130 at market, opening transaction, account number and type. The order is executed properly at a price of 1 1/2, and the customer now has a "long position" in the option.

Now let's say the market moves up and the XYZ OCT 130 Calls are now selling at 4. The customer decides to sell, take a profit, and closes out the position. The order should be entered as Sell 1 Call XYZ OCT 130 at market, closing position, account number and type.

Table 9-1 depicts the positions in the account if the sell order was transmitted improperly:

Transmission Error	Result
Incorrect expiration month, incorrect strike price, or incorrect account number.	The closing transaction will be changed to open. Firm will now have an erroneous short position on the stock record since it sold an option it did not own.
Opening instead of closing transaction	A short and long position for the same option.
Buy instead of a sell	An additional long position is created.
Put for a call	New short position is created.

TABLE 9-1. Results of Transmission Errors

Obviously a myriad of problems can arise if these errors are not rectified. Errors such as the above can usually be resolved prior to the settlement of the transaction, but still may result in money losses to the firm. To prevent these errors, it is customary at many firms to have the Account Executive call the client and confirm the trade. The Account Executive may also compare the confirmation with the information he/she previously posted in the customer's record book, and upon discovery of the error, the necessary trade correction could then be handled in a similar fashion to those for stocks. In addition, some larger firms have developed highly-sophisticated order routing systems that validate open/close codes and other critical components against the account positions before routing the order to the floor. The office would have to contact the Order Support area of Options Operations to rectify an error.

Investors in options may also utilize various strategies in their trading methodology to create "hedge" positions against a previously established option or stock position, or by creating contingency orders.

The operations manager in the branch office should be aware of these types of orders, which if not properly entered and executed, could magnify the problems mentioned previously. Some of these complex orders include:

Straddle. A Put and Call purchased or written on the same underlying security with the same strike price and expiration date.

Spread. The simultaneous purchase of one option of the same type and sale of another on the same underlying security, but in a different series.

Combination. A Put and Call purchased and written on the same underlying security, but with different series.

EXCHANGE FLOOR OPERATIONS

There are two areas to examine with regard to Exchange Floor Operations—trading procedures and processing procedures.

TRADING PROCEDURES

The major exchanges utilize two separate trading procedures for listed option transactions and, as managers, a brief overview of these methods is essential before we discuss the processing and operational balancing aspects of options. The Specialist System is employed by the AMEX, PHLX, and NYSE. The Market-Maker/Order Book Official (OBO) system is used by the CBOE and the PSE.

Let's first look at the specialist system. A specialist is primarily responsible for the following:

Maintaining a fair and orderly market

Handling the order book for orders away from the current market

Conducting the opening rotation for each option class

Ensuring that liquidity exists in option series by supplying capital and trading for his/her own account.

An Order Book Official (OBO) is an exchange employee who performs the first three functions of the specialist while the Market-Maker performs the fourth. A succinct difference exists between an OBO and a Specialist: an OBO can only accept public orders from customers, whereas a specialist may take both customer and proprietary (firm) orders on his/her book.

PROCESSING PROCEDURES

Two different exchange trade processing systems exist currently. The PHLX and PSE function in a "locked-in" trade system, while the CBOE, AMEX, AND NYSE use a clearing "Member-to-Member" matching process.

LOCKED-IN TRADE SYSTEMS

The locked-in trade system requires the floor brokers representing the buyer and seller to meet on the trading floor, agree on the price of the option premium, attach their tickets together, and give them to an exchange employee who reports the information into a dual system. Both parties to the transaction receive a trade acknowledgment ticket, which they can compare to their copy of the trade to ensure that the buy/sell, quantity, price, put/call, series, open/close, account/firm/market-maker information is correct. If the error is identified, it can be rectified by having both parties agree to delete the erroneous information and re-enter it into the processing system. Member firms, therefore, have the capability to make intraday "street-side" corrections up to approximately one hour after the exchanges cease trading for the day. This system, therefore, acts as a last sale reporting mechanism and matching processor before the matched trades are passed on to the OCC.

MEMBER-TO-MEMBER SYSTEM

The "member-to-member" process, as mentioned previously, is utilized by the CBOE, AMEX, and NYSE. Once a trade in executed by the floor brokers representing the member firm, the trade information is transmitted by floor operations personnel of the member firm to their respective Options Operations areas.

At the end of the day, each member firm will forward to the Securities Industry Automated Corporation (SIAC) those option trades executed on the AMEX and NYSE. Once SIAC receives all the executions from the member firms, it will compare the trade information and prepare hardcopy listings of all matched and unmatched trades. An unmatched trade could be the result of an execution being reported as a buy instead of a sell, wrong price, incorrect quantity, wrong firm, etc. The listings are then given to the member firm later that evening. For those trades executed on the CBOE, the exchange advises the member firm directly of its matched and unmatched trades.

All unmatched trades or "breaks" are researched and resolved by night operations personnel at the member firm. Most firms will concentrate on correcting the obvious mistakes, which are due to keying errors. If, in its research, a member firm feels its side of the execution is correct, it will leave the execution alone, and hopefully the contra-broker will discover its error and make the necessary corrections to its side of the trade. AMEX and NYSE corrections are passed back to SIAC, and CBOE trade corrections are relayed back to the exchange. Both SIAC and the CBOE will update their files with the corrections and send the matched trades to the OCC. The OCC will only accept matched trade information.

If any uncompared trades remain, SIAC and the CBOE notify the clearing member. The notices from the AMEX are called ROTNS (Rejected Option Trade Notices), while the notices from the CBOE are known as Advisories. These trade breaks are researched and any corrections are processed. If a difference cannot be resolved, the executing brokers will meet face to face the following morning to decide the issue. The uncompared trades must be resolved as options have a next-day settlement. The matched and unmatched trades are transmitted to OCC and included on OCC's Data Service Tape. Many firms use this Data Service Tape to automate elements of the trade reconciliation process.

Figure 9-9 is an example of a ROTN which could be received by a member firm if an uncompared trade remains.

MEMBER FIRM INTERNAL BALANCING PROCEDURES

In addition to floor options and balancing procedures between member firms, another balancing routine is necessary to ensure that the internal clearing firm's records are in agreement with those of the OCC.

As noted previously, the OCC receives all transactions of matched trades executed on the various exchanges, and updates a clearing firm's open record position. The following transactions will affect a clearing member's open position at the OCC:

REJECTED OPTION TRADE NOTICE	**AMEX Options** American Stock Exchange Inc.	**MAJOR BROKER CHANGE COPY**

1	2-7	8-11	12		13-16	17	18-20	21	22-24	27-29	30-31	32-34	35-38
C O D E	TRANS NUMBER	TIME	B / S		CONTRACTS	P=PUT C=CALL	OPTION SERIES					PREMIUM	
		HR.	MIN.				SYMBOL	EXPIR.	STRIKE PRICE			DOL.	FRACTION
									$				
C													

39-41	42-45	46	47	48	49-52	53-56	57-60		61-70	71-73	74-76	79
CLEAR NO.	EXEC. BROKER I.D.	TRANS (O)(C)	ACCT F.C.S. P.N.	CERT (C)	CONTRA CLEAR NO.	CONTRA BROKER I.D.	TRADE DATE		OPTIONAL DATA	PRIM OCC CL NO.	TRDR CODE	E X C I N C D H
							MO.	DAY				

THIS CONSTITUTES NOTICE THAT THE ABOVE TRADE INPUT WAS REJECTED FROM CLEARANCE PROCESSING AND MUST BE RESOLVED IN ACCORDANCE WITH OPTION RULES.

BUY

BUYING FIRM

[OK] [DK] [OK] [DK]

GIVE-UP BROKER

SELL

SELLING FIRM

[OK] [DK] [OK] [DK]

GIVE-UP BROKER

REMARKS:

TO:_____
(EXEC. BROKER)

_____
OTHER SIDE (EXEC. BROKER)

OPT 2 REV. 1/86

FIGURE 9-9. Rejected Option Trade Notice (ROTN)

Used by permission of the American Stock Exchange, Inc.

A BUY OPEN will INCREASE a clearing member's LONG position.

A BUY CLOSE will DECREASE a clearing member's SHORT position.

A SELL OPEN will INCREASE a clearing member's SHORT position.

A SELL CLOSE will DECREASE a clearing member's LONG position.

You may recall from our review of the Options Clearing Corporation that each morning the OCC provides reports to each clearing member, one of which is called a Daily Position Summary Report. That report reflects all open long and short positions maintained at the OCC. The open long and short position in each option series must be matched versus an internal member firm's records to ensure that if every long position on a firm's books elected to exercise their option, a long position would exist on the books of the OCC, and if the OCC assigned all of a firm's short positions, the firm would have sufficient shorts on its books to allocate the assignments. Position adjustments are processed between the member firm and the OCC to keep these positions in balance.

There are times when a member firm's holdings at the OCC are different from the customer's holdings within the firm. While there are various reasons why this can happen, some of the more frequent ones include:

Streetside trade was not compared by the exchange and thus not passed to the OCC.

Customer transaction was not processed internally or was processed incorrectly.

Open or close information was not processed correctly.

Streetside transaction was processed in a "firm" account at the OCC when it should have been processed in "customer" account or vice versa.

All of these reasons can cause imbalances between the books of the OCC and the member firms, and adjustments are necessary to rectify these situations.

When the Daily Position Activity Report is received, the firm would generate an "external breaksheet." This is a comparison of all cleared option trades as reflected by the OCC from the previous day versus the internal trade information of the securities firm. The breaksheet, therefore, lists any open option breaks between the two sets of records. These must be resolved promptly due to the next day settlement feature of options.

The Control Section within the Options Operations Department should have the responsibility of balancing the internal records to those of the OCC. If these two records are not in agreement, it is conceivable that a position carried in error by the firm could be assigned by OCC. Problems could also arise if the underlying security was going "ex-dividend," which we will discuss later in the chapter.

Firms may utilize another breaksheet to identify imbalances between internal option records and the company's stock record. In some cases, this is known as a "double breaksheet."

The stock record is balanced to the long and short option summary file. After all balancing is completed, all the records will be in agreement, and a firm can be certain that all option exercises and assignments will be accurate.

Personnel in the Control Section research and reconcile the differences highlighted on the breaksheets and make correcting entries to place the firm's internal records in balance. The Control Section will now have to adjust the firm's records at the OCC to coincide with those internally. This is done by what is known as "position adjustments."

The OCC has an on-line system called the Clearing/Management and Control System, or "C/MACS" for short. Each clearing member can access this system via in-house terminals or PC's. Using C/MACS, member firms can input transactions affecting positions at the OCC up until 8:00 p.m., and also have the ability to process inter-broker transfers and exercises.

In Option Operations many entries are made to various accounts each day. Time is critical because of the next day settlement feature of options, and personnel within the department must take great care that the adjustments are accurate. All balances for the mentioned records must be in agreement, both internally and externally, to preclude any incorrect exercises and assignments. Figure 9-10 illustrates the balancing process.

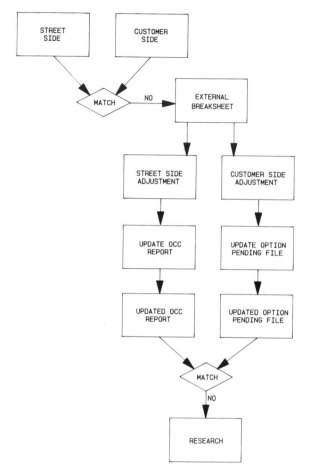

FIGURE 9-10. Option Balancing: Firm and Customer Positions

PROCEDURES FOR EXERCISE AND ASSIGNMENT OF OPTIONS

EXERCISE

When a customer purchases a call or put option, he/she is given the right to buy or sell the underlying security at the strike price. For this right, the customer pays a premium to the writer of the option. The buyer of the call believes the market value of the underlying asset will increase in price, the buyer of the put thinks the asset will decrease, and the writer believes that it will remain relatively the same. Buying or selling the underlying asset before the expiration date of the option contract is called "exercising" the option.

Let's take a closer look at when a client with a call or put may exercise their equity option.

A customer may have purchased a call option on a security with a strike price of $25. If the market moves up, the underlying security might be trading in the marketplace at $35. The client has two alternatives: The client could sell the option itself, which would be trading at a greater premium than when he/she bought it due to the higher market, or he/she could buy the stock (exercise the option) at $25 (strike price) and sell the stock at the then market price of $35. The opposite, of course, would be true for the holder of a put option: If the market value of the underlying security decreased from the strike price, the customer could sell the stock to the writer at the strike price, and then buy the stock in the open market at the lower market value. He/she also could sell the option itself at a higher price. If the holders of the call or put options decide to exercise their option, here is the process which would take place in a securities firm:

Customer notifies his/her Account Executive to "exercise" the option position.

Branch office wires Options Operations where the customer's "long" position is verified.

Options Operations deletes the option position and generates a stock trade (buy for a call or sell for a put).

Options Operations simultaneously wires the branch office (to confirm the exercise is in the processing system) and notifies the OCC to exercise the position.

The OCC accepts all exercise instructions and then randomly "assigns" the member firms with open "short" positions to fill the other side of the transaction.

Figure 9-11 is an illustration of this process.

Exercised equity option contracts settle in five business days, and most firms make it a practice to require their branch office network to meet daily specified time limits to ensure that Operations can process the exercised option before the deadline required by the OCC.

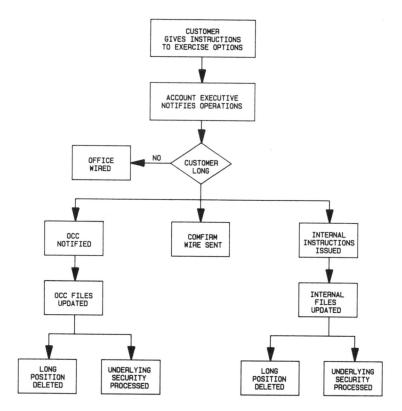

FIGURE 9-11. Equity Exercise Processing

ASSIGNMENTS

The writer of a call or put option may have to respectively sell or buy the underlying security at the strike price, for which they received a premium from the holder, if they are "assigned." At the time the client wrote the option, he/she had a "short" position on the books of the clearing member, and in turn, the clearing member had a short position on the records of the OCC. Upon acceptance of exercise instructions from a member firm, the OCC "randomly" assigns those firms with open short positions to fill the other side of the exercise transaction. Thus, for every option that is exercised, there has to be an option assigned.

The OCC adjusts its records (decreases the open short portions of the member firms), and delivers the assignment notices via a variety of methods to the selected firms the following business day, or T+1. The most common method is through a Direct Data Service Transmission. Your customers should be aware that if they are assigned, the stock trade settlement date is four business days[2] after assignment notification from OCC, since the assignment is made and becomes effective the business day after the exercise is processed by OCC.

Upon receipt of the assignment notifications from the OCC, some securities firms use a random selection method of filling customer assignments, similar to that used by the OCC when assigning the securities firm. Once the assigned option series and the quantities are identified, the computer can scan all the accounts with the open short positions and select those accounts which will be assigned.

Other firms use a "first-in/first-out" process based on the trade date the customer wrote the option contract. The computer will search the option securities record file and identify those accounts to be assigned, based on a chronological methodology. The assignment process, random or first-in/first-out, is decided by the securities firm. The OCC only requests that it have prior approval of the method used by a clearing member, and that it is fair and equitable to all of the clearing member's customers.

Once the customer is selected, several computer outputs are usually generated. A hard copy print out reflecting each series and customer within the series that is assigned can be used for reference purposes. An individual trade assignment report can be transmitted to the branch office servicing the account to notify the Account Executive and the customer of the assignment.

The computer will automatically delete the open option position from the customer's account and enter a buy or sell transaction for the underlying security into the firm's trading system (sell for a call, buy for a put), thereby assuring that the transaction will settle in four business days.

Figure 9-12 provides a flow chart of the assignment process.

---

[2] This will change to two business days effective with the implementation of SEC Rule 15c6-1 on June 1, 1995.

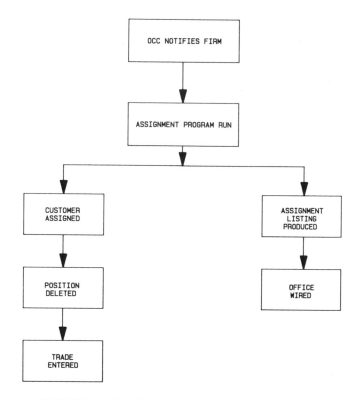

FIGURE 9-12. Equity Assignment Processing

BALANCING OF EXERCISE AND ASSIGNMENT OF OPTIONS

The processing and balancing of both exercise and assignments of options is handled in the Control Section of the Options Operations Department.

The day after an exercise or an assignment of an option, Operations must verify that all entries at the OCC and within the firm have been processed correctly. If not, adjusting entries will have to be made to place all accounts in balance.

The exercise and assignment of index options is the same as that of equity options. However, since there is no underlying security for an index option, the settlement is in cash with the dollar amount to be paid or received based upon the difference between the strike price and the closing price of the index on the day of exercise. Settlement of exercise activity on index options is one day, as opposed to the five business day settlement of equities.[3]

A securities firm may also have a conventional or OTC option assigned by another firm who is the long option. The notification of the assignment and comparison is normally received by messenger from the contra-party. The customer's open position is verified and the option contract is time-stamped.

This is important, since the deadline for conventional option assignments is 3:15 p.m. The comparison is given back to the messenger as a receipt for the exercising firm. The sales office or trader servicing the account is notified, a buy/sell trade ticket is prepared on the underlying security, and the open option position is deleted.

Significant numbers of shares are traded through the exercise and assignment process. This is especially true in periods of high volume, volatile markets, and on expiration weekends. For these reasons, along with the amount of money involved, it is of utmost importance that the balancing of all accounts and the processing of the exercise and assignments be carefully performed.

EXPIRATION WEEKEND

Most of you know the problems and pressures that evolve from expiration weekends. Let's take a look at the entire process.

While most options can be exercised by the buyer at any time from the date of purchase, all options "expire" on the Saturday following the third Friday of the month. The exception is foreign currency options, which expire the Friday immediately preceding the third Wednesday of the expiration month, or on the last Friday of the month in one case of end-of-month currency options. On that Saturday, and the following day, Sunday, Options Operations personnel will have to process and control the expiration and assignment or exercise of those respective options.

One of the most important functions performed on expiration weekend is the balancing of all options expiring "in-the-money." An option is in-the-money when the exercise or strike price is below the

---

[3] This will change to three business days effective with the implementation of SEC Rule 15c6-1 on June 1, 1995.

current market value in the case of a call, and above the current market price in the case of a put. Operations is not usually concerned with any options expiring "out-of-the-money," since they rarely are assigned or exercised.

With the large number of options series expiring in-the-money, clearing members were originally faced with a labor intensive, paper driven, error-prone expiration weekend. To alleviate this

paper crunch, the OCC developed an "Exercise by Exception" routine. In the case of equity options, the OCC will automatically exercise customer option positions 3/4 or more points in-the-money, or firm or market maker positions 1/4 or more points in-the-money, unless instructions are received to the contrary.

For index options, the threshold for customer positions is 1/4 or more points in-the-money, and .01 points for firms on market maker positions. There is no automatic exercise for foreign currency or treasury options, and specific instructions have to be entered by the Account Executive regardless of the in-the-money value.

Customers generally have until 5:30 p.m. on the Friday prior to expiration to issue exercise instructions to their securities firm on expiring options. The Options Operations Department then verifies the customer's instructions, sends a confirming wire to the branch office or trader servicing the account, and advises the OCC of the exercise notice on Saturday.

Let's now look at the basic activities which take place over expiration weekend. On Saturday, the OCC transmits to its clearing members a report reflecting those issues expiring in-the-money and the firm's balance at the OCC. Operations personnel compare those balances to their firm's "pending file" balances and make the required adjustments. They take into consideration the following:

Unresolved "breaks" from the previous day

Inter-broker transfers

Exercises not deleted previously

Trade adjustments.

When everything is balanced, the clearing members then tender their exercise instructions to the OCC. Upon receipt of the instructions, the OCC runs the normal assignment program.

On Sunday, the assignments are received by the member firms. The assignment reflecting the respective series and quantity of the underlying security is then allocated to the appropriate customer and firm account.

The assignment clerk in Options Operations verifies the quantities assigned for each series and inputs the information into the firm's computers. Depending upon the firm policy of assigning options, (random or "first-in/first-out") customers are assigned appropriately. Once the customer is selected, the account's short position is deleted, and a stock trade is generated (sell for a call, buy for a put). Again, this function is usually performed by computer.

Notification of the assignment is then transmitted to the sales office, so that the Account Executive may notify the customer of the assignment on the following business day. All firms try to have the information at their branch office long before the securities markets open, so that customers can take market action to offset assignments if they so choose.

SETTLEMENT OF FUNDS WITH THE OCC

A clearing member firm is responsible for several daily money commitments with the OCC, and it is generally the function of a Clearance Section to ensure that each one is met. In the following section, we will review the process for premium and margin commitments, the Escrow Receipt Depository commitments, and the index exercise and assignment commitments.

Each evening, the OCC determines a member firm's net premium requirements based on the actual purchases and sales from that day's compared option transactions. In general, either the firm will owe funds to the OCC, or it will receive funds. This net requirement is included on the OCC's Daily Margin Summary Report received by the clearing member each morning.

PREMIUM COMMITMENTS

A clearing member must pay any net premium due to the OCC by 10:00 A.M. A member firm must meet this commitment through funds held in an account at a bank. The OCC is empowered to draft the member firm's account at the bank for the amount due. If a member firm is to receive funds, the OCC will make a deposit to the account. The monitoring of the receipt and payment of funds is performed in the Clearance Section. The movement is recorded by issuing journal entries between ledger accounts and specific offset accounts.

For example, a firm may use one bank to interface with the OCC, and another bank to reimburse the first bank for the payments. Two banks may be used, since the member firm may not wish to have idle funds on deposit for an account dealing strictly with the OCC. Any net premium due a clearing member will be paid by 11:00 a.m., unless the member is in a margin deficit situation, in which case the premium will not be paid but held by OCC.

MARGIN COMMITMENTS

A clearing member is obligated to meet margin requirements established by the OCC for each account in which it represents the writer of an option. The clearing member may deposit the underlying stock of the writer, or deposit and maintain the specified amount of margin in cash, or its equivalent, with the OCC. The specific deposit of the underlying security may be made with a bank, trust company, depository, or other custodian which is satisfactory to the OCC under approved agreements. The depository/escrow receipt for the underlying stock is issued to and held by the OCC. Cash, U.S. Government Securities and/or OCC approved bank letters of credit are also acceptable forms of margin. The specific deposit method or "valued securities" deposit will be "marked to the market" on a daily basis at the maximum loan rate.

No stock is valued at a rate higher than 60% of its current market value, nor can the value of any one security exceed 10% of the clearing member's total margin requirement for that account. This latter system is lower in cost and easier to process, and consequently is a popular means of meeting the requirements.

Each evening, as in the case with the net premium requirements, the OCC determines a firm's net margin requirement. Again, this requirement is reported to the member firm on the Daily Margin Report. The member firm may satisfy the requirement by:

Pledging government securities

Pledging letters of credit

Pledging valued securities

Putting up cash

A firm could use valued securities to meet its margin requirements in its customer and firm accounts, provided they are not fully paid for customer securities. A firm may also elect to meet its margin requirements with letters of credit and/or U.S. Government securities (i.e., Treasury bills, bonds, or notes).

The Daily Margin Report reflects the amount of margin on deposit in the account, the amount of margin required, and the amount of margin deficit or excess. Any deficit must be satisfied by 10:00 a.m., while excess margin deposits may be withdrawn between 9:00 a.m. and 2:00 p.m. Excess cash must be requested by 11:30 a.m.

Most firms find that the most cost-effective and easiest method to manage in meeting margin requirements is the pledging of valued securities. Firms will keep a sufficient amount of securities on deposit at a depository as a pledge to the OCC. The bookkeeping is easier to monitor and control, as firms are very familiar with depository processing procedures and accounting methods.

ESCROW RECEIPT DEPOSITORY COMMITMENTS

OCC's Escrow Receipt Depository system (ERD) is an on-line, menu-driven system that allows an approved custodian bank to input depository transactions directly into OCC's Asset Custody system. Real-time editing and data verification are performed against OCC's database immediately upon data entry to the on-line ERD system. If an error is found, the system will display a message on the screen. Errors must be corrected immediately to render the transaction valid and accepted.

The Escrow Receipt Depository system is a book-entry system in which approved custodian banks advise the OCC directly of escrow deposits via C/MACS. A clearing member is responsible for inputting withdrawal entries, except for those receipts covering expired options. These are automatically released from the system by the OCC once it can be determined that the securities pledged are not needed for delivery. By using a similar multipart rollover form, custodian banks can reallocate pledged securities from one series to another. Thus, if a customer has excess securities pledged in one particular option series, but a deficit in another, the excess can be transferred to cover the deficit.

The OCC issues a pending report of all escrow activity which enables both the bank and clearing member to review, reject, or "pend" any item. Rejected or pended items are not processed into the system, and therefore monies are not paid or collected for them.

By means of a signed agreement, each bank specifies its obligations to both the OCC and the clearing member with respect to each escrow position input into the system. The OCC has the necessary authority to effect the settlements for deposits and withdrawals to the bank's escrow settlement account. Once pending ERD items are accepted, all accompanying monies become part of a firm's commitment to the OCC. They are highlighted on the Daily Margin Report from the OCC and incorporated with the daily premium pay or collect figures. Settlement is effected as discussed under "Premium Commitments." However, firms will use an offset account, whereby a journal entry passes the dollar amount on to the identified firm customer.

INDEX EXERCISE AND ASSIGNMENT COMMITMENT

With the exercise or assignment of an index option, a member firm must either receive from, or pay to the OCC, the resultant dollar amount. This amount is reported to the member firm on an "Exercise Assignment Activity Report" from the OCC.

The mechanics of paying or receiving funds are the same as those described under "Premium Commitments." An offset account may also be utilized by a member firm. The balance in the account is reduced by subsequent entries which pass the dollar amount on to the specific customer of the firm.

Figure 9-13 is a basic representation of the settlement of funds a member firm may utilize with the OCC.

SETTLEMENT OF SECURITIES AND MONEY AFTER EXERCISE AND ASSIGNMENT

As a result of option exercises or assignments, delivery and receipt of the underlying securities or money must be effected. We've discussed the mechanics of receipt and delivery of securities in Chapter 3 on Cashiering, so now we'll just briefly go over how the exercises/assignments get into the normal flow of securities processing.

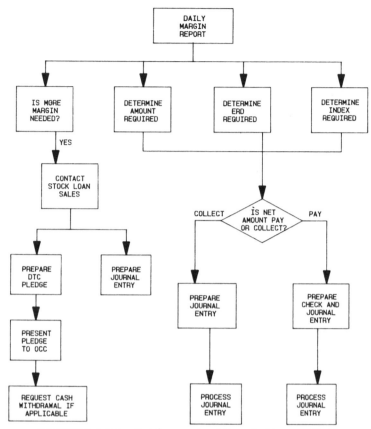

FIGURE 9-13. Settlement of Funds Versus OCC

EQUITY OPTIONS

If the exercise or assignment is for an equity option, the receipt or delivery of the underlying security is usually processed between the OCC and the member firm through a recognized participant stock clearing corporation (e.g., NSCC, Midwest Clearing Corporation, or SCCP). Each clearing member is required to designate one of these approved clearing corporations for the settlement of stock transactions resulting from exercise or assignment. The OCC provides the information to the stock clearing corporation which then updates its records on the holdings of the securities firm. The securities firm updates its records so that customer accounts and the clearing corporation account remain in balance.

INDEX OPTIONS

Index option exercise and assignments are also made directly between the OCC and the member firm. The settlement of funds is described in the previous section on "Premium Commitments" and highlighted under "Index Exercise and Assignment Commitment."

WHAT IS THE IMPACT OF CASH DIVIDENDS, STOCK SPLITS, AND STOCK DIVIDENDS?

Since one equity option contract controls 100 shares of stock at a strike price, an ABC Co. March 60 call controls 100 shares of the underlying security at $60 per share. If this call were to be exercised, the total contract would cost the buyer $6,000 plus commission.

Companies often pay cash dividends or declare stock dividends and stock splits. In most cases, the total value of the contract does not change. The one exception is with OTC options when a cash dividend is declared.

CASH DIVIDENDS

Cash dividends on listed options do not require an adjustment to the contract price, as cash dividends go to the owner of the stock. Thus, if the holder of a call exercises it before the ex-dividend date (four business days prior to the record date), he or she will receive the dividend.

Over-the-counter (OTC) options for both puts and calls are adjusted downward by the exact amount of the cash dividend. Thus an OTC option with a strike price of $60 would become $59.70 on the day the security went ex-dividend with a cash dividend of 30 cents per share.

Other distributions, stock dividends, and stock splits do cause a change in the terms of a listed option contract. A key point to remember is that the dollar value of the original commitment remains the same. In our example of XYZ Co., the contract price was $6,000 (100 shares x $60). Let's now look at a stock split and a stock dividend, and the necessary adjustments to the contract by using our original example.

STOCK SPLIT

If the company decided to split its shares, say 3 for 2, the new adjusted contract would be for 150 shares at $40 per share. It is calculated as follows:

For every 100 shares (options contract), a 3-for-2 split would result in an additional 50 shares (3/2 × 100 = 150 shares).

The contract price of $60 would result in an adjustment to $40 per share (2/3 × 60 = $40).

The dollar value of the contract would remain the same, since 150 shares × $40 = $6,000.

A 2-for-1 split would result in two 100-share contracts at $30 per share, but again the total value would remain the same as that of the original contract.

STOCK DIVIDENDS

The effect of a stock dividend, for example 10%, would result in a contract of 110 shares at $54.50 per share. It is calculated as follows:

A 10% stock dividend would entitle the owner to receive one additional share for every 10 shares held; thus, a 100-share contract would become 110 shares (11/10 × 100 = 110 shares).

The contract price of $60 would result in an adjustment to $54.50 per share (10/11 × $60 = $54.55); however, strike prices are rounded off to the nearest eighth, so the new strike price would be $54.50.

The dollar value of the contract would approximate the same as the original (110 shares × $54.50 = approximately $6,000).

The adjustments for both stock splits and stock dividends become effective on the ex-date. At that time, the internal records (stock records) of a securities firm would be updated to reflect the new positions and price. The strike prices would be adjusted by the various exchanges and the OCC would accordingly modify its records.

For Options Operations Departments, it's important to remember that options have a one-day settlement. Any imbalances between a member firm and the OCC must be resolved promptly for those option series where the underlying security is going ex-dividend the following day. The reason for this is that if a firm were to be assigned a series where the underlying security went"ex," and the firm did not have enough contracts short in its customer account, the firm would lose any dividends associated with the assignment. The firm, of course, would have to pay the customer and incur the loss. Firms also trade options for their own account and errors could result in dramatic losses. As such, the balancing clerks in the department have to keep abreast of which series of options are going ex-dividend and when this will happen.

APPENDIX: GLOSSARY OF OPTIONS TERMS

Equity Call Option. A security that gives the holder the right to *purchase* a fixed number of shares of the underlying security at a fixed price within a specified time period.

Equity Put Option. A security that gives the holder the right to *sell* a fixed number of shares of the underlying security at a fixed price within a specified time period.

Holder. The person who has purchased the option (call or put) through an opening transaction. Holder is said to be *long* the option.

Writer. The person who has sold an option through an opening transaction. Writer is said to be *short* the option.

Opening Transaction. A transaction in which either the seller (writer) of an option or the buyer (holder) *establishes an original position* or increases a previously established position.

Closing Transaction. A transaction in which the holder or the writer reduces a previously opened position.

Exercise Price. The price at which the underlying security may be purchased (call) or may be sold (put). It is also known as the strike, or striking price.

Premium. The amount paid by the buyer of the option to the seller. It is arrived at by an auction between the agents of the buyer and the agents of the seller on the floor of the option exchanges.

Expiration. The expiration date of an equity or index option is the *Saturday following the third Friday* of the expiration month. Foreign currency options expire on the *Friday immediately preceding the third Wednesday* of the expiration month.

Type of Option. Any option on the same underlying security. Puts and calls are types of options.

Class of Option. The same type of option on the same underlying security. All of the puts on a security constitute one class, while all of the calls on the same security make up another class.

Series of Option. Options of the same class that have the same exercise price, expiration month, and cover the same number of shares of the underlying security.

CHAPTER 10

The Margin Department

Any manager in the Operations area of a securities firm usually has some exposure to the Margin Department of the firm. That's because the Margin Department is responsible for the flow of securities and monies to and from a customer's account. The Margin Department interprets regulatory agencies' and firm regulations to ensure compliance, and provides customer bookkeeping and service facilities particularly related to the extension of credit. In this chapter we'll look at the basic definition of a margin transaction, rules and regulations governing margin transactions, how and why customers use margin, what the Margin Department does day-to-day, major problems and how to resolve them. We'll also provide a special Appendix on complex margin terms and transactions that are essential to understanding the work of the Margin Department.

WHAT IS MARGIN ALL ABOUT?

A margin transaction is a security transaction (purchase or short sale) in which a firm lends a customer a portion of the principal amount necessary to pay for the transaction.

The portion of the principal which may be loaned is specified by Regulation T of the Federal Reserve Board (which we'll discuss later). The firm charges the customer interest on his/her loan—usually at a predetermined percentage over the broker loan rate.

"Margin" is the amount of cash or securities which the customer must maintain with the securities firm in order to obtain a loan. When first entering into a margin transaction, the customer will be required to meet an initial margin call, also called a "Reg T" call or simply a "T" call, by putting up margin.

The securities firm must monitor the market value of any securities which the customer has on margin. If the market value drops below levels specified by the regulatory agencies, the securities firm is required to call for more margin (cash or securities). If this "Margin Call" is not met, then the securities firm is required by regulation to liquidate the customer's position. Obviously, good business practice would also dictate that margin credit extended to the customer be closely monitored in order that the firm be protected from loss. Most firms have higher margin requirements than the minimums required by regulatory agencies.

WHY ARE MARGIN TRANSACTIONS ATTRACTIVE TO SECURITIES FIRMS?

Margin accounts are attractive to securities firms because of the revenue stream that they generate to the firms. We noted earlier that the customer pays interest on a margin loan. This is usually based upon the broker call money rate plus a sliding scale of percentages based upon the individual customer's debit balance. As an example, one major firm currently charges the broker call money rate plus from 3/4% to 2-1/4% depending upon the customer's average daily debit balance. The 3/4% is levied upon those customers with an average balance of over $50,000.00. Additionally, it is the experience of securities firms that customers who trade on margin tend to trade much more frequently than do other customers. Consequently, these customers tend to generate much higher commission revenues.

WHY DO CUSTOMERS LIKE MARGIN?

The attraction of a margin account to a sophisticated investor is that it allows him/her to leverage the use of their funds. If, as currently allowed by Regulation T, the customer may borrow up to 50% of the principal amount of a listed equity transaction, then obviously the customer may purchase twice the amount of a particular security for any given amount. Therefore, if an investor sees an attractive situation and is correct in the assessment, they may earn a much larger return by purchasing on margin than by purchasing on a "cash" basis. We will provide illustrations of this later in the chapter.

WHAT ARE THE RISKS?

There are risks to the use of margin, of course. Those risks include the interest cost for the use of the firm's funds and, more dramatically, the risk to the investor should the assessment of a situation be incorrect. In the event that a long position should lose value instead of increasing in value, the investor may face the prospect of being called for additional margin. If the position loses sufficient value, the customer or the securities firm may be forced to liquidate, and only a small percentage of the customer's initial margin may be returned.

In a worst case scenario, if a long position's market value drops precipitously, it is possible for the investor to lose all of the original margin and to wind up owing additional funds to the securities firm. Obviously the Margin Department must be able to monitor customer accounts effectively so as to protect the firm and the customer.

SEC AND FEDERAL RESERVE RULES

The stock market crash of 1929 led to a thorough governmental review of the activities of the securities markets including the extension of credit by securities firms, which for the most part, had not been strongly regulated. This review led to the introduction of two major securities laws: The Securities Act of 1933 and, of most concern to us in this chapter, the Securities Exchange Act of 1934 ("1934 Act").

Among its various provisions, the 1934 Act provided for the licensing of all securities exchanges, the regulation of trading practices, and the promulgation of requirements designed to prevent the manipulation of securities prices and excessive trading by exchange members. The 1934 Act also created the Securities and Exchange Commission as the administrative and enforcement agency for the Act, and directed the Federal Reserve Board, as the U.S. Government's credit policy agency, to set various policies with respect to the extension of credit for the purposes of purchasing securities.

The Board of Governors of the Federal Reserve, exercising the authority granted to them under the 1934 Act, issued four major regulations governing the extension of credit for security transactions, as follows:

1. Regulation X—Rule Governing Borrowers Who Obtain Securities Credit.

2. Regulation G—Rule Governing Securities Credit by Persons Other Than Banks, Brokers or Dealers.

3. Regulation T—Rule Governing Credit by Brokers and Dealers.

4. Regulation U—Rule Governing Credit by Banks for the Purpose of Purchasing or Carrying Margin Stocks

Of the regulations above, the one which concerns us most directly is Regulation T (Reg T). Among its provisions the regulation:

Defines which securities may be margined.

Sets the time frames within which initial margin calls (Reg T calls) must be met.

Allocates to the various securities exchanges the authority to grant extensions of time for payment of Reg T calls.

Establishes and defines the various types of accounts, including the Margin Account, Cash Account, Special Memorandum Account, and others.

Defines such technical terms as loan value, current market value, and others.

Specifies (in Paragraph 220.18, the Supplement to Regulation T) the maximum loan value which may be extended by brokers, and gives the Board of Governors the authority to change that value.

The Fed's adjustments of initial margin requirements have acted to moderate or increase the volume of margin trading. As seen in Figure 10-1, the requirements have ranged from a low of 40% (1937) to a high of 100% (1946). In effect, no margin trading was allowed during the latter period.

By raising the margin requirement, the Fed hopes to reduce the volume of margin trading. Reducing the margin requirement can have the opposite effect, inducing investors to reenter the market. During the 1968 bull market, the Fed raised the margin requirement to 80%, and as a result, margin debt fell from $6.3 billion at year end of 1967, to $4.9 billion at year end 1969. The margin debt ballooned again when the requirement was dropped to 55% in 1971.

The initial margin requirement was set at 50% in January, 1974 and remains at that level at this writing.

Date	Purchases	Short Sales
Oct 15, 1934	45%	Not permitted
Feb 1, 1936	55%	Not permitted
Nov 1, 1937	40%	50%
Feb 5, 1945	50%	50%
Jul 5, 1945	75%	75%
Jan 21, 1947	100%	100%
Feb 1, 1947	75%	75%
Mar 30, 1949	50%	50%
Jan 17, 1951	75%	75%
Feb 20, 1953	50%	50%
Jan 4, 1955	60%	60%
Apr 23, 1955	70%	70%
Jan 16, 1958	50%	50%
Aug 5, 1958	70%	70%
Oct 16, 1958	90%	90%
Jul 28, 1960	70%	70%
Jul 10, 1962	50%	50%
Nov 5, 1963	70%	70%
Jun 8, 1968	80%	80%
May 6, 1970	65%	65%
Dec 6, 1971	55%	55%
Nov 24, 1972	65%	65%
Jan 3, 1974	50%	50%
1974–19	50%	50%

FIGURE 10-1. Reg T Margin Requirements

OTHER REGULATIONS

In setting up the Securities Exchange Commission with the 1934 Act (see Figure 10-2), Congress created an administrative and enforcement agency. Later actions (notably the Securities Act

Amendment of 1964 and the Securities Reform Act of 1975), helped
to strengthen that role considerably. In practice, much of the regulatory work of the commission is delegated to self-regulatory bodies: Exchanges and Securities Dealers Associations. Consequently
the rules of the exchange (or exchanges) to which a particular securities firm belongs also play a major part in the regulatory framework, which determines how the Margin Department operates and
what functions it can or must perform.

Let's look at some of the rules of the New York Stock
Exchange and the National Association of Securities Dealers, two
organizations of which many securities firms are members. Many of
these rules have been created to protect both the securities firm and
the customer from experiencing large losses due to market volatility. These are some of the items with respect to margin that the New
York Stock Exchange addresses in its rules:

Sets initial minimum equity requirements for the purposes of
establishing a new margin account.

Sets maintenance margin requirements for equities and other
marginable securities (whereas Reg T focuses on Initial maintenance requirements). Note: Member firms may, and often do,
set higher maintenance requirements for their customers.

Sets margin requirements for options.

Sets the maximum time frame within which maintenance calls
must be met.

Prohibits "Free-Riding" (the practice of purchasing and then
selling a security position without putting up any money) in
cash accounts.

Sets the time frame within which extensions must be requested from NYSE for securities sold in a cash account.

It should be noted here that a number of these items are addressed in Reg T, but the NYSE and other agencies rules expand upon various points.

A very important rule of the NASD is that which requires the signing by margin customers of a Hypothecation Agreement. This Hypothecation Agreement will generally be one clause of an agreement which the customer will be required to sign before entering into any margin transactions with a securities firm.

The customer agreement normally binds the customer to meet maintenance calls promptly; gives permission for the securities firm to maintain the client's securities in "street" name; and to hypothecate or pledge the securities as collateral for a loan. It also gives the firm the authority to liquidate any customer position at any time necessary to avoid unsecured debits, and binds the customer to payment of margin interest charges. The customer agreement will generally also contain a separate clause allowing the securities firm to loan out the customer's margined securities to other firms or customers, to facilitate short sales. Figure 10-3 is an example of a customer agreement utilized by a major firm.

The thrust or intent of many of the rules of the various regulatory agencies is to avoid a situation in which securities firms or their customers become overextended. The Margin Department in any firm plays a key role in establishing sufficient monitoring mechanisms to ensure that all of the various rules and regulations are applied and adhered to. If that role is properly performed, credit will only be extended as appropriate in a given situation, the customer and the firm will be able to avoid unnecessary loss, and the firm will be able to maintain compliance with regulatory guidelines.

NYSE Rule 431 governs minimum margin maintenance requirements for all instruments traded in a margin account. Figure 10-4 lists the requirements in effect as of September, 1987.

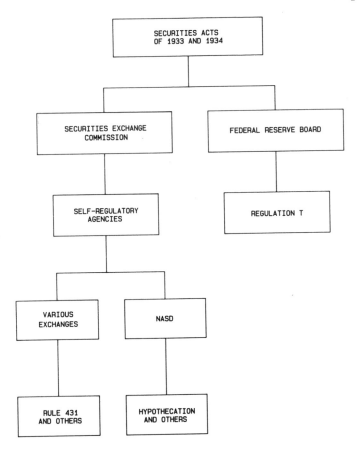

FIGURE 10-2. The Regulatory Framework

In consideration of your accepting and carrying one or more accounts for the undersigned, the undersigned hereby consents and agrees that:

APPLICABLE RULES AND REGULATIONS

1. All transactions shall be subject to the constitution, rules, regulations, customs and usages of the exchange or market and its clearing house, if any, on which such transactions are executed by you (   ) or your agents, including your subsidiaries and affiliates.

DEFINITION

2. For purposes of this agreement, "securities and other property" shall include, but not be limited to, money, securities, financial instruments and commodities of every kind and nature, and all contracts and options relating thereto, whether for present or future delivery.

MARGIN REQUIREMENTS AND CREDIT CHARGES

3. The undersigned will maintain such securities and other property in the accounts of the undersigned for margin purposes as you shall require from time to time; and the monthly debit balance of such accounts shall be charged, in accordance with your usual custom, with interest at a rate permitted by the laws of the State of New York. It is understood that the interest charge made to the undersigned's account at the close of a charge period will, unless paid, be added to the opening balance for the next charge period and that interest will be charged upon such opening balance, including all interest so added.

SECURITY INTEREST

4. All securities and other property now or hereafter held, carried or maintained by you or by any of your affiliates in your possession and control, or in the possession and control of any such affiliate, for any purpose, in or for any account of the undersigned now or hereafter opened, including any account in which the undersigned may have an interest, shall be subject to a lien for the discharge of all the indebtedness and other obligations of the undersigned to you, and are to be held by you as security for the payment of any liability or indebtedness of the undersigned to you in any of said accounts. You shall have the right to transfer securities and other property so held by you from or to any other of the accounts of the undersigned whenever in your judgement you consider such a transfer necessary for your protection. In enforcing your lien, you shall have the discretion to determine which securities and property are to be sold and which contracts are to be closed.

REPRESENTATIONS AS TO BENEFICIAL OWNERSHIP AND CONTROL

5. The undersigned represents that, with respect to securities against which margin credit is or may be extended by you: (a) the undersigned is not the beneficial owner of more than three percent (3%) of the number of outstanding shares of any class of equity securities, and (b) does not control, is not controlled by and is not under common control with, the issuer of any such securities. In the event that any of the foregoing representations is inaccurate or becomes inaccurate, the undersigned will promptly so advise you in writing.

FIGURE 10-3. Customer Agreement

Reprinted by permission of Merrill Lynch, Pierce, Fenner & Smith Incorporated.

CALLS FOR ADDITIONAL COLLATERAL - LIQUIDATION RIGHTS

6. (a) You shall have the right to require additional collateral:

    (1) in accordance with your general policies regarding your margin maintenance requirements, as such may be modified, amended or supplemented from time to time; or

    (2) if in your discretion you consider it necessary for your protection at an earlier or later point in time than called for by said general policies; or

    (3) in the event that a petition in bankruptcy or for appointment of a receiver is filed by or against the undersigned; or

    (4) if an attachment is levied against the accounts of the undersigned; or

    (5) in the event of the death of the undersigned.

    (b) If the undersigned does not provide you with additional collateral as you may require in accordance with (a) (1) or (2), or should an event described in (a) (3), (4) or (5) occur, (whether or not you elect to require additional collateral), you shall have the right:

    (1) to sell any or all securities and other property in the accounts of the undersigned with you or with any of your affiliates, whether carried individually or jointly with others;

    (2) to buy any or all securities and other property which may be short in such accounts; and

    (3) to cancel any open orders and to close any or all outstanding contracts.

You may exercise any or all of your rights under (b) (1), (2) and (3) without further demand for additional collateral, or notice of sale or purchase, or other notice or advertisement. Any such sales or purchases may be made at your discretion on any exchange or other market where such business is usually transacted, or at public auction or private sale; and you may be the purchaser for your own account. It is understood that your giving of any prior demand or call or prior notice of the time and place of such sale or purchase shall not be considered a waiver of your right to sell or buy without any such demand, call or notice as herein provided.

PAYMENT OF INDEBTEDNESS UPON DEMAND

7. The undersigned shall at all times be liable for the payment upon demand of any debit balance or other obligations owing in any of the accounts of the undersigned with you, and the undersigned shall be liable to you for any deficiency remaining in any such accounts in the event of the liquidation thereof, in whole or in part, by you or by the undersigned; and the undersigned shall make payment of such obligations and indebtedness upon demand.

LIABILITY FOR COSTS OF COLLECTION

8. To the extent permitted by the laws of the State of New York, the reasonable costs and expenses of collection of the debit balance and any unpaid deficiency in the accounts of the undersigned with you, including but not limited to attorneys' fees incurred and payable or paid by you, shall be payable to you by the undersigned.

PLEDGE OF SECURITIES AND OTHER PROPERTY

9. All securities and other property now or hereafter held, carried or maintained by you in your possession or control in any of the accounts of the undersigned may be pledged and repledged by you from time to time, without notice to the undersigned, either separately or in common with other such securities and other property, for any amount due in the accounts of the undersigned, or for any greater amount, and you may do so without retaining in your possession or under your control for delivery a like amount of similar securities or other property.

FIGURE 10-3. (*Continued*)

LENDING AGREEMENT

10. Within the limitations imposed by applicable laws, rules and regulations, you are hereby authorized to lend to yourselves, as principal or otherwise, or to others, any securities held by you on margin for any accounts of the undersigned or as collateral therefor, either separately or with other securities. It is recognized that any losses or other detriments, or gains or other benefits, arising from any such lending of securities shall not accrue to the account of the undersigned.

PRESUMPTION OF RECEIPT OF COMMUNICATIONS

11. Communications may be sent to the undersigned at the address of the undersigned or at such other address as the undersigned may hereafter give you in writing. All communications so sent, whether by mail, telegraph, messenger or otherwise, shall be deemed given to the undersigned personally, whether actually received or not.

ACCOUNTS CARRIED AS CLEARING BROKER

12. If you are carrying the account of the undersigned as clearing broker by arrangement with another broker through whose courtesy the account of the undersigned has been introduced to you, then until receipt from the undersigned of written notice to the contrary, you may accept from such other broker, without inquiry or investigation by you (a) orders for the purchase or sale in said account of securities and other property on margin or otherwise, and (b) any other instructions concerning said account. You shall not be responsible or liable for any acts or omissions of such other broker or its employees.

AGREEMENT TO ARBITRATE CONTROVERSIES

13. Except to the extent that controversies involving claims arising under the Federal securities laws may be litigated, it is agreed that any controversy between us arising out of your business or this agreement shall be submitted to arbitration conducted under the provisions of the Constitution and Rules of the Board of Directors of the New York Stock Exchange, Inc. or pursuant to the Code of Arbitration Procedure of the National Association of Securities Dealers, Inc., as the undersigned may elect. If the controversy involves any security or commodity transaction or contract related thereto executed on an exchange located outside the United States, then such controversy shall, at the election of the undersigned, be submitted to arbitration conducted under the constitution of such exchange or under the provisions of the Constitution and Rules of the Board of Directors of the New York Stock Exchange, Inc. or the Code of Arbitration Procedure of the National Association of Securities Dealers, Inc. Arbitration must be commenced by service upon the other of a written demand for arbitration or a written notice of intention to arbitrate, therein electing the arbitration tribunal. In the event the undersigned does not make such designation within five (5) days of such demand or notice, then the undersigned authorizes you to do so on behalf of the undersigned.

JOINT AND SEVERAL LIABILITY

14. If the undersigned shall consist of more than one person, their obligations under this agreement shall be joint and several.

REPRESENTATION AS TO CAPACITY TO ENTER INTO AGREEMENT

15. The undersigned represents that no one except the undersigned has an interest in the account or accounts of the undersigned with you. If a natural person, the undersigned represents that the undersigned is of full age, is not an employee of any exchange, nor of any corporation of which any exchange owns a majority of the capital stock, nor of a member of any exchange, nor of a member firm or member corporation registered on any exchange, nor of a bank, trust company, insurance company or any corporation, firm or individual engaged in the business of dealing either as broker or as principal in securities, bills of exchange, acceptances or other forms of commercial paper. If any of the foregoing representations is inaccurate or becomes inaccurate, the undersigned will promptly so advise you in writing.

FIGURE 10-3. (*Continued*)

EXTRAORDINARY EVENTS

16. You shall not be liable for loss caused directly or indirectly by government restrictions, exchange or market rulings, suspension of trading, war, strikes or other conditions beyond your control.

THE LAWS OF THE STATE OF NEW YORK GOVERN

17. This agreement and its enforcement shall be governed by the laws of the State of New York; shall cover individually and collectively all accounts which the undersigned may open or reopen with you; shall inure to the benefit of your affiliates and your successors, whether by merger, consolidation or otherwise, and assigns, and their respective emloyees and agents; you may transfer the accounts of the undersigned to your successors and assigns; and this agreement shall be binding upon the heirs, executors, administrators, successors and assigns of the undersigned.

AMENDMENTS

18. The undersigned agrees that you shall have the right to amend this Agreement, by modifying or rescinding any of its existing provisions or by adding any new provision. Any such amendment shall be effective as of a date to be established by you, which shall not be earlier than thirty days after you send notification of any such amendment to the undersigned.

SEPARABILITY

19. If any provision or condition of this agreement shall be held to be invalid or unenforceable by any court, or regulatory or self-regulatory agency or body, such invalidity or unenforceability shall attach only to such provision or condition. The validity of the remaining provisions and conditions shall not be affected thereby and this agreement shall be carried out as if any such invalid or unenforceable provision or condition were not contained herein.

HEADINGS ARE DESCRIPTIVE

20. The heading of each provision hereof is for descriptive purposes only and shall not be deemed to modify or qualify any of the rights or obligations set forth in each such provision.

DATED _____   ACCOUNT NO. _____

BY SIGNING THIS AGREEMENT, I ACKNOWLEDGE THAT, PURSUANT TO PARAGRAPH 10 HEREOF, CERTAIN OF MY SECURITIES MAY BE LOANED TO YOU OR LOANED OUT TO OTHERS.

SIGNATURES

CORPORATION   INDIVIDUALS

_____
(NAME OF CORPORATION)

BY _____

TITLE _____
                                                        _____
                                                        (SECOND PARTY, IF JOINT ACCOUNT)

ATTEST _____
CORPORATE SEAL   PARTNERSHIP OR TRUST

                                                        _____
                                                        (NAME OF PARTNERSHIP OR TRUST)

                                                        BY _____
                                                        (A PARTNER OR TRUSTEE)

FIGURE 10-3. (*Continued*)

Instrument	Maintenance Requirement
Equity securities (long)	25% of the current market value
Equity securities (short)	$5.00 per share or 30% of the current market value, whichever amount is greater
Equity securities (short) (selling below $5.00)	$2.50 per share or 100% of the current market value, whichever amount is greater
Equity securities (long and short same security)	5% of the current market value of the long securities
Convertible instruments versus short equity securities	10% of the current market value of the long position
Non-convertible bonds	20% of the current market value or 7% of the principal amount, whichever amount is greater
Non-convertible bonds (short)	5% of the principal amount or 30% of the current market value, whichever amount is greater

	Years To Maturity	*% of Market Value*
U.S. government obligations (U.S. Treasury bonds, bills, and notes)	Less than 1 yr.	1%
	1 yr., but less than 3 yrs.	2%
	3 yrs., but less than 5 yrs.	3%
	5 yrs., but less than 10 yrs.	4%
	10 yrs., but less than 20 yrs.	5%
	20 yrs. or more	6%

Instrument	Maintenance Requirement
Zero Coupons	Same as U.S. government obligations, but subject to 3% of principal as minimum requirement.
All other exempted instruments	15% of the current market value or 7% of the principal amount, whichever is greater.

FIGURE 10-4. NYSE Rule 431

HOW IS MARGIN USEFUL TO CUSTOMERS?

As we mentioned previously, both cash and margin accounts are established according to the rules of Regulation T of the Federal Reserve Board. With a cash account, a securities firm is not permitted to maintain a long term creditor/debtor relationship with a client. Thus in a client's account, all security transactions must be paid for in full, or the securities firm must liquidate the transaction. In addition, short sales are not permitted in a cash account.

In the margin account, Regulation T permits the securities firm to maintain a creditor/debtor relationship with its customer. The firm is permitted to lend the client funds for the purchase of marginable securities (not all securities are marginable), and is permitted to lend the client securities to cover short sales. The securities purchased on margin are held by the firm in "street name" as collateral against the loan of funds. With short sales, additional funds are collected from the client and held against his/her return of the loaned security.

The client will use a margin account to:

Leverage the equity in his/her account; that is, increase the "buying power."

Sell short to earn a profit from a declining market or a declining price in one particular security.

Borrow funds on securities positions at favorable interest rates.

We will look first at an example of the use of leverage. Let's assume that two clients, Bill and Mary, each have $5,000 and want to enter into transactions to buy XYZ Corporation. XYZ is currently trading at $10 per share. Bill has a cash account, Mary has a margin account (note that for simplicity in this and all other examples we will not include commission costs or interest costs in our examples, and also that we will use the current 50% initial margin requirement and, where applicable, the 25% NYSE maintenance requirement):

LEVERAGE:	Bill	Mary
	Cash A/C	Margin A/C
Balance	$5,000	$5,000
	Buy 500 XYZ @ 10	Buy 1,000 XYZ @ 10
	$5,000	$10,000

By using her margin account, Mary has purchased 1,000 shares of XYZ with the same principal amount that Bill has used to buy one half of the number of shares in his cash account. Should XYZ increase in value by $1, Mary would realize a gain of $1,000, (that is, the number of shares owned times the price rise). Bill, on the other hand, would only see a gain of $500. Mary probably feels quite smug at this point.

Leverage, of course, works both ways. Should XYZ move in the other direction by $1, Bill would experience a loss of $500, (500 shares owned times the $1.00 change). Bill would not be quite as uncomfortable as Mary however, as she has purchased twice the number of shares and thus has twice the loss, or $1,000. (It should be noted by the reader that all of the profit and all of the loss in a margin account accrues to the customer. The securities firm is not participating in the transaction with the customer, it is merely financing the transaction for the customer.)

The leverage of a margin account is what makes such an account attractive. It is also the leverage, however, that poses risks to the client and the securities firm.

MARGIN TERMS AND DEFINITIONS

Now let's review some basic margin terminology and definitions:

LONG MARKET VALUE (LMV). The value of the marginable securities held in the margin account based on the previous day's closing price (i.e., number of shares times price).

SHORT MARKET VALUE (SMV). The value of those securities held short in the margin account (and being loaned to the client by the securities firm) based on the previous day's closing price.

DEBIT BALANCE (DR). The dollar amount the customer owes to the securities firm. In a margin account this would generally be related to the funds being loaned to the client by the firm.

CREDIT BALANCE (CR). The funds being held by a securities firm in an account on the customer's behalf. These may be clear funds arising when the client has no further loan from the firm. A credit balance may also arise from a short sale, which then may be required to be maintained in the account to offset the short position.

EQUITY. The net worth of the margin account. The difference between assets and liabilities in the account. Expressed in a formula as: $EQ = LMV - SMV + CR - DR$. Equity is the amount that would accrue to the customer if the entire account were liquidated at current market value.

LOAN VALUE (LV). Established by Regulation T and subject to change by the Federal Reserve Board from time to time. The maximum amount a securities firm may lend to a customer against the market value of marginable securities.

THE INITIAL MARGIN REQUIREMENT. The reciprocal of loan value. The initial margin requirement is the amount that the client must deposit when entering into a new margin transaction, so as to ensure that the securities firm is not loaning more than the Regulation T loan value. If Regulation T were to establish a 30% loan value for purchases in a margin account, the client's required margin would be 70%, a 40% loan value would mandate a 60% T call, and so on.

REGULATION T MARGIN CALL. Also known as a Reg T call or simply a T call. The call issued to a client for initial margin to satisfy a new commitment. The Reg T call is due no later than seven business days following the commitment as prescribed by Reg T. If the call is not met in that time frame, and an extension of time has not been requested from a regulatory agency, the securities firm is required to liquidate the security.

MINIMUM EQUITY REQUIREMENT. The NYSE requires that a customer post a minimum equity of $2,000 to open a margin account. For example, if a client has a cash account with no security position or balance, and he/she wants to purchase $2,000 worth of securities on margin, the T call would only be $1,000. However, the client would be required to post the entire $2,000 in order to meet the equity requirement. Once met, the requirement need not be maintained. However, the client must not withdraw cash or securities from the account if such withdrawal would reduce the equity below $2,000.

MAINTENANCE REQUIREMENT. The amount of equity required to be maintained in the account. This differs from the Regulation T requirement in that it is an ongoing requirement, whereas the Reg T requirement is an initial requirement. The NYSE currently sets the maintenance requirement level at 25% for equity securities. Securities firms may, and often do, set higher maintenance levels for their own protection.

MAINTENANCE EXCESS. The amount by which the equity in the account exceeds the maintenance requirement.

MAINTENANCE CALL. A call by the securities firm for additional maintenance margin. The call is determined by the amount that the maintenance requirement for the security positions exceeds the client's equity in the account. The NYSE states that maintenance calls are to to met "promptly" and, in any event, within fifteen business days. Under the terms of the customer agreements, customers agree to meet their calls promptly and generally give the securities firm complete authority to liquidate at any time, and under any circumstances the firm believes necessary for protection.

SOME EXAMPLES OF MAINTENANCE CALLS

The following examples will illustrate a long account with maintenance excess and another with maintenance deficiency. Let's assume that it is a margin account that has been open for a period of time.

<u>MAINTENANCE EXCESS ACCOUNT</u>

Long Market Value (LMV)	+$16,000
Debit	<u>-$ 9,000</u>
Equity	+$ 7,000
Maintenance Requirement	<u>$ 4,000</u> (25% of $16,000)
Excess	$ 3,000

<u>MAINTENANCE DEFICIENCY ACCOUNT</u>

Long Market Value (LMV)	+$12,000
Debit	<u>-$ 9,200</u>
Equity	+$ 2,800
Maintenance Requirement	<u>-$ 3,000</u> (25% of $12,000)
Deficiency	-$ 200

The latter account does not have enough equity in the account and would incur a maintenance call of $200. When the funds are deposited, they will *reduce* the debit balance and *increase* the equity by said amount. The amount will then reflect the following:

Long Market Value	+$12,000
Debit	<u>-$ 9,000</u>
Equity	+$ 3,000
Maintenance Requirement	<u>-$ 3,000</u>
Balance	$ -0-

UNDERMARGINED ACCOUNT. An undermargined account is one in which the equity in the account is less than the Reg T requirement. This is usually the result of a decrease in the market value of the securities held in the account. For example, if the customer originally purchases $20,000 of securities on margin and deposits $10,000 (50%), the account would have an equity of $10,000 and satisfy the Reg T requirement. If, however, the market value drops to $18,000 the account would reflect the following:

LMV	+$18,000
Debit	-$10,000
Equity	+$ 8,000
Reg T Requirement	-$ 9,000
Undermargin Amount	-$ 1,000

The account is considered undermargined by $1,000. The securities firm, however, would probably not ask the client for more margin, as the equity of $8,000 in the account is well in excess of the NYSE maintenance requirement of 25% of the long market value (.25 × 18,000 = 4,500) and would also, unless the firm has set an extremely high firm maintenance requirement, meet the firm's own maintenance requirement.

RETENTION REQUIREMENT. The retention requirement is a percentage of market value that must be retained in an account in the event of the withdrawal of a listed security, or the percentage of the proceeds that must be retained in the event of the sale of a security. The retention requirement is set by the Federal Reserve Board from time to time, and currently equals the loan value at 50%. When the retention requirement is set at a higher level than the loan value, sales serve to reduce the restriction or undermargining of an account.

MARGIN SECURITY. A margin (or marginable) security is a security which falls into one of the classifications established by the Federal Reserve Board in Regulation T.

OTC MARGIN SECURITY. A security that the Federal Reserve Board has determined to meet certain criteria in order to be marginable. The Federal Reserve Board periodically publishes a list of such securities.

MARGINABLE SECURITIES. The following are some of the various types of securities which may be purchased on margin:

Virtually all stock traded on the major exchanges (i.e., NYSE, AMEX, etc.)

Most equity securities traded in the Over-The-Counter market or NASDAQ system approved by the Federal Reserve Board

Listed Convertible Corporate Bonds

All listed and approved OTC Non-convertible Bonds

All U.S. Government and Agency Bonds

Listed and some unlisted Corporate Bonds

All State and Municipal general obligations and revenue bonds rated BAA or better by Moody's or BBB or better by Standard and Poors

SPECIAL MEMORANDUM ACCOUNT (SMA). All general margin accounts operate in conjunction with a Special Memorandum Account. The SMA and it's use is defined in Regulation T and was formerly called the Special Miscellaneous Account (prior to 1983).

The purpose of this account is to preserve and make available any excess that is generated through market appreciation. SMA may be increased by market appreciation, but is not reduced by market depreciation. Without the use of this account, any excess generated in a margin account would be lost if the market value declined on a subsequent date.

SMA is based upon Reg T excess, which you will recall is the amount a client's equity exceeds the initial Reg T requirement. Let's review an existing account which has this excess:

Long Market Value (LMV)	+$28,000
Debit Balance (DR)	-$ 7,500
Equity (EQ)	+$20,500
Reg T Requirement (50% LMV)	-$14,000
Reg T Excess	+$ 6,500

In the example shown above, the Reg T excess of $6,500 becomes the new SMA figure, assuming the SMA was not previously at a higher figure.

With regard to SMA, it is helpful to understand the following:

SMA is not money, it is credit available to the client.

If the client uses this credit, the debit balance will be increased, as the securities firm is lending funds to the client.

SMA is associated with, but independent of, the computation of Reg T excess since changes to SMA may be made by other activity that credits or debits a client's account.

Only one SMA account is allowed per customer. Any excess in any other account may be transferred to the SMA associated with the margin account.

With respect to the example cited previously for the calculation of SMA, note that if the client withdrew the amount of the SMA by a check, the long market value would remain unchanged. The debit balance would increase, however, by the amount of the check. The equity would be reduced by a like amount, all of the Reg T excess would be used, and the SMA account would be depleted as indicated in the following table:

	PRIOR	ADJUSTMENT	AFTER
LMV	+$ 28,000	(Unchanged)	+$ 28,000
Debit	-$ 7,500	-$ 6,500 (check)	-$ 14,000
Equity	+$ 20,500	-$ 6,500	+$ 14,000
Reg T Rqmt	-$ 14,000	(Unchanged)	-$ 14,000
Excess	+$ 6,500	-$ 6,500	$ 0
SMA	+$ 6,500	-$ 6,500	$ 0

Additional detailed calculation and amplification of some of these concepts can be found in the chapter appendix.

In most firms, computer programs used by Margin Department personnel automatically transfer excess to the SMA each time the margin account is computed and excess is found. In the absence of such programs, the bookkeeper would be responsible for hand figuring the account for excess every day and posting it to the SMA.

WHAT DOES THE MARGIN DEPARTMENT DO?

The Margin Department has many functions, and can be viewed as a combination of a credit control department and a customer service department. It is the custodian of the firm's customer account records, and in that role, is often the focal point for customer inquiry and for the resolution of incorrect or delayed entries to accounts. A Margin Department may generally be broken down into two key areas: 1) Customer Account Bookkeeping/Customer Services; 2) Regulatory and Firm Compliance.

CUSTOMER ACCOUNT BOOKKEEPING/CUSTOMER SERVICES

The Bookkeeping area may be considered the heart of the Margin Department, and is probably the area most of us in the business think of when the Margin Department is mentioned. This is the area that is responsible for the maintenance and correction of customer account records. Whatever the margin clerk (bookkeeper) records or allows to go unchallenged on account records, is what will ultimately appear on the customer's statement of account, and what will be recorded as the firm's official record of that customer's transactions. The bookkeeping area makes possible both the customer service function and the compliance function. It is the individual margin clerk who is responsible for monitoring and posting of entries to the customer's account (helped these days, of course by very complex computer support).

Responsibilities of the bookkeeping area include:

Maintaining a current, complete, and accurate record of the customer's account holdings and balance; to maintain margin calculations so as to provide the customer, the Account Executive, and the firm with timely information as an aid in determining the ability to trade, or monitoring exposure to risk.

Monitoring transactions executed in retail and institutional cash accounts to ensure customer payment/delivery of securities within appropriate timeframes.

Calculating (if necessary) Reg T and Maintenance Calls in margin accounts, and to ensure their payment within the appropriate timeframes.

Maintaining the complete Margin Call Records required by NYSE Rule 432.

Ensuring the prompt transfer of customer accounts between firms as instructed, in compliance with the timeframes dictated by NYSE Rule 412.

Approving the payment of funds to clients either from their cash credit balances, or from excess funds available in a margin account.

Posting and adjusting or monitoring margin interest charges to clients' accounts.

Researching and making journal entries to correct erroneous entries (e.g., account number errors).

Requesting extensions of time from regulatory agencies if the customer is unable for an acceptable reason to meet his/her cash, margin or delivery obligation in the appropriate timeframe, and requests such an extension. (See Figure 10-5 for acceptable reasons for extensions of time.)

Making journal entry transfers of security positions and monies between accounts as instructed and authorized by the customer, and to post any necessary transfer taxes where security ownership changes.

Code Number	Explanation
Regulation T	
01	Unable to contact customer. [Specific efforts must be made to reach the customer to determine why payment was not yet received.]
02	Customer was contacted and advises check is in the mail. [Requires that check was already mailed and is delayed due to postal problems. Customers who are placing their checks in the mail on the seventh business day are not in compliance with the requirements of the Regulations and such action is not acceptable.]
03	Authorization to transfer funds from another account is already in the mail. [Same application as Code 02.]
04	Customer was contacted and advises additional collateral is in the mail. [Same application as Code 02.]
05	Awaiting receipt of securities sold in another account to release funds sufficient to offset purchase requirements in this account. [Same application as Code 02.]
06	Awaiting legal documents or clearance of securities sold from legal transfer.
07	Unacceptable or improperly drawn check received from customer and returned for correction or new check.
09	Customer has been unexpectedly hospitalized or taken seriously ill and is incapable of issuing check. [Illness or hospitalization of customer should be of a nature that makes it impossible for the customer to issue check. Condition must occur after the transaction was made. If condition existed prior to trade date, then reason cannot be used.]
12	COD transaction. Delivery DK'ed by bank for no instructions; customer's address not in U.S. or Canada.
14	COD transaction. Delivery DK'ed by bank for no instructions; customer's address in U.S. or Canada.
15	COD transaction. Broker unable to make delivery; securities in transfer or fail to receive; 35-day item. [To be used only when applying firm is unable to make delivery against payment due to a fail or similar situation and the transaction(s) involved has reached the 35th calendar day after trade date.]
16	Acts of God or other abnormal conditions. [Reason may only be used when exchange staff authorizes it and then for the time period and condition specified by the staff.]
17	Customer's account is coming from another broker and NYSE Rule 412 is being complied with. [Available when the transfer of an account between member organizations is being accomplished in accordance with NYSE Rule 412 and fails, if necessary, will be created to complete the transfer.]
18	Death in customer's immediate family.
19	Awaiting appointment of executor or administrator of deceased customer's account.
20	Transfer of transaction from cash account to another type of account as permitted by Section .4(c)(6) of Regulation T.
21	Any other exceptional circumstances not covered by designated codes. [State circumstances directly on the extension form.]

FIGURE 10-5. NYSE Acceptable Reasons for Extensions of Time

Code Number	Explanation
SEC Rule	
15c3-3(n)	
40	Security has been placed in transfer by a bank for the customer in order to obtain certificate(s) for the amount of shares sold.
41	Customer died on or after trade date. Awaiting appointment of executor or administrator of deceased customer's account.
42	Broker failed in attempting to buy-in because security is in short supply. Broker has open order to buy-in and is trying to complete transaction. [Requires that an open order be maintained until the buy-in of the position is accomplished or otherwise resolved.]
43	Security sold before dividend payable date or a short position was created in customer account due to dividend received directly by customer upon which broker has a claim. Request for extension does not cover a period beyond fourteen days after payable date.
44	Security is held in a foreign depository where settlement procedures or delivery terms are incompatible with the Rule.
45	Security is in for exchange as a result of a merger, consolidation, transfer of assets, exchange offer, recapitalization or other similar transaction or conversion. [Reason established to cover situations where an exchange of securities or similar event is being undertaken by applying firm or delivering agent to accomplish receipt of the security sold.]
46	Certificate delayed in mail during Christmas season or due to a postal strike. [Exchange staff will specifically establish the time periods when this reason is used.]
47	Customers account is coming from another broker and NYSE Rule 412 is being complied with. [Available when the transfer of an account between member organizations is being accomplished in accordance with Exchange Rule 412 and fails, if necessary, will be created to complete the transfer.]
48	Customer has been unexpectedly hospitalized or taken seriously ill and is incapable of delivering security. [Illness or hospitalization of customer should be of a nature that makes it impossible for the customer to deliver security. Condition must occur after the transaction was made. If condition existed prior to trade date, then reason may not be used.]
49	Lost Certificate–Broker lost and is replacing or customer lost and has already commenced proceedings for replacement. If the customer lost, broker must obtain proof that the customer is replacing by obtaining a copy of any required bond or other appropriate proof.
50	Any other exceptional circumstances not covered by the designated codes. [State circumstances directly on the extension form.]
51	Acts of God or other abnormal condition. [Reason may be used only when exchange staff authorizes it and then solely for the time period and condition specified by the staff.]

FIGURE 10-5. *(Continued)*

Code Number	Maximum Number of Days Permitted Per Request	Request to Be Counted Toward Limit	Final on Transaction	Transaction Limit Per Code
Regulation T				
01	7	Yes	No	1
02	7	Yes	Yes	1
03	7	Yes	Yes	1
04	7	Yes	Yes	1
05	7	Yes	Yes	1
06	7	Yes	No	5
07	7	Yes	No	1
09	7	Yes	No	5
12	7	No	Yes	1
14	2	No	Yes	1
15	14	No	No	None
16	14	No	No	None
17	14	No	No	2
18	14	Yes	Yes	1
19	14	Yes	No	5
20	0	No	No	1
21	14	Yes	No	5
SEC Rule 15c3-3(n)				
40	14	No	No	2
41	14	Yes	No	9
42	14	No	No	None
43	14	Yes	No	2
44	14	Yes	No	2
45	14	Yes	No	2
46	14	No	No	None
47	14	No	No	2
48	14	Yes	No	9
49	30	No	No	None
50	14	Yes	No	9
51	14	No	No	None

Source: NYSE Information Memo 82-87.

*Although most of the reasons are self-explanatory, the bracketed remarks are for clarification or to specifically indicate New York Stock Exchange requirements.

FIGURE 10-5. *(Continued)*

REGULATORY AND FIRM COMPLIANCE

It is the Compliance area which uses the customer account records generated by the bookkeeping area, the regulatory guidance given by the Regulatory Specialist, and the firm's own credit policies to determine if an account is in compliance with the relevant rules and regulations. They are responsible for determining if any liquidating action must be taken, or if any violations of the rules have occurred. The Compliance area's role is critical in ensuring that the securities firm is not exposed to loss or regulatory censure.

It should be noted at this point that the Compliance area plays just as strong a role with cash accounts as it does with margin accounts. It is the compliance area which bears ultimate responsibility for ensuring customer and firm compliance with all appropriate regulations. Cash and margin accounts are both established by Regulation T, and under Reg T, a securities firm is not allowed to maintain a creditor/debtor relationship with a cash account in the same way that it is allowed to for a margin account. Thus the compliance area must ensure that all cash purchases are paid for in full, and that sales in cash accounts are covered by the deposit of securities (that is, no short sales).

The specific duties of the Compliance area include the following:

Monitoring all customer accounts to ensure that T Calls, Maintenance Calls, and cash commitments are all met within the appropriate timeframes (see table 10-1).

Forcing the liquidation of those positions in which margin or cash commitments are not met as required (generally done by entering a market order to buy or sell the appropriated position).

Monitoring account trading activity so as to ensure that cash accounts do not "free-ride," and that margin accounts do not make a practice of meeting T calls by liquidating the position that created the call.

Restricting accounts which have engaged in such activity from trading for a period of time, as required by regulation.

Acting as the primary focal point for regulatory agencies, auditing customer activity and the firm's policing of such activity.

Cash purchases	7 business days after *trade* date
Cash sales	10 business days after *settlement* date
Reg T calls	7 business days after *trade* date
Maintenance calls	15 business days

*Securities firms can and freqently do elect fewer days.

TABLE 10-1. Maximum Time Frames for Payments*

With respect to liquidating a customer's position, it should be noted that the firm is obligated to ensure compliance with various regulations. Securities firms are not permitted to give a customer extra time to meet a T call, unless an extension of time has been requested from the appropriate regulatory agency and granted. Failure to liquidate in such an event would place the firm in violation of Regulation T and other various rules, and would subject the firm to fines and/or censure. In addition, the compliance area must act so as to protect the firm from loss. In the event of a rapidly falling market, or in the event that a particular security is rapidly falling in price, the compliance area will liquidate maintenance calls in a time frame considerably shorter than specified above.

What we have discussed are the primary roles performed by the Margin Department. Naturally, the way in which these roles are performed will vary from firm to firm. In an extremely small firm, there may be one or two people who do all of the above with very little computer support. In a very large firm, there may be several departments involved in managing all of these functions, and an extremely complex computer support system will be required. Nevertheless the roles remain the same and the firms' responsibilities to the regulators remain the same. In order to understand the function more clearly, let's look at a typical margin clerk's work day. For the purposes of illustration, we will assume that our margin clerk is operating in a fairly manual environment.

HOW TO PROCESS MARGIN ACTIVITY—RESOLVING PROBLEMS

Our margin clerk's day begins with updating customer account records, for both cash and margin accounts, to ensure that all of the previous day's activity has been taken into account. This includes posting to the account all of the trade activity of the previous day, whether buy or sell. Both the security position and the dollar amount of the trade would be added to the previous balance. While undertaking this activity, or at a later point in the day, the margin clerk examines the client's trading to ensure that no free-riding has taken place in a cash account, or liquidating of security positions which have previously created T Calls. Any deposits or withdrawals of funds or securities are posted. Dividend and interest entries are posted, as are any other entries that affect the customer's security position or credit balance.

Once all activity has been posted to the account, the clerk will "mark to the market" the margin accounts. In this process, the closing prices of yesterday's market are used to compute the long and short market values in the account. The account is then recalculated for equity, buying power, Reg T excess or T calls, and maintenance excess or maintenance calls. If Reg T excess is found, and the value exceeds the SMA previously in the account, then the SMA balance will be updated.

In recalculating accounts, the clerk will normally pay particular attention to those accounts that traded the previous day to see if a T call has been incurred. If a T call was generated, a written call is issued to the client, specifying the amount due and the due date. In cash accounts, if a debit balance arises from a purchase or other entry, or a short position arises from a sale, then a funds or securities due notice would be forwarded to the customer. In most cases, the customer would also receive a phone call, either from the margin clerk or Account Executive regarding the obligation and the due date.

The margin clerk also pays particular attention to those margin accounts holding long securities which have decreased considerably in value, or short securities which have risen considerably in value. In these cases, the clerk will calculate the firm's maintenance margin requirement for the account, and compare it closely to the client's equity. Where there is a deficiency, a maintenance call is issued to the client, and is treated similarly to the T call. In a rapidly dropping market, the margin clerk's first priority will be to examine accounts for maintenance calls, and to issue them promptly. The firm may, in such circumstances, shorten its normal collection timeframes as much as it feels necessary, to afford appropriate protection to the firm.

In reviewing for maintenance calls, the margin clerk should normally be made aware of any particular security which may have had an abnormal price movement. There should also be available some method of determining which accounts may have a major position in that security. In this way, attention can be directed to those accounts which present the most exposure to the firm.

After updating all of the accounts' activity and issuing any needed maintenance or T calls, the margin clerk then reviews all of the outstanding cash transaction due notices, T calls, or maintenance calls. Those which are due, and not met, require further action. In the event of a T call or funds/securities due in a cash account, either an extension would have to be requested from a regulatory agency, if the client has a valid reason for not meeting the obligation, or the position would have to be liquidated (see Figure 10-4). In the event of an overdue maintenance call, the clerk (or supervisor) must decide whether to grant additional time (providing the call had not been open in excess of 15 business days), or to liquidate sufficient securities to cover the call.

Once having ensured that all of the required credit monitoring functions have been performed, the margin clerk will turn to the customer service role. Having previously recalculated the amount that can be provided to the customer or Account Executive with any needed account information such as equity, debit or credit balance, buying power, etc., the clerk also acts on instructions provided. If the customer requested that a check be issued, the margin clerk would review the amount available. In a cash account, the clerk must ensure that the account does not go into a debit. In a margin account, the clerk would review both the SMA and the maintenance excess. The check issued would be no larger than the smaller of the two amounts. (To issue a check for the larger figure would incur either a T call or a maintenance call. To issue a check larger than either figure would incur both calls.) The margin clerk would also ensure that in issuing a check, the client's account does not fall below any minimum equity requirement. If the customer requests that securities be withdrawn from the account, the margin clerk would issue the necessary instructions, provided that after calculation of the retention requirement the account will not go into a Reg T or maintenance deficiency. In undertaking all other instructions and activity as detailed earlier in the chapter, the margin clerk will similarly review the impact of such activity on the margin customer's maintenance or Reg T excess to ensure that no deficiencies are created, and that no debit balances or short security positions are created in a cash account.

Table 10-2 provides a summary of potential problems and suggested solutions.

Problem	Solution
Incomplete or erroneous trade information	Recalculate account once correct information is obtained
Evidence of free-riding or liquidating violations	Restrict account to limited trading or close account
Margin trade in cash account	Obtain hypothecation agreement from client or treat as cash
Margin purchase OTC nonmarginable securities	Treat as cash
Expiring extension	Obtain new extension if permitted or liquidate transactions
"As-of" adjustments	Recalculate margin interest charges
Control/restricted stock held in account	May not be able to be readily liquidated; charge higher maintenance requirements or preclude from margin account
Concentrated security positions (large quantity of one security in an account)	May not be able to be readily liquidated; charge higher maintenance requirements
Inability to contact customer on due date of transaction	Liquidate if insufficient funds available to cover obligation
Insufficient SMA or maintenance excess to allow requested delivery of securities from margin account	Obtain deposit from customer or have customer liquidate securities to raise SMA or excess
Incorrect funds debit or credit to account	Recalculate account to figure SMA or T call and maintenance excess or call; adjust margin interest charge once debit or credit is adjusted
Incorrect deposit or withdrawal of securities from margin account	Recalculate account for correct margin balances

TABLE 10-2. Summary of Potential Problems and Solutions

APPENDIX: TECHNICAL TERMS AND DEFINITIONS

Special Memorandum Account (SMA)

Regulation T permits securities firms to identify and make available to customers, separate calculations of customers' excess margin. SMA is a key concept to understand in margin, since a customer may use his/her SMA to borrow all or part of the funds that would otherwise be needed to cover a margin transaction—purchase or short sale. As we have discussed, a securities firm may lend a client up to 50% (as set by the current loan value) of the purchase price. In addition, if the client has credit available in a SMA, the firm may lend that amount to the client (again, provided that in doing so the customer does not incur a maintenance call, or bring his account below the minimum equity requirement). As a general rule, once a securities firm has made a credit entry to a customer's SMA, the credit will remain there until the customer uses it, by withdrawal or in a transaction. This is true even if the Reg T excess which originally created the SMA disappears, due to a decrease in the market value of securities in the account. Thus there may be an SMA balance in an account, even if there is currently no Reg T excess. This is often referred to as "inflated SMA."

As noted above, the SMA is independent of Reg T excess, as there are other actions in an account that may credit or debit SMA. The following items can change the SMA balance:

Items that Credit SMA Balances

Regulation T excess

Dividends

Deposits of cash in excess of any Reg T calls

Deposits of securities with loan value in excess of any Regulation T calls

Long sales release a minimum of 50% of sales proceeds.

Items that Debit SMA Balances

Regulation T on new commitments

Cash withdrawals

Security withdrawals

ITEMS THAT DO NOT AFFECT SMA BALANCES

Market depreciation

Interest charges

Short dividend charges

Reduction of Regulation T loan value

Let's look at a few of the items that increase the SMA balance and illustrate them in a bookkeeping format.

Example An account with an existing SMA balance of $1,200 received $400 in dividends and the client deposits a personal check for $500. The status of the account before and after is as follows:

BEFORE		AFTER	
LMV	+$34,000	LMV	+$34,000
Debit	-$15,800	Debit	-$14,900
Equity	+$18,200	Equity	+$19,100
Reg T Rqmt	-$17,000	Reg T Rqmt	-$17,000
Excess	+$ 1,200	Excess	+$ 2,100
SMA	$ 1,200	SMA	$ 2,100

The dividend and the cash deposit increased the SMA balance on a dollar-for-dollar basis, since they decreased the debit balance and increased the equity.

A deposit of fully-paid marginable securities would entail a credit to the SMA for the loan value of the securities, as long as no Reg T call is outstanding.

Example A client deposits $5,000 of fully paid marginable equities into a margin account. The loan value (currently 50%) or $2,500 is credited to the SMA as follows:

BEFORE		AFTER	
LMV	+$16,000	LMV	+$21,000
Debit	-$ 6,800	Debit	-$ 6,800
Equity	+$ 9,200	Equity	+$14,200
Reg T Rqmt	-$ 8,000	Reg T Rqmt	-$10,500
Excess	+$ 1,200	Excess	+$ 3,700
SMA	$ 1,200	SMA	$ 3,700

The LMV would increase by $5,000 since the securities are fully paid while 50% or the loan value is credited to the SMA.

The following is an illustration of an event which would decrease SMA:

Example A client is advised by his/her Account Executive that he/she has an SMA balance and decides to withdraw a portion ($2,000) of it. The status of the account would be as follows:

BEFORE		AFTER	
LMV	+$70,000	LMV	+$70,000
Debit	-$37,000	Debit	-$39,000
Equity	+$33,000	Equity	+$31,000
Reg T Rqmt	-$35,000	Reg T Rqmt	-$35,000
Undermargin	-$ 2,000	Undermargin	+$ 4,000
SMA	$ 4,000	SMA	$ 2,000

You will note that the SMA, once given to a client, is not taken away, and that it can be used even if it causes the account to be undermargined by a higher amount.

Customers, we noted previously, may use the SMA to fulfill, either completely or partially, the Reg T margin requirements on new commitments. This is called buying power, and is the result of the SMA balance divided by Reg T margin expressed as a decimal.

The following is an illustration of an account which made use of SMA for such purposes:

BEFORE		AFTER	
LMV	+$67,000	LMV	+$72,000
Debit	-$36,000	Debit	-$41,000
Equity	+$31,000	Equity	+$31,000
Reg T Rqmt	-$33,500	Reg T Rqmt	-$36,000
Undermargin	-$ 2,500	Undermargin	+$ 5,000
SMA	$ 2,500	SMA	-0-

The buying power was $5,000 ($2,500/.5 = $5,000). The SMA balance was decreased by $2,500, or 50% of the transaction. The remaining 50% was loaned to the customer in line with the loan value established by Reg T. The debit balance increased by $5,000. In reality, the securities firm made two loans to the client: 1) as a line of credit from the SMA; and 2) on the marginable security purchased.

In summation, the Special Memorandum Account is a means of noting added credit to a client that would otherwise be lost. It should be understood that the securities firm does not add to or release from the SMA, by taking anything away from the client's margin account. SMA calculations are basically notations, or a vehicle by which margin bookkeepers keep track of a client's added line of credit.

BUYING POWER

Buying power may be defined as the dollar amount of margin securities that a client may purchase or sell short, without incurring a Regulation T call. The formula is as follows:

$$\frac{\text{Available Funds (SMA)}}{\text{Reg T Requirement}} = \text{Buying Power}$$

For example, let's assume that a customer has an SMA of $3,000 and sufficient maintenance excess. The buying power under current Reg T rules would be $6,000, or $3,000/.5 (where the Reg T requirement is expressed as a decimal).

SHORT ACCOUNTS

If a client sells securities short, the client owes the borrowed stock to the securities firm with the sale creating a credit in the account.

Reg T currently requires that the customer deposit margin equal to 50% of the proceeds of the short sale Thus, a short sale of $15,000 would create the following:

Short Market Value ((SMV)	-$15,000
Credit Balance	+$15,000
Equity	-0-
Reg T call (50% of the short sale proceeds)	+$ 7,500

The client would have to deposit $7,500 within 7 business days.

The bookkeeping is similar to that of a long account, except that the equity in the account goes up when the value of the short stock goes down, and the equity goes down when the short stock market value goes up. For example:

STOCK FALLS BY $2,000		STOCK INCREASES BY $2,000	
(SMV)	-$13,000	(SMV)	-$17,000
Credit	+$22,500	Credit	+$22,500
Equity	+$ 9,500	Equity	+$ 5,500

REG T FOR SHORT ACCOUNTS

The initial Reg T requirement (currently 50%) for a short account is computed in the same manner as for a long account. The basic calculations of excess and undermargin in short account bookkeeping are also the same, with the exception of dividends.

In a long account the customer receives a credit for any dividend, while in a short account the securities firm debits the account for the amount of the dividend. The reason for this is that the short account borrowed the security and the owner expects payment for the dividend.

To illustrate the Reg T call requirement, excess and undermargin, we will use a short sale of $22,000 worth of securities.

INITIAL MARGIN

(SMV)	-$22,000
Credit	+$22,000
Equity	-0-
Reg T Call (50%)	-$11,000

Deposit required: $11,000 within 7 business days.

REG T EXCESS

Following the prior example, if the security decreased in value to $20,000 and the customer makes a deposit of $11,000 to satisfy the Reg T call, the account now reflects the following:

SMV	-$20,000
Credit	+$33,000
Equity	+$13,000
Reg T Rqmt (50% of SMV)	-$10,000
Excess	+$ 3,000
SMA	$ 3,000

It should be noted that Reg T excess increases more quickly in a short account than a long account. The reason for this is that the equity is going up, but Reg T is going down. In a long account, an increase in security value results in an increase in equity, but the Reg T requirement also increases.

Thus, the short account profit of $2,000 used in this example resulted in an excess of $3,000. If this were a long account, the $2,000 profit would only result in an excess of $1,000 (50% X $2,000).

REG T RESTRICTION

If a short sale goes against a client, the amount by which the account is undermargin is greater with only a relatively small increase in market value. Thus, if the security value rose to $24,000, the prior account would reflect the following:

SMV	-$24,000
Credit	+$33,000
Equity	+$ 9,000
Reg T Rqmt (50% of SMV)	$12,000
Undermargin	-$ 3,000
SMA	-$ 3,000

A $2,000 decrease in a long account would only have resulted in an undermargin amount of $1,000. In this example, the adverse market increase to the short seller resulted in an undermargin amount of $3,000.

MIXED ACCOUNT

Securities firms consolidate both a long account and a short account into what is called a "mixed account." For both purposes the two accounts are netted.

The following illustrates a long account, short account, and their combination (net) into a "mixed account."

LONG ACCOUNT		SHORT ACCOUNT		MIXED ACCOUNT	
LMV	+$21,000	SMV	-$17,000	LMV	+$21,000
Debit	-$11,000	Credit	+$27,000	SMV	-17,000
Equity	+$10,000	Equity	+$10,000	Credit	+$16,000
				(27,000 - 11,000)	
Reg T Rqmt	-$10,500	Reg T Rqmt	-$ 8,500	Equity	+$20,000
Undermargin	-$ 500	Excess	+$ 1,500	Reg T Rqmt	-$19,000
				(50% LMV + SMV)	
				Excess	+$ 1,000
				SMA	+$ 1,000

The mathematics of a mixed account is simple addition. The reader should note, however, that in a mixed account the customer would be charged interest on the debit balance plus the short market value, or the amount the short market value exceeds the credit balance.

Non-marginable securities purchased in a margin account are included in the cash portion of the account for recordkeeping purposes, but are not included in Reg T computation requirements. Therefore, they would not be included in the long market value of the account. Security firm computer systems are programmed to identify marginable securities just as they are programmed to compute interest charges in a mixed account.

MARGIN MAINTENANCE FOR SHORT ACCOUNTS

The regulatory agencies and NASD use more stringent maintenance requirements for short accounts, and increase the requirements as the market value of the short stock goes down in value. The maintenance requirements imposed by regulatory agencies and NASD on short stocks are as follows:

On stocks selling below $5 per share, the maintenance is $2.50 per share or 100% of the market price, whichever is higher.

On stocks selling at $5 or above per share, the maintenance is $5 per share or 30% of the market price, whichever is higher.

The following example illustrates the maintenance required:

SHORT A STOCK AT	MAINTENANCE PER SHARE
$ 2.00	$ 2.50
4.50	4.50
10.00	5.00
17.00	5.10*
80.00	24.00

*The maintenance is $5.10 per share since 30% of the short market value is greater than $5.

There is a cross-over where the maintenance required moves from $5 per share to 30% of the short market value:

For stocks selling at 16 5/8 per share, 30% is $4.987 so the maintenance is $5.

For stocks selling at 16 3/4, 30% is $5.025 so the maintenance is $5.025.

SHORT ACCOUNT MAINTENANCE CALLS

Let's look at an example, assuming that the stock that the client sold short is valued above 16 3/4, is worth $18,000 and the client has $8,000 cash in the account (Proceeds of sale = $18,000, + $8,000 cash = $26,000 credit balance):

SMV	-$18,000
Credit	+$26,000
Equity	+$ 8,000
30% of SMV	-$ 5,400
Maintenance Excess	+$ 2,600

To ascertain the dollar value to which the short stocks can rise (when the maintenance requirement is 30%) before the account will incur a maintenance call, you divide the credit balance by 1.3 (130%). This is due to:

Credit from a short sale	= 100%
Maintenance	= 30%

Therefore, in the example stated above:

$$\frac{\text{Credit of } \$26,000}{1.3} = \$20,000 \text{ SMV}$$

If the short stocks increased to $20,500, a maintenance call would be issued for $650 as follows:

SMV	-$20,500
Credit	+$26,000
Equity	+$ 5,500
30% of SMV	-$ 6,150
Maintenance Call	-$ 650

RULES THAT GOVERN SHORT SELLING

The NYSE defines a short sale as any sale of a security that the seller does not own, or any sale of a security that is completed by the delivery of a borrowed security. As such, there are two kinds of short sales—a regular short sale and a short sale against the box.

A client in a regular short sale does not own the security. The customer sells it first, with the intention of buying it later. The subsequent purchase is used to repay the loan of the security borrowed to make the original sale.

In a short sale against the box, the customer owns the security, but does not wish to deliver that certificate. Instead, the client sells the security, but borrows another certificate to complete the transaction.

Clients sell stock short because they feel the market will go down. By selling the stock, the customer receives the proceeds from the sale, and if the market price does decrease, the security can be purchased at the lower price. If the subsequent purchase is less than the proceeds from the sale, the client will make a profit.

All short sales (regular or versus the box) must be transacted in a margin account. This is necessary since the short seller has borrowed stock which must be repaid.

As the securities firm holds the stock purchased on margin as collateral in a long account, it also holds the proceeds from the short sale until the short seller repays the borrowed securities. The proceeds from the short sale are thus the collateral.

Short sale orders are conditional upon the securities firm being able to borrow the security. The firm, however, can borrow the stock from the following sources:

The firm's own inventory

Accounts of clients within the firm (with their written permission)

Other firms

Under no circumstances may a securities firm lend a client's securities without prior written authorization.

The SEC requires that short sales of round-lot securities executed on the exchanges must be made on an "up-tick," or a "zero-plus-tick." This rule prevents short sellers from pushing down the market, and requires that the short sale goes against a downward trend in the market.

An "up-tick" can be defined as a sales price that is higher than the previous sales price. Thus, if a sale of a security took place at 50, and was followed by a sale at 50 1/4, the sale at 50 1/4 would be an up-tick.

A "zero-plus-tick" is defined as a sale that takes place at the same price as the previous sale, but the previous sale was higher than the last preceding sale price. For example, let's assume the following sale prices for XYZ Corporation: 60, 60 1/4. The last sale in this sequence of transactions on the exchange would be a zero-plus-tick. Therefore, a zero-plus-tick can only follow an up-tick. The SEC rule requires that the short sale occur on an up-tick or a zero-plus-tick, and does not require the sale be made following an up-tick.

The following will illustrate when a short sale is made by a broker on behalf of the client.

Example A broker receives an order to sell short 200 shares of XYZ. The last sale on the floor of the exchange was at 33 1/2 and occurred on a minus-tick, or one that was lower than the previous sale. The floor broker offers to sell 200 at 33 5/8. The short sale was made at 33 5/8 since it was transacted at a price higher than previous sale of 33 1/2.

One last point on short sales: It is a serious violation of SEC rules for a securities firm to enter a sell order without noting whether it is a long or short sell. Account Executives, therefore, must ask the client at the time the order is placed whether or not the sale is to be a long sale.

BOND PURCHASES IN A MARGIN ACCOUNT

Government, Municipal, and Corporate Bonds may be purchased in a margin account under Regulation T. At one time separate accounts were established for these purchases.

The initial margin requirements for bonds are set by the securities firms, who establish good faith deposits as the initial margin. Reg T does not set the initial margin requirement. The regulatory agencies and the NASD have established maintenance requirements a securities firm must follow. The only exception is with convertible bonds. Reg T requires the same initial margin as required for the underlying equity securities, or currently 50% of the market value.

Maintenance excess computations are identical to those explained earlier in the chapter. The SMA balance may be used to purchase bonds, and follows the principles outlined in that section.

CHAPTER 11

Securities Lending and Borrowing

Most managers know that securities lending and borrowing is an important part of securities firms' operations because it facilitates processing, generates interest income, reduces interest expense, and helps expedite delivery of securities to customers who otherwise might not receive their securities in a timely manner.

This chapter discusses the benefits of securities lending and borrowing to securities firms, basic rules associated with the business, when you should borrow, internal procedures, risks, potential abuses and preventive techniques, and how to measure profitability of the business.

First, let's discuss what lending and borrowing actually is: the lending or borrowing of equities, corporate, municipal and/or government bonds between securities firms and/or other institutions that hold securities as agent for customers or in their own investment portfolios.

Securities firms are permitted to lend to others the securities of customers who owe the firm money from margin debit balance (assuming the customer has signed appropriate agreements permitting the firm to do so). In addition of course, firms can lend securities the firm owns.

BENEFITS OF SECURITIES LENDING AND BORROWING

The benefits of lending and borrowing securities are basically two-fold:

1. It helps facilitate the delivery process by reducing or avoiding fails to deliver from short sales, arbitrage activity, fails to receive, or other "system friction" in the delivery cycle.

2. It provides interest income or reduces interest expense.

Most operations managers understand how the process reduces fails, so let's discuss how securities lending can generate interest income or reduce interest expense.

When Firm A lends securities to Firm B, B usually gives cash to A equal to the market value of the securities. Most firms that borrow securities demand that the lender give back to the borrower a portion of the interest income the lender generates with the cash. The net effect, however, provides the lender with funds at a substantial discount from short-term financing rates.

For example, assume that a firm was financing a customer margin debit of $1,000,000, with a bank loan at a stated broker call rate of 7%. In addition, also assume that the customer is being charged interest over the broker call rate at 8%. In this example, the firm would have net interest income of $10,000.

BANK LOAN FINANCING EXAMPLE

Interest Charged Customers @ 8% on $1,000,000 margin debit balance	$80,000
Less: Bank Loan expense @ 7% on $1,000,000	70,000
Net Interest Profit from Bank Loan Financing	$10,000

In the case of the margin debit being financed by a bank loan, therefore, the firm earns $10,000.

SECURITIES LOAN FINANCING EXAMPLE

Regulators require that customers deposit collateral of 140% of the margin debit balance with the securities firm. In this case, the $1,000,000 debit balance would be collateralized by $1,400,000 of securities. If all the securities are loaned to another securities firm, the firm's net interest profit on this transaction is $34,500, much higher than if the margin debit were financed by a bank loan:

Interest Charged Customers @ 8% on $1,000,000 margin debit balance	$80,000
$1,000,000 of the funds received from stock loan replaces bank loan to finance margin debit, so interest cost:	0
Additional $400,000 security loan is used to reduce other bank loans @ 7%	28,000
Gross Interest Profit	108,000
Less approximate 75% interest rebate on interest savings from securities loaned [.75 (7% × $1,400,000)]	-73,500
Net Interest Profit from Security Loan Financing	$34,500

In the examples above, the financing of the $1,000,000 margin debit with a bank loan provided the firm with net interest of $10,000, and the financing with a security loan provided the firm with net interest income of $34,500, or an incremental interest benefit as to security loan financing of $24,500.

WHAT ARE THE RULES?

The practice of borrowing securities originated with the rules of various regulatory bodies that govern transactions of securities firms with regard to delivery of securities sold. For example, Rule 2440C of the New York Stock Exchange states: "No member or member organization should fail to deliver against a short sale of a security on a national securities exchange until a diligent effort has been made by such member or organization to borrow the necessary securities to make delivery."

Rules such as the one above facilitate processing, and reduce the number of securities that firms would "fail to deliver" to other firms and customers. This expediting of deliveries is in the customer's and firm's interest, as customers receive prompt delivery of securities they bought and firms do not interrupt their transaction flow because of fails to deliver.

The SEC Act of 1934 permits lending of securities between securities firms against a "bona fide" deposit of cash. Other regulations restrict the lending of customer securities to those securities owned by customers who have signed an agreement specifically permitting the firm to lend the securities owned by the customer [see Rule 402 of the NYSE and Rule 240.8 (c) of the SEC Act of 1934].

WHEN SHOULD YOU BORROW SECURITIES?

You should generally borrow securities to:

Avoid fails to deliver

Cover customer and firm short sales

Relend to others

Avoid possession and control deficits

To Avoid Fails to Deliver

Let's say a customer sells through Firm A and Firm A, as agent for the customer, sells to Firm B. On settlement date, if the customer hasn't delivered to Firm A, Firm A will fail to deliver to Firm B. Since money has not changed hands, there is no financing cost to Firm A. But, if Firm A borrows the security from Firm C, makes the delivery, and uses the cash from the delivery as collateral for the borrowed securities, Firm A will generate income in the form of a portion of the interest earned from Firm C.

To Cover Customer and Firm Short Sales

In most circumstances, customers and firms cannot sell short unless they can obtain the securities for delivery against the short. So, if your firm doesn't have excess margin securities in its box, you should borrow the securities. Here, again, your firm will generate interest income and avoid fails to deliver.

To Relend to Others

During the past few years, a number of securities firms have developed "finder" activity as an adjunct to their normal securities lending operation. This activity works in the following manner: Firm A has a borrow/loan relationship with Firm B and calls Firm B to borrow securities. Firm B does not have the security available to lend. Firm A does not have a large staff and therefore, requests Firm B to inquire of other firms to see if the security can be located. Firm B does so, and receives a percentage of the rebate offered to Firm A by the lending firm.

To Avoid Possession and Control Deficits

Rule 15c3-3 of the SEC Act of 1934 requires that firms "promptly obtain and thereafter maintain possession and control of customers' fully paid for securities." There may be times, due to errors, mistakes, bad deliveries and other reasons, when the dynamics of cashiering activity result in possession and control deficits. Firms then may actively try to borrow the securities to eliminate the deficit as quickly as possible.

INTERNAL PROCEDURES—THE MECHANICS OF LENDING AND BORROWING OPERATIONS

In the actual security loan process, loans can be personally solicited by the security loan representative or by phone contact. When a firm receives the request from a broker to borrow securities, the order is checked against the firm's securities available for loan. If available, the number of shares to be loaned is reduced from the firm's security inventory to avoid "overloaning." The borrowing firm is given an immediate confirmation and the order is written up for delivery. Orders are then passed to the Cashiering Department for processing (see Figure 11-1).

As previously noted, borrows of securities are made for a number of reasons, i.e., to achieve timely deliveries of stocks and bonds, which are sold by customers but have not yet been delivered by them to the firm, and to cover customer short sales and firm short sales.

Generally, only a designated function, such as a Securities Lending Department, is authorized to determine from which firm

```
······································· TRANSMISSION RESULT REPORT ··················(AUG 31 '      09:21AM)··········
                                                              MLPF&S GLOBAL EQUITY
································································································ (AUTO) ··············

 DATE    START    REMOTE TERMINAL      TIME    RE-     MODE   TOTAL PERSONAL LABEL              FILE
         TIME     IDENTIFICATION               SULTS          PAGES                            NO.
 AUG 31 09:20AM            602 7585 01'07"    OK      ES     01                                 007
```

```
·····························································································································

  E)ECM  >)REDUCTION   S)STANDARD                      M)MEMORY   C)CONFIDENTIAL  #)BATCH
                       D)DETAIL                                    $)TRANSFER
                       F)FINE                                      P)POLLING
```

FIGURE 11-1. Transmission Result Report

securities should be borrowed. This determination is based on knowledge of which firms have certain securities, historical loan and borrow data, and marketing initiatives. Based on these criteria, representatives prioritize the daily borrowing order from the various firms.

The first concern for a firm that is borrowing securities is to locate availability, to ensure that the firm can make prompt delivery. The next concern is to attempt to borrow from firms who will reciprocate and borrow in turn at a later date. If reciprocal arrangements cannot be made, the borrower will often attempt to obtain a higher portion of the interest income that accrues to the lending firm.

The Cashiering Department decides which securities are needed for delivery purposes. The Cashiering Department usually sends lists of securities that need to be borrowed to the Security Loan Department, and that department then begins the process of borrowing. Constant communication between these two departments is necessary to assure accuracy and promptness of delivery.

EFFECTING CUSTOMER SHORT SALES

In effecting short sales for customers, a firm must generally be in a position to make delivery on settlement date as mandated by various regulations.

In order to do this, certain procedures are usually enforced which entail the following:

The firm's Account Executives must contact the Securities Lending Department before a short sale is effected.

The securities lending representative must fill out a form used to borrow for short sales. This form usually designates the number of shares, type of security, Account Executive and branch (if applicable).

A securities lending representative will then locate the security, either in-house or with another firm.

Upon locating the security, the securities lending representative will notify the Account Executive that the security is available for borrowing. The salesperson must be notified if any inability to borrow occurs in order to inform the customer of a possible buy-in situation.

OPERATIONAL PROCESSES FOR FIRM SHORTS AND RISK ARBITRAGE

Though the operational procedures for firm short sales and risk arbitrage are similar to those discussed for customer short sales, we will discuss these strategies in particular here. The securities lending function must be kept informed as to all risk arbitrage situations. In this situation, securities can very quickly become unavailable. To protect the arbitrage position, the securities lending function must borrow securities from sources which normally would not recall them.

With regard to firm shorts (other than arbitrage items), the potential impact of the order makes it critical. If the short is not covered internally and a borrow is needed, the firm wants to place that borrow with an institution that will give the most in return, either in loan business or rebates.

The most effective way to insure proper coverage of firm short positions is to have an effective communication system between the trading areas and the securities lending function. Compliance with the firm's procedures on short sales is the first critical step.

RISKS INVOLVED IN LENDING AND BORROWING SECURITIES

The major risk involved in lending and borrowing securities is the possible dollar loss if a firm with whom another firm is doing business goes bankrupt. If a firm is lending securities, the lending firm must have cash deposited as collateral for the loans.

If the borrowing firm goes bankrupt and the securities are not returned upon demand, the lender may have to go into the market and repurchase these securities, becoming subject to a potential loss on the differential between the loan money on collateral and the current market price. If the lending firm goes bankrupt and will not return the borrowing firm's cash deposit upon return of the securities, the borrower may have to go into the market and sell these securities. In that case, the borrower would be subject to a possible loss if there is a differential between loan and market price.

To reduce risks and to specify obligations, most firms enter into contracts with all firms with whom they do business. An example of a typical contract is contained in the chapter appendix.

THE "MARKING TO MARKET" CONCEPT

The value of a particular security can change rapidly. Security firms must assure that they always maintain enough collateral to assure they are not exposed to undue risk if the firm they are lending to goes bankrupt. A process called "Marking to Market" is used to accomplish this.

The process works as follows: If Firm A lends $100,000 of securities to Firm B, Firm B deposits $100,000 cash with Firm A. If the market value of the securities increases, say to, $110,000, Firm A is at risk if Firm B goes bankrupt and Firm A has to go into the marketplace to purchase the securities. To limit exposure, firms "Mark-to-the-Market" frequently. In this case, Firm A notifies Firm B of the change, and Firm B sends Firm A a check for $10,000. The actual process is normally accomplished through the use of standard forms through the clearing corporations. A typical form used to "Mark to Market" is illustrated in Figure 11-2.

		MARK TO MARKET		
QUANTITY	DESCRIPTION	SECURITY NO.	REFERENCE NO.	DATE PREPARED
CUSIP NUMBER	TRANS. CODE **LM** CONTRACT DATE	CONTRACT PRICE	VALUE	
	EFFECTIVE DATE	NEW CONTRACT PRICE	VALUE	
BROKER NO. BROKER NAME		NET DIFFERENCE		
		PREMIUM INTEREST ETC.		
MICS ENTRY		FINAL AMOUNT		

FIGURE 11-2. Standard Form for "Mark to Market"

ABUSES IN CONNECTION WITH SECURITIES LENDING ACTIVITIES

In M. F. Educational Circular #424 issued by the New York Stock Exchange in June, 1973, specific irregularities involving securities lending activities were listed. This circular was the result of an investigation conducted by the Securities and Exchange Commission.

The following sections describe the abuses outlined in the circular and procedures that can be used to prevent these abuses.

BORROWING WITHOUT A LEGITIMATE BUSINESS PURPOSE

"A lending organization or its employees may influence employees of other organizations to borrow securities without a legitimate business purpose. The reason may be to provide working cash to the lending broker or simply to improve the record of a stock loan representative."

Prevention Certain borrowing procedures can help prevent this from happening. For example, all borrow instructions should come from areas within the designated cashiering functions. At no time should the securities lending functions be authorized to initiate a borrow request. All borrow requests should be made on a standard stock borrow daily order form and signed by the requesting party and the securities lending representative completing this transaction.

IMPROPERLY FINANCED TRANSACTIONS

"Securities purchased by an employee in a cash account at another firm may be delivered against payment to the employee's firm where he has arranged improperly for the securities to be received as securities borrowed, thus financing a purchase in violation of Regulation T and without the payment of interest."

Prevention This situation may be controlled by having more than one area responsible for the execution of any borrow transaction. These different and distinct areas should determine what securities are to be borrowed and the securities lending function determines from whom to borrow.

INADEQUATE CREDIT ASSURANCE

"Stock borrowed from a broker who is a poor credit risk may be recorded, upon receipt, for the account of a broker or broker of better reputation who is not the actual lender."

Prevention To alleviate this problem, the securities lending function should list on the stock borrow daily order form the securities firms from whom they are borrowing. As borrows are received, they should be compared to a borrow unit by a separate area. If a securities firm that is not on the list delivers stock, the separate area should check with the securities lending area to see if it is a needed borrow. If the item is accepted, a borrow will then be set up from the correct firm.

IMPROPER COLLATERALIZATION

"A stock loan transaction may be improperly collateralized through underpayment or overpayment of the required deposit or a deliberate failure to mark to market."

Prevention Mark to markets should be handled by the cashiering area according to predetermined procedures. They should be done on the day following the transaction. As a result of this, all marks of some minimum amount that reflect loans or borrows from the previous day should be verified by the cashiering area, to insure that they were the result of market fluctuation and not erroneous prices. Any item found to be erroneously priced should be brought to the attention of the cashier.

EXPENSE ACCOUNT MANIPULATION

"Expense accounts and credit cards may be misused by a stock loan representative for his own benefit or to make improper payment to employees of other organizations."

Prevention All securities lending representatives' expense accounts should be submitted on a monthly basis. They should be reviewed and approved by a manager different than the manager of the securities lending area.

In addition to the preventive measures mentioned above, firms should:

1. Establish credit policies related to borrowing and lending activities. Figure 11-3 provides a minimum that should be covered by such policies.

2. Assure that written contracts are reviewed by counsel and are on file before initiating borrowing and lending activity.

3. Assure a definite separation of functions between the Securities Lending Department and the Operations areas. Securities lending and borrowing personnel should not, for example, be phys-

ically located near securities. In addition, under no circumstances should they have responsibility for cash disbursement activities.

Credit Policy

General credit guidelines might be that a major firm should not lend to or borrow from firms unless the following specific criteria are met: NASD or exchange member firms must have a net worth of at least $3,000,000 as indicated on their most recent statement of financial condition. Other criteria might include guidelines to do business only with the following:

National Securities Clearing Corporation

Midwest Stock Exchange Clearing Corporations

Stock Clearing Corporation of Philadelphia

Banks with deposits over $100,000,000

Insurance companies with assets over $100,000,000

Colleges and universities whose portfolio valuation is over $50,000,000

Pension funds whose portfolio valuation is over $50,000,000

In addition to the above, the following should be considered as further control of a firm's credit policy:

1. Do not borrow from or lend to individuals.
2. Do not lend more than $15,000,000 to any one corporation.
3. Do not borrow more than $10,000,000 from any one corporation.

FIGURE 11-3. Establishing Firm Guidelines for Lending and Borrowing Securities

HOW TO MEASURE PROFITABILITY

Just like any other business, Operations Managers should measure how well they are doing in the securities lending/borrowing business. We'll look at a number of different criteria and you will have to determine what's best for your firm. Figure 11-4 provides a sample form that can be used to review the activity on a monthly basis.

The first thing to do is to set some standards, i.e., what do you expect to loan out on average? This number should be a function of at least two things: margin debits and securities borrowed. Total margin debits will tell you how much you potentially could loan, since firms are permitted to loan 140% of the margin debit owed by customers who have signed lending agreements. In the real world, you'll never approach that figure for various reasons (lack of loan consents, fails, shorts, etc.), but it is a good relative barometer. If margin debits are increasing, your loan numbers should be increasing. If you are borrowing securities, the minimum number you should have on loan is the amount you are borrowing, because you can demand that firms you borrow from borrow from you. If they say no, look for firms that will reciprocate.

The average cost of money during the month, times average securities loaned, provides the interest savings to the firm during the month. When you add to that number the amount the firm received on rebates from securities borrowed, you have a "gross interest saved" amount for the month. Now you should look at the firm's cost for this activity during the month:

Rebates paid out on loans

Business development expenses

Securities Lending Department expenses

Cashiering (and other) Department expenses

Clearing Corporation charges

Other

All these expenses should be reduced from the gross interest saved figures to arrive at a reasonable estimate of how much money did the activity really save the firm.

Figure 11-4 shows other information that should be reviewed on a trend basis. Once you gain some familiarity with the numbers, standards for each should be set up and reviewed monthly.

Average security loans

Interest savings @ average cost of money of _____

Rebates received on borrows

Gross interest saved

Less various expenses

    Rebates paid on loans
    Business development operation expenses
    Other departmental operating expenses
    Cashiering Department personnel expenses
    Clearing corporation charges
        Subtotal:
        Net interest saved

Other Information			
	Current Month	*Last Month*	*YTD*
Average margin debits			
Average security loans			
Loans as % of margin debits			
Rebates paid on securities Loaned			
Annualized rebates paid as % of securities loaned			
Average security borrows			
Rebates received			
Securities loaned over (under)			
Securities borrowed			

FIGURE 11-4. Securities Lending Department Profitability Analysis for the Month of: _____

APPENDIX: SECURITIES LENDING AGREEMENT

Agreement dated _____ between _____ of _____, a broker-dealer, as borrower, hereinafter referred to as "Borrower" and _____ of _____, as lender, hereinafter referred to as "Lender," setting forth the terms and conditions under which Lender may, from time to time, lend to Borrower certain securities against a pledge of collateral. Borrower and Lender as the parties hereto agree as follows:

1. *Loans of Securities.*

   1.1 Subject to the terms and conditions of this Agreement, either party hereto may orally initiate a transaction whereby Lender, may, from time to time, lend securities to Borrower. The parties shall agree orally on the terms of each Loan, including the issuer of the securities, the amount of securities to be lent, the basis of compensation, and the amount of Collateral to be delivered by Borrower, which terms may be amended during the Loan.

   Notwithstanding the provisions in this Agreement with respect to when a Loan occurs, a Loan hereunder shall not occur until the Loaned Securities and the Collateral therefor are delivered. The terms "Loan," "Loaned Securities," "Collateral," "Clearing Organization," and certain other terms are defined in Section 15 below.

   1.2 WITHOUT WAIVING ANY RIGHTS GIVEN TO THE LENDER HEREUNDER, IT IS UNDERSTOOD AND AGREED THAT THE PROVISIONS OF THE SECURITIES INVESTOR PROTECTION ACT OF 1970 MAY NOT PROTECT THE LENDER WITH RESPECT TO LOANED SECURITIES HEREUNDER AND THAT, THEREFORE, THE COLLATERAL DELIVERED TO THE LENDER MAY CONSTITUTE THE ONLY SOURCE OF SATISFACTION OF BORROWER'S OBLIGATIONS IN THE EVENT BORROWER FAILS TO RETURN THE LOANED SECURITIES.

2. *Deliveries of Loaned Securities.*

   2.1 Unless otherwise agreed, delivery of Loaned Securities by Lender hereunder shall be made on or before 12:30 P.M. on the day of the oral agreement to lend the securities if such agreement is made before 12:30 P.M., otherwise by 12:30 P.M. of the next Business Day.

   2.2 Lender shall deliver the Loaned Securities to Borrower by either (a) delivering to Borrower certificates representing the Loaned Securities together with duly executed stock or hand transfer power, as the case may be, with signatures guaranteed by a bank or a member firm of the New York

Stock Exchange, Inc., in which event the Lender shall list the Loaned Securities on a schedule and receipt, which Borrower shall execute and return when the Loaned Securities are received, or (b) causing the Loaned Securities to be credited to Borrower's account and debited to Lender's account at a Clearing Organization, as agreed to by the parties hereto, and such crediting and debiting shall result in receipt by Borrower and Lender of a Clearing Organization notice of such crediting and debiting which notice shall constitute a schedule of the Loaned Securities.

3. *Collateral.*

    3.1 Concurrently with the receipt of the Loaned Securities, but in no case later than the close of business on the day the Loaned Securities are delivered, Borrower shall deliver to Lender Collateral in an amount equal to the percentage of the market value of the Loaned Securities as agreed to by the parties (which shall be not less than 100% of the market value of the Loaned Securities) (the "Margin Percentage"). The Collateral shall be delivered by: (a) Borrower transferring funds by wire, (b) Borrower delivering to Lender a certified or bank check representing next-day New York Clearing House funds, (c) Borrower delivering to lender an irrevocable letter of credit issued by a bank as defined in section 3(a)(6)(A)-(C) of the Securities Exchange Act of 1934, (d) Borrower delivering to Lender United States Treasury obligations, (e) Lender causing the Clearing Organization to debit Borrower's account and to make a corresponding credit to Lender's account for the amount of the Collateral, or (f) such other means as are acceptable to the parties thereto.

    3.2 The Collateral delivered by Borrower to Lender, as adjusted pursuant to Section 8 below, shall be security for Borrower's obligations in respect of such Loan, and Borrower hereby pledges with, assigns to, and grants Lender a continuing security interest in, and a lien upon, the Collateral, which shall attach upon the delivery of the Collateral to Borrower.

In addition to the rights and remedies given to Lender hereunder, Lender shall have all the rights and remedies of a secured party under the New York Uniform Commercial Code. It is understood that Lender may use or invest the Collateral, if such consists of cash, at its own risk, but that Lender may not-pledge, repledge, hypothecate, rehypothecate, lend, relend, comingle, with other Collateral or with its own assets, the Collateral, if such consists of other than cash.

3.3 Except as provided in Section 13 hereunder, Lender shall be obligated to return the Collateral to Borrower on termination of the Loan upon tender to Lender of the Loaned Securities.

3.4 If, on any Business Day, Borrower delivers Collateral, as provided in Section 3.1 hereunder, and Lender does not deliver the Loaned Securities, Borrower shall have the absolute right to the return of the Collateral; and if, on any Business Day, Lender delivers Loaned Securities and Borrower does not deliver Collateral as provided in Section 3.1 hereunder, Lender shall have the absolute right to the return of the Loaned Securities.

4. *Fees for Loan.* Unless otherwise agreed, when the agreement to lend securities is made, the parties shall agree on the basis of compensation to be paid in respect of the Loan and the Borrower shall provide the Lender with a written confirmation of such basis of compensation. Unless otherwise agreed, any fee payable hereunder shall be payable (a) by Lender, in the case of Loaned Securities collateralized by cash, (i) before the _____ Business Day following the rendering of an invoice by Borrower, or (ii) immediately, in the event of a Default hereunder by Lender, or (b) by Borrower, in the case of Loaned Securities collateralized other than by cash, (i) before the _____ Business Day of the month following in which the fee was incurred, or (ii) immediately, in the event of a Default hereunder by Borrower.

5. *Termination of the Loan.* Unless otherwise agreed, Borrower may terminate a Loan on any Business Day by returning the

Loaned Securities before 11:30 A.M., New York City time on such day to Lender, and Lender may terminate a Loan on the fifth Business Day following the day on which Lender, prior to the close of business on that day, gives notice of termination of the Loan to Borrower. [Unless otherwise agreed, Lender may terminate a Loan of securities issued or guaranteed by the United States government or its agencies on the second Business Day following the day on which Lender, prior to the close of business on that day, gives notice of termination of the Loan to Borrower.] Unless otherwise agreed, Borrower shall, on or before such termination date, deliver the Loaned Securities to Lender, or cause the Loaned Securities to be credited to Lender's account at the Clearing Organization; provided, however, that upon such delivery by or on behalf of Borrower, Lender shall concurrently therewith deliver the Collateral (as adjusted pursuant to Section 8 below) to Borrower.[1]

6. *Rights of Borrower in Respect of the Loaned Securities.* Until a Loan is terminated in accordance herewith, Borrower shall have all of the incidents of ownership of the Loaned Securities, including the right to transfer the Loaned Securities to others. Lender hereby waives the right to vote the Loaned Securities during the term of the Loan.

7. *Dividends, Distributions, Etc.*

   7.1 Lender shall be entitled to receive all distributions made on or in respect of the Loaned Securities the record dates for which are during the term of the Loan and which are not otherwise received by Lender, to the full extent it would be so entitled if the Loaned Securities had not been lent to Borrower, including, but not limited to: (a) all property, (b) stock dividends, (c) securities received as a result of split ups of the Loaned Securities and distributions in respect thereof, (d) interest payments, and (e) all rights to purchase additional securities.

---

[1] Bracketed clause may be stricken if inapplicable hereunder.

7.2 Any cash distributions made on or in respect of the Loaned Securities, which Lender is entitled to receive pursuant to Section 7.1, shall be paid to Lender by Borrower upon receipt by Borrower so long as Lender is not in Default at the time of such receipt. Upon receipt of payment of any such cash dividends, distributions or interest by Borrower, Borrower shall forthwith pay the same to Lender. Non-cash distributions received by Borrower shall be added to the Loaned Securities and shall be considered such for all purposes, except that if the Loan has terminated, Borrower shall forthwith deliver the same to Lender.

7.3 Borrower shall be entitled to receive all distributions made on or in respect of non-cash Collateral the payment dates for which are during the term of the Loan and which are not otherwise received by Borrower, to the full extent it would be so entitled if the Collateral had not been delivered to Lender. Any distributions made on or in respect of such Collateral which Borrower is entitled to receive hereunder shall be paid by Lender to Borrower forthwith upon receipt by Lender so long as Borrower is not in Default at the time of such receipt.

8. *Mark to Market Margin.*

8.1 Borrower shall daily mark to market any Loan hereunder, and in the event that at the close of trading on any Business Day the value of all the Collateral delivered hereunder by Borrower to Lender shall be less than 100% of the market value of all the outstanding Loaned Securities, Borrower shall deliver additional Collateral by the close of the next Business Day so that the market value of additional Collateral when added to market value of the Collateral shall equal the 100% of the market value of the Loaned Securities. The Collateral may be delivered as provided in Section 3.1 above.

8.2 If the Margin Percentage agreed upon with respect to a Loan hereunder is greater than 100% of the market value of the Loaned Securities, and in the event at the close of trading on any Business Day the value of all the Collateral delivered hereunder by Borrower to Lender shall be less than that Margin Percentage of the market value of all the outstanding Loaned Securities, Lender may, by notice to Borrower, demand that Borrower deliver to Lender additional Collateral so that the market value of additional Collateral when added to the market value of the Collateral shall equal that agreed upon Margin Percentage of the market value of the Loaned Securities. Such delivery is to be made by 11:30 A.M., of the day of Lender's notice to Borrower if such notice is given before 11:30 A.M., otherwise by 11:30 A.M., of the next Business Day, and the Collateral may be delivered as provided in Section 3.1 above.

8.3   In the event that at the close of trading on any Business Day the value of all the Collateral delivered hereunder by Borrower to Lender shall be greater than the Margin Percentage of the market value of all the outstanding Loaned Securities, Borrower may, by notice to Lender, demand that the lender redeliver to Borrower such amount of Collateral selected by Borrower so that the market value of the Loaned Securities. Such delivery is to be made by 11:30 A.M., otherwise by 11:30 A.M. of the next Business Day, and the Collateral may be delivered as provided in Section 3.1 above.

8.4   Each party may mark the values to market pursuant to Section 8.1, 8.2 and 8.3 above (a) by separately valuing the Loaned Securities lent and the Collateral given in respect thereof on an issuer by issuer basis, or (b) by valuing in the aggregate all Loaned Security lent by Lender and the Collateral given in respect thereof by Borrower.

9. *Representations of the Parties Hereto.* The parties hereby make the following representations and warranties, which shall continue during the term of any Loan hereunder:

9.1   Each party hereto represents and warrants that (a) it has the power to execute and deliver this Agreement, to enter into the Loans contemplated hereby and to perform its obligations hereunder; (b) it has taken all necessary action to authorize such execution, delivery and performance; and (c) this Agreement constitutes a legal, valid and binding obligation enforceable against it.

9.2 Each party hereto represents and warrants that the execution, delivery and performance by it of this Agreement and each Loan hereunder will at all times comply with all applicable laws and regulations including those of applicable securities regulatory and self-regulatory organizations.

9.3 Each party hereto represents and warrants that it has made its own determination as to the tax treatment of any dividends, remuneration or other funds received hereunder.

9.4 Borrower represents and warrants that (a) it is a _____ duly organized and validly existing under the laws of _____, (b) it has, or will have at the time of delivery of any Collateral, the right to grant a first security interest therein subject to the terms and conditions hereof, and (c) it (or the party to whom it relends the Loaned Securities) is borrowing or will borrow the Loaned Securities [except for Loaned Securities that qualify as "exempted securities" under Regulation T of the Board of Governors of the Federal Reserve System] for the purpose of making delivery of such securities in the case of short sales, failure to receive securities required to be delivered, or as otherwise permitted pursuant to Regulation T.[2]

9.5 Lender represents and warrants that (a) it is a _____ duly organized and validly existing under the laws of _____, (b) it has, or will have at the time of delivery of any Loaned Securities, the right to deliver the Loaned Securities subject to the terms and conditions hereof, (c) no securities delivered to Borrower hereunder for any Loan have been or shall be obtained, directly or indirectly, from or using the assets of any Plan (which term means (1) any "employee benefit plan" as defined in Section 3 of the Employee Retirement Income Security Act of 1974, as

---

[2] Bracketed clause may be stricken if inapplicable hereunder.

amended, or (2) any "plan" as defined in Section 4975(e)(1) of the Internal Revenue Code of 1954, as amended, if Borrower or any affiliate of Borrower has discretionary authority or control with respect to the assets of such Plan or renders investment advice (within the meaning of 29 C.F.R. Section 2510.3(c)) with respect to the investment of the assets of such plan.

10. *Covenants.*

10.1 Each party hereto agrees that this Agreement and the Loans made hereunder shall be "securities contracts" for purposes of the Bankruptcy Code and any bankruptcy proceeding thereunder.

10.2 Borrower agrees to be liable as principal with respect to its obligations hereunder.

10.3 The Lender agrees either (1) to be liable as principal with respect to its obligations hereunder or (ii) (a) [to provide[3] Borrower prior to any Loan hereunder with a written list of accounts for which it intends to act as agent,] (b) to provide Borrower on request with information available to the Lender concerning the financial status of such accounts and (c) to identify prior to each loan the specific account or accounts for which it is acting in connection with such Loan.

10.4 Borrower has furnished, or promptly upon (and in any event within five (5) Business Days after) demand by Lender shall furnish, Lender with its most recent statement required to be furnished to customers pursuant to Rule 17a-5(c) of the Securities Exchange Act of 1934.

10.5 The Lender shall, if it is a party to this Agreement as a Plan or a trustee of a Plan, so notify Borrower upon the execution of this Agreement. If the Lender so notifies Borrower, Borrower shall promptly notify the Lender whether Borrower or any of its affiliates has any discretionary authority or control with respect to the assets of the Lender or of such Plan (as the case may be), or ren-

---

3 Bracketed clause may be stricken if inapplicable hereunder.

ders investment advice within the meaning of 29 C.F.R. Section 2510.3-21(c) with respect to the investment of the assets of the Lender or of such Plan (as the case may be). If the lender notifies Borrower that it is a party to this Agreement as a Plan or a trustee of a Plan, Borrower and Lender shall comply with the requirements of the Exemption published by the United States Department of Labor at 46 Fed. Reg. 7527.

11. *Events of Default.* All Loans between Borrower and Lender may (at the option of the non-defaulting party, exercised by notice to the defaulting party) be terminated immediately upon occurrence of any one or more of the following events (individually, a "Default"):

a) if any Loaned Securities shall not be delivered to Lender on the specified termination date of the Loan;

b) if any Collateral shall not be delivered to Borrower on the specified termination date of the Loan;

c) if either party shall fail to deliver or return Collateral as the case may be, as required by Section 8 hereof;

d) if either party shall fail to make the payment of distributions as required by Section 7 hereof, and such default is not cured within one Business Day of notice of such failure to Borrower or Lender, as the case may be;

c) if either party shall make a general assignment for the benefit of creditors, or shall admit in writing its inability to pay its debts as they become due, or shall file a petition in bankruptcy or shall be adjudicated a bankrupt or insolvent, or shall file a petition seeking reorganization, liquidation, dissolution or similar relief under any present or future statute, law or regulation, or shall seek, consent to or acquiesce in the appointment of any trustee, receiver or liquidator of it or any material part of its properties; or if any petition, not dismissed within 30 calendar days, is filed against a party hereto (other than by the contra party to this Agreement) in any court or before any agency alleging the bankruptcy or insolvency of such party or seeking any reorganization, arrangement, composition, readjustment, liquidation, dissolution of similar relief under any present or future statute, law or regulation, or the appointment of a receiver or trustee of all or any material part of such party's property;

(f)   if borrower shall have been suspended or expelled from membership or participation in any national securities exchange or association or other self-regulatory organization or if it is suspended from dealing in securities by any governmental agency; or

(g)   if Lender shall have its license, charter, or other authorization necessary to conduct a material portion of its business withdrawn, suspended or revoked by an applicable federal or state government or agency thereof.

12.   *Lender's Remedies.* In the event of any Default by Borrower under Section 11 hereof, Lender shall have the right, in addition to any other remedies provided herein or under applicable law (without further notice to Borrower), to purchase a like amount of the Loaned Securities in the principal market for such securities and may apply the Collateral to the payment of such purchase, after deducting therefrom all amounts, if any, due Lender under Section 7 and 14 hereof. In such event, Borrower's obligation to return the Loaned Securities shall terminate. Lender may also apply the Collateral to any other obligation of Borrower under this Agreement, including distributions paid to Borrower (and not forwarded to Lender) in respect of Loaned Securities. In the event the purchase price exceeds the amount of the Collateral, Borrower shall be liable to Lender for the amount of such excess (plus all amounts, if any, due to Lender hereunder) together with interest on all such amounts at the Prime Rate, as it fluctuates from day to day, from the date of such purchase until the date of payment of such excess. Lender shall have, as security for Borrower's obligation to pay such excess, a security interest in or right of setoff against any property of Borrower then held by Lender and any other amount payable by Lender to Borrower. The purchase price of securities purchased under this Section 12 shall include broker's fees and commissions and all other rea-

sonable costs, fees and expense related to such purchase. Upon the satisfaction of all obligations hereunder, any remaining Collateral shall be returned to Borrower.

13. *Borrower's Remedies.* In the event of a Default by Lender under Section 11 hereof, Borrower shall have the right, in addition to any other remedies provided herein or under applicable law (without further notice to Lender) to sell a like amount of the Loaned Securities in the principal market for such securities and to retain the proceeds of such sale. In such event, Borrower may treat the Loaned Securities as its own and Lender's obligation to return the Collateral shall terminate.

In the event the sale price received from such securities is less than the value of the Collateral, Lender shall be liable to Borrower for the amount of any deficiency (plus all amounts, if any, due to Borrower hereunder), together with interest on such amounts at the Prime Rate, as it fluctuates from day to day, from the date of such sale until the date of payment of such deficiency. Borrower shall have, as security for Lender's Obligation to pay such excess, a security interest in or right of setoff against any property of Lender then held by Borrower and any other amount payable by Borrower to Lender. In calculating this deficiency, there shall be deducted from the proceeds of the securities sold under this Section 13, broker's fees and commissions and all other reasonable costs, fees and expenses related to such sale. Upon the satisfaction of all Lender's obligations hereunder, any remaining Loaned Securities (or cash in an amount equal to the value of the Collateral on the termination date minus amounts which Borrower has received pursuant to this Section 13) shall be returned to Lender. Without limiting the foregoing, the parties hereto agree that they intend the Loans hereunder to be loans of securities and, as such, to be "securities contracts" as that term is defined in the Bankruptcy Code.

If, however, any Loan is deemed to be a loan of money by Borrower to Lender, then Borrower shall have, and Lender shall be deemed to have granted, a security interest in the Loaned Securities and the proceeds thereof.

14. *Transfer Taxes.* All transfer taxes with respect to the transfer of the Loaned Securities by Lender to Borrower and by Borrower to Lender upon termination of the Loan shall be paid by Borrower.

15. *Definitions.* For the purpose hereof:

    15.1 "Business Day" shall mean any day recognized as a settlement day by the New York Stock Exchange, Inc.

    15.2 "Collateral" shall mean, whether now owned or hereafter acquired, (a) that collateral permitted by Rule 15c3-3(b) under the Securities Exchange Act of 1934 and delivered to Lender pursuant to Section 3 or 8, and (b) all accounts in which such collateral is deposited and all securities and the like in which all cash collateral is invested or reinvested.

    15.3 "Clearing Organization" shall mean Depository Trust Company ("DTC"), or, if agreed to by the parties hereto, such other clearing agency at which Borrower and Lender (or Lender's agent) maintain accounts, or a Federal Reserve Bank which maintains a book-entry system.

    15.4 "Loan" shall mean a loan of securities hereunder.

    15.5 "Loaned Security" shall mean any security which is a security as defined in the Securities Exchange Act of 1934, [other than "exempt securities" as defined therein] delivered as a Loan hereunder until the Clearing Organization credits the Lender's accounts or the certificate for such security (or an identical security) is delivered or otherwise accepted back hereunder or until the security is replaced by purchase, except that, if any new or different security shall be exchanged, be deemed to become a Loaned Security in substitution for the former Loaned Security for which such exchange or sale of securities pursuant to Section 12 or 13 hereunder, such term shall include securities of the same issuer, class and quantity as the Loaned Securities, as adjusted pursuant to the preceding sentence.[4]

---

[4] Bracketed clause may be stricken if inapplicable hereunder.

15.6 "Prime Rate" shall mean the prime rate as quoted in the *Wall Street Journal* (New York Edition) for the Business Day preceding the date on which such determination is made. If more than one rate is so quoted, the prime rate shall be the average of the rates so quoted.

16. *Market Value.*

16.1 Unless otherwise agreed, if the principal market for the securities to be valued is a national securities exchange, their market value shall be determined for all purposes (except Section 11 and 12 hereof) by their last sale price on any such exchange on the preceding Business Day or, if there was no sale on that day, by the last sale price on the next preceding day on which there was a sale on any such exchange, all as quoted on the Consolidated Tape or, if not quoted on the Consolidated Tape, then as quoted by any such exchange.

16.2 Unless otherwise agreed, if the principal market for the securities to be valued is the over-the-counter market, their market value shall be determined as follows. If the securities are quoted on the National Association of Securities Dealers Automated Quotations System ("NASDAQ"), their market value shall be the closing sale price on NASDAQ on the preceding Business Day or, if the securities are issues for which last sale prices are not quoted on NASDAQ, the closing bid price on such day. If the securities to be valued are not quoted on NASDAQ, their market value shall be the highest bid quotation as quoted in any of the *Wall Street Journal,* the National Quotation Bureau pink sheets, the Salomon Brothers quotation sheets, quotation sheets of registered market makers and, if necessary, dealers' telephone quotations on the preceding Business Day. In each case, if the relevant quotation did not exist on such day, then the relevant quotation on the next preceding day in which there was such a quotation shall be the market value.

16.3 Unless otherwise agreed, if the securities to be valued are securities issued or guaranteed by the United States government or its agencies, their market value shall be the average of the bid and ask prices as quoted in the *Wall Street Journal* (New York Edition) for the Business day preceding the date on which such determination is made plus accrued interest to such date. If the securities are not so quoted on such day, their market value shall be determined as of the next preceding day on which they were so quoted.

17. *Applicable Law.* This Agreement shall be governed and construed in accordance with the laws of the state of New York.

18. *Waiver.* The failure of either party to insist upon strict adherence to any term of this Agreement on any occasion shall not be considered a waiver or deprive that party of the right thereafter to insist upon strict adherence to that term or any other term of this Agreement. All waivers in respect of a Default must be in writing.

19. *Remedies.* All remedies hereunder shall survive the termination of the relevant Loan, return of Loaned Securities or Collateral and termination of this Agreement.

20. *Miscellaneous.* This Agreement supersedes any other agreement between the parties concerning loans of securities between the parties hereto. This Agreement shall not be assigned by either party without the prior written consent of the other party. Subject to the foregoing, this Agreement shall be binding upon and shall enure to the benefit of the parties hereto and their respective heirs, representatives, successors and assigns.

This Agreement may be cancelled by either party upon giving written notice to the other, subject only to fulfillment of any obligations then outstanding. This Agreement shall not be modified, except by an instrument in writing signed by the party against whom enforcement is sought.

By: _____

_____
Title

By: _____

_____
Title

CHAPTER 12

Branch Office Operations

Every manager who has had the opportunity to work in a branch office appreciates the varied opportunities that experience provided. Branch Office Managers get involved with cashiering, trades processing, legal and regulatory issues, administration, customer service, Account Executive coddling and cajoling, personnel and a myriad of other issues. The typical Operations Manager in a branch office fast becomes a generalist because of the broader perspective required to succeed when you are are far away from "home office" or "main office" support.

In dealing with customers, Account Executives and regulators, the branch Operations Manager often becomes "the firm," because of the nature of the broad responsibilities. These responsibilities fall into the following categories:

Administration

Cash Management

Safeguarding Cash and Securities

Customer Service

Exception Handling/Problem Solving

ADMINISTRATION

The primary function of the branch office Operations Manager is to direct employees in their daily work activities. As such, the nature of the job is similar to a home Office Manager. However, there are other functions that they perform that are solely a branch Operations Manager's responsibility:

Maintaining coordination with all areas of operations and home office operating departments to ensure completion of daily requirements and to resolve operating problems as they occur.

Providing Account Executives with operational direction and assistance, resolving complex order processing or cashiering problems.

Maintaining proper staffing levels for the short and long term.

Evaluating affiliated office expenses and devising methods for effective cost management.

Tracking revenues for P&L statements prepared for the home office.

Establishing error reduction methods to improve office error records and reduce firm exposure.

Providing support and direction to the accounting area in handling bookkeeping related problems and assisting with correctable and collectable items.

Acting as a backup if necessary for all Operations area.

For a better understanding of the nature and scope of a branch Office Operations Manager's responsibilities refer to the organization chart displayed in Figure 12-1. This chart shows a typical operations organization in a branch office. You will note that each area has its own duties, with ultimate responsibility resting with the Operations Manager.

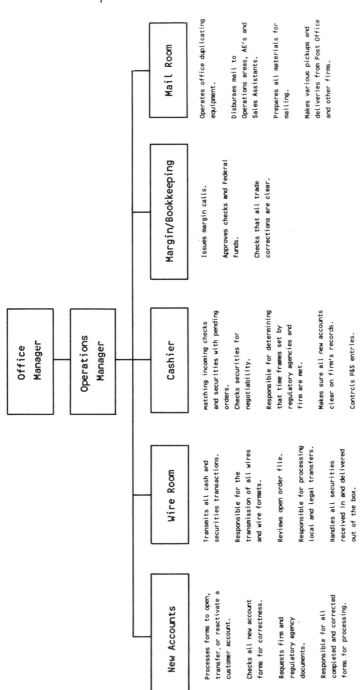

FIGURE 12-1. Branch Office Operations Organization Chart

Additionally, the manager is accountable for various reports that are not a part of the office's daily routine. These are displayed in Figure 12-2.

Report/Activity	Department	Frequency	Description
Local bank account reconciliation	Cashier	Monthly	Balance bank accounts ensure that all funds a being properly deposit and maximum utilizati the funds are achieved
Office box counts	Cashier	Weekly	Ensure that proper fol up is taking place on securities held in the and that no securities being used for unauth purposes.
Review of institutional accounts	Margin/Bookkeeping	Monthly	Ensure that no aged fa are outstanding and th funds owed to the firr being collected.
Review of employee accounts	Margin/Bookkeeping	Monthly	Ensure that no unauth trading or journal entr are taking place.
Confirmation of transfers	Cashier	Monthly	Letters are sent to tra agents on all transfers exchanges over 30 day old.
Preparation of budgets	Operations	Annually	Comply with corporate guidelines in preparati upcoming year's expen

FIGURE 12-2. Nondaily Operational Activities

CASH MANAGEMENT

The establishment of good branch cash management systems is important not only for the daily processing of office business, but more importantly, for the overall cash management functions of the organization. With today's high interest rates, it is extremely important to have maximum usage of all funds passing through the branch office. The goal is to save as much as possible on interest expense while earning as much as possible on interest income.

There are various methods of making the best use of funds flowing through the branch office. The most common of these are Federal Funds (Fed Funds) and Clearing House Funds.

Fed Funds are excess reserves of member banks of the Federal Reserve System that are immediately available and can be moved from one account to another without any delays or additional clearing time. A simple example of the transfer of Fed Funds is shown in Figure 12-3. Because Fed Funds are available on a same day basis, there is no loss of interest to the firm.

Clearing House or next day funds are monies represented by a personal or a corporate check that must go through a local or regional bank clearing function before an account credit is given to payee.

The branch is responsible for insuring that all payments received are either in Fed Funds or Clearing House Funds. These payments must be received by settlement date prior to the closing of the local bank to insure availability.

Aside from the type of funds to be used, the Operations Manager must perform other cashiering functions:

Decide which bank to use for the deposit and withdrawal of funds. Consideration should be given to bank fees, banking hours and location of bank.

Ensure that your account is immediately credited with funds received.

Ensure that all funds being wired into or out of your account are done on a timely basis.

Periodically review all cashiering relationships to ensure that the above requirements are still being met.

Another important part of managing the cash flow in the office is the approval and processing of customer extensions. An extension is the amount of credit that a securities firm may advance to their clients for purchasing securities on margin. Extensions are governed by Regulation T (Reg T), as discussed in Chapter 10.

The Operations Manager should assign one person in the Operations area the responsibility of processing extensions. With the approval of the Office Manager, an extension and/or buy-in letter is sent to the customer with a copy filed in a master file. Typical examples of these letters are shown in Figures 12-4 and 12-5.

The chart displayed in Figure 12-6 lists significant guidelines and valid reasons for granting extension requests.

Corp ——————— *Initiating* ——————— *Local* ——————— *Receiving Fed*
                        Bank   *Fed*   *Bank*

                    10:00 a.m.   10:05 a.m.   10:30 a.m.

                                                                     Receiving
                                                                     Bank
                                                                            11:00 a.m.
                                                                     Customer
                                                                     Notification
                                                                          ?

        Federal Reserve Districts:

1. Boston   7. Chicago
2. New York   8. St. Louis
3. Philadelphia   9. Minneapolis
4. Cleveland   10. Kansas City
5. Richmond   11. Dallas
6. Atlanta   12. San Francisco

FIGURE 12-3. Transfer of Fed Funds

Date: _____

Ref A/C: _____

Transaction: _____

Dear,

Due to the recent transaction(s) in your account, you are required to deposit sufficient funds to satisfy Regulation T of the Federal Reserve Board. To date we have not received these funds.

Regulation T authorizes us, under unusual circumstances, to request an extension of time on your behalf from the New York Stock Exchange. We have today requested from the New York Stock Exchange an extension to _____,on this unpaid purchase call of _____.

In the event that this payment is not received by us by the close of business of the New York Stock Exchange on _____, we will be required to liquidate a sufficient number of the securities purchased to cover the amount due and hold you responsible for any resulting deficiency. This liquidation will take place at the opening of the New York Stock Exchange on _____, or as soon as practicable thereafter.

New York Stock Exchange rules limit the number of extension requests they will grant on behalf of a customer. Should the New York Stock Exchange deny the extension we have requested on your behalf, we will be required to take liquidating action upon receipt of the denial. We hope this information will be of service to you.

If you have any questions concerning this matter, please contact your Account Executive immediately.

Very truly yours,

FIGURE 12-4. Extension Letter

Used by permission of Merrill Lynch, Pierce, Fenner & Smith Incorporated.

Date: _____

Ref A/C: _____

Dear,

On _____, we sold for your account _____

_____.

Pursuant to Rule 15c3-3 of the Securities and Exchange Commission, we are required to take possession of these securities by _____. In the event that these securities are not received by us on that date, we are required to purchase these securities for your account and hold you responsible for any resulting deficiency. This purchase will take place on _____, or as soon as practicable thereafter.

If your records indicate that you have already delivered these securities to us, please notify your Account Executive immediately.

Very truly yours,

By: _____

FIGURE 12-5. Buy-in Letter

SAFEGUARDING CASH AND SECURITIES

As with any other organization, securing the office against theft is of primary importance. Because of the constant flow of cash, checks and securities in the office, the probability of theft is increased dramatically. Therefore, the manager must ensure that proper security measures are in place. The chart in Figure 12-7 shows some of the measures an Operations Manager should take to protect the firm against theft.

Guidelines

No more than five extensions will be granted in any 12-month period to any one retail or institutional customer.

An additional request on the same transaction is counted as a separate request towards the total of five.

Extensions should not be requested for exempt securities (cash accounts).

Extensions should not be requested for funds due for amounts less than $500.00.

All extension requests must be approved by the office manager.

Valid Reasons for Extension Request

Unable to contact customer. (Specific efforts must be made to reach the customer to determine why payment was not yet received.)

Unacceptable or improperly drawn check received from customer and returned for new check.

Awaiting legal documents.

Postal delays in receiving check from customer.

Death in customer's immediate family.

Customer is unexpectedly taken ill and is incapable of issuing check.

Awaiting appointment of executive or administration of decreased customer's account.

Acts of God or other abnormal conditions.

FIGURE 12-6. Granting of Reg T Extensions

Overall, it is important for you as the Branch Office Operations Manager to set up all guidelines for the operations staff as well as the sales personnel. All personnel should be aware of all policies, procedures and deadlines and should be required to adhere to them.

Safeguard	Guidelines	Comments
Safe deposit box at local bank	The bank must allow early access to the securities as well as being located near the office	A close location limits the amount of time your personnel must carry the securities
Secured area for funds to be processed	Limit the cashiering area to authorized personnel only	Reduces the number of people who have access to funds
Limit cash deposits	$100.00 per day per customer	Reduces the amount of cash held in the office
Double check on funds/ securities received	Should be performed by a supervisor or another cashier	Reduces errors and risk of theft
Double-check bank deposit slips	Should be performed by a supervisor or another cashier	Ensures that the cash deposit was received by the bank
Office safe	Do not allow deposits after a specified hour of the day to coincide with local banking hours	Office safe allows exceptions to be made

FIGURE 12-7. Safeguarding Cash and Securities

CUSTOMER SERVICE

NEW ACCOUNTS

The servicing of the customer begins with the opening of the account. In today's complex investment market, there are a vast array of accounts that a customer can open and all require specialized servicing. The chart shown in Figure 12-8 lists the most common types of accounts in which a customer might express interest.

Because the securities industry is so complex, there are many rules and regulations set forth by the various regulatory bodies (SEC, NYSE, AMEX, etc.) that must be followed. This is especially true when opening a new account. As stated in New York Stock Exchange Rule #405 a securities firm is required to "know its customer." Compliance with this rule requires that specific documentation be on file before an account is allowed to do various types of trading.

Account*	Definition	Documents required
Cash	Customer account in which all transactions are paid for in full and the customer takes delivery of securities or leaves them on deposit in the account	New account form
Margin	Customer accounts to which credit is extended by the corporation under "Reg T"; the accounts owe the firm money against securities	New account form, hypothecation, truth and lending letter
Custodian	Cash account with special "securities segregation" features, whereby securities are separately stored in alphabetical order by issue; can be held in customer or street name	New account form, custodian agreement
Commodity	Customer wishes to trade in commodities	Commodity account agreement
Speculative	Individual account with high speculative risk	New account form, financial, net worth documentation
Trade	Nonindividual accounts which use the commodity future market for any purpose except speculation	Commodity hedging agreement
Joint	An account opened by two or more people with common ownership rights in the account	New account form
Joint with right of survivorship	Provides that upon the death of either joint tenant the entire interest in the account shall be vested in the survivor(s) and the estate of the deceased will have no further interest	Joint account with right of survivorship agreement
Joint without right of survivorship	The survivor does not become sole owner of the entire account	Joint account without right of survivorship agreement

*If joint accounts are traded on margin, margin account documents are required.

FIGURE 12-8. Major Types of Accounts

The most common types of documentation are:

Hypothecation (Hypo) Agreement. A written agreement between the customer and securities firm that details the rules under which the account is opened and carried. It is also referred to as a lending consent agreement.

Joint Account Agreement. An agreement that must be signed by all parties to a joint account. Details of the agreement may differ, however one thing remains in common, and that is that any party to the account may make purchase or sale transactions.

Power of Attorney. A signed document that empowers a second party to act on behalf of the signer.

In addition, the manager must know who is authorized to enter orders for an account and if the required documentation from the customer is on file. By accepting orders or instructions from unauthorized personnel you may be opening the door to possible legal actions against your firm. A typical new account form is displayed in Figure 12-9. To properly "know your customer" all information requested must be received.

In addition to receiving and keeping on file the various customer documents, it is important to ensure that the customer has received the various disclosures that pertain to the type of trading that a customer is doing. For example, if the account is trading options, an options prospectus must be supplied to the customer prior to accepting any options orders. Similarly, if a customer is trading on margin, a disclosure must be given as to how and when margin interest will be charged.

As we all know, the opening of an account is not as simple a process as it might seem to be. The flow chart displayed in Figure 12-10 gives you a step-by-step diagram that should be followed when opening an account. With the threat of legal action a very real possibility, it is critically important that the initial stages in the life of an account be handled properly. One "must" that the Operations area should be doing is time stamping all documents, letters, instructions and orders upon receipt. This procedure becomes invaluable during audits (both internal and external), as well as when answering routine questions from Account Executives and customers.

Merrill Lynch

Individual Client New Account Form

New Account # | Transferred From # | Financial Consultant # | Tax ID #

Reference Codes

A Income and Net Worth

A	Under - $ 24,999
B $	25,000 - $ 49,999
C $	50,000 - $ 99,999
D $	100,000 - $ 149,999
E $	150,000 - $ 249,999
F $	250,000 - $ 499,999
G $	500,000 - $ 999,999
H $	1,000,000 - $4,999,999
I	$5,000,000 - and over

Required Documents: ○ Branch DOCS ○ CAD to Client ○ CAD to Branch **Tefra Doc in hand:** ○ Yes ○ No

Participant #1 Tax Reporting Number

Account Title

Mailing Address

Participant #1 Contact Phone Numbers

City | State | Zip

Business Phone ( )

Country

Home Phone ( )

Are all account participants US citizens and US residents? ○ Yes ○ No If **No**, answer these three questions.

Is any account participant or his/her spouse employed by a NASD member or any other financial services company? ○ Yes ○ No If **Yes**, indicate participants below.

Year(s) at Residence | Rent Own

Enter Social Security numbers for secondary account participants.

B Ownership Type

01	Single
02	JT / WROS
03	JT / ATBE
04	JT / TIC
05	JT / COMM
06	UGMA
07	UTMA
08	Trust-Living
09	Trust-Living Bank as Trustee
10	Trust-Testamentary Bank as Trustee
11	Trust-Testamentary
12	Estate-Executor
13	Estate-Administrator
14	Unincorporated Investment Club
15	Committee
16	Guardian
17	Conservator Estate of
18	Conservator Prop of
19	AMUL-GA
20	JT/Surv Mart - WI (Joint Survivor Marital - Wisconsin)
21	JT/Marital - WI (Joint Marital - Wisconsin)

	Country of Citizenship	Residence	Part. has, or has applied for SS#?	Client employed by:	Client's Spouse employed by:	
Part #1			○ Yes ○ No	○ ML ○ NASD ○ Other Fncl Svcs	○ ML ○ NASD ○ Other Fncl Svcs	
Part #2			○ Yes ○ No	○ ML ○ NASD ○ Other Fncl Svcs	○ ML ○ NASD ○ Other Fncl Svcs	#2
Part #3			○ Yes ○ No	○ ML ○ NASD ○ Other Fncl Svcs	○ ML ○ NASD ○ Other Fncl Svcs	#3
Part #4			○ Yes ○ No	○ ML ○ NASD ○ Other Fncl Svcs	○ ML ○ NASD ○ Other Fncl Svcs	#4

Required Account Information *Required for all accounts*

Account Type	Trade Type	Ownership Type	Number of Signatories	Investment Objectives	Account Risk Factor
○ 01 CMA	○ Margin			○ Income	○ Conservative
○ 02 CBA	○ Cash			○ Growth	○ Moderate
○ 03 Subaccount					
○ 10 Ind. Investor Acct.	○ Flex Credit			○ Total Return	○ Aggressive

Authorized Account Individuals Information (Unformatted Accts)

C	TITLE	NAME	FIRST/MI/LAST	SFX	CAPACITY

C AAI Capacity

01	Client
02	JTWROS
03	ATBE
04	TIC
05	COMPRP
06	CUST - MINOR
07	CUST - MINOR
08	TTEE - GRANTR
09	TTEE - GRANTR
10	TTEE - GRANTR
11	TTEE - GRANTR
12	EXEC - EST OF
13	ADMIN - EST OF
14	PART
15	COMM
16	GUARD - BENE
17	CONS - EST OF
18	CONS - PRP OF
19	CUST - MINOR
20	SURPRO
21	MARPRO

Dividend / Interest Usage
○ Hold
○ Monthly
○ As Credited

Disclose Name & Address?
○ Yes
○ No

Does the client authorize Merrill Lynch to disclose their name, address, and securities positions to corporate issuers under a SEC rule designed to permit issuers to communicate directly with non-objecting owners?

Use additional Sheets if Necessary

RULE 405 REQUIREMENT

Client Information (Participant #1)

Annual Salary | Household Annual Income

Household Net Worth Exclusive of Home | % Tax Bracket

Client Gender ○ M ○ F | Date of Birth Month Day Year

Marital Status ○ Married ○ Single ○ Widowed | Number of Dependent Children

Employment Status ○ Employed / Not Owner ○ Homemaker ○ Business Owner ○ Student ○ Not Employed ○ Retired

Years Employed

Employer Name

Employer Address

Type of Business

Position/Title | Occupation

Disability (Hearing Impaired)

Prior Trading Experience ○ Seldom ○ Cash ○ Moderate ○ Margin ○ Active ○ None

Product Experience ○ Mutual Funds/UIT ○ Options ○ Bonds ○ Ltd. Partnerships ○ Equities ○ Futures ○ None

Other Brokerage Firms Dealt With | **Banking Information** Bank Name

Branch Location

Spousal Information (Participant #1)

Name

SS# | Date of Birth

Spousal Employment Status ○ Employed / Not Owner ○ Homemaker ○ Business Owner ○ Student ○ Not Employed ○ Retired

Employer Name

Position/Title

NON-RESIDENT ALIEN INFORMATION (Participant #1)
If client is a non-resident alien, enter passport number and country of issue.

Passport #

Country of Issue

Complete Only If Applicable

CMA Master Financial Service Master CMA

Master Acct. No.

Mutual Fund Advisor — Requested

D Joint A/C Relationship
○ Married
○ Related
○ Not Related

E State Code

F UGMA/UTMA Custodial Age

G Date Living Trust Established

Pledge Collateral
○ 1 Parent Power
○ 2 Mortgage 100
○ 3 Pledge to MLBFS
○ 4 Pledge to Outside Bank
○ 5 Pledge to MLCC (Omega)
○ 6 Pledge to MLIB (Consults)
○ 7 Pledge to MLB&T
○ 8 Pledge to MLNF

D Joint A/C Relationship
Enter relationship of account participants for jointly-owned accounts. See *State Code* below.

E State Code
Enter state of residence. **UGMA/UTMA Accounts:** Enter state whose laws apply, as identified by client.

F UGMA/UTMA Custodial Age
Enter age at which custodianship ends per applicable state's laws. See *State Code* Above.

G Date Living Trust Established
Enter the date on which the trust was established which will be incorporated into the account title when entered into the CIS name and address system.

Business Name *If Sole Owner*

Futures Account Type
○ 1 Speculative
○ 2 Collateral
○ 3 Trade
○ 4 Options Only

Futures Margin Requirement
○ 1 ML Full
○ 2 ML Minimum
○ 3 Exchange Minimum / Speculative
○ 4 ML Trade
○ 5 Exchange Trade

Additional Service Features
○ Invstmt Adv
○ POA
○ DAC/RAP
○ Employee Stock
○ VOCON
○ Consults
○ Escrow
○ ML Employee
○ Multi-Curr
○ Gold Bullion
○ Reactivate

Manager's Approval Required
○ Confidential ○ Discretionary ○ Custodian ○ Asset Power

Managerial Approval

Options
○ Equity
○ Index
○ Foreign Currency
○ Debt
○ HAM (Hold all Mail)
○ TOD (Transfer on Death)

Residential Address of Participant #1 *(If different from mailing address.)*

Use Supplemental Account Information Form for Duplicate Instructions, Registered Investment Advisor Information and Power of Attorney information.

Code 6017R (R 5-94)

SEE REVERSE SIDE FOR APPROVALS SECTION AND ADDITIONAL CLIENT PROFILE SEGMENTS

FIGURE 12-9. New Account Form

Client Information (Participant #2)

Residential Address _____

City _____ State _____ Zip _____

Country _____

Ⓐ Annual Salary	Ⓐ Household Annual Income	Ⓐ Household Net Worth *Exclusive of Home*	% Tax Bracket

| Client Gender ◯ M ◯ F | Date of Birth ⌊ ⌋ Month Day Year | Marital Status ◯ Married ◯ Single ◯ Widowed | Number of Dependent Children ⌊ ⌋ |

Employment Status
◯ Employed/Not Owner ◯ Business Owner ◯ Not Employed
◯ Homemaker ◯ Student ◯ Retired

Employer Name _____

Employer Address _____

_____

Type of Business _____

Position/Title _____ Occupation _____

Prior Trading Experience ◯ Seldom ◯ Moderate ◯ Active
◯ Cash ◯ Margin ◯ None

Product Experience
◯ Mutual Funds/UIT ◯ Bonds ◯ Equities
◯ Options ◯ Ltd. Partnerships ◯ Futures ◯ None

Other Brokerage Firms Dealt With **Banking Information**
_____ Bank Name _____
_____ Branch Location _____

Spousal Information (Participant #2)

Name _____

SS# _____ Date of Birth ⌊ ⌋ Month Day Year

Employment Status
◯ Employed/Not Owner ◯ Business Owner ◯ Not Employed
◯ Homemaker ◯ Student ◯ Retired

Employer Name _____

Position/Title _____

Non-Resident Alien Information (Participant #2)
If client is a non-resident alien, enter passport number and country of issue.

Passport # _____

Country of Issue _____

Reference Codes
Ⓐ **Income and Net Worth**

A	Under - $ 24,999
B	$ 25,000 - $ 49,999
C	$ 50,000 - $ 99,999
D	$ 100,000 - $ 149,999
E	$ 150,000 - $ 249,999
F	$ 250,000 - $ 499,999
G	$ 500,000 - $ 999,999
H	$1,000,000 - $ 999,999
I	$5,000,000 - and over

Client Information (Participant #3)

Residential Address _____

City _____ State _____ Zip _____

Country _____

Ⓐ Annual Salary	Ⓐ Household Annual Income	Ⓐ Household Net Worth *Exclusive of Home*	% Tax Bracket

| Client Gender ◯ M ◯ F | Date of Birth ⌊ ⌋ Month Day Year | Marital Status ◯ Married ◯ Single ◯ Widowed | Number of Dependent Children ⌊ ⌋ |

Employment Status
◯ Employed/Not Owner ◯ Business Owner ◯ Not Employed
◯ Homemaker ◯ Student ◯ Retired

Employer Name _____

Employer Address _____

_____

Type of Business _____

Position/Title _____ Occupation _____

Prior Trading Experience ◯ Seldom ◯ Moderate ◯ Active
◯ Cash ◯ Margin ◯ None

Product Experience
◯ Mutual Funds/UIT ◯ Bonds ◯ Equities
◯ Options ◯ Ltd. Partnerships ◯ Futures ◯ None

Other Brokerage Firms Dealt With **Banking Information**
_____ Bank Name _____
_____ Branch Location _____

Spousal Information (Participant #3)

Name _____

SS# _____ Date of Birth ⌊ ⌋ Month Day Year

Employment Status
◯ Employed/Not Owner ◯ Business Owner ◯ Not Employed
◯ Homemaker ◯ Student ◯ Retired

Employer Name _____

Position/Title _____

Non-Resident Alien Information (Participant #3)
If client is a non-resident alien, enter passport number and country of issue.

Passport # _____

Country of Issue _____

USE ADDITIONAL FORM FOR ACCOUNTS WITH MORE THAN THREE (3) PARTICIPANTS

Approvals

Client Source
◯ Walk-In
◯ Prospect
◯ Call-In
◯ Known Personally
◯ Referral

◯ Existing

Referred By
Name _____
Street _____
City _____ State _____ Zip _____
Account # _____

Initial Transaction
Buy/Sell Quantity _____ Symbol _____
Good Faith deposit waived? ◯ Yes
Deposit _____ ◯ Money ◯ Securities

Financial Consultant's Signature _____ Date _____

Managerial Approval _____ Date _____

Use Supplemental Account Information Form for Duplicate Instructions,
Registered Investment Advisor Information and Power of Attorney Information.
Code 6017R (R 5-94)

FIGURE 12-9. (*Continued*)

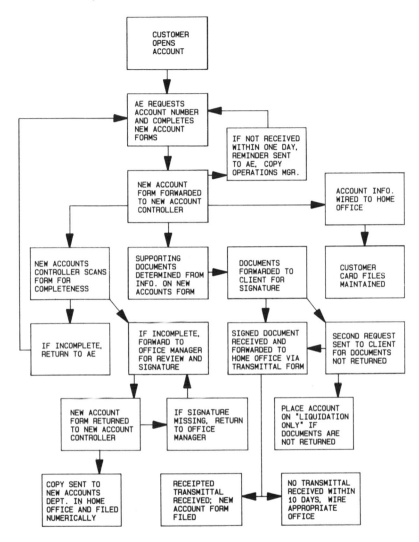

FIGURE 12-10. New Accounts

TRADES PROCESSING

Once you are satisfied that all the necessary documents have been received, and all paperwork has been completed, the actual trading and processing of transactions can begin. The flow chart shown in Figure 12-11 illustrates the procedures an office takes to process a trade. Note that the wire operator (wire room) is an integral part of this process.

It is important to remember that any errors or unnecessary delays during the processing of a trade could conceivably cost the firm money. Mail delays for instance would necessitate a call from the Account Executive to the customer with the confirm information. This will ensure proper settlement of any funds or securities with the customer.

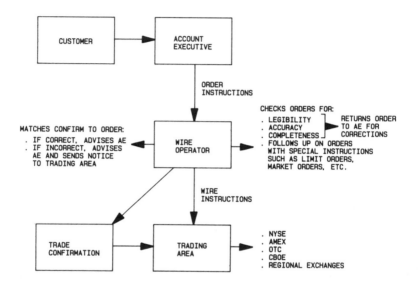

FIGURE 12-11. Processing a Trade

NEGOTIABILITY

Earlier in this chapter we covered the timely receipt and payment of funds. Many transactions require the receipt or delivery of securities, which involves the questions of negotiability. Negotiable securities are securities which permit a transfer of title by assignment of delivery. Any securities being received from the customer must be checked for negotiability prior to releasing the proceeds of a sale to a customer. All registered securities must be properly endorsed and if necessary have the proper legal documents attached. Without these, transfer agents will not change the registration on the securities and your firm will be unable to use them.

Nondetachable securities create problems for your firm in making delivery to the buyers of securities. Any delay in re-registering certificates could also lead to the seller receiving dividends to which they are not entitled. Naturally, this would create additional work for your staff in preparing dividend claim forms.

A legal transfer guide which contains such things as requirements for negotiability should be prepared for the cashier in the office as a reference prior to making payment to a customer. The cashier should be required to check all certificates for negotiability before forwarding them to a central processing area for re-registration. Additionally, a simple checklist should be kept readily available by the cashier so that the requirements for negotiability are satisfied. This list should include the following items:

Make sure the back of the certificate is signed by the registered owner exactly as the name appears on the face of the certificate.

Affix signature guarantee stamp beneath the registered owner's signature.

If stock powers are presented in lieu of certificates being signed, follow the same procedures as above.

Ensure that all legal documents accompany the certificates in the case of certificates that cannot be signed by the registered owner. For example, if the security is multiply-owned and one of the owners is deceased or if the securities are owned by a corporation.

Special care should be taken on bearer certificates to assure proof of ownership. If at all possible, listings should be available indicating certificates and certificate numbers of stolen securities.

EXCEPTION HANDLING AND PROBLEM RESOLUTION

Once a trade has settled (securities are delivered and payments are made) the primary function of the operations staff with regard to servicing the account is complete. However, the job is not over. With any type of paper processing, or for that matter with any operation, there are always errors or exceptions. In this case, the errors can be caused by the Account Executive, the branch Operations area, or the home office Operations area. It is the responsibility of the branch office Operations staff to take the necessary steps to reach an immediate resolution of any problem. There are basically two types of errors: 1) those that require market action to correct, and 2) those that can be corrected without taking market action.

Obviously the market action errors must receive immediate attention and be treated with the priority of a market order. When an error is uncovered, which usually happens when the execution report is compared to the trade ticket, a correction request should be prepared immediately. Many firms are using a standard correction wire format similar to that shown in Figure 12-12.

This wire, after being sent to the proper home office area, should then be kept in a pending file for follow-up until the correction has been made.

Non-market action errors should also receive prompt attention as they may eventually turn out to be a market action problem. Requests for these problems should also be sent on the standard correction wire.

Figure 12-13 lists some of the more common branch office trading errors and solutions.

Although many of the errors that occur in the home office could not have been prevented by the branch office, the quick reaction by a branch office employee in resolving a problem could save the firm considerable amounts of money. The Operations Manager should consider the following measures of preventing or reducing the amount of errors charged to the office:

A properly trained staff should be in place to handle errors and customer inquires. Remember, the branch office is the first resource for customer service.

Cross-training within the Operations staff ensures that a qualified person is always available.

Contact lists of home office personnel should be readily available to help solve problems unanswerable at the local level.

Training manuals and/or job outlines should be available for new employees and as a reference for longer term employees.

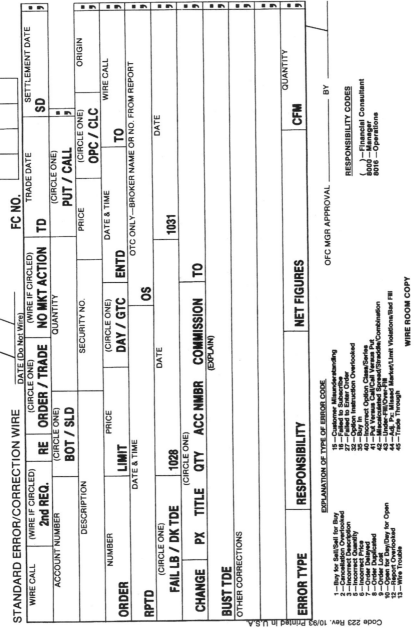

FIGURE 12-12. Standard Correction Wire Format

Type of Error	Action to be Taken
Order entered in reverse (buy should be sell)	Market action
Order entered with incorrect quantity	Market action
Order entered with incorrect security description	Market action
Order entered with incorrect price	Market action
Order entered with incorrect account number	Journal entry
Order entered with incorrect account number	Confirm and billing change
Order delayed	Market action
DK (Don't Know) trade.	Cancel trade or market action
Option orders entered with incorrect expiration month, strike price, type (put/call)	Market action

FIGURE 12-13. Common Branch Office Trading Errors

CHAPTER 13

Operations Management Information Reporting

All Operations Managers wish they had better reporting mechanisms to give them a "picture" of what's happening in the organization. This chapter provides specific information on how to structure Operations reports on processing performance, what volume indicators are important, how to assess Operations impact on regulatory capital charges, what customer information is important, and which primary indicators are reflective of Operations performance. Each section is discussed separately but firms should have one report, containing all the indicators issued on at least a weekly basis.

MONITORING BUSINESS INPUT AND OUTPUT THROUGH EXCEPTION REPORTING

Because of the vast amount of information available to management, it's important that information be presented on an "exception basis" only. The data and reports indicated below are intended to provide the basis for an "information system" for use by Operations Managers. They are designed to provide full disclosure of essential and timely operational and funds flow data for use in determining and controlling the elements affecting security processing, settlement procedures and funds flows affecting net interest income. They consist of information intended as a measure of efficiency, capacity, and control to provide management with status on trend information relative to the indicated department's efforts.

Various stock exchanges, regulatory bodies, and management consultants have for years attempted to develop management information and control systems that would provide information on the operations status of a given brokerage firm. These systems, while "better than nothing," have attempted to measure that status by comparing statistics from one firm to those of another firm, a method often found to be ineffective due to the unique characteristics of firms in the securities industry. Standards should be set, and performance data relative to standards should be presented on a weekly or monthly basis as needed. Whichever system is used should have the following objectives:

1. To function as a control system by providing timely information on the status of various items indicative of processing intensity.

2. To provide "early warning" information on possible future problem areas due to stretching of capacity limits or other reasons.

3. To provide a measure of the efficiency of the processing cycle through the use of funds flow data and other relative statistics.

4. To provide actionable information on funds flows resulting from securities processing and customer activity.

Let's take a look at the various indicators that can be used by firms in these areas: Volume, Processing and Control, Customer Information, Regulatory Capital Charges, and Financing. In each case, examples of reports are given so that a reporting system can be set up.

VOLUME INDICATORS—WHAT'S IMPORTANT?

Figure 13-1 shows what a typical weekly report on volume indicators may look like. As you can see, the report is organized to show historical information. These measures provide information on the volume of transactions being processed through the firm, and contain a number of indicators to highlight potential problem areas at the very beginning of a processing cycle, for example, Purchase and Sales, Stock Record, late reports, and so forth.

REPORTING ON VOLUME IN MAJOR MARKETS

Most firms will want information relative to those markets in which they provide service to customers and/or in which the firm trades. Typical markets are listed in Figure 13-2.

Aside from the volume on these markets, information could be provided relative to the firm's share of the various markets.

Now let's take a look at defining what we are attempting to measure. Each caption below is indexed to the Volume Indicator Report shown in Figure 13-1.

(1) TRANSACTIONS PROCESSED

The event which is counted is any data record entered into the P&S system for clearance in order to confirm the trade and balance the various clearance and settlement accounts of the firm. Any given trade can have one or more executions, so this measure is the one that provides data on actual work that must be done.

(2) TRADES PROCESSED

The event which is counted is all customer agency trades and all principal trades counted on the house side only. It is probably more indicative of sales efforts, whereas "transactions" are more indicative of Operations processing volume.

(3) THROUGH (8)

These items would indicate potential problem areas due to substantial increases in volume, and permit management to respond before the problems flow through the trade processing cycle to the settlement processing cycle. Operations Managers should try to keep these numbers as low as possible.

(9) ANALYSIS OF P&S PURCHASE AND SALE CORRECTIONS BY SOURCE OF ERROR

Highlights P&S corrections by source, providing ability to quickly identify error-prone areas. As soon as you spot problems here you can go right to the offending area.

		Daily Average Current Week	Daily Average Prior Week	Daily Average Last 4 Weeks
(1)	Transactions Processed:			
	Listed - Stocks and Bonds	_____	_____	_____
	OTC Stocks	_____	_____	_____
	OTC Corporate Bonds	_____	_____	_____
	Municipal Bonds	_____	_____	_____
	U.S. Government Bonds	_____	_____	_____
	G.N.M.A. Bonds	_____	_____	_____
	Options	_____	_____	_____
	Syndicate Stocks & Bonds	_____	_____	_____
	Other	_____	_____	_____
	Total	_____	_____	_____
(2)	Trades Processed	_____	_____	_____
(3)	Cancels & Setups	_____	_____	_____
(4)	Number of trades not processed on trade day	_____	_____	_____
(5)	Average time last trade was processed	_____	_____	_____
(6)	Number of days blotters unbalanced at close of business	_____	_____	_____
(7)	Aggregate amount of differences on unbalanced blotters at close of business friday—Debits	_____	_____	_____
	Credits	_____	_____	_____
(8)	Uncompared trades open past settlement date:			
	Items	_____	_____	_____
	Value	_____	_____	_____
(9)	Analysis of P&S corrections processed during the week by *source* of error:			
	Floor NYSE & AMEX	_____	_____	_____
	Block Department	_____	_____	_____
	OTC Department	_____	_____	_____
	N.Y. Communications	_____	_____	_____
	Bond Operations	_____	_____	_____

FIGURE 13-1. Volume Indicators
Weekly Operations Report
Week Ended _____

	Daily Average Current Week	Daily Average Prior Week	Daily Average Last 4 Weeks
P&S and Listed	_____	_____	_____
EDP	_____	_____	_____
Syndicate Department	_____	_____	_____
Municipal Department	_____	_____	_____
Sales Departments	_____	_____	_____
Total	_____	_____	_____

(10) Analysis of P&S corrections processed during the week by *type* of error:

	Daily Average Current Week	Daily Average Prior Week	Daily Average Last 4 Weeks
Account Number	_____	_____	_____
Price or Int. Adjustment	_____	_____	_____
Security Description & Quantity	_____	_____	_____
Commission	_____	_____	_____
Cancellation	_____	_____	_____
Settlement Date	_____	_____	_____
Miscellaneous	_____	_____	_____
Total	_____	_____	_____

(11) Number of corrected customer confirmations _____ _____ _____

(12) Number of corrected broker comparisons _____ _____ _____

(13) Corrected confirmation/comparisons per 1,000 trades processed _____ _____ _____

(14) Stock Record:

	Daily Average Current Week	Daily Average Prior Week	Daily Average Last 4 Weeks
Stock record entries	_____	_____	_____
Stock record errors	_____	_____	_____
Ratio of stock record errors to stock record entries	_____	_____	_____
Breaks created during week	_____	_____	_____
Ratio of stock record breaks to stock record entries	_____	_____	_____
Stock record breaks per 1,000 trades	_____	_____	_____
Unresolved breaks at end of week	_____	_____	_____

FIGURE 13-1. (*Continued*)

		Daily Average Current Week	Daily Average Prior Week	Daily Average Last 4 Weeks
	Analysis of breaks created during week:			
	Active Box Segregation & safekeeping	_____	_____	_____
	DTC	_____	_____	_____
	Customer Rec. & Del.	_____	_____	_____
	Transfer	_____	_____	_____
	Loans	_____	_____	_____
	Other	_____	_____	_____
	Coding	_____	_____	_____
	Keypunch	_____	_____	_____
	Computer Operations	_____	_____	_____
	P&S	_____	_____	_____
	Margin	_____	_____	_____
	Other	_____	_____	_____
	Number of unresolved breaks over 5 calendar day old	_____	_____	_____
	Value of unresolved "short" breaks over 5 calendar days old	_____	_____	_____
	Value of unresolved "long" breaks over 5 calendar days old	_____	_____	_____
(15)	Dividend and Proxy and Reorganization:			
	Number of securities going record	_____	_____	_____
	Number of position affected	_____	_____	_____
	Number of securities paid	_____	_____	_____
	Number of positions affected	_____	_____	_____
	Number of annual reports mailed	_____	_____	_____
	Number of interim reports mailed	_____	_____	_____
	Number of proxy items mailed	_____	_____	_____
	Number of proxy items mailed late	_____	_____	_____
	Number of tenders	_____	_____	_____
	Positions affected	_____	_____	_____
	Number of instructions not processed by tender date	_____	_____	_____
	Value of missed tenders	_____	_____	_____

FIGURE 13-1. (*Continued*)

		Daily Average Current Week	Daily Average Prior Week	Daily Average Last 4 Weeks
	Value of missed tenders			
(16)	Computer Operations Computer usage Number of hours:			
	Production			
	Reruns			
	Development			
	Repair & maintenance			
	Total			
	Available hours			
(17)	Number of Hours Production Reports are Late:			
	Accounting			
	Cashiering			
	Margin			
(18)	Data Preparation:			
	Name and Address			
	Trades			
	Stock Record			
	Cash			
	Security Master File			
	Accounting			
	Other			
	Total			

FIGURE 13-1. (*Continued*)

	Daily Average Current Week	Daily Average Prior Week	Daily Average Last 4 Weeks
Equities			
New York Stock Exchange			
American Stock Exchange			
Pacific Coast Stock Exchange			
Midwest Stock Exchange			
Philadelphia Stock Exchange			
Boston Stock Exchange			
NASDAQ			
Bonds			
New York Stock Exchange			
American Stock Exchange			
Over the Counter			
Options			
Chicago Board Options Exchange			
American Stock Exchange			
Philadelphia Stock Exchange			
Pacific Coast Stock Exchange			
Money Market Instruments			
Certificates of Deposit			
Bankers Acceptance			
U.S. Government and Agencies			
Other			
Mutual Funds			
Bond Funds			
Commodities			
Exchanges			
Redemptions			
Tenders			
International Trades			

FIGURE 13-2. Volume on Major Markets
Weekly Operations Report
Week Ended _____

(10) ANALYSIS OF P&S CORRECTIONS BY TYPE OF ERROR

Highlights P&S corrections by type of error providing the capability to quickly identify reasons for errors. Here again this type of reporting allows errors to be spotted easily.

(11) THROUGH (13)

These items are general indicators of efficiency in P&S processing. This gives you the capability to view the P&S Department's work and make changes very quickly.

(14) STOCK RECORD

The items in this category measure performance in processing and maintaining securities inventories accurately, and indicate the quality of control over stock record input. This is a very important area to keep under control. A big jump in errors and breaks can result in havoc throughout the Operations Departments.

(15) DIVIDEND & PROXY & REORGANIZATION

The items in this category reflect the volume in these departments and provide information on those areas where the firm might have some risk if increases in volume are not supported with more staff or automation.

(16) COMPUTER USAGE

The numbers here could tell you how well your Information Systems area is functioning. If you see big increases in re-runs, you know, e.g. that something is wrong in original processing and you can start asking why.

(17) NUMBER OF HOURS PRODUCTION REPORTS ARE LATE

From the user department's point of view, this item is a measure of efficiency of Information Systems, and indeed it has an effect on other departments' efficiency, cost and control. Dialogue between users and Information System's personnel is necessary to determine which production runs should be considered in the reporting so that meaningful information is provided.

(18) DATA PREPARATION

These items are indicative of the processing load on these areas. Substantial increases would indicate a need for further attention to avoid possible problems later in the processing cycle.

PROCESSING AND CONTROL INDICATORS

Now let's look at specific items that should be reported on in the Operations area for processing and control information. Figure 13-3 shows what a typical weekly report on Processing and Control Indicators might look like. Each caption below is indexed to the report shown in Figure 13-3. These indicators provide information on how efficiently trade and security processing are being completed and how quickly open items are resolved. Aged item increases in unfavorable indicators would indicate a need for attention to the pertinent areas.

(1) ETD—FAILS TO DELIVER, SECURITIES BORROWED AND DVP AS OF FRIDAY

ETD represents "Equivalent Trading Days." In the past, this measure has often been applied throughout the industry as a measure of efficiency in reducing financing costs by reducing a receivable (Fails to Deliver) resulting from security processing. The Fail to Deliver balances at the end of a week were divided by the average daily dollar sales for the week being measured. Thus the ETD for a given week would be arrived at in the following manner:

$$\text{ETD} = \frac{\text{Fails to Deliver Balances at Week End}}{\text{Average Daily Sales for Week}}$$

For the following reasons, however, ETD measuring only Fails to Deliver is not a meaningful measure of securities processing efficiency:

1. *Effect of Borrowing Securities.* Fails to Deliver can and are reduced by borrowing the security from another firm. The effect is to show an improvement in ETD for Fails to Deliver but, in fact, no significant cash flow benefit to the firm, as one receivable (Fails) has merely been replaced by another (Securities Borrowed).[1] This borrowing is done on a significant number of items, making the ETD—Fails to Deliver meaningless.

---

[1] Cash flow may not change significantly but interest expense is favorably impacted by this procedure.

		Daily Average Current Week	*Daily Average Prior Week*	*Daily Average Last 4 Weeks*
(1)	ETD—Fails to deliver, securities borrowed and DVP as of Friday	_____	_____	_____
(2)	ETD—Fails to receive and RVP as of Friday	_____	_____	_____
(3)	Fails to deliver, securities borrowed, and DVP's outstanding	_____	_____	_____
(4)	Fails to receive and RVP's outstanding	_____	_____	_____
(5)	Fail to deliver—7 business days old	_____	_____	_____
(6)	Fail to receive—7 business days old	_____	_____	_____
(7)	Total buy-ins executed against US profit (loss)	_____	_____	_____
(8)	Total buy-ins executed against others, profit (loss)	_____	_____	_____
(9)	Securities loaned contract Value	_____	_____	_____
	Securities loaned market Value	_____	_____	_____
	Securities borrowed contract value	_____	_____	_____
	Securities borrowed market value	_____	_____	_____
	Date of last mark to market	_____	_____	_____
(10)	Items in transfer as of Friday:			
	0 to 30 days old	_____	_____	_____
	30 to 40 days old	_____	_____	_____
	over 40 days old	_____	_____	_____
	Total items	_____	_____	_____

FIGURE 13-3. Processing and Control Indicators
Weekly Operations Report
Week Ended _____

	Daily Average Current Week	Daily Average Prior Week	Daily Average Last 4 Weeks
Value over 40 days not confirmed			
Open items over 30 days old as per cent of total open items			
(11) Reclamation Totals:			
Stock			
U.S. Govt. Bonds			
Other Bonds			
Total			
Reclamation value as per cent of deliveries			
(12) Suspense/Difference Account as of Friday:			
All detail records balanced to general ledger (yes/no)			
Money items open over 3 business days old:			
Debit			
Credit			
Security Differences open over 3 business days old:			
Short value			
Long value			
Option trade differences over 2 business days old:			
Short value			
Long value			
(13) Dividend/Bond Interest as of Friday:			
Dividend Receivable:			
Stock			
Money			
Total			
Bond Interest Receivable			
Dividend Payable:			
Stock			
Money			
Total			
Bond Interest Payable			
Aged Dividend/Bond Interest as of Friday:			
30 days and older			
Dividend Receivable:			
Stock			
Money			
Bond Interest Receivable			

FIGURE 13-3. (*Continued*)

2. *Interrelationship of Customer and Broker Receivables.* From a balance sheet point of view, there is little difference between a receivable from a broker (Fail to Deliver item or Securities Borrowed item) and a receivable from a customer whose standing instructions are "Deliver Versus Payment" (DVP). In each case, a receivable is on the books until the firm delivers the security.

With the advent of Continuous Net Settlement (CNS) systems in clearing corporations, the net balances due from or to a clearing corporation consist of Fails to Deliver and Fails to Receive. These balances are available daily from the various clearing agencies and should be used for purposes of ETD statistics. The Continuous Net Settlement procedures result in a net figure of Fail to Deliver and Fails to Receive being either a net receivable or payable from or to the clearing organization, but that does not take away from the fact that the net figure is made up of certain known receivables and payables.[2]

In addition, efficiency is still a factor under CNS (as it was under previous systems), because firms will still have to finance an item that is not delivered to the clearing agency.

The formula for "ETD—Fails to Deliver, Securities Borrowed and DVP as of Friday" should be:

$$\text{ETD} = \frac{\text{Fails to Deliver, Securities Borrowed \& DVP Balances at End of Week}}{\text{Average daily dollar sales \& DVP customer purchases.}}$$

This is probably a new measurement for many of you, and experience will tell you what is an acceptable ETD for these items. Comparison can be made to "ETD—Fails to Receive and RVP as of Friday" for judgement as to deliveries open versus receives open.

(2) ETD—Fails to Receive and RVP as of Friday

The contraside of (1) above. An indicator of how efficiently other firms and customers deliver to a given firm.

---

[2] Under CNS, the monies are owed to or due from the clearing agency, as opposed to being owed to or due from firms with whom the trade was made.

(3) AND (4) FAILS TO DELIVER, SECURITIES BORROWED AND DVP, AND, FAILS TO RECEIVE AND RVP OUTSTANDING

Another measure of securities processing efficiency looks at the average balances in the major securities processing receivables and payables.

Only experience will tell what the "normal" relationship is, but the goal should be to have the payables at least support the receivables, unless adequate explanations as to trading patterns provide reasons why this should not be.

(5) AND (6) FAILS TO DELIVER, RECEIVE 7 BUSINESS DAYS OLD

These aged items represen t possible potential capital charges and potential exposure to a firm from buy-ins; significant dollar amounts require immediate management attention.

(7) AND (8) TOTAL BUY-INS EXECUTED AGAINST US/OTHERS

These measures are indicative of follow-up on aged items and possible exposure to a firm from the loss experienced on the buy-in.

(9) MARKET VALUE TO CONTRACT VALUE

These items provide information on our "marking to the market" activities for outstanding securities loaned and borrowed. Substantial differences between the market value and the contract value may represent unnecessary financing and risk for a firm. It is important to mark-to-the-market as often as possible.

(10) ITEMS IN TRANSFER AS OF FRIDAY

These items measure the effect of the processing load on the transfer area. An increase in aged items may indicate control problems or heavy volume that should be addressed by more staff, overtime, and so forth.

(11) RECLAMATION TOTALS

This is another measure of efficiency both of the delivery process and effort to reduce DK'd deliveries. DK's represent unnecessary financing costs and should be kept to a minimum.

(12) SUSPENSE/DIFFERENCE ACCOUNTS AS OF FRIDAY

These measures are indicators of control in the delivery processing cycle. An increase in these areas may represent substantial risk exposure to the firm.

(13) DIVIDEND AND BOND INTEREST

These measures are indicative of how well the Dividend Department is responding to the current processing load. A building up of aged receivables results in additional financing costs and a charge to regulatory capital.

CUSTOMER INFORMATION INDICATORS

Firms, of course, will want many different types of information relative to their customer base. Our focus, however, relates to processing information on customer activity. As with the other processing information above, it is useful to set standards of performance and include data on performance relative to these standards to have a meaningful measurement. Figure 13-4 shows a specific report that should be developed on these areas. Following is information on each of the categories referred to in the report.

(1) CUSTOMER COMPLAINTS RECEIVED DURING THE WEEK

This particular area indicates how many complaints the firm is receiving from customers. It is a good indication of how the firm's customers see the promptness or accuracy of error resolution and/or processing. Big increases could mean you have a major problem somewhere in your Operations Departments.

		Daily Average Current Week	Daily Average Prior Week	Daily Average Last 4 Weeks
(1)	Customer complaints received during the week			
(1.a)	Customer complaints unresolved at week end			
(2)	Value of prepayments during the week			
(3)	Value of unsecured debits close of Friday			
(4)	Number of accounts on restriction			
(5)	Number of margin calls issued			
(6)	Number of Regulation T extensions granted during the week			
(7)	Number of Rule 15c3-3 extensions granted during the week			
(8)	Number of Rule 15c3-3 buy-ins during the week			
(9)	Value of customer unsecured short securities as of Friday			
(10)	Value of customer short positions as of Friday			
(11)	Market order turnaround time			
(12)	Items placed in transfer			
(13)	Transfer outstanding 15 days or more			
(14)	Accounts delivered in			
(15)	Accounts delivered out			

FIGURE 13-4. Customer Information Indicators
Weekly Operations Report
Week Ended _____

(1.A) CUSTOMER COMPLAINTS UNRESOLVED AT WEEK END

This information lets a firm know how many complaints are unresolved after a standard period of time. It may be useful to show this information relative to number of days that the customer complaints have been in the firm's possession.

(2) VALUE OF PREPAYMENTS DURING THE WEEK

Customers often sell securities and ask for payment of the proceeds before the end of the five day settlement period. This may be permitted by the regulatory agencies, but firms should understand that they are financing the costs of these proceeds because they will not get paid until settlement date. Increases could mean that your Sales areas are being too free with the firm's monies.

(3) VALUE OF UNSECURED DEBITS CLOSE OF FRIDAY

Large increases here mean that you have customers who owe you money without having securities on deposit. Operations must work closely with the Sales and Legal Departments on collection to reduce interest costs to the firm.

(4) NUMBER OF ACCOUNTS ON RESTRICTION

Accounts on restriction must be watched by the Office Manager and also by the home office (generally, the Margin Department) to assure that inappropriate trading is not taking place in these accounts.

(5) NUMBER OF MARGIN CALLS ISSUED

Margin calls issued, of course, represent potential exposure to the firm. If the firm does not promptly obtain the necessary funds from the customer, it may have to sell the customer's assets which represents potential exposure to the firm.

(6) NUMBER OF REGULATION T EXTENSIONS GRANTED DURING THE WEEK

These extensions represent additional time granted the customer to pay for security purchases. It is important to understand that these extensions represent financing costs and undue exposure to the firm.

(7) Number of Rule 15c3-3 Extensions Granted During the Week

Rule 15c3-3 is discussed in detail in Chapter 3—Cashiering. Customers are required to deliver securities sold short in cash accounts within ten business days, and these extensions represent additional time periods granted because of recognized hardship and other circumstances. Financing costs are incurred if the customer utilizes the proceeds of the sale and if the market value of the securities sold rises, undue exposure might result.

(8) Number of Rule 15c3-3 Buy-ins During the Week

Paragraph "m" of Rule 15c3-3 requires firms to liquidate customers' short positions, resulting from sales in cash accounts, within ten business days of settlement, unless an extension has been approved. The importance of this indicator stems from the exposure which might result from market fluctuations between the settlement and liquidation dates.

(9) Value of Customer Unsecured Short Securities as of Friday

The value of unsecured securities that customers have sold but have not delivered to the firm, represents exposure for the firm. If the market value of the securities, for example, goes up and the customer eventually does not deliver these securities, the firm must go into the open market and buy the securities to redeliver them to the firm to whom they were sold. This could result in a firm having to absorb the difference between the market price on the day the securities were sold, and the market price on the day of a buy-in.

(10) Value of Customer Short Positions as of Friday

The firm is required to guarantee delivery related to sales transactions in customers' bonafide short accounts. Such delivery may be made from existing availability or may necessitate the borrowing of securities. Such positions must be monitored closely to avoid exposure which might result from increases in market value, and the impact on securities loan demand and net capital requirements.

(11) MARKET ORDER TURNAROUND TIME

Customers like to know if and at what price their orders were executed. This indicator provides information relative to how fast the execution areas and the Order Processing Department are executing orders and reporting back to the offices.

(12) ITEMS PLACED IN TRANSFER

The transfer process is a cumbersome one in most firms and this indicator gives an idea of what activity is going on in that department. Significant increases or decreases in this area may provide information relative to appropriate staffing levels.

(13) TRANSFERS OUTSTANDING 15 DAYS OR MORE

This is a suggested standard (15 days) to measure how long the transfer process is taking. If outstanding transfers rise over a period of time, Operations Managers will have to work with the offending Transfer Agents to speed up the process.

(14) & (15) ACCOUNTS DELIVERED IN/ACCOUNTS DELIVERED OUT

This tells a firm how many accounts are being received from other firms and/or delivered out to other firms. A significant increase in accounts delivered out versus accounts delivered in could be an indication of other processing delays that are causing customer dissatisfaction.

REGULATORY CAPITAL CHARGE INDICATORS

This is a very important area—one where Operations Managers must be particularly careful, because large increases in these numbers could restrict the firm from using capital for more productive efforts. To understand better why these areas are so important, let's take a few minutes to discuss the difference between "financial" capital and "regulatory" capital.

Financial capital refers to that amount of equity and/or debt that a given firm has to finance its business. Regulatory bodies, such as the Securities and Exchange Commission ("SEC"), the NASD and/or many of the exchanges, have provisions that require member firms to maintain a certain amount of what is referred to as "regulatory" capital. Regulatory capital is financial capital less any items that are not considered "liquid" as defined by the NASD, SEC or an exchange. In addition to reducing financial capital by items that are not considered liquid, the regulators require firms to reduce financial capital by certain items which may represent exposure to the firm and eventually, exposure to customers of the firm. After all the "regulatory charges" are subtracted from financial capital, a figure is arrived at that is used in the industry and referred to as "net regulatory capital." It is this sum that is used to determine the level of customer or trading activity in which a firm may engage. The minimum dollar amount of regulatory capital varies depending upon the type of business the firm is engaged in.

Figure 13-5 shows a report that should be used to measure how Operations processing is impacting regulatory capital charges. Basically these items result from processing delays on securities differences in the books and records of the firm. Now we'll discuss each of the items referred to by number in the report.

(1) VALUE OF SHORT SECURITY DIFFERENCES OVER 7 BUSINESS DAYS

If firms have aged short security differences, they may be required to buy-in the securities with a resultant loss to the firm.

(2) VALUE OF LONG SECURITY DIFFERENCES WHERE POSITIONS HAVE BEEN SOLD

This category tells the firm what liquidated security differences may have to be purchased to satisfy a claim.

(3) VALUE OF GOOD FAITH DEPOSITS OUTSTANDING MORE THAN 11 BUSINESS DAYS

This represents the amount of money that firms have extended to other firms who are the syndicate manager for a given underwriting. If these good faith deposits are not returned to the firm, they again represent exposure.

	Capital Charge Items	Daily Average Current Week	Daily Average Prior Week	Daily Average Last 4 Weeks
(1)	Value of short security Differences over 7 business days old	_____	_____	_____
(2)	Value of long security Differences where positions have been sold	_____	_____	_____
(3)	Value of good faith deposits outstanding more than 11 business days from S/D of underwriting	_____	_____	_____
(4)	Free shipments of securities over $5,000 and all free shipments over 7 business days old	_____	_____	_____
(5)	Unresolved debits in suspense accounts	_____	_____	_____
(6)	Aged fails to deliver (Muni, over 24 business days old, all other over 14 business days old)	_____	_____	_____
(7)	Aged dividend/bond interest receivables over 30 calendar days old	_____	_____	_____
	Total Capital Charges Items	_____	_____	_____

FIGURE 13-5. Regulatory Capital Charge Indicators
Weekly Operations Report
Week Ended _____

(4) FREE SHIPMENTS OF SECURITIES

Firms sometimes send securities through the mail, or through agents, for delivery to clients. The SEC has mandated that, because of the potential exposure, firms must reduce their regulatory capital by the value of these shipments.

(5) Unresolved Debits in Suspense Accounts over 7 Business Days

The entire dollar amount of unresolved debits in suspense accounts over seven business days old must be subtracted from regulatory capital, because it represents potential exposure to the firm.

(6) Aged Fails to Deliver

Significant aged fails to deliver may indicate that the firm is having trouble delivering securities to another securities firm. Since it is possible that the delivery will not be completed, the firm may be subject to market risk. The rules mandate that capital be reduced by any existing liquidating deficit, plus a percentage of the market value of the underlying securities.

(7) Aged Dividend and Bond Interest Receivables

These unsecured receivables represent potential exposure to the firm and again are subtracted from regulatory capital.

FINANCING INDICATORS

Most of you know that securities processing impacts the financing needs of securities firms—favorably or unfavorably. If you are more efficient than other firms in the delivery process, you get paid faster and can reduce borrowing costs. In addition, many securities firms have their Operations areas manage day-to-day bank loans, replenish cash accounts, lend and borrow securities, and perform certain other tasks that non-securities firms usually give to the Treasurer's Office.

This section shows you which indicators you should look at closely to spot important trends. Figure 13-6, Financing Indicators, shows a report that should be used to measure how well cash management activities are being performed. The specific indicators discussed below (and referred to in the sample report shown in Figure 13-6), reflect the financing necessary as a result of securities and money flows associated with securities processing, firm trading, and customer activity.

		Daily Average Current Week	Daily Average Prior Week	Daily Average Last 4 Weeks
(1)	Cash-In-Banks			
	Targeted			
	Actual			
(2)	Drafts Payable			
(3)	Securities Flow Receivables:			
	Fails to deliver			
	DVP's outstanding			
	Securities borrowed			
	Total			
(4)	Payables:			
	Fails to receive			
	RVP's Outstanding			
	Securities Loaned			
	Total			
(5)	Ratio of F/D, DVP and S/B to F/R and RVP and S/L			
(6)	Securities Loaned Balances as % of margin debits			
(7)	Customer Balances			
	Margin debits			
	Cash debits:			
	(Non-C.O.D.)			
	Total debits			
	Free credits			
	Other credits			
	Total Credits			
(8)	Firm Trading Positions			
	Long:			
	Money market			
	Stocks			
	Bonds			
	Subtotal			
	Short:			
	Money market			
	Stocks			
	Bonds			
	Subtotal			
	Net			

FIGURE 13-6. Financing Indicators
Weekly Operations Report
Week Ended _____

		Daily Average Current Week	Daily Average Prior Week	Daily Average Last 4 Weeks
(9)	Financing Summary Overnight Financing— Money Market:			
	Repurchase agreements	_____	_____	_____
	Dealer loans	_____	_____	_____
	Subtotal money market	_____	_____	_____
	Broker loans	_____	_____	_____
	Secured	_____	_____	_____
	Unsecured			
	Subtotal broker loans	_____	_____	_____
(10)	Day Loans:			
	Syndicate	_____	_____	_____
	Operational	_____	_____	_____
	Total Day Loans	_____	_____	_____
(11)	Immediate Credit Drafts	_____	_____	_____
(12)	Interest Rates Average rate experienced on broker loans			
	Lowest rate			
	Highest rate	_____	_____	_____
	Average published (WSJ) loan rate for broker loans	_____	_____	_____
	Average published (WSJ) high rate for broker loans	_____	_____	_____
	Average rate experienced on dealer loans			
	Lowest rate	_____	_____	_____
	Highest rate			
	Range of dealer loan rates offered			
	Lowest	_____	_____	_____
	Highest	_____	_____	_____
	Average rate experienced on repurchase agreements			
	Lowest	_____	_____	_____
	Highest	_____	_____	_____
	Average rate experienced on commercial paper			
	Lowest	_____	_____	_____
	Highest	_____	_____	_____

FIGURE 13-6. *(Continued)*

(1) Cash-in-Banks

Targeted levels for general ledger cash balances should be established periodically. This item reflects efforts to meet those targets. These should be reviewed at least weekly to be sure the firm is not leaving excess cash idle.

(2) Drafts Payable

These funds are the dollar values of outstanding drafts issued on "zero balance" and other accounts. They eliminate bank loan costs in some cases, and in others they provide reduced interest costs. Target levels should be established and the reports should provide a measurement of how well you are doing.

(3) and (4) Securities Flow Receivables and Payables

These are the major dollar amounts of receivables and payables resulting from securities processing, as previously discussed.

(5) Ratio of F/D, DVP and S/B to F/R, RVP and S/L

A ratio of related receivables and payables also previously discussed. Experience should provide a "norm."

(6) Securities Loaned Balances as % of Margin Debits

This is one measure of success in the security lending field. Experience will provide information as to a "norm." The more securities the firm can lend, the lower its financing costs will be.

(7) Customer Balances

Cash debits represent financing costs and should be kept as low as possible. Operations should provide more detailed information to the Sales areas to reduce these debts. Free credits provide free financing to the firm.

(8) Firm Trading Positions

These positions are a significant component of financing requirements and provide data necessary to review changes in net financing. Big increases in long positions will provide a need for financing. Short positions will result in high securities borrowed or Fail to Deliver amounts.

(9) Financing Summary

A summary of money borrowed on a short-term basis organized by type of borrowing. This is important because one form of financing may be less expensive than another.

(10) Day Loans

A summary of total day loans taken. These day loans can cost between .25% and 1% of the principal amount borrowed; excessive use of day loans is wasteful. If Operations Managers see this amount rising, they should investigate other means of satisfying daily financing requirements.

(11) Immediate Credit Drafts

When firms deliver a security out of town, to a location where they do not have an office, they often use an agent bank and borrow money equal to the face amount of the delivery. This is a "contingent liability" and is as costly as a bank loan.

(12) Interest Rates

This is a recap of interest rate experience on financings. Data published in newspapers and other financial publications is provided to allow a measure of efforts.

CHAPTER 14

New Product Support

How many of you have received a telephone call from your boss that goes something like this: "Marketing wants to introduce a new security that gives customers the ability to "put" to the issuer and carries a variable interest rate. They're asking if we can support it within two weeks!" You probably start thinking can the dividend system handle it? Is the Reorganization Department prepared for it? How will we clear it?

During the 1970s and 80s, the proliferation of new products has been phenomenal. Just consider some of the major ones:

Asset Management Accounts

Money Market Funds

Tax Shelters

Standardized Equity Options

Floating Rate Notes

Zero Coupon Bonds

Put Bonds

Limited Partnerships

All of these products required operational support, which brought to the surface some basic problems. In today's environment, a marketed financial product is already considered to be in the beginning stages of obsolescence.

Therefore, the need to evaluate quickly the operational impact and support requirements prior to a new product's implementation, is crucial. However, because of the rush in the industry to introduce new products, operational support areas find themselves hard-pressed to meet the time demands of this pace. At many firms, the typical new product support process (if one exists) simply does not provide the operations area with enough time to support new products adequately.

In this chapter we'll review a case study and look at problems that come up when you have inadequate planning for a new product, discuss what to look for in preparing to support a new product, how to organize to support new products, and show how to set up a new product support procedure.

CASE STUDY

As an example of some of the problems associated with the introduction of a new product, let's take a look at a real product.

The case concerns the sale of new put bonds issued by an Industrial Development Authority, and we'll use an issue date of September 15, 1995.

The bonds were tax-exempt tender bonds which had interest rates adjusted quarterly. They were redeemable at each quarter, prior to and including the fixed rate date, at the option of the bond-holder.

The processing of the quarterly tender feature put the managing underwriter into a new type of business, that of a Tender Remarketing Agent. The steps involved were as follows:

1. Fifteen business days prior to the interest payment date, clients to whom the underwriter sold the bonds had to be notified by mail of these upcoming quarterly tender and interest payment dates.

2. On the fifth business day before the quarterly interest payment date, the underwriter announced a tentative interest rate to be paid on the bond for the next quarterly interest period.

3. On the fourth business day before the quarterly payment date, bondholders had to notify their Account Executive by phone if they wished to tender the bonds. This notice had to be given no later than 4:00 P.M., Eastern Standard Time on that fourth business day.

4. On the third business day before the quarterly interest payment date, bondholders wishing to tender had to deliver the physical notes to the managing underwriter's home office headquarters in New York.

PROBLEMS

Here are some of the complications which were incurred with this issue.

1. The firm had the responsibility of notifying all clients who purchased the bonds of the upcoming quarterly tender and interest payment dates on the 15th business day prior to interest payment date. A list of all bondholders who chose to have the securities firm retain their securities was in existence. Unfortunately, due to lack of procedural planning, the firm had no record of those clients who chose to take physical possession of the securities. Therefore, there was no way of contacting these clients. If the support areas were contacted, informed and consulted, prior to the product implementation, they could have advised those writing the prospectus to recommend that customers not take physical delivery, but rather maintain the bonds long in their account. The firm would then have a record of all clients who had purchased the bonds, and could notify each one on a timely and accurate basis.

2. With the introduction of this new product, the underwriter for the first time was acting as a Tender Remarketing Agent. Prior to this, the calling of bonds was always the job of the issuer. With these bonds, the customer gains the option of tendering the bond at par with accrued interest. The underwriter, as tender agent, assumed the responsibility of receiving and delivering the securities under restricted time-frames. This was a unique, new role for the underwriter, further complicating its operational functions and responsibilities.

3. The following complications arose regarding the physical delivery of tender bonds. Receipt of all tendered securities had to take place on the third business day before the quarterly interest payment date. Payment by the firm had to be in Fed Funds on interest payment date. Frequently, the securities were not received in the prescribed time-frame, and the firm could not effect redelivery vs. payment. The buyer of these new securities did not submit payment until delivery was effected, resulting in a loss of interest to the firm. If the firm had kept all bonds long in each customer's account, the firm would have eliminated all the receive/deliver complications. Very simply, a bookkeeping entry could have been made, Fed Funds received as scheduled, and interest would not have been lost by the firm.

In summary, this example demonstrates some of the problems that can arise because of the lack of a new product support process. If one was in place, appropriate planning could have eliminated the serious problems that subsequently arose.

WHAT TO LOOK FOR

New products will have a different impact on operations, depending upon the degree of complexity of the product and the flexibility of a firm's systems and operations support process. Some new products are derivative, and can be supported through an already existing operating mechanism. Others, such as asset management accounts, are totally new concepts that require completely new mechanisms to handle them. As such, the time needed to prepare for these two types of products can vary significantly.

In order to prepare for new product introduction, the Operations Manager should ask the following questions:

Which Operation Departments will be affected?

What are the systems support requirements?

What are the unique processing features in terms of clearing and settlement?

What are the regulatory requirement/controls that will have an impact on how the products will be processed?

What are the customer service requirements?

What organizational support is needed other than operations?

What technical and operational staff is needed to facilitate processing?

What are the training requirements for the support staffs?

The only way to solve the "crisis atmosphere" usually associated with new product introduction is to set up a new product introduction process and always stick to it.

Such a step-by-step "how to" program will better service customers and increase operations efficiency in any firm by integrating the needs of Marketing and Sales.

ORGANIZING FOR NEW PRODUCT SUPPORT

How a given firm organizes for new product support will vary depending on the size of the firm and the culture of the firm, i.e., formal or informal, structured processing or unstructured processing. There are generally three ways to set up the process: 1) a separate New Product Support Department in the Operations area that is responsible for coordinating Operations, Sales, Marketing; 2) a New Product Unit within each functional area of Operations, Sales, and Marketing; or 3) a New Product Committee structure.

SEPARATE NEW PRODUCT SUPPORT DEPARTMENT

The New Product Support Department would coordinate the formal process of planning for the introduction of a new product. Input would be received from the various areas of the firm most closely involved in the product's development such as Marketing, Information Systems, and Operations. In this way, support areas would have a central location to find out about new products, and to interface with the product originators to ensure that appropriate support is fully planned for. Additionally, the support areas would be able to contact the New Product Support area for those "after the fact" products that are launched without any prior notice. The New Product Support Department would be able to relieve the Operations Departments of the cumbersome work of finding out about the specifics of the new product: how it operates, rules and regulations, and so forth. Another advantage to this approach is having a pool of trained staff familiar with both the firm and the new product process.

NEW PRODUCT SUPPORT WITHIN FUNCTIONAL AREAS

Because of the diverse nature of the products the firm services, one new product area may not be capable of supporting all new developments. In addition, the specialization of the different divisions of the firm may call for more decentralization. With the new product development completely decentralized, there is greater likelihood that product projects will match the capabilities and market needs of the originating area, and will receive stronger commitment from them. Therefore, some firms will dedicate a New Product Support Section within an Operations Department, and within a Marketing or Sales Department. Ideally the two will work together to ensure the smooth implementation of the new product.

NEW PRODUCT COMMITTEES

The use of a "New Product Committee" is another way to manage the introduction of new products. Representatives from the major impacted areas of the firm should be on the committees. Although each area will have specialized representatives that will participate, the major areas that should be included on a committee of this nature include Operations, Systems, Marketing, Compliance, Finance and Sales. The committee would be responsible for approving new product suggestions, and would also act as a "task force" to foster the development of the product.

Because of the task force format, all affected areas can be represented and can contribute to the design of the product. This is especially significant for Operations personnel, who can discuss with the product originators those aspects of the product which they feel should be modified or adjusted.

The committee format also has the advantage of being flexible. Either a permanent standing committee can be formed, or an ad hoc process can be adopted. The committee format has the advantage of opening lines of communication between various members of the firm who otherwise might not communicate often.

A New Product Committee can be a very important forum for the Operations Manager to participate in the new product support process. In a firm where a formal new product department or process does not exist, the committee is one way to ensure that Operations has a voice in the critical area of product support.

To summarize the divergent choices facing the decision of optimum organization and placement of a New Product Support area, refer to Figures 14-1 and 14-2 which list some advantages and disadvantages of the organizational alignment for new product support.

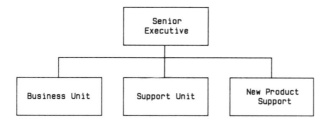

Advantages

Greater control and coordination of all the firm's programs or innovations.

Senior management is kept aware of ongoing new product activities.

Resources available for new product development can be concentrated where outcome is likely to be most advantageous.

Responsibility for new product is clear-cut.

Disadvantages

New product ideas are not necessarily attuned to the products, markets, and operational capabilities that are familiar to the business units.

Because of its separation, the unit may become isolated.

There is a potential for friction in the interactions between departments, especially in the handling of the transition of new products to the line organization.

FIGURE 14-1. New Product Support as a Separate Document

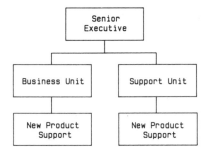

Advantages

New products developed at the divisional level are more likely to meet the customer needs, market opportunities, and operational and technical capabilities.

Business unit-wide market involvement and operational commitment to the new product program may increase chances of success when the product has been conceived, born, and nurtured at this level.

Job is being performed at the "doing level" instead of the thinking level.

Disadvantages

Interfacing with all other areas of the firm that may be involved with new product development is not always possible.

New product development may become too limited to one area's operational methods.

Senior management may not be aware of new product activities, and therefore support may not be as great.

Resources to support new product development are more restricted.

FIGURE 14-2. New Product Support as Part of a Business Unit

NEW PRODUCT SUPPORT PROCESS

The following is a proposed New Product Support Procedure: refer to the flow chart (Figure 14-3) as we discuss the process.

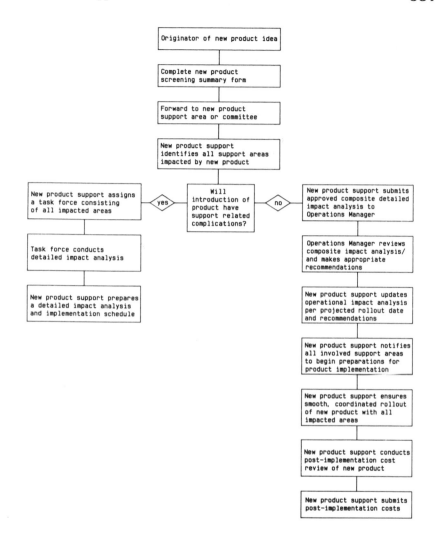

FIGURE 14-3. New Product Support Process

Responsibility	Procedure
Representative from Originating Unit	1. Complete the New Product Screening Summary Form (see Figure 14-4).
Originating Unit Representative	2. Forward completed Screening Summary and the preliminary prospectus to the New Product Support Section.
New Product Support Section	3. Identify all support areas impacted by the new product.
New Product Support Section	4. Conduct Preliminary Operations/ Impact Analysis integrating all support areas (see Figure 14-5) and the originating unit representative and proceed to step 8; if the product causes support related complications then proceed to step 5.
New Product Support Section	5. Assign and coordinate a Task force consisting of all impacted support areas.
Task Force	6. Each member of the task force conduct a Detailed Impact Analysis and a Proposed Implementation Schedule (see Figure 14-6). Upon completion, submit to New Product Support Section.
New Product Support Section	7. Prepare a composite Detailed Impact Analysis and Proposed Implementation Schedule.
New Product Support Section	8. Submit approved composite Detailed Analysis and Proposed Implementation Schedule to Manager/Director of the originating unit and all other impacted areas through their representatives.

Manager/Director of	9. Review the composite Originating Unit recommendations/changes and refer back to New Product Support Section.
New Product Support Section	10. Update Operational Impact Analysis as required to reflect projected rollout date and appropriate recommendations/modifications.
New Product Support Section	11. Notify all involved support areas to begin preparation for product implementation.
New Product Support Section	12. Ensure smooth, coordinated, rollout of new product with all involved support areas.
New Product Support Section	13. Conduct post-implementation analysis. Submit to operations manager and the director of originating unit.

Note: When a task force is assigned, it should consist of representatives from those support areas areas impacted by the new product. Members should be selected from the following potentially affected areas:

All Impacted Support Areas
New Product Support Section
Originating Unit Representatives
Information Systems
Legal Counsel
Law and Compliance
Financial Advisory
Risk Analysis
Tax Advisory
Audit Review
Financial Reporting & Control
Sales
Marketing

Product Name _____   Date submitted _____

Originating Department(s) _____   Scheduled Implementation

Date _____

Originating Department Representative _____

Project Number _____

Product Category

_____ Current/Current	Improve current product for existing market
_____ Current/New	Modify current product to appeal to new market
_____ New/Current	Add to current product line for current customers
_____ New/New	Introduce entirely new product to attract new customer base

Product Description (Briefly describe the new product)

Who are the potential customers for this product/service?

What client needs will this product or service satisfy?

How will this product or service better meet these needs?

Does the product have any unique features?

Do you foresee the product causing any operating complications? (for example, unusual settlement procedures).

The first step in completing the New Product Screening Summary is to describe the new product concisely and then to answer the five questions following the product description.

The purpose of these questions is to provide the New Product Support area with the minimum amount of information to conduct a preliminary impact analysis.

FIGURE 14-4. New Product Screening Summary

DERIVATIVE AND NEW PRODUCTS

In today's securities industry, there are usually two types of products to which the Operations Manager will be exposed. The first is the totally original product, one that is unlike any other product the firm or even the industry might offer. The second is the derivative product that is a variation of an existing offering.

Product Name _____ Date Submitted _____
Originating Department(s) _____ Scheduled Implementation _____

Date _____
Originating Department Representative _____
Project Number _____

Product Category

_____ Current/Current   Improve current product for existing market
_____ Current/New   Modify current product to appeal to new market
_____ New/Current   Add to current product line for current customers
_____ New/New   Introduce entirely new product to attract new customer
                                 base

Product Description

Projected Areas of Impact

Degree of Impact					Minimal Impact		Maximum Impact			Comments/ Recommendations
List Operating Departments	1	2	3	4	5	6	7	8	9	10

Name of Individual Completing Study _____

Department _____ Floor _____ Extension _____

The preliminary Analysis determines if a product will cause support related complications, if the product is projected to exhibit various complications refer to a Task Force for further detailed Impact Analysis Evaluation.

FIGURE 14-5. Preliminary Impact Analysis

Product Name _____ Date submitted _____

Originating Department(s) _____ Scheduled Implementation

Date _____

Originating Department Representative _____

Project Number _____

Product Category

_____ Current/Current   Improve current product for existing market

_____ Current/New   Modify current product to appeal to new market

_____ New/Current   Aid to current product line for current customers

_____ New/New   Introduce entirely new product to attract new customer base

Product Description

Task Force

Consists of individuals from support areas affected by product. Members will be selected from the potentially affected areas listed under each department.

Department	*Floor*	*Extension*
All affected		
operating areas		
Legal Counsel		
Law & Compliance		
Financial Advisory		
Tax Advisory		
Risk Analysis		
Audit Review		
Financial Reporting/		
Accounting		
Sales		
Marketing		

Impact Analysis Evaluation

(The following should be submitted for *all* areas of impact):

Projected costs, capital expenditures, staffing, equivalent involvements, compensation and benefits, occupancy costs, training requirements and customer service requirements.

Final Recommendation

Estimated Development Time

Action Plan—Responsibility/Schedule/Duration

FIGURE 14-6. Detailed Impact Analysis and Proposed Implementation Schedule

The first question the manager may ask is how to differentiate between the two. Although each firm will have specific guidelines which are unique to their operation, some general guidelines for pinpointing a "new product" are the following:

It addresses a customer group not currently served by the firm.

It requires the creation of a financial investment not currently offered by the firm.

It requires a delivery system not currently used by the firm.

It may have a significant impact on existing firm systems or operations at either the headquarters or branch level.

An idea for modifying an existing product or service, which does not meet any of the above criteria, would be considered a derivative product or a product enhancement. As such, it would require a different approach from both the New Product Support area and the Operations area.

Some of the areas that would need to be addressed when looking at a new product are:

Is a new system required?

What are the time-frames for product implementation?

What are the costs of the product versus anticipated profits?

Who are the potential customers?

Are Legal and/or Regulatory requirements impacted?

Are there unique processing features?

What are the expenses and/or cash flow implications of offering the product (for example, unusual settlement procedures)?

Will the anticipated volume require a new Operations support area?

Will there be any major processing problems associated with the product that would be difficult to resolve?

The derivative or product enhancement will necessitate a different set of questions. Because the product is a modification of an existing one, systems and procedures may already be in place. The

New Product Support area will need to focus on what the differences are. Some of the questions to ask are:

How does the enhancement compare to the existing product?

What programming requirements or modifications will be necessary?

Were the problems with the current product resolved by the enhancement?

Will there be anticipated volume increases?

Does the derivative product repeat processing problems found in the parent product?

Are any problems with the parent product resolved by the enhancement?

These questions will clarify and focus the process, and serve to prepare the way for a smooth transition to the product's implementation.

NEW PRODUCT EVALUATION

One of the duties of a New Product Support Department should be the evaluation of the product after its implementation. This aspect of the process often is neglected because of time constraints, but it is a crucial step. The evaluation will serve to assess both the profitability of the product, as well as the ease of its implementation. The vital information learned from the evaluation will assist in both the development and implementation of future products.

How well does the supporting system operate?

_____

_____

If system problems occurred, what was the nature of the problem?

Downtime _____

CRT Access _____

Reports _____

Processing Functions _____

Other _____

What costs were associated with processing the products?

Personal _____

Equipment _____

Space _____

Overtime _____

Travel & Expense _____

Advertising _____

Systems Development _____

Errors/Write-offs _____

Exposure _____

Did the product serve the needs of the anticipated client base?

FIGURE 14-7. New Product Evaluation Form

Was volume the same, greater, or less than anticipated?

If greater or less, what impact did this have on profitability?

Was a profitability study conducted? If so, what were the results.

Did the product cause any unique processing features?

If so, what was the impact on the operation?

What problems were encountered that could be avoided in the future for a similar product?

FIGURE 14-7. (*Continued*)

The time frame of one year after product implementation will give all areas involved in the product processing time to become familiar with the product's concept, as well as any problems associated with its implementation. (See Figure 14-7 for a sample New Product Evaluation Form.)

With the influx of new products in the securities industry today (see Figure 14-8 for a partial listing of products offered by a full service securities firm), operations support areas must meet the processing demands within required time constraints. Effective planning and preparation are the keys to survival in today's increasingly competitive financial services world.

Equities Products
o Over the counter
o Listed
o New issues

Options Products
o Stock options
o Options on commodity futures
o OTC options
o Debt options (T-bonds, T-notes, T-bills)
o Managed options service

Mutual Funds
o Capital appreciation/ small growth fund
o Municipal bond funds
o Tax managed trust
o Option income funds
o Specialty funds
o Equity funds
o International bond funds

Fixed Income
o Corporate Bonds
   Convertibles
   Deep discount
   Junk
   Zero coupon
   Capital note
   Variable rate

o Money Market Instruments
   Insured CD's
   Commercial paper

o Government Securities
   TIGR'S
   Bills
   Notes
   Bonds
   Agencies
   Mortgage-backed securities

o Municipal Bonds
   Short-term paper
   Tax-free commercial paper
   Bonds
   Zeros
   Deep discount

Bonds Funds
o Taxable Trusts
   Short-term CD trust
   Intermediate-term corporate zero coupon
   Government guaranteed trust
   Long-term corporate bond trust
   Long-term equity income trust
   Long-term preferred stock trust
   Long-term treasury trust

o Tax Free Trusts
   Short term tax free trust
   Intermediate floating rate
   Intermediate municipal trust
   Long-term specialty funds
   Bond fund swap program

Margin
o General margin account
o Non-purpose loan

Money Market Funds
o Ready assets trust
o Institutional funds
o U.S.A. government reserves
o Government securities fund
o Tax exempt funds
o Retirement reserves money funds

Incremental Share Services
o Discount brokerage service
o Stock purchase plans
o Automatic investment of dividends

Financial Planning

Retirement Accounts
o Self-directed IRA
o Rollover IRA
o Mutual fund IRA
o Keogh

Special Transactions
o Installment sales
o Rule 144/145 transactions
o S-16 registrations

Tax Advisory/Investments
o Tax planning

o Tax investments
   Energy
   Real estate
   Venture capital
   Equipment leasing

Insurance
o Term
o Permanent
o Group health
o Pension
o Individual disability

Annuities
o Fixed
o Variable
o Structured
o Group

Financing
o Mergers & acquisitions
o Investment banking

Securities Research
o Fundamental research
o Investment strategy
o Fixed income research
o Market analysis
o Investment guides

Institutional Services
o Block trading
o Risk arbitrage

FIGURE 14-8. General Products and Services Offered by Full Service Securities Firms

CHAPTER 15

Customer Service

The Customer Service area often is the only contact a customer has with a firm after the customer buys or sells through the Account Executives. Using other industries as an example, how many times have you bought from General Motors, Ford, or General Electric, and come away with a favorable or unfavorable impression of the company after speaking with its Customer Service area?

A firm is often judged by a customer on how promptly and courteously the customer's problem is resolved. Therefore, from the operations manager's viewpoint, it is important that the Customer Service area, however small or large, provide a high level of responsiveness.

This chapter will discuss the organization of a Customer Service area, what to look for in selecting employees for this function, training and equipment needs, workflow, control, and recordkeeping.

ORGANIZATION

The structure of the Customer Service area depends on the size of the operation. In a large firm, Customer Service might be a separate department, structured hierarchically with different reporting levels. A smaller firm, on the other hand, might have a less extensive Customer Service area, or Customer Service areas which are part of other operating departments, such as a Dividend or Transfer department. Let's look at both scenarios.

LARGE FIRM

In a Customer Service area that is part of a large firm, the head of the department might have several managers in a direct reporting line. They, in turn, might manage several supervisors who could be directly responsible for the Customer Service Representatives. There could be separate units handling branch inquiries and client inquiries, or even special units handling aged or management items (items referred from regulatory agencies or senior management).

The organization chart shown in Figure 15-1 gives an example of this type of sctructure.

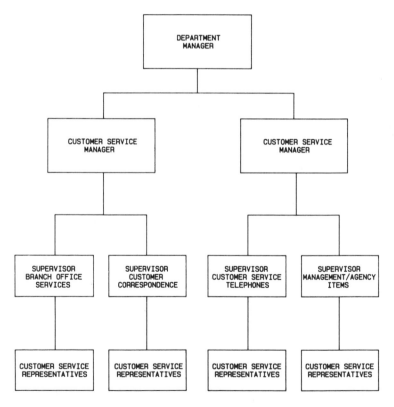

FIGURE 15-1. Customer Service Department—Large Firm

SMALL FIRM

In a smaller firm, the Customer Service area might be either a separate entity on a smaller scale with fewer reporting levels or part of another operating department, such as the Dividend Department or a special product area. In addition, the Customer Service area might be functioning from a branch office or regional level.

Figure 15-2 depicts a typical organization structure of a Customer Service area in a small firm.

The major responsibilities of Customer Service supervisors and representatives are shown in Figure 15-3.

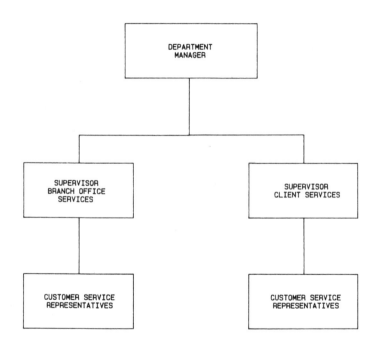

FIGURE 15-2. Customer Service Department—Small Firm

Customer Service Supervisor	Customer Service Representative
Reports statistics to management	Acts as liaison between branch offices and operating departments
Monitors aged items	Compiles statistics
Ensures correspondence meets professional standards	Researches and responds to customer and branch office inquiries/complaints
Ensures prompt resolution of management/ agency items	Handles customer and branch phone inquiries
Supervises Customer Service Representatives	

FIGURE 15-3. Responsibilities in a Customer Service Area

SELECTING THE CUSTOMER SERVICE REPRESENTATIVE

The selection and training of a Customer Service Representative is important because these employees are often the "front line" in dealing with customers. In addition, the representative needs to work well with internal clients, such as branch office personnel and home office personnel, who are responsible for processing the customer's transactions.

Some of the characteristics that should be looked for when selecting a person for this role are:

Good oral communication skills

Good written communication skills

Ability to maintain an even temperament under pressure

Ability to adapt to changing roles

Ability to work well with others

The job of a Customer Service Representative is usually subject to a high degree of turnover. It can be used to give employees a useful broad background on the firm's operations, but managers should prepare and plan for significant job rotation.

TRAINING THE CUSTOMER SERVICE REPRESENTATIVE

Because the Customer Service Representative in the securities industry requires at least a working knowledge of many aspects of the securities business, it will be necessary to provide training that will give the representative a broad perspective of the business. Some of the areas that should be considered here are:

Employee orientation to the firm

Introduction to securities

Introduction to securities operations

Introduction to branch office operations

In addition, there are various specialized courses the employee in this department should be exposed to:

Personal computer courses

Telephone etiquette

Interpersonal skills

Effective business writing

Specialized courses related to functions

It is also a good idea to design a training manual for the representative. This manual should include problem-solving procedures, definitions of common industry terms, organization charts, contact lists, sample letters, and any information directly related to the firm. Not only will this be a valuable training tool, but the manual will serve as a handy reference for the representatives in performing their daily functions.

EQUIPMENT USERS' GUIDES

These are guides explaining the use of various types of equipment usually found in Customer Service areas. For example, a guide that explains the use of terminals dispensing market data information, such as Quotron, Telerate, and Reuters terminals, would explain to the Customer Service Representative the basic procedures necessary to obtain the information. The type of guide can usually be written specifically for the needs of the department, since not all market data vendors' features are applicable to a Customer Service area. The guide should be concise and clear, giving directions that are simple and easy to follow.

The following is a brief list of the type of users' guides a typical Customer Service area might employ:

Market data terminal guide

Internal systems guides which give directions on the use of internal data systems to obtain customer account information.

Guides explaining the use of the personal computer, these would include the handbooks published by the vendor explaining the use of the hardware, as well as directions on the use of the various software packages.

Form letter handbook describing the form letters used by the department with samples of each.

REFERENCE BOOKS

Standard reference works should be available for use by the department, including:

Dictionaries

Thesauruses

Internal organization contact lists

Zip code books

Business writing handbooks

Because working in a Customer Service area in a securities firm requires knowledge of so many specialized areas, various publications and reference books dealing with the industry are necessary. The Customer Service Representative should be familiar with these standard works. The following is a brief checklist of the most important guides that the Customer Service Representative should have a good working knowledge of:

Standard & Poor's Dividend Guide. Gives dividend information on the majority of announced dividends. Includes rate, record date, ex-date, and payable date. Published on a daily, weekly, monthly, and yearly basis.

Standard & Poor's Stock Guide. A brief synopsis of various companies, what they do, stock symbols, market price range, and financial information.

Financial Guide. A listing of major corporations and their transfer agents.

In addition to these standard works, there may be other reference guides that are applicable to a Customer Service area, such as bond guides, or tax information updates. The manager should determine which ones will be particularly helpful.

EQUIPMENT NEEDS

Timely and informed responsiveness should be one of the most important goals of the Customer service area. To help the staff reach that goal they should be provided with the best equipment to do so. Listed below are some of the equipment needs that are important:

Adequate telephone lines

Automatic call directors

Market data terminals

Terminals for accessing customer files

Facsimile machines

Microfiche readers

Personal computers/local area network

The type and amount of equipment will depend on the volume of transactions processed by the area. The objective is to provide the appropriate equipment to allow the representatives to accomplish their tasks in a responsive manner.

WORKFLOW

Work is received in the Customer Service area in many ways. Customers may forward written correspondence, telephone the area to discuss a problem, or personally visit the area. Inquiries will also come from branch offices or other operating departments within the firm.

STEPS IN RESOLVING PROBLEMS

When an inquiry is received, it should first be reviewed by a supervisor and then assigned to a Customer Service Representative. The work assignments can be by account number, geographic area, or by even distribution among the representatives.

Upon receipt of the item, the representative attaches an inquiry form which provides client name, account number, date received, and space for notations. In addition, the representative usually will log in the problem on a control sheet.

If the Customer Service area has a computer reporting system, the representative will fill out a form and/or enter the data directly into the computer system. An example of this type of form is illustrated in Figure 15-4. The example used is a three-part form which will allow for the tracking of the item from its initial receipt, and referral to the final closing of the item. In a simpler operation, manual logs may be utilized which are kept on a daily basis by one clerk for the entire unit.

After logging in the item, the representative will review it to decide which steps are necessary to resolve the problem. It might be a simple problem requiring only minimal research, or a more complicated item requiring referral to a branch office or another operating area of the firm. In a small area, the representative may be responsible for contacting the branch or department directly and ascertaining the information necessary to resolve the problem. In the latter scenario, the representative should document each conversation to assure accuracy and completeness.

If the item is referred to another area, the date of the referral should be noted, as well as the date returned. When the problem has been resolved, the customer should be sent a written response. A copy of the letter should be attached to the completed item, the log updated, and the item filed.

Figures 15-5 and 15-6 provide schematic diagrams of workflows in a Customer Service area. Figure 15-5 provides an overview of how work is received and resolved. Figure 15-6 provides more detail on the steps taken by the Customer Service Representative to resolve problems.

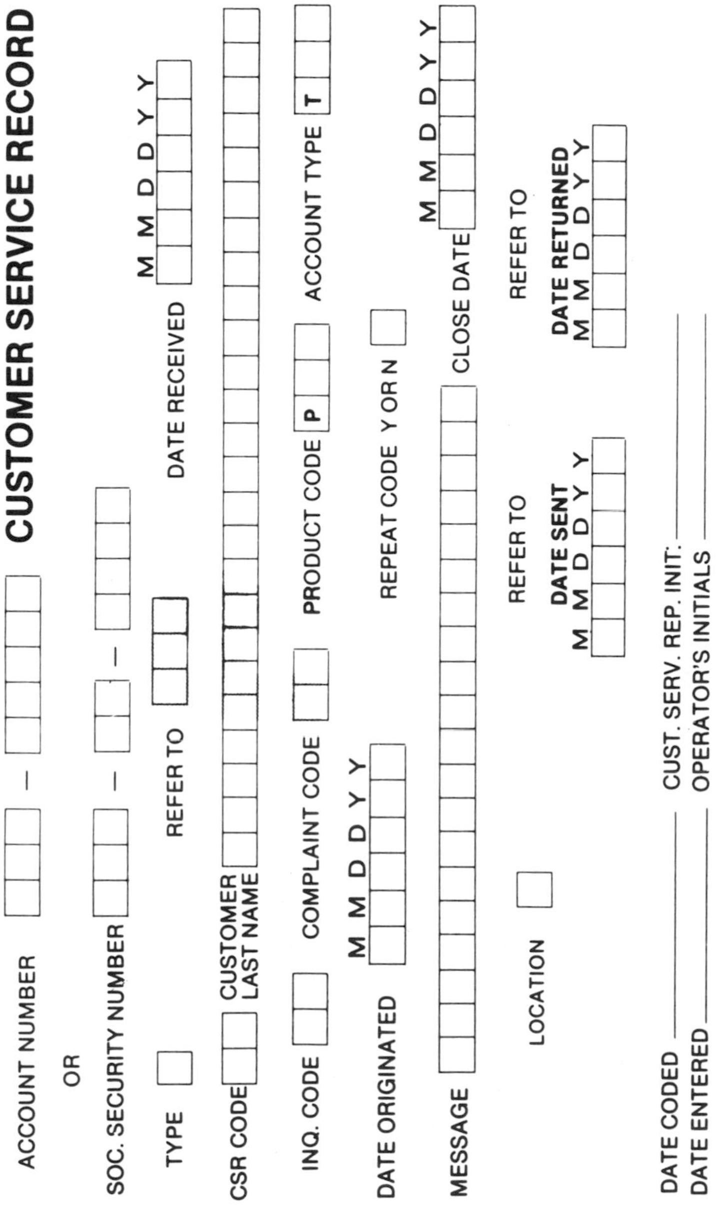

FIGURE 15-4. Customer Service Record

¹The client's account number.

²The type of item: inquiry or complaint.

³The branch office or operating department the item is referred to.

⁴The date the item was received by the Customer Service area.

⁵The Customer Service representative coded by number.

⁶The client's last name.

⁷The number assigned to each type of inquiry. For example, 03 would be an inquiry or dividend entitlement, 14 on lost certificates.

⁸The number assigned to each type of complaint.

⁹The product the item refers to.

¹⁰The type of account, for example, retain or institutional.

¹¹The date of the customer's letter.

¹²Whether the item is a repeat item.

¹³Any comments the Customer Service representatives wishes to note, for example, previously worked on by J. Smith.

¹⁴The date the item is closed.

¹⁵The date the item is referred to a branch office or operating department for response.

¹⁶The date returned from referral.

¹⁷The date the Customer Service representative fills out the Customer Service record.

¹⁸The Customer Service representative's initials.

¹⁹The date entered into the system.

²⁰The operator's initials.

FIGURE 15-4. (*Continued*)

MOST COMMON TYPES OF PROBLEMS

A Customer Service area in a securities firm receives a wide variety of inquiries and complaints. However, there are certain categories of complaints and inquiries that seem to reoccur frequently. Figure 15-7 gives a general idea of the most common problems received, grouped by type.

These, of course, will not cover every type of item that is received by a Customer Service area. However, it is a good probability that at least some will be encountered on a daily basis.

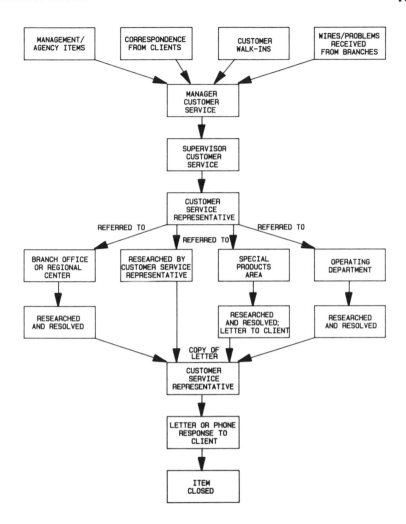

FIGURE 15-5. Customer Service Workflow

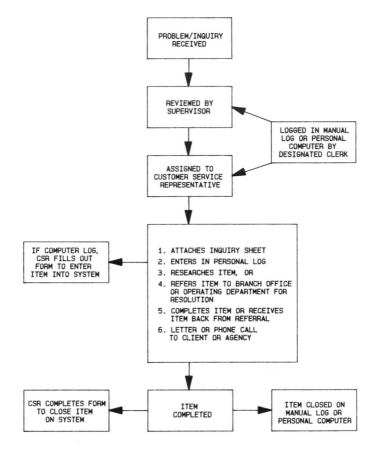

FIGURE 15-6. Steps in Problem Solving

AGED ITEMS

Aged items result when the resolution of a problem or inquiry exceeds the firm's accepted turnaround standard. If the standard is 15 business days, then those items that still remain open after this time should be considered aged.

Service-Related	Trade-Related	Transfer
Duplicate record requests	Unauthorized trades	Request for delivery
Confusion in reading or interpreting statement	Execution price	Lost certificate
Name and/or address change	Money loss	Broker to broker transfer requests
Dividend/Interest	*Deposits*	*Branch Office*
IRS reporting	Missing funds	Rude treatment
Dividend entitlement	Incorrect credits	Request to close account
Interest calculation		
Short pay dividends		
Special Products		
Inquiries/problems relating to special problems or account types offered by the firm		

FIGURE 15-7. Common Customer Service Problems

It is important that the manager review the open item reports and determine the disposition of all aged items. Along with management/agency items, aged items should be treated as priority. It is usually not necessary to create a special unit to handle these items. However, it should be one of the supervisor's main duties to be aware of these items, and make every effort to ensure their prompt resolution. In addition, the supervisor and manager should be available to lend their assistance to the representative, both with their expertise and in eliciting cooperation from other areas of the firm when necessary.

By carefully monitoring and controlling aged items, the manager can ensure that they do not escalate into major problems. There is always a possibility that aged items could evolve into management or agency complaints; therefore it is the manager's responsibility to closely monitor them, and step in when necessary to effect their resolution.

Management/Agency Items

Customers will often appeal to the various regulatory agencies governing the securities industry in an effort to have their problems resolved. Among these agencies are the Securities and Exchange Commission, the various stock exchanges, and the National Association of Securities Dealer. As an alternative, some clients will often write or call senior management of the firm in an attempt to resolve their problems.

These items are classified as management/agency items, and as such, are subject to priority handling. When they are received they should be segregated, logged in, assigned to a representative, and resolved as soon as possible. An attempt should be made to solve these inquiries within the allowable 15 business day time-frame. Although this may not be possible for all items, every effort should be made by the manager to closely monitor these items and ensure their prompt resolution.

If the organization of the Customer Service area allows for it, a special person could be designated to handle management/ agency problems. Or if there is a special unit dealing with aged items, management/agency items might be included as part of that unit's responsibility.

There are two special considerations in preparing a response to these items. First, the response should be directed, under the manager's signature, to the regulatory agency with a copy to the client. Second, it is a good policy to have the response reviewed by the Compliance area of the firm before it is sent to the customer.

CONTROL

It's important to have a system to control the status of all inquiries. The degree of sophistication employed will depend on the size of the operation and the resources available. Control can range from simple manual logs of all inquiries or complaints to an intricate computer system designed not only to track items, but to assign them a place in the overall scheme of the firm's productivity standards.

Some of the data necessary for this tracking include:

1. Date of receipt of the item
2. The type of inquiry
3. To whom the item was referred
4. Present status
5. Date the item was closed
6. The amount of time it remained as an open item

Figure 15-8 gives an idea of one type of control log and the information that can be extracted from it.

Date: 10/25

Complaint Codes	Current Week		Prior Week		Change from Prior Week	Ytd Items
	Items	*Percent*	*Items*	*Percent*	*Prior Week*	*Items*
Dividend/Interest						
Short pay	4	1.0	4	1.3	+ 0	20
IRS report	17	4.3	10	3.3	+ 7	46
Entitlement	15	3.8	25	8.4	− 10	73
Auto reinvestment	5	1.2	1	0.3	+ 4	13
Category subtotal	41	10.3	40	13.3	+ 1	152
Transfer						
Delivery of securities	40	10.2	24	8.1	+18	104
Missing documentation	1	0.2	3	1.0	− 2	6
Broker to broker	27	6.0	21	7.0	+ 6	97
Office to office	3	0.7	1	0.3	+ 2	8
Category subtotal	71	17.1	49	16.4	24	215
Deposits						
Missing funds	16	4.1	7	2.3	+ 9	37
Returned checks	2	0.5	0	0.0	+ 2	6
Wire funds	1	0.2	1	0.3	+ 0	2
Category subtotal	19	4.8	8	2.6	+11	45
Reorganization						
Tender offer	2	0.5	3	1.0	− 1	7
Missing proceeds	2	0.5	1	0.3	+ 1	7
Category subtotal	4	1.0	4	1.3	+ 0	14

FIGURE 15-8. Customer Service Department Weekly Operating Statistics by Complaint

RECORDKEEPING

Closed files are usually kept on premises for a period ranging from 18 months to 2 years. This is necessary since many items are repeat items requiring referral to the original. Files are usually retained for a period of 4 to 7 years. Since space considerations usually rule out storage of these items within the Customer Service area, they are frequently stored in the firm's warehouse.

CHAPTER 16

Human Resource Strategies for Training and Development

One of the most important aspects of your position as an Operations Manager is to assure that the professional and technical development of your staff is not neglected. This is especially important in today's operations environment, where new business is transforming the area almost daily.

This chapter will explore some Human Resource strategies which will assist you in developing your staff. We will look at training, which is one of the most important tools a manager possesses. We will also focus on developmental strategies, such as Performance Evaluation Techniques and the Employee Profile, which will assist you in focusing on employee strengths and weaknesses in order to make your operation as efficient as possible.

TRAINING IN AN OPERATIONS AREA

Because the securities industry environment is changing so rapidly, the need for training cannot be emphasized enough. You, as an Operations Manager, have a critical need to bring your staff immediately up to par by providing training that will meet your employees' needs to do the present job more efficiently, as well as giving them a sound introduction to new products and procedures.

To give just one example of the rapidly expanding and evolving operations environment, let's look at the increased presence of

United States securities firms in the global securities marketplace. This international presence poses a major training challenge for the Operations Manager. Some of the questions your staff would need to have answered are: How do currency fluctuations affect clearing? Is foreign securities processing different from domestic and how do the rules of foreign exchanges differ from the NYSE and AMEX? These are just a few of the questions that the Operations Manager must address to meet the challenge of an expanding field. The best way to do this is by rapid and effective training.

In order to assist you in achieving this goal, we will focus on providing a core curriculum for an Operations area. We will discuss the courses and programs available, what should be covered in each and some different types of training methods that will be of assistance.

TYPE OF TRAINING

In the securities business, training usually focuses on two major types: technical and developmental. Technical training focuses on skills training, the basic requirements needed to perform the job. An example of technical training would be a basic Dividend course, which covers such topics as balancing and reconciling cash and stock dividends. Developmental training, on the other hand, concerns itself more with interpersonal managerial skills, and is therefore geared to first-line supervisors and managers. Some examples of developmental programs are courses on motivating the employee, how to delegate responsibilities, and the use of constructive criticism.

DEVELOPING A CORE CURRICULUM

Let's take a closer look at some classes that Operations Managers should be aware of when assessing the training needs of their staff. Although not all of these courses will be applicable to your area, they will give you an idea of how training can assist you in providing the basic and advanced skills necessary to keep pace with your needs. We'll look first at a core curriculum designed to enhance the technical skills of the operations employee.

Included will be a basic curriculum as well as courses that are more specific to the different operational areas of a securities firm (see Figures 16-1 and 16-2). To give you an idea of how training can be utilized to answer the questions posed by new aspects of the business, we'll include courses designed for the global marketplace (see Figure 16-3). We will also include courses that focus on more complicated products, such as Options and the Money Market, which will give you an idea of what courses of this nature should be included (see Figure 16-4).

These course descriptions will assist you in ensuring that the training provided for your employees will be useful and relevant to the operations environment. Also included will be developmental programs designed to give a sound foundation in managerial techniques to your supervisory and managerial staff (See Figure 16-5). Because the securities industry has become so dependent on computer technology, courses in the operation of the personal computer should also be a part of the core curriculum.

Compare these technical and developmental curriculums to those offered by your firm. Make sure that the major points are covered. Remember that there are also financial training institutions in most major cities that offer courses of the nature described. Some examples of these types of institutions would be the New York Institute of Finance and The Securities Training Corporation in New York, both of which offer comprehensive detailed training on all aspects of the securities industry. In addition, many colleges and universities offer financial courses that may be of help to your staff. Explore these institutions as a means of supplementing what may already be offered by your firm.

Course	Who It Is For	Content
Employee orientation	New employees or those new to the Operations areas of the company	The history and language of Wall Street The various departments, positions, and functions of a securities firm The history and organization of your firm The principal securities products Why and how corporations issue stock The rules and regulations governing security trading
Introduction to securities operations	New Operations employees or experienced Operations employees who need a more thorough concept of the interrelationship of the various Operations areas.	How an order is processed How different types of trades are processed Introduction to margin How the Cashiering Department operates How the Stock Record Department operates The Proxy Department The functions of the Dividend Department The Clearing Corporation Depositories and their functions
Introduction to securities	Employees new to firm or the Operations areas	Types of issues Common and preferred stock Rights and warrants The over-the-counter market Mutual funds The NYSE and AMEX Round lots Odd lots Short sales Corporate, municipal, and government bonds Reading and understanding financial statements Introduction to options Opening and conduct of customer accounts

FIGURE 16-1. Core Curriculum Technical Training Basic Courses

Course	Who It Is For	Content
The Cashiering Department	Cashiering personnel or those involved in related departments	Cashiering operations including functions of each area and their relation to other processing departments Negotiability rules Regulations affecting cashiering such as Regs. T and U, SEC Rule 15c 3-3 Receives and delivers Fail to deliver or receive
Introduction to dividends	Dividend personnel and those desiring a better knowledge of dividend processing	Introduction to dividends The concept of ex-dividend date Cash dividends Stock splits Identifying and correcting errors Tax consequences and record keeping Foreign dividends Due bills
Introduction to bonds	Employees working with bonds or those needing more information about the bond market	Definitions of bonds Bond yields Factors affecting yields How bonds are rated Trading terms and techniques Bonds funds
Introduction to margin	New margin employees or those who interface with the Margin Department	Definition of margin Margin operations processes Margin rules and regulations Margin calls Margin bookkeeping Short sales
The Stock Record Department	Stock Record personnel and those affected by Stock Record operations	Functions of the Stock Record Department Causes of and solutions to "breaks" Daily stock record take-off Monthly stock record Trial balances Suspense accounts—definition and reconciliation DTC reconciliation

FIGURE 16-2. Technical Training Specific to Operations

Course	Who It Is For	Content
The transfer process	Transfer personnel and those desiring a better knowledge of transfer procedures	Good delivery rules Rules for negotiability for registered and bearer securities Importance of signatures and certificate registration Legal transfer requirements Use of stock/bond power Missing, lost, or stolen certificates

FIGURE 16-2. (*Continued*)

Course	Who It Is For	Content
Foreign Exchange Markets	Employees working in International Operations	Calculating foreign exchange profits and losses Foreign exchange forecasting Economic, political, and financial factors affecting rates Relationship between foreign exchange market and Eurocurrency markets Money market activities leading to foreign exchange transactions
Processing Foreign Exchange Transaction	New employees in International Operations	Settlements in foreign currency Variations in dollar settlements Foreign exchange regulations Internal controls Exposure monitoring
International Securities Clearing	Employees involved in clearing foreign securities	Negotiability of international equities American depository receipts (ADRs) Settlement abroad vs. foreign currency Foreign dividends and rights Clearing through Euro-clear and Cedel

FIGURE 16-3. Technical Skills Training—Global Financial Markets

Course	Who It Is For	Content
Introduction to Options	New employees who need a basic understanding of options	Definition of options History of option trading Terminology Basic concepts of puts and calls Advantages and disadvantages of option trading Option strategies The options markets
Introduction to the Money Market	New employees who require a more detailed knowledge of the money market	Basic definition U.S. Treasury instruments Repurchase agreements Commercial paper Bankers' acceptances Certificates of deposit Domestic and Eurodollar CDs Calculating yield

FIGURE 16-4. Core Curriculum: Specific Products

OPERATIONS MANAGER TRAINING

We have discussed a core curriculum for your staff. Now let's look at courses designed for you as an Operations Manager. The programs noted in Figure 16-6, or ones of a similar nature, should be the center of an Operation Manager's training curriculum. All aspects of the position are covered, from administrative duties to Human Resource management.

By supplementing these courses with additional technical ones relating to products, you have a thorough base for your own professional development.

ENSURING COURSES ARE JOB RELATED

As you may have noted, the course contents in Figures 16-1 through 16-4 are very specific to the job. This is a very important point to emphasize. A prevalent complaint about training is that employees receive information that is, in effect, extraneous to the job they are performing.

Course	Who It Is For	Content
Basic Functions of Supervision	First-line supervisors	Definitions of the basic role of the supervisor Demonstration of various supervisory styles Delegation techniques Ways of motivating the employee Techniques of effective discipline
Effective Presentation Skills	First-line supervisors and managers	Methods to improve poise, vocal quality, topic organization, time consideration Method of effectively utilizing visual aids Techniques for utilizing individual strengths for presentations
Interpersonal Skills for Manager	First- and second-line managers	How to give recognition Methods of constructive criticism Communicating goals and priorities Providing direction and feedback
Effective Business Writing	First- and second-line managers	Time-saving techniques to improve memos and reports Clarity Brevity Use of effective words Editing techniques Techniques of persuasive writing
Interviewing Techniques	First- and second-line supervisors and managers	Methods of analyzing job positions prior to the interview How to develop effective questioning, listening, and evaluating techniques Understanding the legal requirements for conducting an interview

FIGURE 16-5. Core Curriculum: Developmental Training

One way of ensuring that the courses and programs attended by your employees are job related, is to be involved in the design of the course. When training professionals do their research to develop programs for your area, make sure that there is input from the employees who are actually performing the job function. You should also make sure that you have final approval of the course.

In cases of classes that have already been prepared, especially developmental classes, a careful assessment of your employees' needs should be measured against the objectives of the course. You should ask yourself whether the performance you wish to develop or change in your employee will be affected by the class. Also ask if the course fits the employees' needs. This is very important if training is to be an effective tool for employee development.

MANAGEMENT SUPPORT

It is important that the manager be totally committed to the necessity of training. One would think this is an obvious point, but many times managers will only give lip service to the learning needs of their employees, and no real effort will be made to provide a work environment supportive of the ideas and skills learned in class.

It is important that the employee receive positive follow-up from the manager. Often training is done in a vacuum by an area of the firm that is unable to provide assessment of the effectiveness of their courses. At this point, the manager must step in to provide follow-up reinforcement to the employee. This is especially necessary in developmental training. Supervisors are taught people skills to assist in dealing with staff. However, when they go back to an environment that negates what they have learned, an environment that is not conductive to fostering people skills such as motivation and constructive criticism, all the effort expended by the trainer will be in vain.

TRAINING METHODS

Figure 16-7 gives a brief synopsis of some of the methods used by training professionals. You might wish to review those training methods and, with your own area in mind, try to pick courses that utilize the most effective methods for your employee population.

For example, if only a few new bookkeepers need to be trained, as opposed to a large number, computer based instructions may be a good choice.

Discuss these methods with your training professionals, so that you will be able to determine the most effective training method.

PERFORMANCE APPRAISALS

You, as an Operations Manager, will be required at various stages in your career to give or review performance appraisals. The performance appraisal process is essentially a management tool which provides you with information about how your objectives are being met at the operational level. At the same time, it provides the employees with valuable information about the way management views their performance and the contributions they have made to the organization.

Because performance appraisal is so important to the employee's professional development, and therefore to the manager's goal of achieving an effective operation, it should be a critical component of your Human Resource strategy. Unfortunately it is a tool which is sometimes misused. The supervisor and manager often shy away from the formal appraisal process. They find it difficult to focus

Course	*Content*
Essentials of Effective Management	Basic organizational information
	People-management skills
	Motivating the employee
	Developing the employee
	Approaching problems in a systematic way
	Establishing positive interdepartmental communication
The Budgeting Process	Introduction to the firm's budgeting process
	Assigning costs to action plans
	Planning and executing an accurate budget
Introduction to Compliance	Review of common compliance problems
	How to recognize common compliance problems
	Developing and implementing solutions

FIGURE 16-6. Core Curriculum: Operations Manager Training

Course	Content
Introduction to Administration	Review of reports essential to running the office Personnel administration Human resource issues
Introduction to Legal Issues	Legal problems common to the branch office Guidelines for dealing with legal issues
Termination	How to prepare for a termination Proper documentation Conducting termination interviews How to manage an unpleasant situation professionally
Delegation	The importance of delegation Assessment of subordinate's abilities Overcoming obstacles to effective delegation Step-by-step action plan for effective delegation
Business Planning	Definition and purpose of business plans How to write and develop a useful business plan Establishing objectives Establishing time frames Developing strategies to put plans into effect
Performance Appraisal	Job analysis Components of a performance review Common mistakes Use of feedback Guidelines for conducting the performance review Role playing
Interviewing Skills	Job analysis Questioning techniques Legal requirements Planning the format of the job interview Evaluation techniques
Managing Time Effectively	Time management techniques Specific solutions to time problems Managing crisis Changing ineffective use of time on and off the job

FIGURE 16-6. (*Continued*)

Type	Description	Advantages	Disadvantages
On-the-job	Experienced employees demonstrating job functions to new employees	Totally job-related Low cost Convenient	Bad habits are passed on Can disrupt regular workflow No control of training environment
Computer-based training	Method utilizing the personal computer to affect job knowledge	Not disruptive Self-paced Actual job simulation Content is standardized and controlled Provides immediate reinforcement	Difficult to use for developmental training Costly
Classroom presentations	Formal method whereby instruction is imparted by means of formalized presentations	Large groups of people can participate Techniques such as slides, overhead projectors and videos can be used Can be used for developmental training	Disruptive to regular workflow Time-consuming Not related to real life

FIGURE 16-7. Training Methods

objectively on the strengths and weaknesses of the employee. They look on the appraisal as a chore, and fail to see it as part of their overall strategy for achieving their management objectives. Therefore, they often postpone or neglect conducting an evaluation.

In order to assist you, we will provide some guidelines in preparing an employee evaluation. We will give some suggestions on how to fill out an appraisal with a sample form provided. By following the process step-by-step, you and your supervisors will feel more comfortable with the appraisal process, and will be able to utilize this valuable tool more effectively.

Refer to Figure 16-8, which is a sample Performance Review Form. Explanations giving specific directions in filling out the form are listed on page 426.

GLOBAL OPERATIONS SERVICES
PERFORMANCE OBJECTIVES & APPRAISAL

Use this form to establish and review performance for employees in grades 12-31.

EMPLOYEE NAME	GRADE	TITLE	
GROUP MANAGER	DEPARTMENT NAME/APPRAISER		APPRAISAL YEAR

* PERFORMANCE RATING LEGEND
DNM - DID NOT MEET REQMNTS, MM - MET MOST REQMNTS, MR - MET REQMNTS, ER - EXCEED REQMNTS, FE - FAR EXCEEDS REQMNTS

POSITION SUMMARY

This section is completed by your supervisor/manager. Listed are the major functions your position performs and the clients (internal/external) to whom you provide service.

FIGURE 16-8. Performance Objectives and Appraisal

---

1. OBJECTIVE/RESPONSIBILITY: CRITICAL [   ]   IMPORTANT [   ]

> The objective listed here and in the following boxes, reflects the major duties
> associated with your position. Objective setting occurs during the first quarter of
> the calendar year for all employees. New hires should receive their objectives
> within the first 90 days of employment. If you take on new responsibilities during
> the year, they should be added to this portion of the Performance Plan.

STANDARDS

> The standards indicate the level of acceptable performance to achieve a Mets Requirements
> for each of your listed objectives. They indicate how and how well you are expected to
> perform your job and the results you are to achieve. The purpose is to give you and your
> supervisor/manager a yardstick for measuring your performance. Your standards will be
> specific and measurable.

MID-YEAR REVIEW

> This section is completed at mid-year (June). Your performance during the first six
> months is described against the objectives and standards that were established
> during the first quarter. Your supervisor/manager will specify examples of how you
> far exceeded, exceeded, met, met most, or did not meet the standards. The
> mid-year review is an opportunity for you and your supervisor/manager to discuss
> your performance and to modify your objectives and standards.

> Your supervisor/manager will check one of the seven boxes below which reflects
> your performance for that given objective during the last six months.

* PERFORMANCE RATING FOR MID-YEAR REVIEW

DNM [   ]   MM [   ]   MR [   ]   MR+ [   ]   ER [   ]   ER+ [   ]   FE [   ]

YEAR END REVIEW

> This section is completed at the end of the assessment period. Your performance is
> described against the objectives and standards that were established during your
> objective setting meeting at the beginning of the first quarter and at mid-year. Your
> supervisor/manager will specify examples of how you far exceeded, exceeded, met, met
> most, or did not meet the standards. The year end review is a summary discussion
> between you and your supervisor/manager about your past year's performance.

> Your supervisor/manager will check one of the seven boxes below which reflects
> your performance for that given objective during the assessment period.

* PERFORMANCE RATING FOR FULL YEAR REVIEW

DNM [   ]   MM [   ]   MR [   ]   MR+ [   ]   ER [   ]   ER+ [   ]   FE [   ]

FIGURE 16-8. (*Continued*)

AREAS FOR IMPROVEMENT

Identify specific actionable items which will improve the employee's performance and overall growth and development.

MID-YEAR REVIEW

> At mid-year, your supervisor/manager identifies opportunities that will help you
> achieve your career objectives, add to your skill base, capitalize on your strengths and
> overcome your weakness. These opportunities might be training, job rotation, project
> assignments, additional responsibilities, etc. Also listed, are the steps you will
> undertake to pursue the development opportunities for the coming assessment period.

FULL YEAR REVIEW

> Your supervisor/manager identifies opportunities that will help you achieve your career
> objectives, add to your skill base, etc. These opportunities might be training, job rotation,
> project assignments, additional responsibilities, etc. Also listed, are the steps you will
> undertake to pursue the development opportunities for the coming assessment period.

EMPLOYEE COMMENTS

After the appraisal meeting between the manager and employee, the employee is encouraged to provide any comments
regarding this appraisal and/or his/her overall performance. (additional paper may be used).

OBJECTIVE AND STANDARD SETTING

COACHING SESSIONS HELD THROUGHOUT THE YEAR

MID-YEAR REVIEW

FULL YEAR REVIEW

> At the conclusion of the performance assessment, (both mid-year and year end) you are encouraged to
> comment on your own performance, as well as to express your opinions on the review process and
> coaching sessions your supervisor/manager held with you during the year.

FIGURE 16-8. (*Continued*)

PERFORMANCE SUMMARY

Summarize the employee's overall performance. Include specific examples relating to performance dimensions which are critical to success in this position, such as; Initiative, Teamwork, Responsiveness to Clients, Quality of Work, Knowledge of Work, Reliability, Interpersonal Skills, etc. Additionally, make sure to include performance discussion and review for any ad hoc and/or unplanned projects.

MID-YEAR SUMMARY

This section is completed at mid-year. Your supervisor/manager will list specific examples of what makes you an effective employee, special talents that you have exhibited and also your weakness as related to the performance dimensions.

Your supervisor/manager will check one of the seven boxes below which reflects your overall performance during the last six months. Because Merrill Lynch has very high expectations of performance, an "MR" rating is considered positive and reflects that you are doing what is expected of you.

OVERALL PERFORMANCE RATING

Select the rating below which reflects the employee's overall mid-year performance. Keep in mind the relative importance of each objective/responsibility and the associated performance in selecting the overall rating.

DNM	MM	MR	MR+	ER	ER+	FE
☐	☐	☐	☐	☐	☐	☐

FULL YEAR SUMMARY

Listed here are specific examples of what makes you an effective employee, special talents that you have exhibited and also your weakness as related to the performance dimensions.

Your supervisor/manager will check one of the seven boxes below which reflects your overall performance during the assessment period. Because Merrill Lynch has very high expectations of performance, an "MR" rating is considered positive and reflects that you are doing what is expected of you.

OVERALL PERFORMANCE RATING

Select the rating below which reflects the employee's overall year end performance. Keep in mind the relative importance of each objective/responsibility and the associated performance in selecting the overall rating.

DNM	MM	MR	MR+	ER	ER+	FE
☐	☐	☐	☐	☐	☐	☐

FIGURE 16-8. (*Continued*)

SIGNATURES
At this point the employee's performance has been thoroughly evaluated and discussed with the employee.
The employee should retain a copy of the appraisal with all signatures.

OBJECTIVE SETTING

EMPLOYEE   DATE   MANAGER/APPRAISER   DATE

NEXT HIGHER LEVEL MANAGER   DATE

MID-YEAR REVIEW

EMPLOYEE   DATE   MANAGER/APPRAISER   DATE

NEXT HIGHER LEVEL MANAGER   DATE

FULL YEAR REVIEW

EMPLOYEE   DATE   MANAGER/APPRAISER   DATE

NEXT HIGHER LEVEL MANAGER   DATE

FIGURE 16-8. (*Continued*)

SECTION A

JOB REQUIREMENTS

This column will list the major responsibilities and goals of the job. If a job description is available, you may wish to utilize it in preparing this column.

ACHIEVEMENT MEASURES

List the specific results or objectives you expected the employee to accomplish. It's a good idea to include time frames if applicable.

RESULTS ACHIEVED

This column will focus on how well the employee has met the achievement measures that have been set for the job. Specific examples should be used if possible. This aspect of the appraisal will give you, as the manager, valuable information regarding how your broader objectives are being met or not met on the daily operational level. You can then ensure that your first line supervisors can address any problems before they impede the achievement of your objectives.

SECTION B I.   EMPLOYEE'S STRENGTH AND
II.   AREAS FOR IMPROVEMENT

These two areas should focus on the employees outstanding abilities and major strengths, as well as those areas needing improvement. This area is usually the one found to be most difficult by reviewers. Listed below are some questions to ask yourself that will assist you in providing direction, and focusing on strengths and weaknesses.

Is the employee's work accurate and complete?

How effectively does the employee accomplish things?

Can the employee effectively set priorities?

How does the employee meet deadlines?

To what extent is the employee able to get full cooperation from others?

How well does the employee follow established procedures?

How persuasive and diplomatic is the employee?

Has the employee improved since the last review?

What are the frequency and types of mistakes made?

What major areas need development?

How flexible is the employee in adjusting to changing work situations?

To what extent does the employee suggest alternative courses of action?

How well does the employee keep you informed?

By taking the time to really concentrate on these questions, it should become much easier to fill out this section of the form. Try to think of specific instances where the employee exhibited the desirable, or undesirable behavior. This will give the employee a better understanding of what you require. Give encouragement when work is done well, discuss problems and reasons for errors, and state specifically what can be done to improve performance.

III. TRAINING AND DEVELOPMENT

List here any courses that the employee should take to improve his/her performance. The actual listing of the courses on the performance appraisal form will reinforce the manager's commitment to training and provide the employee with a concrete way to improve performance.

IV. NEXT CAREER STAGE

At this stage in the performance appraisal discuss with the employee his/her aspirations for next career move. Give concrete feedback on whether the goal is attainable and what needs to be done by the employee to develop his/her skills to attain the goal.

If you feel that the employee's strengths do not warrant the career path the person wishes to follow, explain specifically why the employee is not suited to the position, and provide alternate routes the employee can follow.

These are some general guidelines in conducting an effective Employee Appraisal. An Operations Manager cannot afford to neglect using and requiring the use of these techniques by subordinates if your goal is truly to make your operation as successful as possible.

THE EMPLOYEE PROFILE

The Employee Profile is another valuable tool to assist the manager in assessing employees. The Profile is a form designed to give specific information about the employee; such items as educational background, work history and skills are included. It serves several valuable functions:

Assists the manager and supervisors in promotional decisions.

Gives the manager an overall picture of the employee base.

Assists the manager in redeploying the work force in times of heavy volume, or when warranted by organizational change, via its synopsis of employee skills and previous experience.

Consolidates employee data that may be found in several different locations, thereby saving the manager time.

Highlights skill or training deficiencies. (For example, a clerk involved in balancing activities should be familiar with the personal computer; the profile can highlight a discrepancy of this nature and training can be supplied.)

Assists in planning future operational strategies with greater efficiency through a better knowledge of the employee base.

These are a few of the important benefits an Operations Manager can realize from using an employee profile. Together with the performance appraisal, it gives a current picture of his/her organization. Strengths and weaknesses become readily apparent. The manager becomes aware of where he/she can go in the organization to draw on the knowledge needed to meet his/her objectives.

The supervisor of each unit should sit with the employee to gather the necessary information. If this is not convenient, a member of your staff can be assigned to obtain a profile of the complete organization.

The supervisor should concentrate on specific skills, such as personal computer or word processing expertise. In addition, any job-related experience the employee has, such as a sales or customer service background, should be listed.

The employee's most apparent strengths and weaknesses should be listed. The Performance Appraisal, which will be attached, can supply any details required.

CONTROL

The easiest way to control the information received is through the utilization of the personal computer. This will make the storage and retrieval of information easier, as well as allowing you to extract only the portions of information needed at any given time.

Although it will be time consuming to input all the information at first, especially with a large department, once the information is on the computer, updating becomes a much easier task. In addition, a print out of all the employees in a unit can be made for use by your supervisors, which will assist them in controlling their own personnel functions.

CHAPTER 17

Records
Management

Have you ever looked around your area and been dismayed by the amount of paper? Computer printouts and other papers are piled high on desks and in corners, microfiche is unorganized, and boxes are precariously placed in any available space. If the records that are so vital to processing your business are not readily available, valuable time is lost searching for them. That's why the management of records and information is such an important task for the Operations Manager.

This chapter will explore how to set up a new records management program or improve one that is already in place. We will address:

The need for a records management program.

The problems caused by inadequate record management.

How to analyze records requirements.

The benefits of microfilm, microfiche and image processing.

WHY DO WE NEED RECORDS MANAGEMENT?

There is an increasing emphasis being placed on productivity and management of information within Operations Departments. However, information is often lost or misplaced. Without proper organization, identification and consistent arrangement, controlling hard copy-reports or microfiche is virtually impossible. In any large-scale operation, paperwork is often created in the guise of record keeping. Computer-generated reports also fall under the "paperwork" category. Frequently information is redundant and stored in many areas in the Operations Department. This is especially so in large firms where increased specialization often leads to duplication of records. Therefore, it's important that Operations Managers carefully examine the record retention needs in order to ensure maximum productivity. The following sections will discuss some of the factors that create problems unique to operations.

The Growth of Information and Inadequate Storage

As securities firms grow, so does the amount of information stored. Just look at your area to see the number of pages filed each year, and you will realize the need for a coherent records management system. Operations areas are especially prone to this paper crunch because so many functions are still performed manually. The increasing market volume of recent years has only intensified the amount of information and records produced. The old filing and storage systems of the past are just not adequate to meet the new needs.

Cost

Paper and files take up space, and occupancy costs are a significant expense in most Operations departments. In addition, a poor records management system results in higher labor costs because of the time spent in research.

Regulatory Requirements

Your firm probably has a number of internal policies regarding how long and where you must keep certain records. In addition, there are various regulations governing the amount of time securities firms must keep certain records available. In particular, SEC regulation 17A-4 requires firms to have certain records retained for a specified amount of time. The usual retention period is six years, the first two years of which the records must be kept in an "easily accessible place." All of these requirements contribute to the need for an organized records management program.

HOW TO ANALYZE REQUIREMENTS

Before deciding the type of system you should have, where it should be, what records should be kept and for how long, there are a number of questions that need to be answered:

1. What specific records are kept by your department?
2. How do you classify your records; e.g., by customer, propriety, internally required, externally required, etc.?
3. What is the frequency of use of the records; e.g., daily, once a week, monthly?
4. What is the age of the records; e.g., active, six months to one year, one to two years, two to five years, over five years?
5. What medium is the record kept in; e.g., paper, microfiche, microfilm, etc.?
6. How many copies of the record do you keep?
7. Who uses the records; e.g., your department personnel, other personnel?
8. What storage devices are the records kept in?
9. How much space is required?
10. Are copies often made from the records?

Figure 17-1 shows a form that may be useful to you in gathering the above data. After gathering the above information, you will be in a position to analyze your requirements. The next step is to determine whether you should keep the records onsite or at a warehouse location.

ONSITE VERSUS WAREHOUSE LOCATION

There are some records that must be kept close by for some period of time. There are other records, however, that you can choose to keep onsite or send to a warehouse manager. Some areas to consider after you determine which records could be stored in either manner are:

Department Name: _____ Date: _____

Type of record: (A) Report: Computer _____ Paper _____ Film _____ Other _____

    Report/Record Number and/or Name: _____

    (B) Report: Paper _____ Fiche _____ Film _____ Other _____

Is report or record received or generated? _____

Purpose of report or record _____

How many pages or pieces of paper? _____

How Stored? File drawers _____ Boxes _____ Shelves _____ Other _____

How is report/record received or generated:
    Daily _____ Weekly _____ Monthly _____ Other (specify) _____

  2. If a report, what percent is used? _____

  3. Is this the best media for your needs?   No _____ Yes _____

  4. How many times a week do the people in your unit have to refer to this report/record?
    _____

  5. When you refer to the record/report do you make notes on it which must be referred to at some future time?   No _____ Yes _____

  6. Is there a legal retention for this report/record in the unit? _____ If so, how long? _____

  7. How long do you keep this report/record in the unit? _____

  8. Is this report/record kept an additional length of time in another area of the department?
    No _____ Yes _____

  9. How long? _____

10. Is this record/report sent to offsite storage?   No _____ Yes _____
    If yes, how long is it stored offsite? _____
    Is the record/report ever recalled from offsite storage?

    No _____ Yes _____

11. If yes, how often? _____

FIGURE 17-1. Records/Information Form

1. Are you able to provide onsite storage with proper facilities?

   Do you have sufficient space?

   What will it cost?

   What filing equipment would you need? (See Figure 17-2 for suggestions.)

   What will your future needs be?

2. Can you provide appropriate security for the records?

   What original documents are kept?

   Are disaster recovery plans in place for fire, flood, theft?

   Do you need computer or communications facilities?

3. How efficient will your onsite facility be?

   How important is the need for immediate access?

   What is the cost of your office space compared to warehouse space?

   What are personnel requirements?

   Do you have the necessary management expertise?

If you conclude that onsite storage contributes to the productivity, customer service and other objectives of your department, you then should consider such factors as file retention procedures, storage media and management.

FILE RETENTION

File retention procedures can be developed from the analysis discussed earlier in this chapter (Figure 17-1). Retention schedules should be reviewed and revised annually so that records no longer needed can be disposed of promptly.

Specifications for retention dates can be noted on Records Retention Charts to identify outdated records that can be destroyed or placed in an inactive file. Figure 17-3 provides a sample of a Records Retention Chart. Departments that have personal computers connected by a local area network can use their system to keep track of record retention data, record contents and other information to keep the files updated.

Equipment Type	Description	Advantages	Disadvantages
5-drawer vertical files	Cabinet containing drawers that can be pulled out	Effective for storing small volumes of files Easy to relocate Drawers can be locked	Requires more floor space than other types of equipment Simultaneous access to more than one drawer difficult or impossible Misfiles cannot be readily identified
5-drawer lateral files	Cabinet in which drawers are opened from the side	Good for small-volume storage Easier access Easy to relocate Drawers can be locked	Drawer can be difficult for shorter people to access Simultaneous drawer access is prevented by safety interlock Misfiles can't be readily identified
Fixed lateral files	Files are accessed from the side instead of the top and shelves are fixed in place, either open shelf or with retractable doors	System can be 7 or 8 tiers high which allows more space efficiency Multiple users can be accommodated simultaneously When used with color coding equipment misfiles can be rapidly identified	Open shelf units cannot be locked More difficult to relocate
Modular suspension equipment	Folders are contained in 4–6″ wide boxes that are suspended from a freestanding framework containing steel rails	Multiple users can be accommodated simultaneously Boxes facilitate easy shifting of records in the files	Units remain open at all times
Rolling or mobile files	Pendaflex files are stored in mobile carts	Materials are within easy reach for quick reference Files can be easily moved Ready access to files	Only small volumes can be stored

FIGURE 17-2. File Equipment Selection

DESCRIPTION	RETENTION PERIOD	
	EASILY ACCESSIBLE	REQUIRED
CUSTOMER SERVICE INQUIRY	2	6
NEW ACCOUNT INFORMATION	2	Life of Account/6
ORDER FORM	2	6
CORRECTION NOTICE	2	6
CUSTOMER CONFIRMATION	2	6
TRANSFER AGENT INSTRUCTIONS	2	6
OPTION ORDER FORM	2	6
OPEN ORDER CONFIRMATION	2	6
DELIVERY TICKET	2	6
ORDER FORM	2	6
SPECIAL ORDER REQUISITION	2	6
CUSTOMER STATEMENT	2	6
PAYMENT DUE NOTICE	2	4
JOURNAL ENTRY (SECURITIES)	2	6
JOURNAL ENTRY (MONEY)	2	6
GOV'T./MONEY MARKET ORDER	2	6
GOV'T. BOND ORDER	2	6

FIGURE 17-3. Records Retention Chart

RECORDS MANAGEMENT

The manager responsible for updating records must be familiar with internal firm policies and external regulatory mandates. The manager also has the following considerations:

Space requirements
Security requirements
Storage media

Retrieval media

Storage procedures

The manager will also provide orientation to new employees on the systems used for records management, and develop a procedure manual defining responsibilities and action steps associated with all retrieved records.

MICROFILM VERSUS HARD COPY

Whenever possible, microfilm or microfiche should be used instead of storing the original documents. If the original documents are required to be kept, they should be kept at a location that provides the lowest space costs. There are various types of microfilm that can provide significant savings in space requirements, improve customer service, and improve efficiency.

MICROFILM

This is a particularly economical mode which can store 300 pounds of paper per one pound of microfilm. Moreover, one reel of microfilm requires only 2% of the storage space of paper records, retaining the same amount of information. The microrecording operation usually involves 16 mm or 35 mm film to photograph documents which can be reduced in varying degrees.

MICROFICHE

This is a 4 × 6" sheet of film containing microimages arranged in a grid pattern. This has become the leading format for microfiche application in Operations Departments over the past several years. Many firms prefer to use microfiche over other formats available because of its convenience. Microfiche's biggest advantage is that images are generally easy to find and read. Data is retrieved by using a reader printer which displays and copies records.

UPDATABLE MICROFICHE

This is a new format which enables the user to add a page at a time. As convenient as a file folder, this mode permits multiple users to have simultaneous access to copies of the master. It provides users with most of the advantages of microfiche with the additional advantage of updatability.

ELECTRONIC FILING SYSTEMS

Electronic filing systems should be considered by managers in medium to large size firms. This system uses a retrieval technique that permits random filing of documents in a given batch. Documents are filmed on high speed microfilmers, which automatically stamps an image location on each document, and also positions an image mark beneath each document as it is being filmed. The document locations are keyed into a computer index file for later reference. Retrieval is accomplished by accessing the computer index. Once the computer displays the desired document image location, the researcher pulls the document. An index determines the film "address" or location of the record. This enables records to be located quickly and easily, and provides prompt customer service and cost savings.

ADVANTAGES OF USING MICROFILM

SAVINGS IN SPACE REQUIREMENT

With a microfilm operation, both input and output retrieval use at least 25% less space than the paper file area. The capability of system expansion reaches over 200% without having to utilize additional operating floor space, which of course, results in significant cost savings. In addition, the maximization of floor space improves the overall work environment in the operating areas and improves employee morale.

RAPID INFORMATION RETRIEVAL

Information retrieval will increase significantly because of the very rapid retrieval speeds of the equipment.

IMPROVED FILE SECURITY

Duplicate files can be produced at the time when you are converting from hard copy to micrographics. The duplicate should be stored in a secure location in order to safeguard against loss, misplacements, or destruction. This helps streamline business operations, because when a roll of film is lost the duplicate can be easily retrieved.

The department will run more smoothly when you pay more attention to the handling and storage of records. Practically speaking, micrographics is an advantageous method for research and retrieval because of the cost and retrieval access capability.

IMAGE PROCESSING

I believe image processing will soon replace microfilm and microfiche as the most advantageous way to store certain records. Image processing captures electronically a very clear image of many types of paper. The technology can be used for all types of forms used in the industry (e.g., new accounts, hypothecation agreements, legal transfer documents, stock and bond certificates, journal entries, and order tickets).

There are a number of legal questions that need to be addressed related to use of image processing as "an original" in many courts, but acceptance will probably come with time.

CHAPTER 18

Planning for Emergencies

If Operations Managers tried to prepare for all conceivable emergencies, you would spend more than most firms can afford and still not cover every potential emergency. You should, however, develop systems and plans that cover common emergencies to assure the safety of personnel and firm assets.

Unfortunately, little preparation is usually given to what can be a serious problem, and could considerably hamper or completely shut down operations. For example, a transit strike, a power outage or a fire, if not properly prepared for, would seriously affect the normal work flow. The Operations Manager may have a tendency to overlook this problem because it is not usually considered a part of daily management responsibilities. However, failure on a manager's part to properly prepare for emergency situations could result in serious injuries, exposure, violation of regulatory compliance and infractions of the law.

This chapter will give you guidelines for handling emergency situations. The topics covered will include: personal safety, protection of the firm's assets, disaster planning, and what to do in specific types of emergencies.

PERSONAL SAFETY

There are a number of basic measures that can be used to assist personnel in the event of "minor" emergencies. It's simply a matter of having facilities available to react quickly. Figure 18-1 lists those items that should be on hand for both daily first aid use and for any major disaster.

First Aid Equipment	*Major Disaster Requirement*
Bandages/gauze	Cots
Aspirins	Blankets
Smelling salts	AM/FM radio with weatherband
Antiseptics	Flashlights
Antacids	Extra batteries
First aid manual	Portable TV

FIGURE 18-1. First Aid and Disaster Requirements

CPR

Classes in Cardiovascular Pulmonary Resuscitation (CPR) are available through your local Red Cross organization. Training in this life saving technique should be as critical as any technical operations training.

At least two people in a department, or on a floor, should be skilled in CPR. The manager should consider only a licensed or certified instructor to give this course. Similarly, a registered nurse could give training in the Heimlich (choking) Maneuver, as well as a first aid course which addresses methods of treating burns, cuts, etc. Posters which depict the Heimlich Maneuver are available from the local Red Cross, and should be prominently displayed. All or any of these items could be instrumental in saving someone's life.

Quick and easy access to critical phone numbers may also save a life. Are the phone numbers of the Medical Department, Internal Security Department, and Fire and Police Departments clearly labeled on each phone? If not, steps should be taken to ensure that this is done as soon as possible. Of course, if your firm has firm-wide procedures for responding to emergencies, you should make sure that all of your employees are familiar with them.

PROTECTION OF THE FIRM'S ASSETS

Many of the steps you take to protect employees also protect firm assets. For instance, a sprinkler system protects personnel and assets against fire, and security systems protect personnel and assets against theft. However, there are specific measures that should be taken to protect the assets of the firm.

Obviously, the steps you take would depend on the type of assets involved. One example of this type of protection measure would include vaults for the protection of securities, and offsite location storage for critical records. Let's look in further detail at some considerations for assuring security in a vault:

Type and thickness of vault doors and walls.

Type of door locks (e.g., time locks).

Type of combinations (are there dual combinations with separate areas each maintaining one?)

Is there an alarm system to the Police Department or a security agency?

Are guard stations set up to prevent unauthorized access?

Is there a key card access for employees working in the area?

Are there lockers set up outside the vault area for employees' personal belongings?

Naturally, security systems are not infallible. In much the same way as the Fire Department requires periodic fire drills, the various systems that have been put in place to protect the firm should be tested.

Figure 18-2 lists types of problems concerning the physical protection of your employees and assets.

Problem	Consequence	Solution
Destruction of critical records	Potential legal actions and regulatory violations	Store copies of critical records at offsite locations Establish a master list of all critical records
On premise losses	Inability to deliver securities	Establish mini vault to safeguard securities during working hours
	Additional paperwork in filing for replacement certificates	Allow only authorized personnel to handle
Employee safety	Physical injury or fatalities	Establish fire drill procedures
	Potential lawsuits	Know and obey Fire Department regulations
	Increase in insurance	Have first aid kit available Have designated employees trained in lifesaving techniques such as CPR and first aid; have posters displayed for Heimlich (choking) maneuver
Equipment and/systems failure	Inability to process work	Provide adequate backup power for electrical failure Provide backup system during system failure Prepare employees to process work manually if necessary Have overtime task force available if necessary
General emergencies	Serious injury, exposure, regulatory violations, and infractions of the law	Listing of all office personnel phone numbers and emergency phone numbers, i.e., Medical Dept., Fire Dept., law enforcement agency Listing of all equipment with serial numbers for insurance purposes

FIGURE 18-2. Safety Guidelines

DISASTER PLANS

Once your security systems are all in place, the next step in preparing for emergencies is the development of a disaster plan. A disaster plan will prepare a firm/operation to continue functioning with a minimal amount of confusion during an emergency. Emergencies can range from the very serious (fires, earthquakes, bombs), to the less serious (blackouts, transit strikes, and other disturbances).

PREPARATION OF THE PLAN

Because of the varying degrees and types of disasters, a general plan can be developed which can be followed in any emergency. More detailed plans should be developed to handle specific situations. The general plan should encompass the following:

Selection of a key individual in the department who is assigned the responsibility of coordinating disaster control efforts with other departments.

Development of a disaster control plan outlining steps to be taken in various emergencies.

Preparation of a disaster Control Organization Chart (see Figure 18-3) which lists all key management individuals with home telephone numbers.

Others items that should be considered and implemented if possible are alternate headquarters, public relations, medical care and welfare, and a warning system.

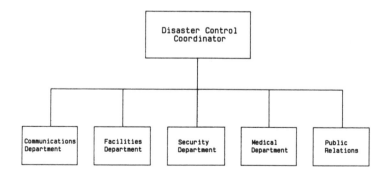

FIGURE 18-3. Disaster Organization Chart

Alternate Headquarters It is conceivable that a disaster could render a headquarters unusable. A common solution for organizations having more than one location is to designate an alternate headquarters. For example, an organization with a main office and branch locations could shift operations depending upon the need. Additionally, departments could be shifted from one operations area to another.

Public Relations Disasters are considered newsworthy by the media, and for that reason, the plan should include provisions for the orderly release of information. Also, a radio station should be designated for employees to listen to for information concerning their situations.

Medical Care and Welfare Almost any type of disaster can result in the disability of individuals due to injury or sickness. For that reason, emergency numbers should be available for the Fire Department, local hospital and your internal Medical Department, if one exists. Also, an emergency medical kit, which would include blankets, bandages, antiseptics, ice or cold packs, and so forth should be kept in each area.

Warning System A method of warning those occupying the facility when an emergency condition exists should be provided for in the plan. The best example of this is a public address system.

Because information regarding status during an emergency is difficult to obtain, the development of checklists, as displayed in Figures 18-4 and 18-5, will be extremely helpful.

1. Section/unit reporting. _____

2. Number of management personnel present. _____

3. Number of clerical personnel present. _____

4. Are there sufficient personnel present to complete essential jobs listed for your area? ___

    a. If answer to 4 is "No," how many additional people are required?
    _____

    b. List essential jobs not covered:
    _____
    _____

5. Are you missing documents that are essential to your operation? _____
   If answer is "Yes," list missing documents:
   _____
   _____

6. Are banks, agents, depositories, or other institutions essential to your operation open
   and capable of doing business? _____
   If answer is "No," give details: _____
   _____
   _____

7. Do you have any communication problems (include messengers)? _____
   If answer is "Yes," give details:
   _____
   _____

8. Describe other details you think should be brought to the attention of management.
   _____
   _____

Prepared by: _____

Date: _____

Forward to Department Administration as soon as possible and begin of preparation of Checklist #2.

FIGURE 18-4. Emergency Checklist 1—Situation Evaluation

1. Section/unit reporting. _____

2. Have all essential personnel who are not present been contacted? _____

3. What is your estimate of the number of personnel, not present, who will report for work tomorrow? _____

4. What is your estimate of the total number of personnel who will be present tomorrow?
   _____

5. What is the number of hotel accommodations you will require.

   _____ Tonight   _____ Tomorrow night.

6. If you are not receiving Information Systems support, can you operate without it? _____
   If answer is "No," list type of support or documents necessary:
   _____
   _____

7. Do you anticipate operational problems resulting from outside agencies, such as banks, agents, depositories? _____
   If answer is "Yes," explain:
   _____
   _____

8. If lack of transportation is the cause of the emergency, check the following:
   a. If available, have instructions for use of firm transportation been supplied to all personnel and necessary reports been completed? _____

   b. Has the use of car pools been explored? _____

   c. Have the alternate routes of transportation been explained to all personnel? _____

9. Do you have any suggestions that may help in this or future emergencies of this kind?
   _____
   _____

   Prepared by: _____ Date: _____

   Forward to department administration as soon as completed.

FIGURE 18-5. Emergency Checklist 2—Continued Operations
Capabilities

TYPES OF EMERGENCIES

Now let's look at some specifics of planning for emergencies like transit strikes, blackouts, and disasters that impact the Data Center.

Transit Strikes

The major problem presented by transit strikes is getting people to work and back home again so that processing continues without significant interruption. Transit strikes often occur only for a day or two, but they can go on for months. It is important, therefore, that careful planning be done long before the advent of a strike, because when the strike comes, every other firm in your area will be trying to obtain the same resources (buses, hotel rooms, etc.) that you are trying to obtain.

Here's a list of the major elements of a basic plan for a transit strike:

Appoint a transit strike coordinator and a contact person in each major department.

Compile a list of all essential employees; i.e., those that you must have at work to maintain operations.

Review the demographics of your employee base to see where the majority of affected employees live.

Arrange for private bus transportation for critical employees. Bus companies will usually help in establishing routes of travel, and strategic pickup or dropoff spots.

Arrange for car-pooling of employees, and reimburse employees for expenses connected with this activity.

Arrange for blocks of rooms in hotels for critical employees who are unable to utilize the private buses, car-pools, or alternate means of transportation.

Communicate, communicate, communicate: It is very important that all employees know and understand the procedures in place to assist them.

Blackout

Planning for blackouts has some of the same characters of the transit strike plan. There are a number of other specific steps, however, that should be reviewed for this type of emergency. All departments should have flashlights, batteries, and a portable radio. Computer Operations area have unique needs in this type of emergency:

Backup power in the form of generators is the major way to handle this type of emergency. If your building is too small for this backup, then arrangements should be made to move employees to another site.

Use the telephone for processing order information and other contact with employees and customers.

Establish procedures for the manual processing of critical work and a means by which the information can later be processed into the computer files.

Communicate, communicate, communicate: Employees will be very nervous during a blackout emergency. Be prepared to calm them immediately with specific information as to what happened, and how you will continue to operate.

DATA CENTER DISASTER AND RECOVERY

Disasters that affect your firm's Data Center range from the minor, like blackouts that can be planned for by installing backup generators, to major ones that could require operating the systems at another site. In any event, the best way to prepare for a disaster that could cripple the Data Center is to have a plan in place for recovery. The importance of having a disaster recovery plan for data center operations in the securities industry cannot be overemphasized. Trading is taking place at various times during the day, and changes in the price of financial assets can occur rapidly. In the event of any disaster, you must be able to process customer orders as soon as possible to protect customers and your firm from market exposure.

The plan for recovery should include these phases:

1. Steps to protect life and property.
2. Steps to resume critical processing.
3. Steps to resume normal processing.

Depending upon the size of your firm (volume, applications, etc.), and the number of Data Center sites, plans to provide for another site to resume processing could include the following alternatives:

Another Data Center in the firm

A Service Bureau

A joint venture arrangement with one or more firms

A standby facility owned by your firm that could be rapidly equipped for processing

The adequate preparation for disaster recovery may seem expensive, but it has to be viewed as a cost of doing business in this industry. In most cases, I recommend that firms provide their own backup facilities. Service bureau and joint venture arrangements generally do not provide the same level of assurance that is necessary for recovery.

Some of the major areas that should be included in recovery plans include:

Procedures for first aid and notification to authorities

Procedures to notify management and Account Executives

Procedures to switch communications traffic

Procedures for data retention and backup

Procedures for physically moving to another site

Procedures for restarting applications

To accomplish all of this there should be a number of different inventories available in an offsite location, that can be easily accessed:

Applications. A listing of all applications systems, what they are run on, what area they support, where they are run, and operating system used. This listing should prioritize all the applications as to their importance to the business (see Figure 18-6).

Hardware. An inventory of all data processing and communications equipment. The inventory should indicate type, manufacturer, model, number, and location (see Figure 18-7).

Software Systems. A listing of all software systems including version used, release number, vendor location, number of copies (see Figure 18-8).

Supplies/Peripherals. A listing of all supplies and peripherals used including paper, tape, Disc Access Storage Device (DASD), printers, forms, and so forth. This should include vendors, amount and usage requirements.

Documentation. Libraries that contain documentation on operating systems, library maps, data set conventions, job flow, and other information should be maintained offsite.

Personnel. A listing of all personnel, with names, addresses and telephone numbers, job title, and expertise should be available to management.

PRIORITY	APPLICATION	BUSINESS AREA	HARDWARE	OPERATING SYSTEM	LOCATION

FIGURE 18-6. Applications Systems

DEVICE NAME	TYPE	MANUFACTURER	MODEL	NUMBER	LOCATION

FIGURE 18-7. Hardware Inventory

SOFTWARE	VERSION	RELEASE	VENDOR	LOCATION	# OF COPIES

FIGURE 18-8. Software Systems

CHAPTER 19

Information Systems
in Securities Firms

The paperwork crunch of the 1960s caused several U.S. securities firms to fail due to their inability to process their business efficiently and accurately. Other firms that survived the crunch received numerous customer complaints, and visits from regulators when those firms' "back office" and "data processing" functions were not accurate or timely.

Since then, leading edge firms have understood that efficiency in Information Systems (I/S) and Operations is key to customer satisfaction, compliance with regulatory bodies, and supporting new products. Furthermore, firms that stress innovation and cost reduction are focusing on the strategic role that Information Systems plays relative to Operations, Trading, Sales, and Investment Banking areas.

Securities firms are in transition. One of the driving forces of that transition is integrating the Information Systems function with Operations to minimize costs, and to provide Trading, Sales, and Banking with the flexibility to meet the changing needs of the marketplace. The crash of October, 1987 led to a lack of investor confidence, lower volume in the sales and trading business, reductions in Operations budgets personnel, and a flattening of the I/S spending patterns of the early and mid-1980s. Efficient and effective information gathering, processing and distribution will be the differentiating factors among tomorrow's successful securities firms. Successful firms will have to make the technological leap from transaction processors to information processors.

In this chapter we'll discuss the evolution of Information Systems in the securities industry, review the issues that have been driving the growth of I/S, and show how to build a model to manage that growth.

EVOLUTION OF I/S IN THE SECURITIES INDUSTRY

Over the past two decades, the typical securities firm's I/S resource has changed as fundamentally as the business has. Let's consider some of the areas of major change:

Information Systems departments have had to broaden their focus. They have had to continue supporting operations' transaction processing, and at the same time, have had to acquire a thorough understanding of complex information/business issues (interest rate swaps, trading analytics, hedging strategies, mortgage-backed securities and non-U.S. securities) in order to provide support to revenue areas dealing in those products.

Information Systems managers, analysts, and programmers have had to support their firms' compliance with increased book entry settlement practices, such as NYSE Rule 387 on electronic confirmation and book entry settlement for corporates and equities, MSRB's requirements for municipal issue book-entry settlement, and the conversion of FNMA and FHLMC pools from physical to wirable form in 1984-85.

I/S representatives have had to cope with greater demands for processing, as well as support of their firms' international expansion, especially in European and Japanese markets, where support systems often had to be set up to work in tandem with systems in the home office.

I/S has experienced a substantial increase in calls for assistance from revenue generating end-user areas, where analytical product support on minicomputers and networked PC's has been the issue, often catching I/S staff off guard, as their expertise has been mainframe-based transaction processing.

In today's environment, systems are often developed for specific products or functional areas. Innovation occurs as a rule within entrepreneurial pockets of the organization. Long-term I/S planning and firm-wide goals often suffer as a result. In several firms, many end-user areas have their own programmers and do not have frequent contact with I/S at all. Their applications development is market-oriented, quick in delivery, and because turnaround time is crucial, end-users developing programs "don't have the time" to adhere to generally accepted rules and procedures of coding, testing, and user acceptance protocols. They develop market-focused applications such as cold call databases, new issue calendars, institutional and hypothetical portfolios, high-yield security master files, high-yield investor name and address and trade history files, mortgage research and analytics files, history files on commodity price fluctuations, and so forth.

Furthermore, I/S has been told to join the cost-cutting and contingency plan efforts of the major firms by generating more productivity gains, and planning for disaster/recovery events to assure continuous systems performance in the event of major catastrophes.

TODAY'S ENVIRONMENT

In the post-crash environment, profit margins are extremely narrow, and traditional sales and trading revenues are down, as is trading volume (see Figure 19-1). The most aggressive firms are cutting back their Operations areas and scrutinizing their Information Systems expenses.

At the same time, there is growing recognition that major core systems developed in the 1970s are badly in need of modernization. In addition, many of the new systems written to support the rapidly expanding product base of the industry are not connected to each other, or to core systems. This has led many firms to start work on architecture reviews so that a cohesive foundation of support systems, often "real-time" and "on-line," is put in place.

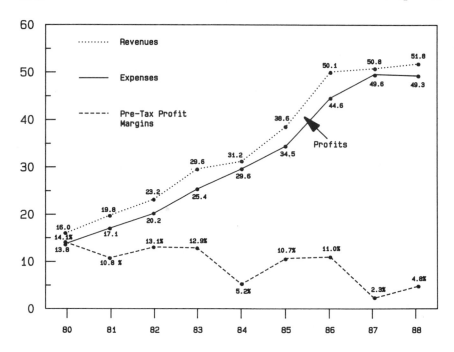

FIGURE 19-1. Security Industry Revenue and Profit Trends
Used by permission of the Securities Industry Association.

AUTOMATION BENEFITS ALL AREAS

Almost all areas of the typical securities firm benefit from the increased automation of crucial functions: processing areas, control areas, and revenue producing areas. Table 19-1 summarizes these.

Because of the significant increase of new products and new technologies that permit end-users to develop mini-systems, recent systems development has often occurred at the expense of an integrated systems architecture. Integration would support such firmwide concerns as risk management, credit review, customer information, product costing, and compliance. All of these areas involve integrated management information reporting. The lack of integrated systems limits what can be achieved in many key development areas. We will discuss how to develop an integrated architecture in Chapter 23.

	Automation	Benefit
Processing Areas		
Margin	On-line updating of customer positions, prices, federal and house calls, and customer debits.	Provides Account Executives with timely information and allows for more prompt action on violations.
Account transfer	Automated monitoring of Rule 412 activity to track accounts and positions in and out of the firm.	Reduces exposure and allows customer trading more quickly.
New accounts	On-line entry and updating.	Accounts will be in the data base when trades are made. New standing delivery instructions can be added as they are received, resulting in a reduction of fails and DKs; allows settlement instructions to be immediately updated, potentially reducing errors and fails.
Control Areas		
Credit review	On-line reports of trades exceeding customer/firm limits.	Enables quick action for credit review of trades which violate restrictions.
Treasurers	On-line updating of settlements, monies, and securities.	Provides current view of financing needs for the finance desk.
Revenue Producing Areas		
Sales	On-line updating of client positions.	Provides Account Executive with real-time view of client positions and account balances resulting in more timely investment analysis.
	On-line tracking of securities in transfer.	Allows Account Executive to know at any time the status of securities out to transfer.
Trading	On-line position trading.	Permits traders to see immediately the status of various positions.
	On-line risk analysis.	Provides updated view of risk and exposure.

TABLE 19-1. Automation Benefits

Because of the need for systems integration (driven by business unit information requirements), overall I/S spending growth in the securities industry is likely to continue. This growth is caused by both supply and demand factors. Advances in technology have made it possible for financial markets to expand, but the growth of these markets has in turn necessitated further I/S investments. (See Figure 19-2 for an illustration of I/S spending in the securities industry.)

DRIVERS OF GROWTH IN INFORMATION SYSTEMS: THE SUPPLY SIDE

Improved technology capabilities have enabled securities firms to offer new products and services, to make internal operations more efficient, and to enhance the performance of professional employees. The supply of technology can be categorized in four broad classes: mainframes, software, mini- and microcomputers, and telecommunications.

MAINFRAMES

Mainframe computer systems have the ability to access large complex data files that reside in sophisticated storage devices, and to process this data more rapidly than other types of general business computers. The industry's asset management accounts are examples of such an application. A large number of transactions must be posted to millions of accounts each day, and the results must then be accessible to thousands of computer terminals.

Mainframe technology advancements have made it possible to use information systems to automate applications which require the central processing of large amounts of data. Mainframe computers, and their peripheral devices, have also made it possible to offer such high-value services at low cost. This type of technology will, of course, continue to provide the central processing required in support of internal functions, as firms move to strengthen their management information systems (MIS) reporting, on-line settlement, order execution, and so forth.

SOFTWARE

Advances in software technology have resulted in an increased use of I/S. This has occurred not only because sophisticated data-

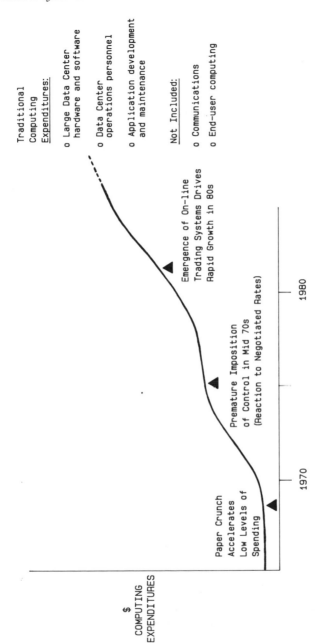

FIGURE 19-2. Computing Expenditures

Used by permission of Nolan Norton & Company.

bases have made information available as never before, but also because the information can be manipulated as never before. Relational database software, so necessary in real-time processing, allows capital markets firms to increase risk management techniques, bid on swap opportunities in hours instead of days, develop sophisticated "what-if" scenarios, and a host of other trading related activities necessary in today's 24 hour global marketplace.

Data management techniques now allow data to be maintained separately from applications, so that users in all areas can access information for their particular needs: traders can get prices during the day—and so can Account Executives and Operations personnel; sales personnel can relate different accounts for marketing—and so can Operations personnel for margining. The list goes on, but you can see that the importance of information processing has grown relative to transaction processing.

The implications of the increased use of I/S in securities firms are far reaching, because so many databases are being created within the systems that were developed in the 1970s. The result is that many firms are beginning to recognize the need for a standardized systems architecture foundation. This is a complex and expensive effort, but one that must be accomplished to allow end-users to gain the efficiencies offered by the latest software technologies. It requires strategic planning by I/S and Operations and the business units of Sales, Trading, and Banking to understand their information requirements. Such an effort, however, will permit the Information Systems resource to be more responsive, reduce manual tasks, give users the capability to do their own coding, and make on-line integration of systems files a reality. This will provide better information to customers, Account Executives and traders more rapidly and, eventually, allow firms to organize differently.

Mini- and Microcomputers

The emergence of mini- and microcomputer technologies has had a significant impact on I/S in the securities industry. These technologies have made it possible to place processing power at the end-user's site, thus freeing up the mainframes to support applications which truly require central, large scale processing. As a result, end-users, supported by intelligent terminals and local area networks, now perform many of the tasks which were once the responsibility of I/S. These tasks range from mundane error checking during data entry, to sophisticated computerized analytics in support of fixed income trading. The growth of end-user investments, and specifically of mini- and microcomputer and local area network investments, has been a significant factor in the trends of I/S spending levels (see Figure 19-3).

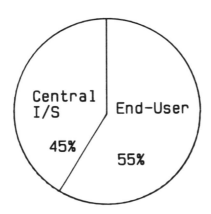

The majority of computer power is also in the hands of end-users.

FIGURE 19-3. End-User Driven Spending Exceeds Central I/S Expenditure Levels in Leading Organizations

Used by permission of Nolan Norton & Company.

TELECOMMUNICATIONS

Telecommunications has always been an important segment of Operations and Information Systems. From the early use of telex equipment in transmitting customer orders, to the use of satellites in broadcasting data streams between exchanges and securities firms throughout the world, telecommunications has played an important support role.

Advanced telecommunications technologies and lower cost applications now, however, have added to the demand for I/S. Firms can now connect remote locations to central mainframes, and/or download information from mainframes to regional centers. This permits the regional centers to be as up-to-date with information as the home office. It also permits the home office to obtain information regarding the activities of personnel in the regional centers. Global trading activities now occur on a twenty-four hour basis, because of advanced communications capabilities that allow the same information systems applications to be used in London, Tokyo and Hong Kong as in New York and Los Angeles.

Telecommunications, when combined with advances in other technologies, also permits firms to establish trading and sales activities in other countries without the expense of "brick and mortar" facilities previously required. In addition, fewer personnel are necessary because updating, reconciliation and manipulation of data, can be accomplished via a central site.

DRIVERS OF GROWTH IN INFORMATION SYSTEMS: THE DEMAND SIDE

We talked earlier about the industry's product and market growth. This has led to a significant increase in the demand for I/S support for new fixed income processing, mergers and acquisitions, futures, and options. Risk and exposure systems need to be developed to monitor customer and firm risk, and customer service requirements have also increased as a result of this new environment. In addition, external links to industry processing institutions requires significant upgrading of systems support. Let's take a closer look at how these areas have increased the demand for I/S support.

FIXED INCOME SECURITIES

Mortgage-backed securities are securitized collections (pools) of mortgages purchased by GNMA, FNMA, FHLMC and others, and then brought into the secondary market by securities firms. Securitization of mortgage debt led the way for securitizing automobile loans and credit card debt, and to the development of "stripped" mortgage-backed securities (instruments where either principal only or interest only portions are sold).

Treasury securities have also spun off derivative products. Treasury strips, selling principal or interest only, and zero coupon treasuries selling at a deep discount, and paying nothing until full principal is repaid at maturity, are other examples of products that have developed in the past 15 years.

Municipal bonds have also been sold as zero coupon issues, and have been packaged with other "munis" in offerings known as Unit Investment Trusts.

Information Systems has had to be responsive in quickly developing applications that support these derivative products. However, the response has been technically uncoordinated because so many systems are old, technology has changed, and business unit's focus has been on the short term.

FUTURES AND OPTIONS

The areas of financial futures and options as products have also accelerated in the past 15 years, as more investors try to hedge their securities positions and make an extra profit, or offset potential losses by taking options or futures positions. Not only does I/S need to develop systems to process futures and options transactions, but it also needs to provide supportive analytics to traders and sales personnel, and to their clients who are trading these products.

MERGERS AND ACQUISITIONS

Mergers and acquisitions resulting in the issuance of debt instruments, especially high yield or "junk" bonds, call for extra support from I/S departments because data, spreadsheets, analytics, and forecasts must be created for bidding on a deal. Analogous support must be available to Investment Banking, Trading, Sales, and to Syndicate Clearance once the securities come to market.

RISK AND EXPOSURE

As these products proliferate and are traded, they may create certain exposure risks that need to be managed. For example, mortgage-backed securities trade on forward settlements: that is, when you trade them, you agree to a settlement date in excess of the normal five day settlement period. This factor creates significant credit and exposure windows for the firm, as it is committed to buy securities at today's market for a client who will not pay until some time later. Furthermore, the average mortgage-backed security trade is for at least several million dollars. I/S therefore has a particular burden, that of creating and implementing on-line, real-time credit exposure monitoring systems, so that the firm's credit review committee can view such large forward settlement trades as they happen, and prevent trades for a customer whose financial situation may be troubled, or who for other reasons should not be doing the trade.

I/S also needs to provide information on all these transactions to the Director of Compliance, to make sure that trading is done in only those accounts whose investment objectives allow such activity. I/S must also provide information on trades to the Margin or Credit Department, which ensures that the customer pays the proper amount to settle the transaction.

LINKS TO INDUSTRY PROCESSORS

Securities firms have also seen rapid growth in electronic links to industry processors. Links to the Exchanges and NASD are quite familiar to most of us, however, firms are now electronically linked to The Depository Trust Company, the National Securities Clearance Corporation, regional depositories and clearing organizations, and the Options Clearing Corporation for automated Institutional Delivery System confirmations, book entry comparison, clearance and settlement of corporates, equities, municipals and options.

Many firms doing international business are linked to Cedel and Euroclear, and their London offices are linked to the London Stock Exchange for trade execution and reporting.

The conversion of FNMA's and FHLMC's to wirable form has increased the major firms' use of the Fed Wire system for the delivery of these securities. The ongoing conversion of mortgage-backed securities will increase the major players' links with the new Mortgage-backed Securities Clearing Corporation.

Most of the foregoing examples have arisen relatively recently in the industry, and illustrate the significant demand that product and market changes have made on the I/S department to support new businesses.

CHANGES IN THE END-USER COMMUNITY

As previously discussed, much processing has already migrated from central operations to the end-user community. Technologies are emerging which enable end-users to perform their own systems and processing support.

In response to this technology trend, I/S personnel are being assigned to work directly within functional areas. Internal technical support is one of the greatest needs in the end-user community. This also means that I/S personnel need to acquire in-depth business area knowledge, if they are to obtain credibility in the business units where they work.

The potential benefits of this trend include more responsive I/S support, reduced backlogs, and better prioritization. At the same time, precautions must be taken to assure appropriate access to data and systems integration. Here's a five-point program that should help to assure conformance to firm guidelines:

1. Develop an End-User Technology Review Program to test and review what end-users are producing for adherence to corporate level guidelines on software, hardware, architecture, and data management.

2. Assign I/S personnel directly to end-user groups. The I/S personnel are familiar with the firm's I/S policies, can provide technical expertise, and will become significantly more knowledgcable about the end-user's business through this assignment.

3. Ensure that the I/S personnel assigned to end-users functionally remain part of the I/S community. This will permit automation in end-user areas to occur that is process-oriented rather than task-oriented, and will facilitate the sharing of innovation across areas.

4. Measure return on investment. All technology investments must make economic sense. They must either demonstrably provide greater revenues, or add value in a different way. End-user expenditures should be measured in the same way as the I/S expenditures.

5. Develop an end-user "help desk" in the central I/S group. This type of support builds credibility from the business units, and enables the growth of end-user computing to occur within an overall design.

IMPLICATIONS OF I/S GROWTH

Building information systems and services is an extremely costly venture, and must be managed like any other significant firm resource. I/S and business managers must determine how much of their future I/S investments should be directed at internal systems integration and how much should support the firm's activity in the marketplace.

At the same time, the securities industry has experienced a shift in emphasis during the 1980s, away from transaction based revenue and towards asset management revenue. I/S must respond with databases for relationship management, and with systems for regulatory and compliance reporting.

Furthermore, since the crash, securities firms have been examining their payrolls and functions, and have eliminated a number of middle management decision support layers in order to reduce expenses and streamline the organization. I/S must develop systems that correspond to the needs of this trimmer, flatter organization, where personnel will need easy access to information across traditional boundaries.

For example, in fixed income sales and trading areas, high-yield bond analysts want to have access to data pertinent to investment grade fixed income instruments. Traders in government securities wish to see the results of quantitative analysis done by equity researchers in order to get a better feel for market trends. Investment Banking analysts packaging new deals want to look at trading statistics and analytics in the secondary market, for both companies and market sectors, to help in evaluating the likelihood of a new issue's success.

Whether supporting internal integration or market participation, I/S investments will be expected to yield a tangible return. Let's look at two areas where most would agree that I/S investment has produced tangible returns.

First, I/S investments have resulted in the profitable survival of many firms. Whether the I/S investment has permitted the firm to cope with exploding transaction volumes, or has provided a competitive advantage (as with the asset management account), I/S has often provided the tools for survival in a highly competitive environment. I/S has been able to develop the applications and systems to support the new products of the 1980s: strips, zero coupons, new options products, swaps, and so forth, so that the firm can thrive and profit from being involved in a variety of markets. Second, since these I/S investments have helped drive the shift from institutions to markets, the value of the I/S investments can be shown to have passed through to the customer. The alert Account Executive with on-line updates of customer balances and positions, as well as indications of customer interest, can match opportunities to customers and reduce the possibility of missing markets.

Clients doing extensive institutional business benefit from research and analytics available on-line as a means to profitable trading, hedging, and portfolio strategies. Since all of the highly competitive firms are doing this for the same customers, the customers benefit from a variety of analytical and decision support information tools.

Because of the increased level of I/S expenditures, however, securities firms executives are now demanding that I/S investments submit to rigorous financial analysis. Proposals for new investments will be submitted to return-on-investment analysis, and specific action plans with deliverables will be asked for. Most firms are recognizing that investments in I/S need to be measured on tangible evidence of corporate financial benefits. The benefits can be increased revenues, cost containment, or product support at declining life cycle stages (see Figure 19-4), but more formal controls will be enforced on I/S managers and end-users of the I/S resource.

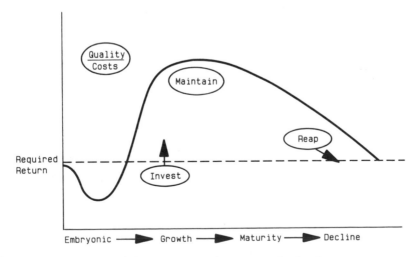

FIGURE 19-4. Production Life Cycle
Used by permission of Nqlan Norton & Company.

BUILDING AN I/S MANAGEMENT MODEL

Because I/S has become such an integral part of the securities firm, it's important to plan with the business units how to manage the I/S resource. This can only be done at senior levels, and the impetus will probably have to come from the I/S organization.

In working with the business units, I/S managers need to approach the model in the same way business unit managers approach an analysis of their business—answer the questions they might ask about the marketplace. For example, they would want to know: What are our costs? Are we spending in the right areas? What's our competition doing? What is the quality of the product? What do external suppliers provide? Do we have the right people?

These questions can be grouped into three major areas:

1. Are we spending money in the right areas?

2. Does computing support meet our requirements?

3. Where are we weak?

ARE WE SPENDING MONEY IN THE RIGHT AREAS?

To answer this question, you need to know how much you are spending and with whom. How does the cost compare to the competition? Is it productive? Is it being spent for the right reasons? Let's look at ways to answer these questions:

	INFORMATION SOURCE	FUNCTION
How much are you spending?	3-5 years of actual expense data	Market data services workstations
	Vendor invoices	Consultants
	General Ledger	External timesharing and data communications
		Internal communications
		Production
		Development
		Administration
		Maintenance/ Enhancement

	INFORMATION SOURCE	FUNCTION
		Hardware
		Research and Development
With whom?	3-5 years of actual expense data	Internal I/S costs
		External consultants
	Vendor invoices	
		Business unit I/S costs
		External timesharing
		Market data vendors

How Does the Spending Compare to the Competition's?

Source data here should be obtained from I/S industry consultants to be creditable in the business units. The areas that should be examined include:

Total I/S costs

Expenses per employee

Expenses per revenue dollar

Number of I/S employees

Business unit I/S expenses (development and maintenance)

Hardware expenses

Type of hardware

Communications expenses

Technologies utilized

Areas of expenditures by major product

Is the Spending Productive?

This is always a difficult question to answer, but there are a number of industry benchmarks that can be used to measure development, maintenance and enhancement, and production. For discussion purposes, let's define these activities:

Development. Automating a function previously not automated, automating a business need which is not part of an existing system, replacing an existing system.

Maintenance and Enhancement. Changes made to obtain or exceed service levels intended in original requirements, such as recovering from a system's crash, fixing a bug, improving storage efficiency or system throughput, or fixing a system to meet changing business needs.

Production. CPU, disk, tape, print, and network costs associated with the operation of a system.

Now let's look at possible ways to measure the productivity of these activities:

Development The methodology here could focus on work spent on a sampling of major products recently implemented. Then use some industry accepted measure to analyze your firm versus others. For example:

MEASURE	DESCRIPTION
Functionality	A measure of system size based on: input types output types internal file types external interface file types processing functions
Duration	Length of development project (days/ months)
Manpower	Average number of equivalent people working on the development project over the project's duration
Functional Point per Full-Time Equivalent	The average amount of system functionality created per person over the duration of the systems project
Function Point per Man Month	The average amount of system functionality created by month over the duration of the systems project

Maintenance and Enhancement Using the definition above, one industry standard measures the dollars spent on maintenance and enhancement divided by the dollars spent on production. Approximately $.65 of maintenance spending is required for each $1.00 of development spending.

Production Data center productivity can be measured by looking at used capacity that can be compared to industry standards that predict staffing and technology requirements. Two areas that can be measured are: 1) actual spending versus expected spending and 2) expenses versus utilized capacity.

ARE YOU MAKING THE RIGHT INVESTMENTS?

Here you need to review where you have been investing, by product and by area, determine if you have obtained appropriate returns, and determine if you should continue spending patterns. A matrix model such as that in Figure 19-5 can assist in the analysis.

Further analysis can show how the spending has occurred, for example, on development, maintenance and enhancement, and production. The business units and I/S managers can then determine if they want that pattern to continue. This is called "application portfolio management."

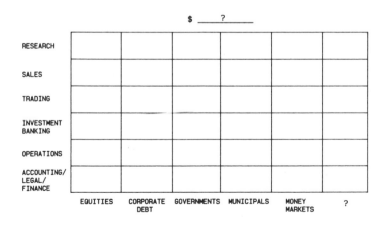

FIGURE 19-5. 1994 Total I/S Spending

DOES COMPUTING SUPPORT MEET OUR REQUIREMENTS?

It's important to look at a number of areas to answer this question. For example: How much support is provided? What is the quality of support? How much support is provided by outside suppliers?

HOW MUCH SUPPORT IS PROVIDED?

Computing support could be looked at as the amount of "attempted coverage" to a business function. Attempted coverage is the amount of automation provided as a percent of what is, and could, or should be automated. In other words, not every function in an area needs automation. I/S needs to work with users here to determine what business functions can, and should be automated, to provide the most cost effective use of the I/S resource. The functions within the major areas of Research, Sales, Trading, Operations, and Administration should first be identified and then analyzed. An analysis could also be performed by product area. In all cases the results of the analysis can then be measured against competitive benchmark data and your firm's desired resource allocation.

WHAT IS THE QUALITY OF I/S SUPPORT?

Quality, like beauty, is in the eye of the beholder. Both technical quality (by asking the I/S community) and functional quality (by asking the end-users) should be measured. The following sections describe criteria for measuring both.

INFORMATION SYSTEMS PERSPECTIVE: TECHNICAL QUALITY ATTRIBUTES

Design Attributes

1. Modularity and Logical Processing Flow
2. Functional Consistency with User Requirements
3. Logical File/Database Structure
4. Data Storage and Access Techniques
5. Quality Controls and Validation

6. Operations Requirements
7. Hardware/Software Usage
8. Ability to Integrate/Interface
9. Transaction Execution
10. Data Entry
11. Security Features
12. Adherence to Standards

Maintainability Attributes

1. Quality of Documentation
2. Determination of Problems and Change Control
3. Maintenance and Enhancements
4. Available Test Data

Operating Attributes

1. Ease of Operations
2. Outages and Reruns
3. Determination of Problems
4. Technical Currency

User Perspective: Overall Functional Quality Levels Functional quality can be measured against the following and compared against industry benchmarks.

Research, Sales and Trading Professional Support

1. Ease of Use in Getting Started
2. Ease of Use in On-Going Operation
3. Performance
4. Functional Capability
5. Security/Recovery
6. Flexibility
7. Overall Performance

Operations and Administration Functional Quality

1. Data Accuracy
2. System Reliability
3. Data Accessibility
4. Output Presentation
5. Summary Reporting
6. Documentation Quality
7. Detailed Reporting
8. Data Currency
9. Data Security
10. Overall Performance

HOW MUCH SUPPORT IS PROVIDED BY OUTSIDE PROVIDERS?

Your firm uses outside suppliers to some extent: Do you know how much? Quotron, Reuters, Telerate and others provide all sorts of I/S services to securities firms. It's important to know what kinds of information services they provide and at what cost, that is, monetary, and at what integration expense. Too many outside suppliers could put your firm in the position of being unable to integrate information necessary to manage the business.

In any event, the knowledge gained by this analysis will help you to evaluate the need for integration, if you decide to continue with the current level of outside suppliers, as illustrated by Figure 19-6.

FIGURE 19-6. Integrating Information

WHERE ARE WE WEAK?

Some items to consider in assessing weaknesses include:

1. Funding
2. Data Center Operations
3. Personnel
4. Level of I/S Focus of Business Issues
5. Architecture Condition

1. Funding. Business and I/S managers need to review funding for I/S to determine the appropriate amount of spending at a macro level. There may be reasons to cut back spending such as:

Reduced business activity

Need to assimilate recent growth

Lack of well-thought-out plans

Or to increase spending such as:

Expanding markets

Expanding product opportunities

Need to modernize systems portfolio

Potential I/S revenue generation

In any event, there should be a process in place to constantly analyze project funding. The process could be managed through a Steering Committee consisting of I/S and business unit personnel, product management meetings, financial commitment control procedures, and so forth.

2. Data Center Operations. As development applications are put into production, your data center operations become critical. Many of the systems used in the securities industry must never "fail." As more and more trading systems become on-line and real-time, this becomes particularly important. Some areas that managers need to review are:

Data center capacity

Hardware technology

Communications facilities

Recovery facilities

Cost of production

Performance and reliability standards

3. Personnel. Skilled I/S professionals always seem to be in short supply. Areas that should be reviewed include:

Internal I/S turnover versus industry I/S turnover

Projected growth of I/S staff levels

Skills inventory assessment

Career planning and development programs

Training resources

Compensation

4. Level of I/S Focus on Business Issues. It is critical that the business units decide how the I/S resource is used. The I/S community may be doing excellent technical work, but not in the areas that are important to business units. This is another area where I/S Steering Committees can be very useful.

As spending on the I/S resource increases, business unit managers will have more of a say on how and where the funds are spent. Organization structures that align the I/S personnel with the appropriate business units can be helpful here, because the I/S groups can then culturally be part of the business units. This allows for an effective development process from the definition of objectives to system implementation.

Business Unit and I/S Project Analysis

1. Business Unit Defines Objectives
2. Business Unit and I/S Analysis
3. I/S Pilot
4. Business Unit and I/S Analysis
5. I/S Refines Pilot

6. Business Unit Sign-Off
7. I/S Implementation

   5. Architecture Condition. This is an area where many firms in the securities industry are vulnerable today. As spending increases have occurred in the last decade, major new systems have been added to firm's systems portfolios. In addition, hardware/software technology choices have expanded, data architecture alternatives have grown, and language choices have multiplied. To assure that your firm maintains flexibility in markets, in access to customers and in new product generation, I/S managers must define and construct a computing architecture that does not constrain business alternatives (see Figure 19-7).

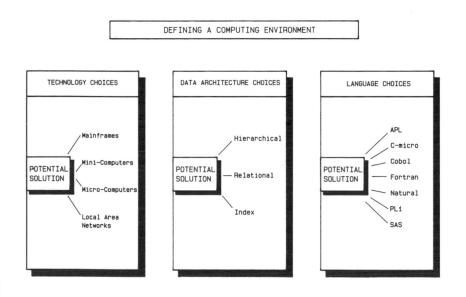

FIGURE 19-7. Defining a Computing Environment
Used by permission of Nolan Norton & Company.

CHAPTER 20

Systems Supporting Securities Firms' Operations

Because of the vast amount of paperwork associated with Operations processing, most securities firms dedicated Information Systems resources to Operations at a very early stage. Major investments were made in the 1960s, and 1970s, to process increased volumes of trading, reduce manual labor and satisfy regulatory requirements. Figure 20-1 depicts the major files and processes that are at the heart of a securities firm's automation of Operations' functions.

In this chapter, we'll review the major functions involved in processing a trade and give a system-by-system review of the Operation's functions automated in securities firms, including objectives of the system, the system architecture, major data elements, major functions, and possible weaknesses.

MAJOR FUNCTIONS IN PROCESSING SECURITIES TRANSACTIONS

In earlier chapters we discussed in detail the major departments and functions in Operations. A trade starts with a customer calling an Account Executive and requesting a buy or sell order. Specific information was required before processing: customer name, account number, buy or sell, quantity, commission, type of security, delivery instructions, and so forth.

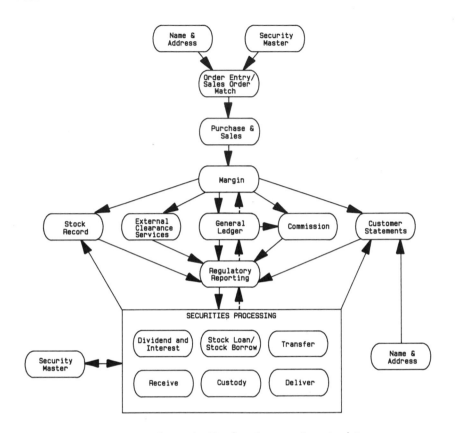

FIGURE 20-1. Generic Trades Processing Architecture

Simple buys or sells rapidly become more complex when calculations involving margin or accrued interest must be performed. These calculations are done whenever a trade involves a loan, or certain debt instruments. In addition, the value of margin accounts must be recalculated every day to ensure that each account maintains sufficient equity, and to calculate interest charges and credits.

After the order is taken by the Account Executive, it is given to the Operations area. The order is then entered, usually electronically, and routed to an execution location (trading desk, exchange or OTC market). The order is often again entered at the execution location to maintain an audit trail and match the original order to the trade, once it is executed. The latter function is critical in cases where trades are not executed immediately, or when they are executed partially or incorrectly. Problems usually occur when the customer requests more complex orders, such as stop limits, GTCs, partial fills, spreads, or straddles.

The Purchase and Sales Department (P&S) coordinates the trade processing tasks after its execution. The functions of the department include preparing confirmations, comparing orders versus executions, and comparing the firm's records against contraparties. Once an order is received, communicated, executed and reported, the P&S Department calculates the customer's charges or credits, and the monies due to exchanges, clearing corporations, and others. The Account Executive's commission is then calculated and recorded in the firm's records.

Since the Account Executive must be able to answer customer questions at any time regarding the status of pending orders, the P&S area must be able to match executions to pending orders in a timely manner. Executed trades must be allocated to the proper accounts. If an execution can't be matched to an order, the mismatch (called an "exception") is referred to clerks to solve the problem. If everything appears to be in order, a confirmation is sent back to the originating Account Executive, who can either notify the customer of a successfully executed transaction, or reject the confirmation as not having matched the original order.

After the P&S Department processes the trade on the firm's books and records, major files are updated: Security Master, Name and Address, Margin, Dividend, and Securities Processing. The Securities Processing area is responsible for the receipt or delivery of securities and monies, and for updating the firm's records relating to where the securities are kept, delivery instructions, payment instructions, and so forth. In addition, other files, such as External Clearance Systems, General Ledger, and Management Information Systems are updated as required.

Now that we have reviewed the basic functions involved, let's take a look at the key systems that support operations in a securities firm, including: Name and Address, Security Master, Stock Record, Order Entry and Sales Order Match, Purchase and Sales, Customer Statements, Margin, General Ledger, Commission, Dividend and Interest, Transfer, Stock Loan and Borrow, External Clearance, Regulatory Reporting, and Management Information Systems. For each of these systems, we'll present the major objectives of the system, the basic architecture, major data elements, major functions and possible weaknesses.

NAME AND ADDRESS SYSTEM

System Objective: Maintains customer account data required for the processing and settlement of trades and the gathering of marketing information.

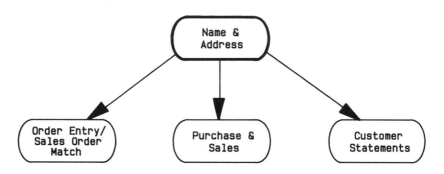

FIGURE 20-2. Name and Address System Architecture

Major Data	Name/Title
Elements:	Address
	Social Security Number/Tax ID
	Delivery Instructions
	Confirm and Statement Disposition
	Account Number
	Account Classification
	Account Type (e.g., Cash, Margin, IRA,
	Delivery/ Receipt vs. Payment,
	Discretionary, Institutional, Retail)
	Agent Information
	Country Code
	State Code
	Citizenship
	Date of Birth
	Occupation

Beneficiary Information and Tax ID
Tax Status
Account Currency
Tax Withholding Information
Bank or Credit References
Financial Information
Margin Exposure Limitations
Investment Data (e.g., Guidelines, Objectives, Constraints, Trading Authority and Instructions, Approved List of Securities, Credit Limits)

Major Functions: Add and delete customer accounts and modify all relevant fields.

Possible Weaknesses: Inability to relate account information for Sales Marketing; inability to update standing instructions for prompt delivery.

SECURITY MASTER SYSTEM

System Objective: Maintains descriptive security information on all securities products processed by the firm.

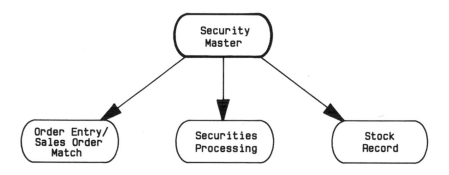

FIGURE 20-3. Security Master System Architecture

Major Data	Asset ID (CUSIP Number and/or Special ID)
Elements:	Asset Description

Asset Type

Issuer Code

Eligibility Codes for Clearing Corporations/
    Depositories State/Country of Issue Code

Fixed Income Information (e.g. Original
    Purchase Date, Maturity Date, Sinking Fund
    Schedule and Payment Data, Coupon Period
    and Rate, First Premium Call Date and
    Price, Par Call Date, Private Placement Put
    and Call Features)

Pricing Service Codes

Pricing Matrices

Pricing Parameters for System Derivation of
    Price

Quality Rating

Expiration Dates

Special Qualifications (e.g., Ex-Legal, In-Default)

Corporate Action Information

Major
Functions: Update descriptive security information with all relevant fields; add information on new issues.

Possible
Weaknesses: Inability to distinguish between products; inability to handle digital price feeds; inability to process multiple currencies.

STOCK RECORD SYSTEM

System Objective: Maintains and updates all security positions for customer, firm and "street-side" locations. Provides capability to balance long and short positions with exception reporting.

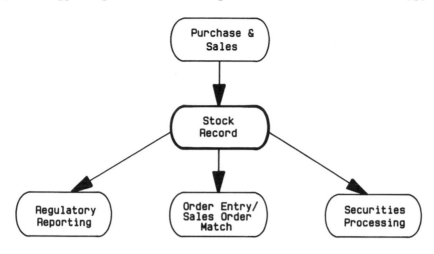

20-4. Stock Record System Architecture

Major Functions:	Monitor, track, adjust activity and net positions of securities.
Major Data Elements:	Security number Account number Quantity (long/short) Divident reinvestment indicator Name of indicator Last activity date Segregation quantity
Possible Weaknesses:	Inability to provide real-time view of stock record; inability to view historical data for adjustment purposes.

ORDER ENTRY AND SALES ORDER MATCH SYSTEM

System Objectives: Processes all orders, tracks and monitors orders from the time they have been entered into the system until they have been executed (also referred to as the Order Match System). This includes edits, routing to the appropriate execution location, and matching executions against open orders.

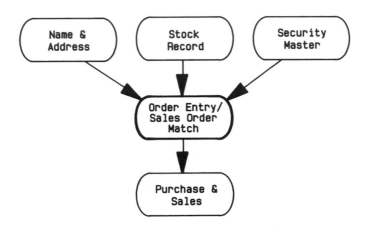

FIGURE 20-5. Order Entry and Sales Order Match System Architecture

Major Data
Elements:

Security Number
Symbol
CUSIP Number
Buy/Sell
Account ID
Contrabroker
Units/Shares/Value
AE Number
Trader
Trade date
Settlement Date
Transaction ID
Status
Limit Order Information
Order Type

Major *Functions:*	Stores and tracks status of eligible orders. Routes orders to appropriate execution location. Rejects orders back to source if vital information required for execution is missing. Provides correction capabilities to correct matched or unmatched trades and orders. Matches executed trades against open orders.
Possible *Weaknesses:*	Systems often lack masks; order tracking may differ by product; re-entry of orders at different locations is error-prone.

PURCHASE AND SALES SYSTEM

System Objectives: Facilitates processing, comparing and matching of all transactions. It also provides customers with confirmations, and the contraparty with comparisons pertaining to the transaction.

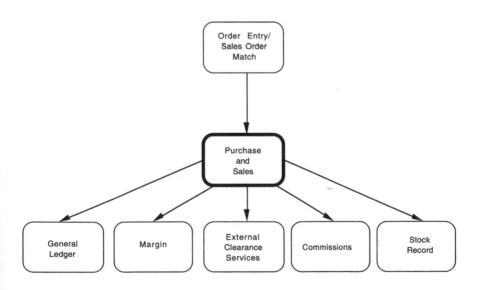

FIGURE 20-6. Purchase and Sales System Architecture

Major Data *Elements:*	Account Number Security Number Buy/Sell Quantity Principal/Agent Net Money Commission/Markup Accrued Dividend/Interest Contrabroker Settlement Date Regulatory Fees Commission Schedules (based on quantities 　　and price)
Major *Functions:*	Validates key data in trade record (e.g., securi- 　　ty number, branch, quantity, price, buy/sell, 　　etc.). Calculates commission credits, principal, net, 　　money, other charges, etc. Maintains trade records for correction between 　　trade and settlement dates. Creates firm and customer records for margin 　　and accounting systems. Produces daily activity reports. Produces trade confirmations.
Possible *Weaknesses:*	Inability to accommodate unique products; 　　inability to provide same-day error correc- 　　tions; lack of exception reporting; lack of 　　multi-currency reporting.

SECURITIES PROCESSING SYSTEM

System Objectives: Maintains and updates customer and "street-side" information regarding custody, receive and deliver requirements.

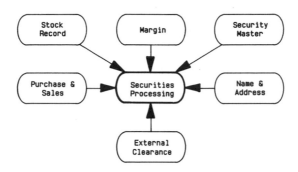

FIGURE 20-7. Securities Processing System Architecture

Major Data Elements:	Account Name
	Account ID
	Custody Requirements
	Delivery Instructions
	Security Number
	CUSIP Number
	Security Description
	Quantity
	Denominations
	Dividend/Interest Information
	Reorganization Information
	Stock Loan/Stock Borrow Information
	Margin Requirements
Major Functions:	Receives and delivers securities.
	Coordinates with transfer agent for each security to effect registration.
	Deposits securities in Inventory Control System and is responsible for the processing requirements for dividend/interest collection, corporate reorganizations, coordination of loans of securities to other brokers and custody requirements.

Possible
Weaknesses:
Inability to utilize available securities; inability to access information on-line.

CUSTOMER STATEMENTS SYSTEM

System Objectives: Compiles necessary information and prints out statements reflecting customer activity for a specified period of time. The basic information provided to customers on their statements includes: customer name, social security number, cash balances, security positions (quantity, market price, original cost and current value), all activity for the time period, dividend/interest postings, corporate actions, and so forth.

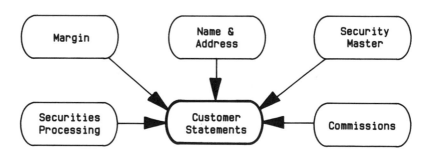

FIGURE 20-8. Customer Statements System Architecture

Major Data
Elements:
Name
Address
Account Number
Account Classification
Security Number
Security Positions
Market Value
Cash Balance
Total Equity in the Account
Account Executive
1099 Tax Reporting Information
Transaction Information

Major Functions:	Produces statements for all customers which include purchases and sales, bookkeeping movements, valued closing positions and opening and closing balances. Produces monthly and year-to-date 1099 tax reporting information.
Possible Weaknesses:	Inability to relate accounts; inability to process multi-currencies; inability to price all prod - ucts.

MARGIN SYSTEM

System Objectives: Records customer activity and controls credit extended to customers. It complies with various regulations regarding collateralization of margin transactions, customer payments and proper segregation of customers' securities.

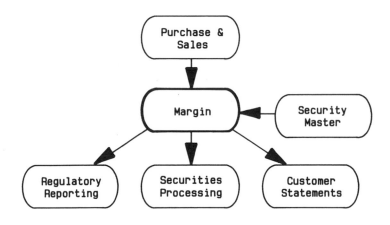

FIGURE 20-9. Margin System Architecture

Major Data Elements:	Account Number Account Status Security Number

> Security Type
> Trade Settlement Date
> Margin Requirements
> Margin Balances as of Trade Date, Short and
> Long
> Market Value
> Closing Prices
> Security Positions

*Major
Functions:*

Ensures that all customer accounts comply
 with the various requirements for using
 margin.
Identifies customer buying power.
Identifies margin call requests.
Calculates margin interest.

*Potential
Weaknesses:*

Inability to access customer data separately
 from firm data; inability to provide exception processing information identifying risk
 exposure.

GENERAL LEDGER SYSTEM

System Objectives: Provides accounting records for trades, cash
receipts/payments, assets, liabilities, expenses, and so forth.

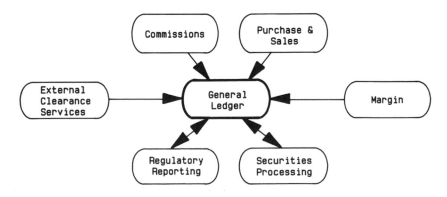

FIGURE 20-10. General Ledger System Architecture

Major Data Elements:	Debit/Credit Balances
	Assets and Liabilities
	Money Differences (number of items and dollar value)
	Financial Statement Adjustments
	Commissions
	Trading and Investment Account Gains/Losses
	Other Income Items
	Commodities Income
	Payroll Expense
	Floor Brokerage Clearing Expense
	Overhead Expense
	Tax Tables Information
	Sub-ledgers
Major Functions:	Income, expense and balance sheet accounts are maintained for each organization entity in the firm. A uniform chart of accounts is used to allow the results of each entity to be consolidated into the closing statement each month.
Possible Weaknesses:	Inability to have one entry affect all ledgers; inability to accommodate multi-currencies.

COMMISSION SYSTEM

System Objectives: Calculates commissions for each purchase and sale. Tables of algorithms are maintained for each product and used by the system to calculate commissions for that product. The Commission System also handles a variety of payout structures and amounts to calculate commission compensation for individual traders and sales personnel.

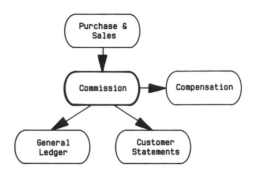

FIGURE 20-11. Commission System Architecture

Major Data Elements:	AE/Trader ID Number
	Security Number
	Security Type
	Security Quantity
	Security Price
	Type of Trade
	Schedule Tables (e.g., Payout, Bonus, Special Payouts)
Major Functions:	Calculates AE/Trader commissions which include splits and commission sharing arrangements, product overrides and bonus schedules.
	Provides information to the compensation (payroll) system.
Possible Weaknesses:	Inability to provide appropriate product information.

DIVIDEND AND INTEREST SYSTEM

System Objectives: Tracks dividends declared by issuing corporations on outstanding stocks and interest payments on outstanding bonds. It records the dividend and interest payments on stocks and bonds that the firm holds for customers and credits the appropriate accounts. The system also tracks record date, ex-date, and payable date for security positions and transactions.

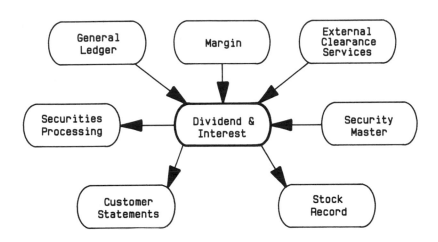

FIGURE 20-12. Dividend and Interest System Architecture

Major Data Elements:	CUSIP Number Security Number Account Number Dividend/Interest Detail Record (includes Record Date, Ex-Dividend Date, Pay Date, Rates and Type of Dividend) Tax Information
Major Functions:	Dividend/Interest Master File (Security Records)—maintains dividend/interest information for all securities including when payment is to be made, amount of payment and type of payment. Pending File (Customer's Record)—establishes customer and firm holdings.

Possible   Inability to capture foreign corporation data;
Weaknesses: inability to track corporate reorganizations;
                       inability to balance receipts against disburse-
                       ments.

TRANSFER SYSTEM

System Objective: Enables the Securities Processing area to
monitor all activity in both customer and firm accounts relating to
the transfer of securities.

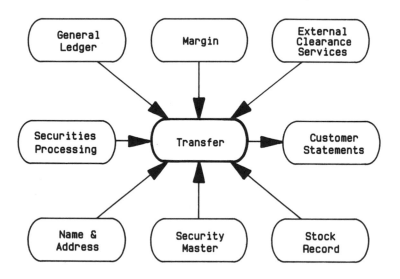

FIGURE 20-13. Transfer System Architecture

Major Data   Security Number
Elements: CUSIP Number
                      Quantity
                      Legal Code
                      Tax Indicator
                      Denomination to Transfer
                      Customer Account Number
                      Customer Name and Address
                      Social Security Number or ID Number

Major Functions:	Provides various systems with status of customer/firm securities in the process of transfer.
Possible Weaknesses:	Inability to access transfer agent workflow.

STOCK LOAN/BORROW SYSTEM

System Objectives: Processes securities for loaning to or borrowing from individuals and institutions.

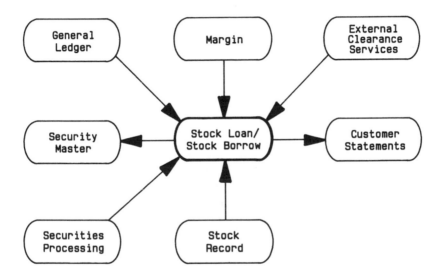

FIGURE 20-14. Stock Loan/Borrow System Architecture

Major Data Elements:	Security Number
	Security Description
	Security Type
	Security Quantity
	Security Price
	Customer Holdings
	Firm Holdings
	Account ID
	Financial Agreement

Major	Daily market-to-market
Functions:	tracking of principal, customer holdings and
	fails
	Allocation of borrows and receives

Possible	Inability to mark-to-market on a timely basis;
Weaknesses:	inability to differentiate firm versus cus-
	tomer holdings.

EXTERNAL CLEARANCE SYSTEM

System Objectives: Interfaces with depositories and clearing corporations where securities firms exchange information on purchases and sales, make deliveries and make payments for securities. The system also interfaces with vendors where participating firms deposit securities, thereby enabling book entry settlement of transactions, stock loans, account movement, and so forth.

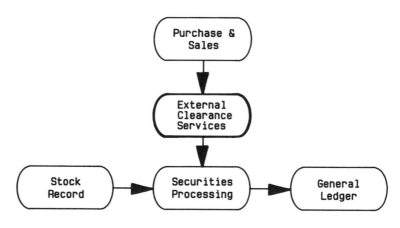

FIGURE 20-15. External Clearance System Architecture

Major Data	Order Number
Elements:	Security Symbol
	Buy/Sell
	Quantity
	Contrabroker

Executing Broker
Units/Shares/Value

Major   Ensures that the securities positions across
Functions: multiple clearance firms are in balance.

Possible   Inefficient interface with clearing corporations;
Weaknesses: redundant applications; lack of exception
                 reporting.

REGULATORY REPORTING SYSTEM

System Objectives: Provides information for FOCUS and other
regulatory reports required by the firm, and responds to requests for
information from regulatory and legal authorities.

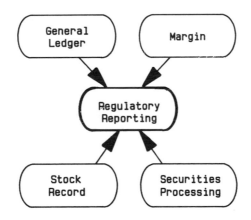

FIGURE 20-16. Regulatory Reporting System Architecture

Major Data   Name and Address Files
Elements: Customer Profile
                 Relationships and Households Among Account
                       Holders
                 Proprietary Accounts
                 Trade Date/Settlement Date Activity
                 Firmwide Balances and Positions

Major *Functions:*	Tracks customer and firm trading, cash and margin activities for regulatory reporting purposes.
Possible *Weaknesses:*	Inability to track regulatory information in format required by regulatory and legal authorities.

MANAGEMENT INFORMATION SYSTEMS

System Objectives: Supplements the operating reports produced by other systems and sub-systems, generating exception and control reports for management. Reports can focus on financial and regulatory analysis, cash management, error control, risk management and capital planning, budgeting and forecasting.

Major *Functions:*	Collects information from all systems in the architecture; provides management information for control and performance measurement.
Possible *Weaknesses:*	Inability to provide information by products; inability to provide information on a real-time basis; inability to organize captured data for usefulness.

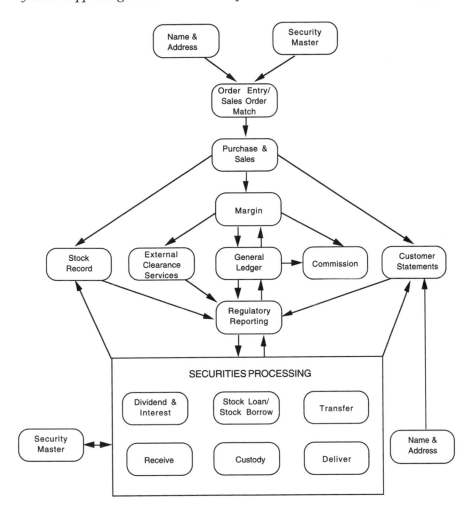

FIGURE 20-17. Management Information Systems Architecture

CHAPTER 21

Functional Responsibilities of Information Systems Departments

In many firms, the users of Information Systems services have little exposure to the work that I/S personnel perform. Users generally only see the final result, and this lack of exposure to the processes necessary for an I/S department to be successful often leads to a complete misunderstanding of the nature of major functions performed by I/S personnel.

In this chapter we will discuss some of the major functional responsibilities that an I/S department must perform well in order to be effective. The specific areas discussed are Systems Planning, Systems Development and Data Center Operations, including workflow management, inventory management, resource monitoring, documentation control, and recovery operations.

SYSTEMS PLANNING

Most I/S managers know that while specific systems development efforts may produce intended results, many firms, in the past, did not give enough thought to the potential value of Information Systems in realizing corporate objectives. In recognition of the potential value of I/S, firms now expend considerable effort in planning to assist in the realization of business objectives, long term competitive advantage, profit and growth.

The process and results of an effective plan provide a firm with the following benefits:

I/S efforts (and expenses) are linked to corporate objectives.

I/S implementation activities are prioritized based on corporate strategies.

Business unit participation in the development of systems results in greater user satisfaction and increased benefits to the business.

I/S expenditures and activities are measured in terms of their contribution to the achievement of corporate objectives.

A systems plan is a series of integrated feasibility analyses which describes major systems development activities over the planning horizon for a business activity. In this scenario, systems development activities are defined as major modifications to existing systems, and/or the design and installation of new application systems to meet specific business needs. The systems plan is a derivative of the business plan, supportive of the goals contained in the business plan, and identifies the role of the system in attainment of business objectives on a cost-justified basis.

Regardless of the cultural or stylistic differences among various firms, well-developed plans have certain fundamental components that are common across all firms.

A definition of the firm's business environment, strategic business objectives, and key business strategies.

A definition of the major system applications which business units see as most important to be implemented, including costs and benefits.

A statement of the telecommunications, hardware, and maintenance costs to support the existing business.

A specification of the hardware and software necessary to meet the future demands of the business at lowest total cost.

An estimate of personnel requirements, including system analysts, programmers, and systems software and operations personnel.

A description and analysis of alternative means of providing adequate service, for example, regionalization versus centralization of hardware, and distributed processing.

A schedule for implementation of new application systems.

A clear definition of the organizational structure required to implement the plan.

A definition of major milestones in the plan's implementation, with a description of what will be accomplished at each milestone, when the milestone will occur, and how much money will have been expended when the milestone is reached.

A detailed set of actions for implementation of the plan, with clear definition of authority and responsibility for various parts of the plan.

SYSTEMS DEVELOPMENT

The I/S area should have a standard framework for carrying out systems development efforts, and specifying the products that will result from these efforts.

THE NEED FOR A STANDARD METHODOLOGY

I/S and business unit managers generally agree that the most important criteria for developing successful systems are:

1. Meeting users requirements.
2. Completion on schedule.
3. Completion within budget.

Those same managers also agree that few systems development efforts meet all three of these criteria. Failure to do so can be attributed to the following causes:

Failing to fully understand user requirements before translating those requirements into a systems design.

Failing to involve the user in the development process.

Accepting design changes without a corresponding revision of the project schedule and budget.

Failing to establish checkpoints at which the progress and performance of the project is reviewed.

Failing to communicate to each of the project participants their duties and responsibilities.

Attempting to plan the entire project in detail during the initial stages.

Failing to evaluate alternative system designs for cost-benefit trade-offs.

Most of these failures are the result of not understanding that building new systems requires procedures for controlling a management process. In order to define, develop and produce the product (i.e., the new information system), many diverse interested groups must be consulted, unfamiliar procedures must be analyzed, technical resources must be brought to bear, and a creative solution must be found. Confronted with such problems, firms normally develop management processes to help ensure that resources are used effectively and efficiently. One basic problem-solving approach to the development of major application systems is shown in Figure 21-1. This Phase Structure approach segments the total development process into a series of distinct parts in order to facilitate management of the process. Let's review what happens in each of the phases.

PHASE I: REQUEST FOR SERVICE

The purpose of the Request for Service is to provide a procedure for users of the I/S service to record a request and, after discussion with I/S, to receive an estimate of the resources required to satisfy the request. If a decision to proceed is then made, existing I/S plans are adjusted to reflect the new project. The specific objectives of this phase are:

1. To record a user request on an I/S Request for Service form and communicate it to I/S personnel.

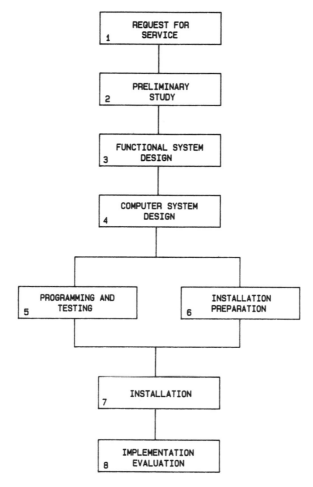

FIGURE 21-1. Systems Planning Phase Structure

2. To estimate and record the resources and timeframe required to satisfy the request and to classify it.

3. To discuss with the user the disposition of the request in light of existing I/S plans.

4. To adjust existing plans, and document the resource commitment if approval is received.

The Request for Service is the first step in the process of planning for new projects, whether they are new systems or enhancements to existing systems. I/S response to the request should be as immediate as possible after consulting with the user to get a good estimate of the resources required to fulfill the request.

The disposition of the request should first be discussed between the user and I/S. The user may decide to cancel the request, to add the request as a project following other scheduled work for their area, or to insert the request ahead of other projects.

PHASE II: PRELIMINARY STUDY

The purpose of the Preliminary Study is to assess the costs and benefits of the proposed system, in order for management to make an investment decision with respect to the system. It is important that a cost/benefit analysis be performed in consultation with appropriate staff early in the development process, before significant time and resources are expended in system design. The objectives of the Preliminary Study are:

1. To more clearly define the problem.

2. To identify alternative solutions to the problem.

3. To assess the economic, technical, and operational feasibility of each alternative.

Both Phase II, Preliminary Study, and Phase III, Functional Design, call for study of the existing process or system. The difference between the two studies is the degree of detailed examination of procedures, responsibilities, data, forms, and so forth. The Phase II study is done to gain an understanding of the system—enough to determine feasibility for cost-benefit purposes. The Phase III study is done to obtain a very detailed understanding of all aspects of the present system, in order that they be considered in the functional design.

Having gained a general understanding of the present process or system and its problems, user requirements for a solution are developed by interviewing users and identifying their needs. Given the general user requirements, alternative system solutions are identified for example, manual versus automated, end-user computing versus mainframe, or on-line versus batch processing. Finally, a Systems Proposal is prepared which documents the findings of the study and presents recommendations.

The Preliminary Study must be carried to sufficient depth to permit a credible analysis of the existing situation, and of the possible alternatives to be developed. However, as noted, an extensive study of the present system, and a detailed specification of the functional requirements for the new system, are deferred until the recommendations of the System Proposal have been reviewed and approved.

The Project Manager has overall responsibility for administering this phase; i.e., planning, coordinating, reporting, and reviewing task outputs. This phase is highly dependent on systems analysis skills for studying the present system, determining user requirements, and developing and evaluating alternative system designs. There is heavy involvement of users throughout the phase. Finally, the System Proposal is reviewed by I/S and user managers responsible for authorizing further development.

Two outputs are produced during the phase: a System Proposal, and a Project Plan. As discussed, the System Proposal documents the findings of the study and presents recommendations. The Project Plan is prepared upon authorization and approval for further development. The Plan consists of a detailed schedule, a statement of responsibilities and budget for the next phase, and a more general schedule and cost estimate for the remainder of the project.

PHASE III: FUNCTIONAL SYSTEM DESIGN

During the previous phase, the Preliminary Study, the output was a proposal outlining the general design approach for a system solution to the user problem. The Functional System Design phase commences upon approval of the recommendations contained in the proposal. During this phase, the system is designed in detail— system inputs, processing logic, and outputs are specified completely. However, the design process takes place at the functional level, in that the system is described from the user's perspective; that is, it is described in terms of the functions to be performed, not from the I/S perspective in terms of computer programs, files, and job streams. The emphasis of this phase is on determining what functions must be performed, not how to perform those functions. Thus, the output of this phase must be completely understandable to the user. The objectives of this phase are to:

1. Understand the present system in detail as a basis for specifying the new system.

2. Design the new system in sufficient detail to obtain user agreement as to the system definition, and to enable the system to be designed.

3. Develop a plan for the remainder of the project.

The first major task within the Functional System Design phase is to perform an in-depth study of the present system or process. The objective of this task is two-fold: First, it provides some assurance that user requirements are not overlooked. In addition, it facilitates identification of opportunities for improvement of present manual or automated systems.

Having developed an in-depth understanding of the present system, the next major task is to define the new system in greater detail. Specifically, source documents, report layouts, screen formats and transactions, and other system inputs and outputs are defined, along with the processing logic needed to produce the outputs from the inputs. The contents of the logical files are defined, and manual and automated controls are designed for maintaining system integrity.

After developing the functional system design, the relative roles and responsibilities of the users and I/S in the remaining project phases are made explicit. Specifically, the data conversion plan is determined, user acceptance criteria are defined, and the installation plan is developed. This way, the users know what is expected of them in the remainder of the project.

Upon completion of the above tasks, the project plan is updated by defining Phase IV in detail. A phase-end report is prepared in which the functional system specifications are documented. Finally, the phase outputs are reviewed for user acceptance, and signed-off before initiating the next phase.

There is a significant need for systems analysis skills for investigating the present system, developing functional requirements, and defining user acceptance criteria. There is heavy involvement of users throughout the phase, and the participation by I/S Data Center staff is essential. Finally, the phase outputs are reviewed along several dimensions, with user and I/S management responsible for final approval of the phase as suggested in the review matrix depicted in Figure 21-2.

The main output of this phase is the Functional Specifications document. This document contains a functional description of the system in terms of its input, processes, and outputs. It forms the basis for Phase IV, Computer System Design. In addition, user requirements are finalized during this phase, and the project plan is updated.

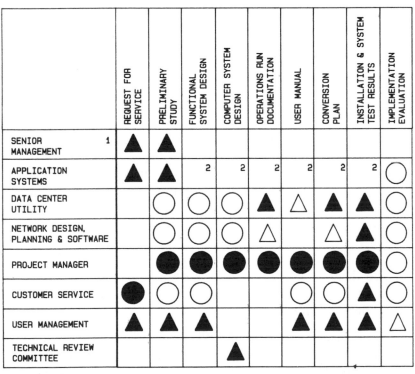

	REQUEST FOR SERVICE	PRELIMINARY STUDY	FUNCTIONAL SYSTEM DESIGN	COMPUTER SYSTEM DESIGN	OPERATIONS RUN DOCUMENTATION	USER MANUAL	CONVERSION PLAN	INSTALLATION & SYSTEM TEST RESULTS	IMPLEMENTATION EVALUATION
SENIOR MANAGEMENT ¹	▲	▲							
APPLICATION SYSTEMS	▲	▲	2	2	2	2	2	2	○
DATA CENTER UTILITY		○	○	○	▲	△	▲	▲	○
NETWORK DESIGN, PLANNING & SOFTWARE		○	○	○	△		△	▲	○
PROJECT MANAGER		●	●	●	●	●	●	●	○
CUSTOMER SERVICE	●	○	○			○	○	▲	○
USER MANAGEMENT	▲	▲	▲			▲	▲	▲	△
TECHNICAL REVIEW COMMITTEE				▲					

○ PERFORM   ¹ FOR PROJECTS ABOVE DETERMINED COST LEVELS

● PARTICIPATE   ² NORMAL LINE MANAGEMENT REVIEW IS ASSUMED

△ INFORMATION REVIEW

▲ REVIEW AND APPROVE

FIGURE 21-2. Systems Planning Review Matrix
Copyright by Nolan Norton & Company.

PHASE IV: COMPUTER SYSTEM DESIGN

The previous phase—Functional System Design—produces as output a functional description of the desired system. The Computer System Design phase transforms the Functional Specifications into specifications for computer programs, master file, intermediate files, and manual controls and procedures. In effect, the system functions are mapped onto the programs and procedures. The objectives of this phase are to:

1. Develop a computer system design—comprising program specifications, master file definition, and intermediate file definitions—from the Functional System Design.

2. Design the data conversion system.

3. Develop detailed internal specifications.

4. Develop unit and system tests.

5. Plan the remainder of the project.

The key activity within this task is converting the functional description of the system into a description in terms of process flows. Additional activities within this task include developing logical and physical file structures, defining intermediate file structures, and identifying data control and other procedures.

After developing the overall system design, several major tasks are performed:

1. The data conversion system is designed. The conversion system transforms data from its present form and location to its required form and location.

2. A test plan encompassing both unit and system tests is developed. At the same time, a tentative program development plan is prepared. The development plan specifies the order in which programs are to be developed.

3. The internal structure of each program is determined from the external program specifications.

Upon completion of the above tasks, several phase-end tasks are performed, such as planning the remainder of the project, preparing the system specifications, and reviewing the specification documents before approving further development.

Other I/S areas including Network Design, Planning and Software, and the Data Center, provide assistance in the development of the production and conversion systems. Additional project participants are consulted with respect to those aspects of the system which impact them. Finally, the system is reviewed along several dimensions with I/S management responsible for final approval of the system. Note that with the exception of the Data Conversion System Design, and the development of the test plan, user involvement during this phase is minimal.

Two primary outputs are produced during this phase: the System Specifications and Internal Program Specifications. The System Specifications document is a description of the system in terms of its programs and program flow, logical and physical master file structure, intermediate file structures, and data control procedures. In addition, this phase documents a system test plan for the remainder of the project. The Internal Program Specifications describe the internal structure of each program—production, conversion, and test to be developed. These two outputs form the basis for the Programming and Testing, and Installation Preparation phases.

PHASE V: PROGRAMMING AND TESTING

During the previous phase—Computer System Design—user requirements are translated into specifications for a computer system comprising programs, procedures, and files. Each program is designed in sufficient detail to enable program coding. The computer system is augmented by data conversion programs for converting the data to its required form and location. Finally, a comprehensive system test plan is developed for ensuring that the system performs in accordance with its specifications.

The Programming and Testing phase is initiated upon approval of the System Specifications Document generated during the previous phase. The purpose of this phase is to code and test all application and conversion programs in preparation for installation of the new system. The objectives of this phase are the following:

1. Code, compile, and test the programs identified in the System Specifications Document, using established standards and conventions.

2. Perform an integrated systems test to demonstrate that the system performs in accordance with its specifications.

3. Produce the System/Program Documentation.

4. Provide input to the Installation Preparation and Installation phases as required.

Each program is coded and tested individually. System testing is performed to ensure the proper execution of all programs in an integrated environment.

The System/Program Documentation is also produced during this phase:

1. Programs and JCL (Job Control Language) listings are generated and, upon approval, placed into the Technical Library and the appropriate computer libraries.

2. System and program descriptions are produced by abstracting from the documentation in the project file and other information as necessary.

3. Unit and system test results are produced and added to the System/Program Documentation.

The Project Manager is primarily responsible for administrating this phase. The phase is heavily dependent on the programming activity for coding, testing, and integrating the programs of the new system. The Project Manager or staff must also be available to answer any questions of interpretation, and approve any required changes to the design specifications. Because of the highly technical nature of this phase, user involvement during the phase is limited. However, users do review the test results.

There are three outputs which are produced during the Programming and Testing phase:

1. Production System.
2. Conversion Activities.
3. System/Program Documentation.

PHASE VI: INSTALLATION PREPARATION

Installation Preparation is performed in parallel with Programming and Testing, and prior to the Installation phase. Objectives of this phase include:

1. Plan the Installation phase in detail.
2. Prepare Installation Guide.
3. Order any forms required by the system.
4. Monitor the status of any special equipment purchases, or installation already ordered (Phase IV).
5. Prepare the User Manual and develop the User Training Program.
6. Prepare the Operation Run Book Documentation, and develop a Data Center Operation and telecommunications review.
7. Initiate conversion and generate the master files.

The Project Manager must coordinate the activities of this phase with the parallel programming and testing effort. Users are heavily involved during the phase, and are usually responsible for any data collection and conversion required for generating the master file. Data Center Operations and Technical Services provide assistance as required, and assure that any special equipment ordered is on schedule.

The principal outputs produced during the phase are the following:

1. User Manual. The reference/training manual for the users of the system.
2. Operation Run Book Documentation. The reference manual for personnel in the Data Center who must operate, control, and support the system.

3. System Master File. The portions of the master file which are feasible to convert prior to Installation.

4. Installation Guide. A manual for installing the system, including training schedules, training materials, and user test schedules.

PHASE VII: INSTALLATION

Initiation of the Installation phase requires approval of both the Installation Preparation phase and the Programming and Testing phase. The purpose of this phase is to install the new system, converting the system from a developmental to an operational status. The objectives of this phase are:

1. Perform required training.

2. Perform Data Center operations acceptance testing.

3. Perform user acceptance testing.

4. Transfer the system to full production status.

The Installation phase, particularly user acceptance testing, will typically take one of the following three forms to ensure the appropriate production environment:

1. Parallel operation. The old and new systems are operated in parallel until the new system is accepted by the user.

2. Staged conversion. The system is installed in parts, e.g., by organizational unit or by system function.

3. Pilot operation. An immediate conversion is made to the new system; the old system is maintained as a backup.

Once the system satisfies the user acceptance criteria and is certified by the Data Center as ready for Production Status, the system enters a moratorium on modifications and a period of monitored production. During this period, the operation of the system is closely monitored to ensure that all procedures are being followed, and problems with the system are detected and resolved. Upon completion of this transition period, the system enters full production status. Thereafter, any users requests for enhancements or maintenance are handled as normal work requests.

Four outputs are produced during this phase:

1. Operational System.
2. System Documentation.
3. Approved Data Center Operations Run Book Documentation.
4. Approved User Manual.

PHASE VIII: IMPLEMENTATION EVALUATION

Initiation of the Implementation Evaluation phase requires sign-off by the User and Data Center of the Installation phase, and commences after transferring the system into full production status. The purpose of this phase is to evaluate the performance of the operational system against the original objectives and its projected cost-benefit analysis.

The objectives of this last phase of the system development methodology are as follows:

1. Evaluate functional performance of the new system.
2. Evaluate cost performance and efficiency of the new system.
3. Analyze the system development process utilized.
4. Prepare a written report to the end-user.
5. Develop recommendations regarding system and procedural enhancements.

The principal output produced during this phase is a written management report which covers the following:

1. Documentation and evaluation of the new system performance in terms of user effectiveness and operational efficiency.
2. Evaluation of performance (actual versus projected) for user costs, user benefits, and computer costs.
3. Evaluation of conformance to the system development methodology process, structure, and timetables.

4. Recommendations for system enhancements or procedural enhancements.

DATA CENTER OPERATIONS

Data Centers must provide high levels of support to all users. In securities firms, the performance of the Data Center is the lifeline of Sales, Trading, and Operations. Customers, traders, and sales personnel need information, on-line in many cases and, for batch systems, within very tight timeframes. Let's look at the work that goes on in the Data Center to meet these objectives.

WORKFLOW MANAGEMENT

Workflow management involves the forecasting and scheduling of individual jobs that are required to be run, and how work flows through the Data Center to the user. There are at least two types of schedules involved: 1) master schedule and 2) monthly/weekly schedule.

Master Schedule The master schedule should forecast for at least one year all systems which will be run and approximately when they will be run. It should schedule a job from the time it reaches production control to be logged in until it is no longer in the control of the Data Center. Clearly all usage cannot be predicted. Estimates should be made for "on demand" jobs, preventive maintenance, change installation, and so forth. The master schedule should have two parts: the equipment and the people to run the equipment. All systems should have resource requirements associated with them. Thus, if a new system is proposed, the master schedule will enable the Data Center manager to determine whether or not it is feasible to run the system.

Monthly/Weekly Schedule This schedule expands on the master schedule. Run times and estimates are more precisely defined. "On demand" work is more accurately estimated. Intra-data center movement of tapes, disks, and so forth are defined precisely for all jobs. In the event a resource is lost during the day, the monthly/weekly schedule should include alternate processing schedules by system priority. Since most sophisticated equipment can be reconfigured dynamically, this schedule should produce a configuration map to best suit the job mix and service level requirements. The monthly schedule should be regularly compared to the actual processing, and variances should be analyzed to improve the schedule.

In addition to job scheduling, shift workflow control procedures should be implemented. The shift workflow control procedures are concerned with utilizing the personnel and equipment in the most efficient manner possible in order to accomplish the work. These procedures deal with the management of Data Center operations on a minute-to-minute basis. They include such things as turnover from shift to shift, acceptance and maintenance of run books, recovering from certain problems, and so forth.

INPUT/OUTPUT CONTROLS

Procedures and controls should also be established to anticipate, receive, validate, and reconcile data from the user community. When data is not received on time, or does not proof properly, the I/S Control area should immediately contact the end-user. Just as the jobs or the input is logged in, so the output should be logged out after it has been checked for validity, appearance, and adherence to schedule. In many firms, this is known as the report compliance system. Often data entry and its associated controls are found within this function.

INVENTORY MANAGEMENT

Keeping up with the individual pieces of hardware, and versions or levels of software, becomes a complex problem as the organization matures. Unless a formal inventory control system is in place to identify exactly what resources the firm has, and where they are located, the management of change can become a true nightmare.

SYSTEMS SOFTWARE INVENTORY

This system identifies every piece of system software within the installation. It is important in large, complex environments since it is not unusual to find 70 - 100 pieces of system software in those installations. Different releases of software have different features. An applications programmer may wish to use a feature of the telecommunications handler not available, except on a particular release. It's necessary, therefore, to have a mechanism to track releases and their features. In addition, there may be interdependencies among pieces of system software. Installation of a certain release may require other software to be updated. The system software inventory includes such information as:

Vendor name and address

Whether the software is in test, installation, or production

Software version, release and level

Installed fixes, object code modification or other modifications, along with who, when and why

Other required hardware or software

Responsible person

Associated problems along with their resolution

APPLICATIONS INVENTORY

The applications inventory is a complete list of all production applications for the Data Center. It is similar to the systems software inventory, however it contains some unique information, including:

When it is run (linking it to the various schedules)

Any scheduling considerations relating to other jobs or systems

User contracts for both distribution and problem management

Original author or vendor

The minimum hardware/software configuration required to run the system

HARDWARE INVENTORY

The hardware inventory is analogous to the system software inventory. However, the number of items inventoried is normally much larger. In a larger installation, it's not uncommon to have thousands of pieces of hardware counting all terminals, lines, modems, and so forth. The same type of information is maintained as we described for the system software inventory and in addition, the hardware inventory includes:

Physical location

Other units to which connected

List of all options and how they are installed

Financial information such as current rental, current purchase prices, purchase options, service or maintenance fees, and any complicated contractual obligations (lease-back or walk-away deals)

RESOURCE MONITORING

This is a very technical area within the Data Center. The basic statistics are gathered and normalized to do chargebacks, performance measurement, tuning, and even portions of capacity planning. Often, the utilization statistics, which represent job, resource and utilization measurements, may come from 20–30 separate sources, among them: the vendor's machine accounting, database systems, time-sharing systems, hardware monitors, recovery management facilities, I/O logs, data entry logs, job setup sheets, special forms logs, and manpower time reporting procedures. This data must be combined, normalized to a common base, and validated to provide an accurate accounting base.

This monitoring of resources helps determine which resources are used most frequently, how the Data Center responds to "downtime," when resources most frequently fail, and so forth. Some of the areas that need to be monitored are:

CPU utilization by time

CPU utilization by system

Operating systems failure and recovery times

On-line systems availability

Hardware failures

On-line systems response times

Production reports volume

Production reports schedule

On-line transactions

Batch transactions

Time of production jobs

Aside from helping Data Center management reallocate resources on a timely basis, the above data is also needed to "chargeback" expenses to users (if a chargeback system is used).

DOCUMENTATION CONTROL

Documentation Control assures that the integrity of documentation in the Data Center is maintained. This function controls creation, modification, access and use of documentation, and libraries in the Data Center.

A library control system will manage the cataloging of all systems into the various system libraries. The system is responsible for:

Controlling the location and content of all libraries

Maintaining the procedures under which data sets are accepted as production

Enforcing data set naming conventions

Maintaining library maps

Ensuring that media is properly prepared

Ensuring that files are reorganized correctly

RECOVERY CONTROLS

Recovery procedures attempt to assure that the integrity of data sets and systems can be reconstructed. Within this set of procedures, there are a number of levels of complexity.

Procedures must be in place to recreate any data sets lost or corrupted by program failure. These are system specific and are generally included in the systems run book. These individual job rerun procedures may be extremely complex, since 40 or 50 separate steps can be required to return to the step which was processing prior to the need to reinitiate the job.

Elaborate backup and recovery procedures require that all sensitive and all production data sets can be copied for security purposes. These copies are normally stored onsite.

As the organization becomes more sophisticated, it develops off-site storage on files and special forms. This off-site storage is usually concerned with the destruction of the primary Data Center.

Procedures must be in place and tested which ensure that the entire data processing installation is backed up, and can be recreated in the event of a catastrophe. While the likelihood that this will occur is small, the consequences of loss are significant. Normally the highest level of backup and recovery is associated with the disaster recovery plan addressed later in this chapter.

CHANGE MANAGEMENT

Change Management includes the procedures and controls required to ensure that the Data Center operates in a predictable, trouble-free manner. Data Center managers often think that this is intended only for large organizations. Actually, it should be introduced in firms with as few as 10–15 terminals. By the time the organization has 100 terminals, procedures and attitudes are hard to change. Some of the areas to consider are problem recording and tracking, user help desks, change requests, and acceptance testing.

PROBLEM RECORDING AND TRACKING

Problem Recording is designed to recognize the existence of a problem and record relevant data in a central problem log. The problem log is a central facility for monitoring problems until they are resolved.

Problem Tracking is part of problem management. It monitors problem status from the time it is entered into the log until it is ultimately resolved. At any time the Problem Tracking function should be able to report such things as:

Who reported the problem

When it was reported

The impact of the problem

Who is working on it

If it is a duplicate problem

When it is expected to be resolved

Interim action required

USER HELP DESK

The User Help Desk is an organization within the Data Center designed specifically to aid users. The initial problem reporting, problem tracking, and problem determination are accomplished here. In addition, service level and status reports are issued by the User Help Desk. By definition, it should be user-friendly, and should serve as the focal point of all user inquiries and information regarding production systems.

CHANGE REQUESTS AND CHANGE CONTROL

The change request is a request that the production environment be modified. The change request must be logged and tracked until it is either installed or rejected. Once it is installed, it must be monitored to ensure it does not result in problems. Change control attempts to log, track, and monitor changes to the production environment in order to aid the problem-resolution process. Change coordination, a part of change control, attempts to schedule the installation of changes in order to have a minimum impact on the production environment.

ACCEPTANCE TESTING

Before programs and data sets are catalogued into production libraries, the application must be formally tested and accepted by the Data Center. The procedures must be reviewed early to ensure that they can be run without a programmer "helping" the system through. Procedures should be designed to ensure that the new system will not harm any part of the production environment.

Acceptance testing addresses a major interface between the systems and programming group and the production services group. The development group is anxious to get the system into production in order to satisfy the user. However, since the Data Center is ultimately responsible for the day-to-day activities involved in production, the Data Center needs to have the final authority to determine whether to run the system.

SECURITY/DISASTER RECOVERY

Physical Security Physical security involves protecting the physical plant. It includes fire protection, backup power, installation access control, theft prevention, sabotage protection, and so forth. In short, it includes all procedures necessary to assure the safety of the Data Center, its contents, and the personnel who work there.

System Security System Security is a set of system designed guidelines, control procedures, and auditing procedures directed at assuring integrity of both application systems and system software. System Security focuses on the interrelationship between applications, the operating system, and the end-users. It assures that access to the telecommunications network is adequately controlled and that one application does not destroy another, or that one application does not destroy a piece of system software. Change control procedures discussed earlier are also important here.

Information Security Information security is a set of policies, standards, and procedures accompanied by specific software products which are designed to allow access to data only when appropriate authorization exists. This is an important but difficult task, since information might reside on mainframe media, on a floppy disk (in someone's desk), or even in a processing queue waiting to be transmitted via satellite to some remote location.

Disaster Recovery Plan A disaster recovery plan is a highly detailed set of instructions designed to recover from a catastrophe. Most disaster recovery plans assume the worst. They attempt to specify what the data processing organization should do in the event the Data Center is completely destroyed. They consider who to call for first aid and how to notify the proper authorities. In addition, they specify which routines are critical for the Data Center to process. Each of these routines should have a contingency processing plan of its own as a part of the disaster recovery Plan. This would refer to alternative processing plans. In summary the disaster recovery plan incorporates all of the problems or issues which must be addressed in order to resume processing in the event the Data Center is destroyed. Chapter 18 provides much more specifics on a disaster recovery plan.

CHAPTER 22

Information Systems Organization and Administration

Most readers realize that organization structures, that is, "who reports to whom," change fairly frequently. The "organization chart" is often outdated as soon as it is printed. This is because organizations evolve, grow and mature. The same is true for departments within organizations, for example, Sales, Marketing, Operations, and Information Systems. There is no "right" or "wrong" structure. Most successful firms try many structures over a period of years. There is however, one constant in all the change—firms organize to achieve corporate objectives. They also put administrative functions in place as departments grow in importance.

In this chapter, we will look at organization structures of Information Systems: trends, considerations for determining an organizational structure, and what typical organization structures look like. We will also look at the administrative functions of Information Systems: funding processes, the use of steering committees, development of human resources, account management, charge-back processes, and data administration.

I/S ORGANIZATION TRENDS

When securities firms first started investing in Information Systems technology, most firms put responsibility for managing the I/S resource in Finance or Operations. This appeared logical since these two areas were the most significant users, as initial I/S commitments were aimed at automating operations tasks, producing payroll, or automating general ledger activity. As the sophistication of technology expanded and the range of applications increased, other areas of the firm began to realize the potential benefits of technology. Sales and Trading areas in particular began to see that technology could provide them with tools to process their business more efficiently. This increased demand led to the separation of I/S from the Operations or Finance areas into an independent organization within the firm.

During the expansion of the late 1970s and early 1980s, I/S areas experienced rapid, and often uncontrolled staff and expense growth, as they tried to keep up with technology and user demands. The job market for programmers and analysts was characterized by strong competition and a high rate of turnover. As a result, many firms depended on the use of outside consultants to meet their programming needs. Furthermore, Sales and Trading areas quickly discovered that they could go directly to outside consultants and have their applications developed on a much "faster" basis, circumventing the I/S area completely.

Most firms soon discovered that I/S costs were rapidly getting out of control, that priorities needed to be set for I/S investments, and that the investments could be strategic. Today security firms expect their I/S area to be "run like a business," with accountability for the expenditures and resources that are utilized, to deliver quality service and products to users, and to produce a return on investment at targeted levels. As a result, many firms now realize that the organizational structure of I/S areas should be designed in light of the business objectives of Marketing, Sales and Trading, with appropriate corporate controls for strategic investments.

Richard Nolan points out in *Managing the Crisis in Data Processing* (Harvard Business Review, March-April, 1979), that there are six stages or phases in Information Systems evolution and management as shown in Figure 22-1. Let's look at what happens in each of these stages:

Stage 1. The computer is brought into the organization to perform administrative tasks, fulfill a computation need, and show that the company uses the latest technology.

Stage 2. The computer becomes contagious and more uses are found for it to pay for itself. The new uses create internal demand for more computing power. At a certain point the computer system is saturated with applications, expenses keep increasing, while computer managers' skills remain the same and a crisis is at hand.

Stage 3. To evolve from the crisis, management institutes controls: Systems application and documentation are restructured, users are charged for computer services, the importance of the I/S function is recognized, and a top management position is created to direct the I/S area.

Stage 4. Control tasks are refined and made the responsibility of I/S management. Payback appears as computer resource efficiency rises at a greater rate than costs.

Stage 5. The various components of the computer resource (hardware, software, databases, communications and applications) are integrated based on the firms objectives and technology needs.

Stage 6. Applications reside where the business needs them as the firm balances distributed and centralized technology. Controls are in place to monitor expenses, activity, and performance.

It's important to recognize where your firm is in the growth stages to understand which organizational structure is most beneficial.

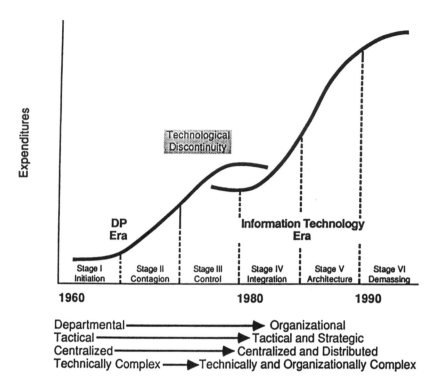

FIGURE 22-1. I/S Management Fundamentally Changes
Used by permission of Nolan Norton & Company.

Notwithstanding the above, however, more and more firms are decentralizing, or establishing matrix reporting relationships between I/S and business units. This has come about for the following reasons:

1. Business people emerging from universities are much more computer literate than ever before.

2. Business managers are beginning to see the I/S resource as an indispensable tool in providing products to customers and markets.

3. Systems applications are changing more rapidly in response to shorter market windows and technology shifts, and firms want I/S and users to work more closely together.

CONSIDERATIONS FOR DETERMINING AN ORGANIZATION STRUCTURE

Before organizing the I/S area's units, it's important to also consider where the I/S organization itself should be in the securities firm. As mentioned previously, there are few "right" or "wrong" answers; the key consideration is supporting the firm's objectives. Some objectives will call for centralization, that is, have the area report to a corporate executive at the same level as business unit executives. Others will call for decentralization of some or all of I/S and have the I/S area report to a business unit. Still others will call for a matrix management structure with solid-line reporting to the I/S executive, and dotted line reporting to the business unit.

Figure 22-2 provides 10 corporate objectives along with a suggested organizational emphasis for the I/S area's development and maintenance functions. The management of the Data Center and shared data should almost always be centralized at the executive management level.

Primary Corporate Objectives	*I/S Organizational Emphasis*
Control (cost/regulatory)	Centralize
Develop business unit–I/S management experience	Decentralize/matrix
Support business units	Decentralize
Support administration area	Centralize
Support product area	Matrix
Support market area	Matrix
Support strategic investments	Centralize
Vertical integration	Decentralize
Create business unit–I/S Interaction	Decentralize/matrix
Achieve economies of scale	Centralize

FIGURE 22-2. Considerations for Determining I/S Organizational Structure

TYPICAL I/S ORGANIZATION STRUCTURES

I/S organizations in securities firms today will, of course, differ depending on the objectives and the size of the firm.

Let's look at two possible structures: a large firm organized by support areas, and a small firm organized by systems functions. While it is also possible for a large firm to organize by systems functions, the trend is to organize by support areas and decentralize. Smaller firms may not yet have, or perceive the need for this change. (As you might imagine, most firms' organization structures will be a hybrid of the two presented here. There is no "right" or "wrong" way.) We will briefly discuss the major components in each of these structures and examine some of the advantages and disadvantages to their use. You should keep in mind, however, that although we are looking at each component separately, they are highly interdependent and interactive.

A LARGE FIRM ORGANIZED BY SUPPORT

Applications groups may be organized by user area supported, by product or business line, and by major product or technology type. In addition, programmers and analysts may be permanently assigned to these areas, or they can be treated as a resource pool and assigned on a project-by-project basis. I/S Project Managers within the applications development groups often have a user project manager as well.

Figure 22-3 shows an organization of the application groups by user area supported, which is typical in a large securities firm. Let's take a look at the major groups and the work they support.

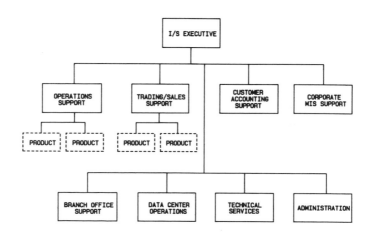

FIGURE 22-3. Organization by Support

Operations Support The Operations Support group in an I/S organization provides the systems support for securities processing, from the time an order is entered until it is settled. It is responsible for developing the systems and applications that automate the processing of orders, receive and deliver instructions, transfer instructions, dividend/interest payments, stock loan and borrow, cashiering, clearance, and so forth. These systems generate many daily reports, either on-line or in hard copy, from which Operations personnel carry out their daily functions. In the typical large securities firm, most of these systems are in place and the I/S focus is on production, maintenance, and application development.

Trading/Sales Support The Trading/Sales Support group in an I/S organization is primarily responsible for providing support to the revenue generating areas of the firm. This support will generally include:

Trading and Sales analytic systems

New product support

Trading desk support

Market data systems support

Research support

External interfaces

The I/S staff responsible for Trading/Sales support have frequent interaction with their users, and must be highly responsive to the users' needs. Applications frequently have to be delivered in short timeframes, and data often must be available on-line, real-time.

Customer Accounting The Customer Accounting group is responsible for the systems and applications that support the processing of customer account information. This will include:

New accounts systems

Margin systems

Customer statement systems

Special product account systems support, such as for IRA, Keough, and asset management accounts

There are multiple users of this I/S group. For example, a Sales area will access customer accounting systems to find out what a customer's balance is, or look at a record of the account activity. An Operations area will monitor margin accounts and generate maintenance calls to a customer. A Customer Service area will access a customer's statement to respond to an inquiry, or resolve a discrepancy.

CORPORATE MIS SUPPORT

The Corporate MIS Support group is responsible for providing the financial and administrative systems support to a firm. This includes:

Financial systems that generate profit and loss and balance sheet information

Financial reporting systems for tracking and monitoring expenses

Cash management support

Human resource systems support

Legal and compliance support

Corporate asset management support

Essentially, these are the business management records of the firm, which are used for various control and reporting functions. Management reports are generated to evaluate business performance of specific areas, as well as the overall business.

Branch Office Support The Branch Office Support group of an I/S organization is responsible for delivering technology to the branches. It ensures that branch office activity is incorporated into the Operations, Sales/Trading, and Customer Accounting systems, so that regardless of where an order originates, it is processed in the same efficient manner. Likewise, when an Account Executive in a local office wants to use a home office bond analytics application to provide information to a customer, the I/S Branch Office Support group must make sure that it is available. This group must be responsive to the particular needs that are unique to the Branch Offices, and provide the same level of support that home office personnel receive.

Technical Services The basic mission of this group is to provide systems software and network support to Data Center and applications development personnel. It is usually responsible for monitoring systems software performance, testing, installing and coordinating new software releases, performance reporting, and capacity planning. Some firms put these responsibilities in an Administrative area and also include quality control, architecture planning, data management, facilities planning, and contract negotiations with vendors.

ADVANTAGES VS. DISADVANTAGES

The organization structure above provides dedicated applications support to specific areas of the business by structurally aligning applications groups with user areas. Data Center Operations and Technical Services remain centralized to obtain economies of scale and for control purposes. As with any type of organization structure there are both advantages and disadvantages.

Advantages

Applications groups will maintain an awareness of the current needs and level of satisfaction of their users through frequent, direct contact.

Applications groups will hear first hand about future business directions of user areas and can prepare to support them.

Business knowledge of a particular area is cultivated in I/S personnel, enabling them to anticipate user needs.

I/S management can control service delivery more easily, by knowing who is responsible for supporting a particular area, and monitoring the user satisfaction of that area.

End-users are less likely to go outside of the organization to have their needs met when they have dedicated I/S resources available.

Centralization of Data Center functions allows the firm to benefit from lower production costs, utilize systems more fully, and monitor performance more accurately.

Centralization of Technical Services assures consistency in the I/S planning and quality control efforts. Opportunities to utilize new technologies can be more easily identified, and users have a source to find out about new developments.

Disadvantages

Multiple units could be inputting data into the same systems, thereby increasing the chance for errors.

Larger staffs could be required because of inability to share expertise.

Redundant systems efforts could develop as separate applications groups attempt to satisfy user demands.

Management may have to take special efforts to promote interrelationships between the separate support groups to maintain necessary integration.

I/S policies and procedures must be in writing and monitored consistently.

A SMALL FIRM ORGANIZED BY SYSTEMS FUNCTION

Systems Development This group typically includes both the systems analysts who work with users in defining system requirements, and the programmers who produce the applications from these specifications (see Figure 22-4). In this structure, this group will generally work on the development of new systems. They will usually have a broad expertise in major systems used throughout the firm.

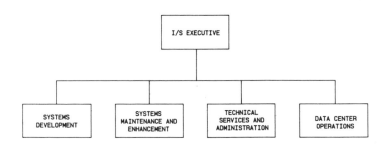

FIGURE 22-4. Organization by Systems Function

Systems Maintenance and Enhancement This group may include some analysts, who together with the programmers, work on maintaining and enhancing existing applications and systems. This type of structure can be an effective means of segregating types of skills needs in these positions which arise because of the familiarity often required to enhance older, complex applications and systems.

ADVANTAGES VS. DISADVANTAGES

As with the previous structure, there are both advantages and disadvantages to organizing the I/S area on this functional basis.

Advantages

The organization can accomplish the basic I/S requirements with fewer resources.

I/S staff in each area are familiar with all of the activities that take place on a firmwide basis and are more easily interchangeable.

A smaller management hierarchy is required.

Disadvantages

Developers and programmers could be isolated from users, and therefore not be as familiar with the users' business needs.

Users are more likely to go outside of the I/S organization to consultants to meet their needs.

I/S staff become specialized in one function, such as development or maintenance.

Support is not dedicated to user groups, and may not be as responsive to business demands.

I/S ADMINISTRATIVE FUNCTIONS

There are a number of functions that need to be performed within the I/S organization that are administrative in nature. These include funding processes and steering committees, human resource management, account management, chargeback processes, and data administration.

FUNDING PROCESSES AND STEERING COMMITTEES

Securities firms face two big challenges in managing the financial aspects of I/S activities: managing the expenditures to coincide with business objectives, and fostering business user responsibility for the level of the expenditures. From the I/S manager's point of view, he or she is constantly searching for ways to satisfy management's objectives, and to obtain agreement on the appropriate projects to underwrite and the appropriate level of expenditures.

Historically, securities firms monitored I/S expenditures in the central data processing group. Departments prepared their budgets for compensation, benefits, professional fees, communications, space, training, and so forth. Development managers met with users to determine what the users wanted in the coming year, estimating staffing levels and associated expenses. Senior I/S management used that information to talk to managers in the Data Centers and obtain their estimates of Data Center expected expenditures resulting from the various projects. Budgets were then prepared and negotiations with senior management produced a final budget.

As I/S expenditures grew and demands by different business units for major projects increased, so did frustration at all levels. Business users began demanding more input to the I/S funding process and I/S managers experienced the frustration of working on major projects, and then having the business unit complain that the results were not what they had asked for, costs were higher than they agreed to, or the project was taking too long. To resolve these issues, securities firms are aggressively setting up I/S steering committees to ensure that the I/S resource is aligned with the business strategy. The increasing competitive importance of I/S applications is causing technology leadership and direction setting to be conducted at the highest levels of securities firms. The steering committee is generally responsible for two activities: establishing strategic direction of I/S investments, and monitoring progress of significant investments. Let's look at how a typical committee might be set up.

STEERING COMMITTEE MEMBERSHIP

The membership of the steering committee should consist of the senior I/S executive and the senior business people, for example, the heads of Trading, Sales/Marketing, Investment Banking, and the Chief Financial Officer. Staff support should be provided by the senior I/S executive. It's important that the I/S executive take the time to explain to the other executives the "business" of I/S. Over time they will become more familiar with the work, and terminology, but initially it must be recognized that that the I/S world is considered "esoteric," "different," "too techy," and so forth by the business unit managers. Once they understand that I/S management is openly willing to listen to their thoughts and ideas, and professionally answer their questions, they will be more inclined to participate in the process.

ISSUES

It is important to gain agreement early as to what the mission of the Steering Committee is. As an example, it could be stated that the mission of the Steering Committee is to establish the strategic direction for I/S and be responsible for the monitoring of major investments. The functions performed by the committee should consist of direction setting, funding, and monitoring.

DIRECTION SETTING

Direction setting involves making decisions that will affect the nature and availability of systems resources over a two- to three-year period. Critical decisions include:

Setting scope of objectives for major projects.

Determining relative investment priorities.

Establishing appropriate investment and staffing levels.

In this function, the business unit executives need to define the business strategies and business priorities, and then the I/S executives need to identify the appropriate systems capabilities necessary to meet the objectives of the business strategies.

Funding In general the committee should be responsible for:

Investments with strategic implications.

Projects impacting multiple business units.

Projects over a defined dollar cost.

Monitoring The objective of monitoring is to determine if the firm should continue to invest in particular systems as originally planned, and to ensure that the original objectives are being met. This means that the I/S executive must present reports to the committee, with input from users, that include status of major milestones, cost, headcount, functionality, technology changes, and so forth.

PROCESS

Meetings should probably be held on a quarterly basis, and the first few meetings will be the most important, as the business unit executives will determine quickly whether or not the process is working. The first meeting should be used to gain agreement on overall objectives and to provide the committee with a current status report of budget, headcount, resource allocation, and major projects. This should be a fairly detailed review of "where we are," strengths, weaknesses, and present priorities. Discussions should then focus on gaining consensus for priorities and investments.

Agreement should then be obtained on how the process will work at future meetings, and what information should be provided to the committee prior to meetings. Specific steps should include:

1. Determine meeting dates.
2. Determine information to be provide by:
   Status of major projects
   Staffing report
   New project requests

3. Determine new project request information needs:
   Sponsor
   Purpose/Need
   Financials

    Staffing

    Equipment

    Consultants

    Benefits

    Action Plans

4. Approval/Disapproval/Redirection.

The committee process is time-consuming, but offers firms an excellent method for using the I/S resource as a competitive advantage in the marketplace.

HUMAN RESOURCE ACTIVITIES

Many I/S departments have set up a dedicated Human Resource function reporting directly to the manager of I/S. Other functions in the securities firm, such as Operations, Trading, and Sales have been around for many years. The I/S function, however, has only existed for the last 20-30 years, and some firms are only now beginning to develop core Human Resource activities for the I/S professional.

I/S professionals have traditionally focused on developing their technical skills. The recent growth in importance of I/S to overall firm activities necessitates a broadening of those skills to include general business knowledge and general management expertise. In achieving their objectives, business professionals tend to look at markets, organization goals, and measures of profit and loss. I/S professionals need to be trained in these skills as their work broadens from a purely technical emphasis. To accomplish this task, securities firms are offering a broad array of training, compensation, and diversified management systems dedicated to the I/S professional. Some of the areas that securities firms are focusing on include:

    Intern Programs

    Orientation Programs

    Attitude Surveys

    Organizational Analysis

    Career Path Management

Compensation Analyses

Team Building

Motivational Analysis

Effective Writing

Leadership Skills

Technical Training

Project Management

Annual Needs Surveys

General Business Curricula

Strategic Planning

CHARGE-BACKS AND ALLOCATIONS

In trying to understand product profitability, business unit profitability, to gain control over expenses, or to foster greater accountability, many firms are charging business units directly for the expense of their I/S areas. I/S areas now have to set up mechanisms whereby all of their costs are allocated in some manner to business units. This is generally done through a financial unit assigned to the I/S department from the firm's central finance area, by a controllership function, or simply by assigning the task as an administrative function to I/S. If the firm is organized with I/S as a central unit, the process is more complicated than when I/S is decentralized and reporting to the business units. Even in decentralized firms, however, central areas such as the Data Center require negotiation with the business units.

The most important part of any charge-back system is to gain agreement between business users and I/S on a number of factors that are crucial to the success of the process. This will require significant interaction between the users and I/S, but it is worth spending the time up front to avoid disagreements later. Some of the more important issues to be examined are:

Will all costs be included (e.g., fixed and variable)?

What formula will be used to charge back expenses (e.g., volume, project expense, headcount, product)?

How often will the methodology be reviewed and changed, if appropriate?

What level of service will be provided?

A suggested process that can easily be implemented is the following:

Define services rendered to the business units.

Develop unit costs.

Define the relationship between user/product costs and volume.

Define how data gathering will take place.

Define the reporting and analysis process.

In developing agreement with the business units the first time a chargeback process is instituted, it's important to keep the process simple—sophistication will come in time. As an example, systems development could simply be charged out by allocation of person-hours on a project. Administrative costs of the department could be assigned in the same manner. Data Center costs could be grouped by usage of CPU, DASD, tape, and print, and all costs charged back by these four categories.

USE OF ACCOUNT MANAGERS

In some firms, the increased specialization of I/S applications by user or product group, and the increased competitive importance of I/S, is giving rise to the creation of Account Managers within the I/S group. The account manager generally supports one user group and addresses their needs across other I/S functional groups—applications development, operations, I/S administration, and technical services. In securities firms, the account manager may also take a particularly active role in defining applications needs for users. This may be desirable if users are less knowledgeable of I/S capabilities, or if market windows for an I/S application are particularly short and dictated largely by competitive "catch-up."

DATA ADMINISTRATION

Most readers are aware of the many different types of data used in securities firms systems applications development. Figure 20-1 in Chapter 20, for example, shows the many applications used in the basic trades processing cycle.

In addition to the data used in those applications, there are many other data files used by securities firms. End-user computing has proliferated the growth of databases in forms not readily accessible by others in the firm who could have a use for the data. This growth of data files has led many firms to set up a Data Administration unit within the I/S area.

If we step back for a moment, it is fairly easy to categorize the major sets of data in securities firms into three broad categories: transactions, positions, and "other."

TRANSACTIONS	POSITIONS	OTHER
Trades	Customer Accounts	Market Data
Cash Receipts/	Proprietary Accounts	Research
Withdrawals	Customer Documents	General Ledger
Securities Buys	Cash Positions	Human Resources
and Sells	Security Positions	Legal/Compliance
Dividends		Marketing
Interest		Investment Banking
Reorganization		
Activity		
Corrections		

To accomplish the task of monitoring the integrity of data, and to simplify accessibility to data throughout securities firms, particularly as the industry moves from batch processing to on-line processing, firms are establishing principles to which all systems groups must adhere. These principles are based on the generally accepted theory that data files are a firm asset, that is, they do not belong to any one system or user group. The principles are:

1. Data will be kept separate from the applications that update them.

2. Common data dictionaries will be used to ensure consistency and eliminate redundancies.

3. Access to data will be controlled and standardized.

4. Data recovery mechanisms will be standardized to minimize impact on on-line, real-time performance.

5. Data sent to or received from external parties will be encrypted and decrypted.

6. Database management systems will be standardized throughout the firm.

The Operations, Producing and Administrative areas of a securities firm are diverse in their activities. Each of these areas may have separate stand-alone data files, particularly PC files, that will not be subject to the above principles. However, when any of the data are necessary for firmwide processing, everyone must adhere to these principles.

Planning for Tomorrow's Information Systems

The future Information System's environment in the Securities Industry will be significantly different than today's environment. In some cases, the changes will be driven by cultural changes in society: demand for varied career experiences, demographic shifts, and further development of the "knowledge worker." In other cases, the changes will be driven by technology: further development of micro-computing, increased capacity and capability of mainframes, advances in communications, continued sophistication of software, and continued emphasis on user friendly software and hardware. If there is one message common to all the areas discussed in this chapter, it is that the industry's Information Systems' managers will have to change, from being very good at transaction processing, to being very good at information processing.

In this chapter, we'll look at what the future environment will be with respect to architecture and how to plan for it, organizational issues, emerging technologies, and the role of the future I/S executive.

TOMORROW'S ARCHITECTURE AND HOW TO PLAN FOR IT

If you refer back to Chapter 20, the "architecture" shown for systems that process Operations functions is based on a "batch orientation": the order entry system takes trade data, performs the order entry functions, passes it on to P&S, and then to Margin and so forth, until the firm's books and records are updated during a night's cycle, and then new books and records are available, hopefully by the beginning of the next business day. During the day, all sorts of transactions occur, are accumulated, and held until the night cycle is ready to start again. Volumes increase, problems occur, and Data Center managers hope they can get through the evening in time to have the firms' books and records ready to service customers, traders, and salespeople the next morning. If the above scenario sounds familiar to you, you have plenty of company.

Today, many firms are reviewing the way their systems process the data relative to operations functions, because most firms' architecture for operations processing is still batch-oriented. Databases are often redundant, and need to be replaced by structures which support all applications, whereby each application "strips" the data required and then performs the application.

Before we take a look at what tomorrow's architecture may look like, let's give a definition to architecture for discussion purposes: the way in which data, the software and hardware that process data, the systemic availability of the data, and the methods used to access the data are integrated.

THE FUTURE ARCHITECTURE ENVIRONMENT: BUSINESS-DRIVEN

Yesterday's architecture was built on the technology then available and limited business requirements. Control and processing were the issues, and "batch" systems were built on available technology. Today, the business requirements are significantly different and technology permits database applications in real-time. The business demands information where the customer wants it, in the form the customer wants it, and when the customer wants it.

The future architecture will have more varied users of data, greater accuracy of data, and multiple systemic use of data. To begin to build the new architecture, firms must review business plans, understand the present technology environment, and set up plans to migrate to a new architecture that will meet the business objectives.

REVIEWING THE BUSINESS OBJECTIVES

Any redesigning effort needs to be preceded by a review of the firm's business strategy. The vision of where the business is headed needs to be agreed upon before work can begin on designing and implementing the technology base that will support it. Figure 23-1 illustrates the areas that need to be included. All business units and support units (e.g. Operations, Finance, Human Resources) need to be included in the assessment to understand where the business is going.

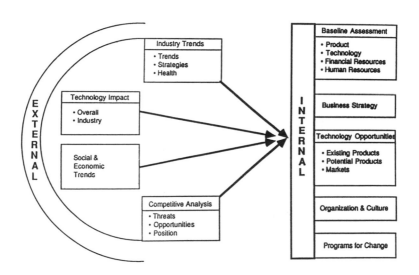

FIGURE 23-1. Components of a Vision
Used by permission of Nolan Norton & Company.

WHERE ARE WE TODAY?

To understand where they are today, I/S managers must take inventories of a number of different areas starting with data—specifically what data is used by the firm. If we go back to the discussion in Chapter 22 on data administration, we can develop the data inventory as follows:

TRANSACTIONS	POSITIONS	OTHER
Trades	Customer Accounts	Market Data
Cash Receipts/	Proprietary Accounts	Research
Withdrawals	Customer Documents	General Ledger
Securities Buys	Cash Positions	Human Resources
and Sells	Security Positions	Legal/Compliance
Dividends		Marketing
Interest		Investment Banking
Reorganization		
Activity		
Corrections		

Inventories should then be built for the software and hardware, including telecommunications support, that use the data:

Hardware. Mainframes and other computers, including workstations/end-user PC's; tape and disk access storage devices; telecommunications hardware, including satellites, fiber optics networks and land lines, and access mechanisms.

Software. Operating systems, applications systems, and administrative systems, e.g., library tools, CASE tools (computer-aided software engineering), and artificial intelligence tools.

The next step is to inventory the availability of the data, including currency and accuracy. This step will tell you who inputs the data, who controls it, and who can change it. Additional facts must be gathered as to retention, frequency, security, usage, volume, location, and mediums used to access the data.

Taken as a whole, these above actions will give you a good idea of "where you are" with regard to architecture.

MIGRATION

A review of the business strategy, discussed earlier, will provide a basis for proceeding with the new architecture. As discussed in Chapter 22, principles must be agreed upon by I/S and business unit managers. A number of such principles, again based on the premise that data is a firm asset, are:

1. Data will be kept separate from the applications that update it.

2. Common data dictionaries will be used to ensure consistency and eliminate redundancies.

3. Access to data will be controlled and standardized.

4. Data recovery mechanisms will be standardized to minimize impact to on-line, real-time performance.

5. Database management systems will be standardized throughout the firm.

After agreement is reached on corporate objectives and business plans, the I/S executives need to examine the following questions, all related to data, with the objective of providing information to manage the business:

1. Where does the data come from?

2. Which data is important and for what purpose?

3. How important is the accuracy of the data?

4. How important is the currency of the data?

5. What locations does the data need to be available to? What users?

6. Who controls the data?

7. What systems use the data?

The result will be an architecture design driven by the firm's business strategy as shown in Figure 23-2.

The final step for building a plan for the future architecture is to set up a migration plan. The plan needs to lay out the implementation steps over time and consider benefits, costs, funding, alternatives, personnel requirements, and management controls necessary for success. Specific steps need to be detailed (with choices available where appropriate) for the design of applications, data communications, and technology. In addition, however, management programs must also be specified dealing with administration, policies, standards, and control mechanisms.

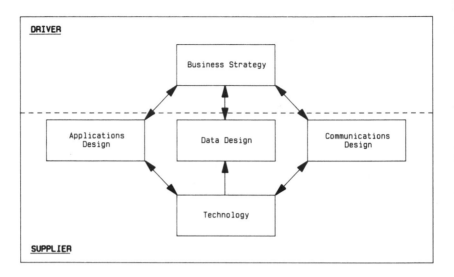

FIGURE 23-2. Target Architecture

ORGANIZATION ISSUES

In many firms today, the I/S organization is still hierarchal and functions are centralized. The background and reasons for this are part cultural and part technical. On the cultural side, many firms' entire organizations are hierarchal, and the I/S structure simply follows the other parts of the firm. On the technical side, I/S is still viewed by many managers as complex, specialized, and not part of the mainstream of the business. Many firms also have experienced high expense growth in I/S and believe that a centralized structure helps control costs.

This is changing however, and for good reasons. In the future, I/S organizations will be far less hierarchal and more decentralized. Some of the reasons driving this change are:

1. *Architecture.* The technology and business needs in the past were such that many systems that were built called for a centralized approach. The primary business need was processing orders and related paper flow, and the technology resulted in batch processing systems. Data was centralized, applications were dependent upon when they could use the data, and mainframes did all the processing. Today's technology and

business needs permit much greater decentralization. Business needs call for use of I/S resources in many more areas than simply processing of trades. Technology permits separation of data from applications, and PC's do much of the processing.

2. *Hardware/Software.* Hardware and software are now available at reduced expense, so that the proliferation of the supply has been dramatic. Minicomputers, PC's, and local area networks can now store and process vast amounts of data that previously could only be done on a mainframe. Software is now easily available to end-users, while previously it was only available to the technicians in I/S.

3. *End-User Involvement.* The technology is becoming so user friendly that end-users all over the firm are demanding access to data and systems to manage their functions. The end-users are demanding that they have direct access to the I/S resource, without going through third party I/S personnel.

4. *Business Demand.* The business units in securities firms now view the I/S resource as critical to their success. In addition, they want to directly manage the costs, like they manage the other parts of their business, such as Sales and Marketing. New products in the industry require rapid support turnaround times, and the business units believe they will get better response times if the resource reported directly to them.

These are only some of the reasons. Societal changes are occurring that are driving other parts of the firm towards decentralization. This is occurring because the availability of information now makes the hierarchal structure less necessary. Managers can access information much more quickly, and therefore do not need as many supervisory layers as they did before.

It's not yet clear what the organizational "structure" of securities firms' I/S departments will look like. In fact, the form of the structure will vary dependent upon business needs. The most likely scenario, however, will be that applications groups will report directly or be matrixed to business units. Systems development is now so important to the business units that they are demanding direct responsibility for the I/S resource. In addition, it is becoming increasingly important that I/S development personnel understand the business they support, and the new alignment will provide a mechanism for that to occur.

There will also be increased use of project teams, where managers will be removed from their line positions for the life of a given project. Use of Steering Committees will also increase, consisting of I/S and business unit personnel, to direct the deployment of the I/S resource, and to monitor progress of major projects.

A centralized I/S structure will not go away completely however. Communications and mainframe support will emerge as a "utility" serving various business units. Management controls will also reside in the utility, as will data administration, applications standards setting and policies for vendor selection.

EMERGING TECHNOLOGIES

The use of the word "emerging" here is appropriate, only because the technologies listed below are starting to be used by securities firms. In fact, many of them have been in existence for years. Their usefulness has grown in recent years, however, and it is important that you at least understand how they can be of assistance. Here are twelve technologies that will become important to the industry in the 1990s.

1. *Voice Mail.* As a way of cleaning up the office and eliminating the "telephone tag" that we all play in our firms, voice mail may become more common. Essentially the technology allows you to leave a voice message in the "mail box" of the person you want to speak to, rather than depend on a message slip that may get lost. It also gives you greater room for an extended message, and since the recipient's mail box is private, allows for confidential communications. In addition, it permits you to send the same message to several groups of recipients simply by changing the address code that you dial on your telephone. Voice mail also allows you to request electronic return receipts, as proof that the other party has received your message, and it will let you forward received messages to third parties, as well as store important messages that you want to save.

2. *Electronic Mail.* Electronic mail lets you receive any number of communications over a PC that is connected either on-line, or via a dial-up arrangement with another party.

   In some firms, salespeople are directly linked to their customers through electronic mail systems. Customers may receive daily overviews of market trends, as published by a firm's chief economist, pricing and trading histories, or on-line results of product research and analysis (instead of someone going to the expense and trouble of mailing this material). Salespeople may also send ideas for suggested trades to their customers, showing prices, yields, and basis point gains with graphic illustrations.

   On the Operations side, some firms are giving their customers added value and a day's advantage in processing payments, by sending their day's trade activity, both on-line and real-time, with an end of day summary or trade recap. Someday, when electronic transmission is fully acceptable to regulatory bodies, it may replace the paper confirmations that we presently mail.

3. *Teleconferencing.* There is perhaps no line of work where executives travel to meetings and product seminars as much as in the securities industry. That is, of course, because the home office is generally in a major city, and the major firms have customers, branches, and regional offices throughout the world. Teleconferencing, where you can hear and see your colleagues in other locations as they speak, permits the same type of interaction you can have at a conference where everyone is physically present. Most of the same interchanges and comments are possible. Its advantage is that it offers a way to reduce the time and expense required for travel, and permits direct communication that may not otherwise occur, due to the busy schedules of participants. Teleconferencing will probably never replace the benefits of personal contact, but in situations where that aspect or confidentiality is not needed, savings can be significant.

4. *Laptop Computers.* PC technology has led to the development of even smaller and more powerful computers. Laptop com-

puters, with the power and memory capacity of many of today's desktop PC's, are becoming a preferred item for the Investment Banking analyst, or more senior investment banker, who needs to spend a lot of time on the road, and wants to do spreadsheet or analytical work anywhere, anytime.

These devices can be connected to the home office through modems, so that information can be passed back and forth, and they can be connected to printers to show the results of analyses. Some laptops are being provided with lightweight printers even today. Before long, the laptop may come equipped with its own cellular telephone with a microchip, and the user will not be restricted by the nearness of a suitable telephone for sending or receiving information.

5. *Handheld Computers.* Over time, the handheld computer, no bigger than the average paperback book, will become as common as calculators are today. Uses in the securities industry will be similar to other industries: checking on messages while traveling, leaving messages, communicating electronically with customers, checking on inventories, accessing firm data, and so forth.

6. *Local Area Networks (LAN).* Local Area Networks are common even today. Through a combination of computers and communications devices, they permit users of previously unconnected PC's to become part of groups that would naturally interact in the normal course of business. Software and applications can be more easily shared and at significantly reduced expense.

7. *Workstations.* In a sense, these are high powered PC's which can be connected to Local Area Networks, mainframe computers, and various minicomputers. Once the architecture design work that we discussed earlier is accomplished, workstations will be able to pick and choose among a host of applications, functions, and processes applicable to business management. Even today, the workstation user can do word processing, calculations, spreadsheets and analytics. In the future, they will access the firm's trade database, product database, or any other databases to perform an almost limitless number of ad hoc activities supporting Sales, Trading, Operations, and Management activities.

8. *Image Processing.* Many of you have seen the television commercials for the auto-insurance claim where the claim, the photo of the accident, and the investigation report are all filled out on the spot, and immediately sent to the insurance company's Claims Evaluation area—not by overnight mail or interoffice—but electronically, with the visual quality of the original, enabling a claim judgement to be rendered within hours, instead of days or weeks. Image processing transmits electronically the clear image of a form, certificate, or picture.

   This new technology offers the potential of significantly reducing the incredible costs associated with paper processing. In addition, image processing will significantly reduce the time spent by Operations personnel in research, the time spent by Account Executives and support personnel in processing new accounts, trading authorization forms, claim letters, and so forth.

   There are a number of legal questions that need to be addressed related to the admission of "image" documents in the judicial system, but acceptance will come over time, and the industry will gain enormous productivity benefits.

9. *Expert Systems.* These systems are another subset of artificial intelligence systems and they can be extremely useful in the securities industry. The systems combine data, standards of measurement, and logical choices to provide exception processing, or analytic analysis of the data in extremely short timeframes. Work that would otherwise take days to accomplish by large numbers of people can now be performed in hours. Applications to the industry are in compliance monitoring, credit analysis, swap portfolio engineering, securities lending, marketing reviews, and so forth.

10. *CASE Tools.* Computer Aided Software Engineering Tools offer the potential of significant increases in systems development productivity. Today, many of the tools are very expensive and require extensive training, installation, and vendor assistance. This will change, however, as the technology develops. The software has become available due, in part, to the advent of inexpensive computing power, that is, speed, storage, and memory. They are very useful for building new systems in a

"greenfields" approach, particularly those with a database design. Productivity gains in the analysis-design-code-test work that you are all familiar with will be significant, when some of the present issues associated with standards are resolved.

11. *Multimedia.* The availability of inexpensive multimedia hardware and improved authoring software will enable firms to create more effective training programs and on-the-job aids for many clerical, administrative, and customer service positions. The obvious benefits of this approach are multiplied when the implications of "Work Force 2000" projections are considered.

12. *Internet.* Competitive advantages will accrue to those firms which best utilize the increasing availability of interactive access to product, market, regulatory, technology, and economic information. The super-skilled drivers of the "Information Super-Highway" will be technically competent "Corporate Librarians." Many more casual "drivers" will make active use of the growing base of on-line information becoming available.

MANAGEMENT ISSUES FOR EMERGING TECHNOLOGIES

The aforementioned emerging technologies will create opportunities to provide new and improved services to the firm and its customers. The rush to technological glory, however, must be tempered by the I/S executive's objective analysis of business priorities, competitive initiatives, organizational capabilities, ongoing support responsibilities, budgetary guidelines, and a myriad of issues associated with the use of each new technology.

One painful reality, is that many issues which the I/S executive worked to resolve for the firm's more centralized and non-interactive environments must be addressed again, in light of the additional exposure that employing new technology creates. This is especially true in the areas of privacy, security, recovery, and end-user support.

Here are a few illustrative examples of issues which must be addressed if new technologies are to be successfully employed:

Voice Mail, Electronic Mail, Teleconferencing Technologies

Privacy Issue. It is vital to insure restricted access to information on the system for corporate, legal, and individual needs. The I/S executive, in cooperation with the Legal and Human Resources departments, must define and develop both policy and enforcement mechanisms, to insure that corporate guidelines for communication privacy are adhered to.

Security Issue. Information being processed over "public," or between/within private networks, is subject to compromise or loss. As in centralized computing/telecommunications environments, policies and practices for LAN/distributed computing facilities must be uniformly defined and enforced.

Client Acceptance Issue. The implementation of electronic communications should be consistent with the client's ability and desire to utilize such a facility. The I/S executive must insure that clear expectations are developed relating to the services offered and service level being provided, and that interaction with the client environment (e.g., human factors, technological, legal, and procedural views) are consistent with business requirements.

Lap-Top Computer, Handheld Computer, Local Area Network, and Workstation Technologies

Data Sharing/Security Issue. Data is a significant resource of the corporation, and ready access to it presents both an opportunity and an exposure for the corporation. It is incumbent upon I/S to provide ready access for those having a need and a right-to-know. It is also incumbent upon the I/S executive to provide protection of that information from non-authorized users. A policy and mechanism to enable data owners the ability to control access and sharing must be established. Standards and controls are concurrently required to protect the data from unauthorized destruction, replication, and alteration.

Data Redundancy Issue. Multiple distributed platforms and removable media create the potential for different "versions" of corporate data. Management and Operational decisions must be based upon representations of the data where the accuracy, currency, and source (version) of the information is explicit. A policy and a development standard are needed to effect this requirement.

Help Desk Support Issue. The proliferation of hardware and software alternatives enables "local" organizations to adopt new technology for which local technical support is limited, or non-existent. The I/S executive must establish a policy to determine which technologies will be "corporately" supported, and the method and level of service which will be provided.

Software Licensing Issue. The method of acquisition and dissemination of distributed platform software (e.g., workstation/LAN) across the corporate enterprise should address software licensing restrictions and pricing policies. The I/S executive should establish a clear policy and mechanism for the purchase and distribution of workstation and/or LAN software. Economic advantages may also be gained by providing centralized purchasing of workstation, PC, and LAN hardware.

Disaster Recovery Issue. In the event of a disaster, essential business systems operating on local platforms require the same level of recoverability as is currently provided for centralized applications. The recovery issue is compounded by the multiple hardware/software/network configurations, which are operating within the enterprise, and which are geographically dispersed. The creation of common/shared recovery facilities, either in-house or through a third party, should be considered for effective cost management. In support of this process, the executive must establish the policy, procedures, and technical capability to support business units to comply with the profile(s) of centrally maintained disaster recovery facilities.

Expert System and Case Tool Technologies The use of both expert systems and CASE tools within non-academic and non-R&D environments has been, at best, checkered. What we know is that some exceptionally gifted people can use these tools to build successful applications. What has not been adequately demonstrated is that the "typical" business enterprise, with its competing business priorities and mix of personnel, can consistently create and maintain cost-justified systems with these tools.

The above discussion is not intended to be exhaustive in either its breath or depth. It is meant to illustrate that the opportunities to employ emerging technology must be evaluated by I/S management in light of the co-requisite tasks and capabilities they require.

ROLE OF TOMORROW'S I/S EXECUTIVE

Most discussions on this subject start off with trying to give a title to the senior I/S executive. In fact, the functions he or she will perform are far more important than the title. Some titles that may be used are "Chief Information Officer," "Director of Technology," "Director of Information Systems," and there are others. My personal choice is Chief Information Officer, because the business he or she is responsible for is managing information.

Tomorrow's executive will be a facilitator versus today's director, a broad-based manager rather than a technician, an integrator versus an autocrat. He or she will emphasize teamwork while rewarding individual performance, emphasize strategies while facilitating tactical change, and emphasize research and development without losing focus on production. The major roles will focus on general management issues, architecture integration issues, research and development, vendor relationships, and mechanisms to facilitate the use of technology.

GENERAL MANAGEMENT ISSUES

The CIO of the future will be a member of the firm's executive committee and the board of directors. His or her time in this area will be spent on strategic issues, organizational issues, and control issues. On strategic issues impacting I/S, the executive will respond to questions such as:

What are the firm's business plans?

How should I/S resources be organized and deployed to support these plans?

How is the firm's architecture for the future going to be built?

On organizational issues, the CIO must decide how to structure the utility, how to integrate development personnel into the business units, how to gain adherence to policies and procedures, and how to compensate I/S personnel.

On control issues, the I/S executive will focus on the:

Process for setting priorities for development

Process for selection of new technology

Process for funding of maintenance and development

Process for "buy or make" decisions

Process for charge back methodologies (if appropriate)

Process for performance/productivity measurement

ARCHITECTURE

This is clearly one of the most important areas the future I/S executive will be responsible for. He or she is the only executive who can direct this effort through the maze of problems, costs, and complexities associated with redesigning basic systems for the future, while meeting today's production demands. In preparing for a decentralized world, he/she must put the mechanisms in place that will ensure adherence to centralized corporate policies, procedures and standards for data that will permit decentralized applications. The integration of data, the software/hardware that process data, the systemic availability of data, and the methods used to access data, is a major task that must be managed by the CIO.

RESEARCH AND DEVELOPMENT

The technology in the securities industry is changing rapidly as it is in many other industries. The Chief Information Officer must dedicate his/her time to understanding these changes as they impact the industry. We will probably see more joint ventures, particularly with universities and industrial firms, to reduce the costs of such research. Some of the more important areas that need to be examined include image processing, artificial intelligence, and CASE tool methodologies.

VENDOR RELATIONSHIPS

There is growing recognition among securities firms that suppliers of technology are important to the success of the business. This recognition is common in industrial firms today, but is only now gaining acceptance in the securities industry. In addition, many firms are examining their production facilities to see if services can be provided by other firms more efficiently and less expensively. Whatever conclusions the individual firms make, the emphasis will be on cost and quality. Some of the major areas that will be examined include: facilities, mainframe computers, minis and micros, disk access storage devices, communications equipment, and communications network management.

FACILITATING THE USE OF TECHNOLOGY

Many firms talk about the importance of integrating the use of technology into their business, but few spend substantial time on doing it. The process takes a serious effort on the part of senior management, and the CIO will lead that effort.

Here are eight steps that the CIO should consider when developing a program for facilitating the use of technology within a firm:

1. Training programs directed at administrative or business personnel.

2. Financial information to provide cost/benefit analyses.

3. Reward systems for successful implementations as well as "nice tries."

4. Flexibility in systems design to generate greater usage.

5. Free use of PC's at home or office.

6. User help-desks to solve problems quickly.

7. Basic software programs applicable to user work functions.

8. Information programs to alert users to new functionality.

Implementation of T+3 Settlement in the United States

BACKGROUND

In October 1987, the Dow Jones Industrial average declined by almost one third, representing a total loss in the value of outstanding U.S. stocks of approximately one trillion dollars. While the U.S. Clearance and Settlement system is among the safest in the world, events immediately following the market break of 1987 demonstrated that much can be done to improve the safety and soundness of the U.S. market place. The heavy volume and volatility during October 1987 exposed many brokers/dealers to potential market and credit risk, before they could settle trades five business days later, (the standard settlement period for corporate securities in the United States). In addition, the sharp decline in securities prices during that period and October of 1989, left a number of brokers/dealers vulnerable to loss from positions of their customers, who were unable or unwilling to meet their settlement obligations. As a result, many in the industry were concerned with the ability of those brokers/dealers to meet their obligations to clearing corporations, and the resultant threat to the entire financial system if a clearing corporation was unable to meet its financial obligations.

Stock markets "crashed" all over the world during October of 1987, and in March of 1988 the Group of Thirty, a consultive organization based in London, held a symposium to review what could be done to prevent systemic risk in the areas of Clearance and Settlement in the world's securities markets. The Group of Thirty later formulated a number of recommendations that were offered as standards for clearance and settlement for securities transactions worldwide. One of these recommendations was to have all countries settle their securities transactions on Trade Date + 3. The United States formed a Working Group, under the aegis of the Group of Thirty, to review the recommendations of the Group of Thirty.[1] The U.S. Working Group concluded that while the U.S. was in compliance with many of the Group of Thirty recommendations, the U.S. should consider moving to a Trade Date + 3 Settlement date (from the present Trade Date + 5 Settlement), and settle all transactions in Same Day Funds. In 1991, the Securities and Exchange Commission (SEC) asked John W. Bachmann, Managing Principal of Edward D. Jones & Co., to review the recommendations of the U.S. Working Group and to identify practical solutions. Mr. Bachmann formed a Task Force of senior executives from the Securities Industry, and in May of 1992, presented his findings and recommendations to the Commission. The Commission then published the "Report of the Bachmann Task Force on Clearance and Settlement Reform in U.S. Securities Markets" and asked for comment from practitioners.

BACHMANN TASK FORCE RECOMMENDATIONS AND SECURITY INDUSTRY RESPONSE

The Securities Industry Association (SIA), representing over six hundred securities firms headquartered throughout the United States and Canada, responded in detail to the Bachmann Task Force recommendations.[2] The following is an excerpt from the Securities Industry's Association's response to the SEC on the Bachmann Task Force report, and is presented here so that readers understand the initiatives now taking place in U.S. Securities Markets to reduce risk, and increase safety and soundness in the marketplace.

---

[1] The author was a member of the Working Committee of the Group of Thirty.

[2] Excerpted from September 15, 1992 SIA response to SEC's request for comment on the Bachmann Task Force Report. The author is the SIA adviser to the SIA's Clearance and Settlement Committee and was responsible for preparing this SIA comment letter.

BACHMANN RECOMMENDATION #1

Shorten the settlement cycle. If time equals risk, then less time between a transaction and its completion reduces risk. A shorter settlement cycle will also uncover potential problems sooner, before they mushroom or begin to cascade throughout the industry.

SIA Comment This recommendation calls for a shortened settlement cycle, from T+5 to T+3 for corporate and municipal securities by July 1, 1994, to reduce systemic risk. SIA endorses this recommendation, but believes a significant amount of work needs to be done to meet this time frame.

As the report points out, there are important "building blocks" that must be in place when T+3 becomes effective:

Automated payment mechanisms to facilitate timely payments to and from retail investors.

Interactive ID processing to require T+1 affirmation of institutional trades.

SIA believes the Task Force's recommendations on the following also must be in place at the time the settlement cycle is shortened:

Book-entry only settlement among financial intermediaries and between financial intermediaries and their institutional clients.

Depository eligibility for new issues.

Efforts are underway in the industry to implement these important steps, and SIA believes that SEC endorsement of these efforts will prove critical to their success.

SIA also believes successful implementation of this recommendation will require a T+1 comparison system between brokers and dealers for all products and a review of the impact upon investors of SEC rules 15c3-3, 15c3-1, and 10b-10, Federal Reserve Regulation T and MSRB Rule G-15(a).

Additionally, SIA believes settlement risk reduction (an objective of the Task Force and of Group of Thirty efforts) can be favorably impacted by providing appropriately capitalized regulated investment organizations with access to the Federal Reserve securities wire. There exists today significant settlement concentration risk within the U.S. Government Securities market. The basis for this risk is that there are only three member banks of the Federal Reserve that provide non-bank settlement services for this huge market. SIA believes that, at a minimum, consideration should be given to provide direct access to the Federal Reserve securities wire for primary dealers. Market makers, secondary dealers, and brokers could be provided access through a recognized registered clearing corporation. This direct access enables maximization of netting benefits, as well as standardized comparison procedures, and uniform risk management and collateralization methods.

SIA believes this recommendation's impact upon retail and institutional investors is significant and positive. SIA looks forward to working with the SEC to implement the building blocks and legal steps necessary to assure success.

BACHMANN RECOMMENDATION #2

Revise the ACH system. If retail trades must settle more quickly, then the wiring of funds to and from customers should be a practical, inexpensive, and reliable alternative. Steps are currently being taken to eliminate the rescission aspect from the settlement process.

SIA Comment SIA endorses this recommendation. The flow of funds both to and from customers should be expedited, and ACH could be a viable electronic payment mechanism for retail transactions, particularly for small firms that rely largely on checks for payments to and from customers. In order to make ACH suitable for timely settlement of retail securities transactions in a T+3 environment, a number of changes are required. One of these changes requires the creation by the National Automated Clearing House Association (NACHA) of a new ACH transaction code (SCT) which would enable broker/dealers, with written customer consent, to secure payment electronically, directly, promptly, and without a 60-day rescission privilege. Unfortunately, the membership of NACHA voted down this proposal, which would have been scheduled for an April 1993 implementation. The defeat of this new alternative for accelerating retail payments for securities presents a major obstacle to T+3 settlement. In view of this development, SIA will renew its efforts to have the proposal approved. SIA requests the SEC to work with the appropriate banking authorities to obtain their support for the proposal.

Another change requires revision of Regulation E of the Federal Reserve to make it consistent with the Electronic Funds Transfer Act, which SIA has formally requested. If approved, however, the Federal Reserve, Securities and Exchange Commission and the Commodity Futures Trading Commission (CFTC) need to interpret this exemption, so that broker/dealers can know with some precision when the use of ACH is exempt form Regulation E.

SIA also believes that before ACH can become a viable alternative to check payments, the industry will need significant information and education efforts to familiarize the retail brokerage community and its customers with the benefits of ACH. If the rescission issue can be successfully addressed, SIA will work enthusiastically with all interested parties on this educational challenge.

The next step, to assure all participants in the investment process of fair access to the benefits of accelerated payments, would be to enable all appropriately capitalized regulated investment organizations to have the safety and security of membership in the Federal Reserve System's money wire. SIA believes this change will provide another vehicle to accelerate the flow of funds to and from investors within the safety of the Federal Reserve's processing system.

SIA requests the SEC to encourage the Federal Reserve, the CFTC, and NACHA to approve the above changes to facilitate the move to a shortened settlement cycle.

BACHMANN RECOMMENDATION #3

Require an interactive ID process. To permit days to pass before verifying an institutional transaction is as much of an anachronism as the physical certificate. All trades should be confirmed by T+1. Requiring all institutional market participants to immediately verify their transactions would reduce settlement risk materially.

SIA Comment Depository Trust Company (DTC) and users of DTC's Institutional Delivery (ID) system have done excellent work in developing an interactive option for the ID system. This facet of the system will facilitate the affirmation of institutional transactions by T+1, one of a number of essential prerequisites for a T+3 settlement cycle. As the report mentions, DTC's proposed system will process data upon receipt and distribute reports on request, thereby allowing participants to be as interactive as they choose.

The DTC ID Focus Committee consists of broker/dealers, banks, money managers, and institutional users of ID affiliated with Investment Company Institute, Investment Counsel Association of America, the Bank Depository User Group and the Industry Standardization for Institutional Trade Communication. SIA is in active communication with this Committee and encourages its excellent work.

Early affirmation (T+3) is a prerequisite for moving settlement date from T+5 to T+3. The initial implementation of ID required extensive promotion, education, and encouragement by industry utilities and broker/dealers. This same multi-pronged effort will be needed for the implementation of Interactive ID. SIA is convinced that institutional customer acceptance and use of the system for early affirmation of trades will not occur without a regulatory mandate. This was accomplished in the initial implementation of ID by New York Stock Exchange (NYSE) Rule 387 and other SRO rules.

DTC has the reporting capability on compliance with NYSE Rule 387 and provides compliance reports to the National Association of Securities Dealers (NASD) and the NYSE. DTC, however, does not have regulatory authority to assure that institutional customers submit data on trade date to the system and affirm by T+1. If institutional customers do not affirm early enough to settle by T+3, the industry will have an interactive option for the ID system, but will not have accomplished the Task Force's safety and soundness objectives.

SIA believes the industry needs substantial regulatory support from the SEC, SROs, Federal Reserve, the Department of Labor (ERISA accounts), and perhaps others mandating that institutional customers affirm trades by T+1 to reduce settlement risk.

BACHMANN RECOMMENDATION #4

Include Tax-exempt Bonds. Municipal bonds are an important part of the U.S. securities market and as such should be included in this effort, though any delay in the implementation timetable for the recommended changes should not impact the date for implementation for corporate securities.

SIA Comment As stated in the report, municipal bonds are an important part of the U.S. securities market, and should be included with corporate securities in the efforts to improve safety and soundness in U.S. clearance and settlement systems. The Municipal Securities Rulemaking Board (MSRB) has recently approved rule amendments to require automated confirmation/affirmation, automated comparison and book-entry settlement of essentially all inter-dealer, and institutional customer transactions in depository eligible securities. The MSRB has proposed an implementation schedule for these changes starting in January 1993 through July 1, 1994.[3] The MSRB recently requested comments[4] on a suggested revision of CUSIP eligibility standards. These revisions would make nearly all issues, including those under $250,000 in par value, eligible for CUSIP numbering, a prerequisite for depository eligibility. SIA applauds the MSRB actions in the above areas as they are processing municipal securities. The relevant depositories, MSRB, SIA, and industry members are aggressively pursuing increased depository eligibility for existing municipal securities and a T+1 comparison system.

SIA urges the MSRB to mandate depository eligibility for new municipal issues. The Legal and Regulatory Sub-Group of the U.S. Working Committee of Group of Thirty is working with interested parties to develop such a uniform rule for adoption by SROs for corporate securities, and SIA urges the MSRB also to work on the development of such a rule for municipal securities. SIA recognizes there may be a variety of economic or other factors unique to the municipal market in this regard, and believes enabling regulation can deal appropriately with these concerns. While SIA hopes exceptions to such enabling regulations are kept to a minimum, there is no valid reason to exclude municipal securities from this significant step that is so necessary to achieve the Task Force's objectives of safety and soundness.

SIA encourages the SEC to continue to be an advocate of the progressive steps taken by MSRB to reduce risk and increase safety and soundness in U.S. markets, and to work with depositories to mandate depository eligibility for all municipal issues. SIA also

---

[3]   See MSRB Reports, Vol. 12, No. 1 (April 1992)

[4]   See MSRB Reports, Vol. 12, No. 2 (July 1992)

encourages depositories, clearing corporations, industry members, and MSRB to continue their efforts directed at reducing risk and inefficiencies in the municipal marketplace.

BACHMANN RECOMMENDATION #5

Settle all transactions among financial intermediaries and between financial intermediaries and their institutional clients in book-entry form only and pay for them in same-day funds.

SIA Comment SIA concurs with the Task Force's conclusion that street-side book-entry settlement enjoys widespread support in the industry. SIA applauds the efforts in this regard of industry members, depositories, clearing corporations, SROs, MSRB, Federal Reserve and SEC, and encourages all interested parties to continue to remove any obstacles to street-side book-entry settlement. This issue is important to T+3 and is strongly connected to the Task Force's recommendation on depository eligibility, and SIA encourages all regulators to keep any exceptions to eligibility in enabling regulations to a minimum.

DTC and NSCC have jointly issued "A Same-Day Funds Settlement System Proposal for Industry Evaluation" that has recently been released for industry comment. SIA applauds DTC, NSCC, the Federal Reserve and SEC efforts in this area, and is actively supporting this effort. SIA believes this effort will eliminate the overnight credit risk inherent in the current next-day funds environment and assure finality of payment.

SIA supports the objectives of the proposal, but believes further discussion needs to take place regarding a number of technical issues including:

participant liquidity

collateral haircuts

concentration within the settling bank system

criteria for choosing a settling bank

debit caps

impact on agreement-to-pledge loans

implication of same-day funds for all payments to and from participants and paying agents.

SIA encourages the SEC to approve all regulatory changes necessary to implement these recommendations.

BACHMANN RECOMMENDATION #6

Make all new securities depository eligible. Today all but a very few securities can be eligible for deposit in a depository. Such eligibility should be mandatory.

SIA Comment SIA supports the Task Force's recommendation that all new corporate and municipal securities coming to market be depository eligible. The Legal and Regulatory Sub-Group of the U.S. Working Committee of the Group of Thirty (Working Committee) is working closely with the various SROs and MSRB to draft a uniform rule for depository eligibility of new issues. SIA strongly encourages these efforts, as SIA believes that mandatory depository eligibility of new issues (along with settlement of all transactions among financial intermediaries and between financial intermediaries and their institutional clients in book-entry form only) is a critical component of T+3 settlement. SIA also strongly supports the work of depositories to make existing issues depository eligible, and encourages them to include money market instruments in this effort.

SIA supports the Working Committee's proposal that the Commission adopt a disclosure requirement under the Securities Act of 1933 that would require issuers in registered offerings to indicate in the prospectus whether the securities are depository eligible, and, if not, the reasons why such eligibility was not obtained and the potential impact on the liquidity of the securities.

"Flipping," the practice of selling into an underwriter's syndicate bid in violation of underwriting agreements, is presently being monitored through the delivery of physical certificates. SIA supports the implementation of a solution to monitor flipping in a mandated depository eligibility/book-entry only environment. SIA is actively working with the industry to develop a viable solution.

SIA urges the SEC to work towards making all new corporate and municipal securities depository eligible.

BACHMANN RECOMMENDATION #7

Implement or expand cross-margining. If available data is organized in a more useful way between and among markets and clearing agencies, and cross-lien agreements are arranged, clearing agencies should be able to see evidence of hedging and thus be able to set credit requirements accordingly. This enhancement can have a profound effect on the liquidity of key market participants at critical times.

SIA Comment SIA strongly agrees with the Task Force's conclusion that the withdrawal of liquidity was the single greatest risk on October 20, 1987. In support of the report's key theme of safety and soundness in the clearance and settlement system, SIA believes one of the most important efforts participants, regulators, and investors should sponsor is the expansion of cross-margining and the implementation of a system to coordinate the payment of funds for each participant across all domestic markets.

This effort not only addresses the question of marketplace liquidity, but by improving the actual "mechanics" of settlement, industry utilities can maximize the potential for certainty of payment from participants, while participants will be relieved of the costs (both direct and opportunity costs) of financing inefficiencies that occur today in settling multiple market transactions.

This endeavor will require the cooperation of all domestic clearing and depository organizations and the support of the SROs, the Federal Reserve Bank, the Commodity Futures Trading Commission, and the Securities and Exchange Commission. There are a number of legal and regulatory barriers to these goals because of various federal and state laws and clearing corporation and depository rules.

These goals are vital to reducing risk in the U.S. financial system, and they are in the nation's best interest to implement. SIA will continue to work with all relevant organizations to facilitate changes necessary to achieve the above objectives, and strongly encourages the SEC's support for them.

BACHMANN RECOMMENDATION #8

Monitor all market activity. Today, data about markets is fragmented though interdependencies increase. Information on the financial markets should be gathered, examined, and made publicly available so all interested parties can better understand risks.

SIA Comment The report contains a lengthy discussion which makes clear that the Task Force is concerned about the fragmentation of market information, and in particular, the lack of information available to clearing corporations respecting "off exchange" risks of clearing members. The SIA believes the SEC, having adopted the risk assessment rules, 240.17h-1T and 240.17h-2T, will have a basis to meet the concerns expressed by the Task Force.

It remains to be seen whether the information to be reported to the SEC under those rules will be relevant or useful if shared with clearing corporations or the public at large, since such information will not include any information about the financial condition of customers and counterparties of clearing members and other reporting institutions.

We believe that clearing systems should continue to rely primarily on clearing member deposits, margin, marks-to-market, debit caps, and other traditional methods, as well as continuing the effort to implement coordinated payments and cross-margining, as the most appropriate clearing system risk-reduction tools. Clearing corporations and depositories should continue to have high financial standards and financial reporting requirements for members, and should continue to develop systems that measure market risk of members' positions.

BACHMANN RECOMMENDATION #9

Be prepared to streamline the handling of physical certificates. The desire of individual investors or institutions to hold physical certificates need not slow down an accelerated settlement process. Because the trend is toward fewer and fewer investors taking physical delivery of certificates, we have come to the conclusion that it is not necessary to immobilize certificates at this time. However, should certificate processing prove a barrier to implementation of these recommendations, then as a minimum, investors holding securities should be required to deliver them before entering a sell transaction.

SIA Comment SIA concurs with the Task Force's conclusion that (to reduce risk and increase safety and soundness) ". . .it is not necessary to immobilize certificates at this time." SIA believes that systemic risk emanating from retail clients selling certificates which are not in the system is small, and does not contribute significantly to the risks addressed in the report.

While certificate processing may be cumbersome and inefficient, there is no apparent evidence that the retail investor's selling
securities before returning them to the system, or failing to deposit
them in the system before settlement date, represents systemic risk
to the marketplace. In addition:

> The number of investors requiring certificates has declined sig-
> nificantly over time, and can be expected to continue to
> decline with industry efforts directed to that goal.

> Financial intermediaries and industry utilities continue to
> develop capabilities to effect street-side settlements where
> retail investors have failed to deliver certificates on, or prior to,
> settlement date.

> Physical certificates are subject to the risk of being lost or
> stolen, but this is a risk assumed by retail investors or their bro-
> kers. It is not a systemic risk.

The Task Force "...strongly encourages the SEC to explore the
possibility of requiring retail investors to return their certificates to the
system before trading can occur." SIA believes such an effort is
unnecessary at this time and such a requirement would create undue
hardship on retail investors. Markets often move quickly, and
investors who hold certificates outside the system would be preclud-
ed from exercising the right to immediately liquidate their holdings.
SIA concurs with the Task Force's conclusions that the physical movement of securities is inefficient and immobilization should
be the preferred route for U.S. securities markets. SIA will continue
to work with industry members and utilities to accomplish this goal
through education of investors regarding the inconvenience and
their risk associated with physical certificates.

BACHMANN RECOMMENDATION #10

Monitor flipping. "Flipping" is the practice of selling into an
underwriter's syndicate bid. It is a violation of underwriting
agreements and can destabilize a public offering. Flipping
presently is being monitored through delivery of physical certificates. The ability to monitor this practice should not be lost
in a certificateless environment.

SIA Comment SIA supports the Task Forces's recommendation that the ability to monitor "flipping" should not be lost in a certificateless environment.

The present practice of monitoring flipping, where manual methods are used for tracking physical certificates during a new public offering, represents an obstacle to the Task Force's recommendation that all new securities issued be depository eligible and transactions be settled in a book-entry only environment. Flipping occurs when certain investors participate in new issues and immediately trade out the position. This can adversely affect the market during the stabilization period, and if not effectively monitored, can lead to increased costs of raising capital.

An industry committee addressing this concern has developed a number of alternatives for capturing relevant transaction information and concluded that capturing customer information and developing an automated new issue sub-account reporting system appears to be an effective solution. These alternatives are now in the conceptual design stage.

SIA believes strong regulatory support will be needed when the final design is available, and encourages the SEC to require SROs to provide that support so the flipping issue is not an obstacle to depository eligibility and book-entry processing.

The SIA letter also noted that T+1 comparison systems for products that do not yet compare on T+1 need to be implemented, and that various rules and regulations (discussed below) need to be reviewed carefully for reinterpretation before a T+3 settlement rule is implemented.

After reviewing the responses received regarding the Bachmann Task Force Report, the Securities and Exchange Commission proposed for comment Rule 15c6-1 under the 1934 Act, changing the settlement date for most corporate securities transactions from T+5 to T+3. After the comment period expired, in October of 1993, the Commission adopted new Rule 15c6-1 under the Securities and Exchange Act of 1934 establishing three business days as the standard timeframe for broker/dealer trades, effective June 1, 1995. The Rule excludes municipal securities transactions, but the SEC asked the Municipal Securities Rulemaking Board to implement a rule to change the settlement time for municipal trades to T+3 at the same time as implementation of Rule 15c6-1. It is expected, therefore, that municipal securities transactions will settle within the same T+3 settlement timeframe as corporate securities effective June 1, 1995.

Rule 15c6-1: T+3 Settlement On October 16, 1993, the Securities and Exchange Commission adopted Rule 15c6-1, which established three business days as the standard settlement timeframe for broker/dealer trades, effective June 1, 1995. The precise wording of the Rule is as follows:[5]

240.15c6-1 Settlement Cycle (a) Except as provided in paragraph (b) of this section, a broker or dealer shall not effect or enter into a contract for the purchase or sale of a security (other than an exempted security, government security, municipal security, commercial paper, bankers' acceptances, or commercial bills) that provides for payment of funds and delivery of securities later than the third business day after the date of the contract unless otherwise expressly agreed to by the parties at the time of the transaction.

(b) Paragraph (a) of this section shall not apply to contracts:

(1) for the purchase or sale of limited partnership interests that are not listed on an exchange or for which quotations are not disseminated through an automated quotation system of a registered securities association;

(2) for the sale for cash of securities by an issuer to an underwriter pursuant to a firm commitment offering registered under the Securities Act of 1933, or the sale to an initial purchaser by a broker/dealer participating in such offering; or

(3) for the purchase or sale of securities that the Commission may from time to time, taking into account then existing market practices, exempt by order from the requirements of paragraph (a) of this rule, either unconditionally or on specified terms and conditions, if the Commission determines that such exemption is consistent with the public interest and the protection of investors.

---

[5] Reprinted from the Federal Register, Vol. 58, No. 196, October 13, 1993.

WHAT THE RULE INCLUDES AND EXCLUDES

WHICH SECURITIES TRANSACTIONS DOES THE RULE INCLUDE?

Securities and Exchange Commission (SEC) Rule 15c6-1 (the Rule) establishes three business days as the standard settlement timeframe (T+3 Settlement) for broker/dealer trades, effective June 1, 1995.

The Rule includes broker/dealer transactions in corporate fixed income and equity securities, limited partnership interests listed on an exchange, securities issued by investment companies, and private-label mortgage backed securities. To-be-announced (TBA) trades of mortgage pass-through securities are required to be settled within three days after a specific pool is identified for delivery under the contract.

WHICH SECURITIES TRANSACTIONS ARE EXCLUDED FROM THE RULE?

The Rule excludes broker/dealer transactions in exempted securities, government securities, municipal securities,[6] commercial paper, bankers' acceptances, commercial bills, limited partnership interests not listed on an exchange, new issues of securities sold for cash pursuant to a firm commitment offering,[7] and mortgage backed securities issued by government agencies and government sponsored enterprises. There are certain other securities transactions (e.g., listed option contracts) that are unaffected by the Rule since they already settle within the timeframes designated by the Rule.

---

[6] The SEC has asked the Municipal Securities Rulemaking Board to develop a plan to have municipal securities settle in the same timeframe and on the same effective date as securities subject to Rule 15c6-1. In August 1994, the Municipal Securities Rulemaking Board filed with the SEC proposed amendments to MSRB rules G-12 and G-15, which establish three business days as the standard settlement timeframe for regular-way transactions in municipal securities to be effective on the same date that SEC Rule 15c6-1 becomes effective.

[7] The Rule permits the Commission to exempt, by order, additional securities transactions from the scope of the Rule. As of the date of this publication, the securities transactions listed above are exempt. Industry participants, however, are currently discussing a number of open issues with the Commission such as:

Consideration should be given to eliminating the present exemption for new issues if the Commission and the Industry find ways to resolve the concerns related to delivery of a prospectus at the time of a new issue sale.

Consideration should be given to exempting International securities and permitting them to be settled within the settlement date convention of the country of origin.

In addition, the Rule allows brokers/dealers to agree that set-tlement will take place in more than three business days, when the agreement is expressed and reached at the time of the transaction. This provision is intended to apply only to unusual transactions.

STATUS OF MAJOR BUILDING BLOCKS

Industry participants believe that a number of "Building Blocks," i.e., processes that are necessary to facilitate T+3 settlement, should be in place prior to the implementation of Rule 15c6-1. These Building Blocks and their status as of September 1994 are discussed below:

> *Settle all transactions among financial intermediaries and between financial intermediaries and their institutional clients in book-entry form only.*

Status: In June 1993, the SEC approved uniform rule changes filed by the American Stock Exchange, Boston Stock Exchange, Chicago Stock Exchange (formerly Midwest), National Association of Securities Dealers, New York Stock Exchange, Pacific Stock Exchange, and Philadelphia Stock Exchange. These rule changes mandate book-entry settlement of transactions between financial intermediaries in depository eligible securities with limited excep-tions permitted. The rule changes became effective August 10, 1993.[8]

In January 1993, the MSRB amended Rule G-12 (f)(ii) to require book-entry settlement of essentially all interdealer transac-tion in depository eligible securities. In July of 1993 the MSRB amended Rule G-15 (d)(iii) to require all DVP/RVP customers' trans-actions in depository eligible securities to be settled by book-entry, with limited exceptions. In addition, in July of 1994 the MSRB amendment to Rule G-15(d)(ii)[9] to require essentially all DVP/RVP customer transactions that are eligible to be confirmed/acknowl-

---

[8] Securities Exchange Act, Order Approving Changes Relating to the Book-Entry Settlement of Securities Transactions; Release No.34-32455; File Nos. SR-Amex-93-07; SR-BSE-93-08; SR-MSE-93-03; SR-NASD-93-11; SR-NYSE-93-13; SR-PSE-93-04; and SR-PHIX-93-09, dated June 11. 1993.

[9] MSRB Reports Volume 14, Number 2, March 1994.

edged in a confirmation/acknowledgement system operated by a registered clearing agency, became effective.

MAKE ALL NEW SECURITIES DEPOSITORY ELIGIBLE

Status: In August 1994, the MSRB filed with the SEC proposed amendments to MSRB Rule G-34 which require that brokers, dealers, and municipal securities dealers apply for depository eligibility within one business day of the date of sale of a new issue municipal security. The proposed rule change exempts (i) issues not meeting the eligibility criteria of the depository and (ii) issues maturing in 60 days or less. It also provides a temporary exemption until July 1, 1996, for issues under $1 million in par value.

The Legal and Regulatory Subgroup of the U.S. Working Committee of the Group of Thirty is drafting a model rule, to be adopted by all exchanges and the NASD, which would require depository eligibility for exchange listed and NASDAQ quoted issues. The draft rule would generally require each exchange and the NASD to receive a representation from the issuer prior to listing that the issue is acceptable for deposit in a securities depository registered as a clearing agency under the Securities Exchange Act of 1934. Until the "Flipping" issue is resolved, this representation will not mean that every new issue will be immediately required to be transferred by book-entry only. The current draft rule proposes that a new issue will be deemed accepted by a securities depository, eligible for book-entry transfer and therefore required to be transferred by book-entry only, on one of three dates:

1. On the date the issue is deposited and credited to the account of the managing underwriter; or

2. If the issue is not so deposited on the initial distribution date, on a date selected by the managing underwriter within 3 months after the initial distribution date; or

3. If such a date is not received by the depository from the managing underwriter, on the business date following the expiration of 3 months after the initial distribution date.

Once agreement is reached on the wording of the draft depository eligibility rule, it is expected that the exchanges and the NASD will take whatever steps are necessary to have their rule approved for filing with the SEC. *Please note that this current draft is subject to further revision.*

FLIPPING

Status: "Flipping" is the practice of selling securities into the managing underwriter's syndicate bid in the period immediately following the effectiveness of an initial public offering. Flipping is presently monitored through the delivery of physical certificates. In May 1993, the Flipping Focus Group Design Committee was established to develop alternative solutions for monitoring flipping in an automated environment. The Committee has recommended that DTC develop an IPO Tracking System, and create an omnibus account to maintain IPO positions. The Committee's report defines how the proposed IPO Tracking System could operate, and discusses proposed reporting requirements for broker/dealers and agent banks. The report was distributed in August 1994 to the brokerage and banking communities for comment and to broaden support for this proposal. After receiving industry comments and appropriate action from the regulating agencies, the Committee intends to ask DTC to begin developing detailed specifications.

TRADE DATE PLUS ONE (T+1) COMPARISON

Status: In August 1993, National Securities Clearing Corporation (NSCC) implemented a new comparison system for municipal securities in which trade data is compared on the evening of trade date, and the results are reported back to dealers on T+1. There still exists, however, concern over the relatively low percentage of municipal trades that actually compare on the night of trade date. The MSRB is working with the agencies responsible for enforcement of MSRB rules to arrange for a special enforcement effort on rule G-12(f)(i).

NSCC has filed regulatory changes that mandate the acceleration of trade input submission of Corporate Bonds and Unit Investment Trusts to trade date, from trade date plus one, to enable T+1 comparison for these products. Implementation is scheduled for October 1994.

An on-line comparison system has been developed at the New York Stock Exchange (NYSE) to further streamline the trade comparison process. In November 1993, the NYSE proposed that a Trade Date Comparison System should be implemented by June 1995. This program is being implemented in conjunction with the National Securities Clearing Corporation and the American Stock Exchange (ASE). Trade Date Comparison is part of the NYSE's technology plan, and the Exchange has already begun to implement intraday comparison systems.[10]

REQUIRE AN INTERACTIVE ID PROCESS

Status: The existing ID and international ID systems were replaced by a single, new interactive system in June 1994 with SEC approval. Except for changes to the ID processing schedule, and to ID trade input edit routines, all features of the new system will be optional.[11] Current users may choose to use the new interactive features or remain in the current batch mode. This system will deal with front office issues and provide the necessary link to back office processing. The new ID system will contain several enhanced functions as requested by users.

Industry participants have organized two advisory committees related to ID and T+3 implementation. The first committee will recommend cut off times for the new system to facilitate T+3 settlement, and will also review supporting regulations. Representation on this committee comes from the broker/dealer, banking and investment manager communities. The second committee will suggest changes to the current ID manual in order to better reflect a general use of ID confirmations for the confirmation of any type of security. The composition of this committee consists of representatives from the broker/dealer community.

Settle all transactions among financial intermediaries and between financial intermediaries and their institutional clients in Same Day Funds.

---

[10] Securities exchange Act Release No.34-34153, File No. SR-NYSE-94-08; date June 3, 1994 and Securities Exchange Act Release No. 34-34298; File No. SR-Amex-94-13; dated July 1, 1994.

[11] Securities Exchange Act Release No. 34-34199, File No. SR-DTC-94-04; dated June 10, 1994; Order Granting Accelerated Approval of a Proposed Rule Change to Implement the Interactive Capabilities and the Electronic Mail Features of the Enhanced Institutional Delivery System.

Status: In July of 1992, DTC and NSCC distributed to the industry a "Same Day Funds Settlement Proposal for Industry Evaluation". In July of 1993, DTC and NSCC released to the industry a memorandum incorporating user recommendations for changes to the proposal. In July of 1994, DTC and NSCC released a memorandum "Same Day Funds Settlement System Conversion," which details plans for the conversion. DTC and NSCC expect full implementation of a Same Day Funds System by December of 1995, or shortly thereafter.

In August of 1993, the U.S. Working Committee of the Group of Thirty assembled a "Principal and Income Task Force" to present recommendations to the industry on how principal and income payments should be processed in a Same Day Fund environment. The recommendation of that task force, and the timeframe for implementation, have been endorsed by the Industry. These four recommendations include the following:[12]

1. Effective January 1, 1995, all new issues must be made depository eligible by meeting depository requirements, and must be structured so that all payments to depositories of principal and income must be made in same-day funds on payment date. Such issues can be certificate or book-entry-only (BEO) form. Underwriters must work with issuers to structure each new issue so that it meets depository eligibility criteria.

2. Effective for payments made on and after January 1, 1995, paying agents on all depository-eligible issues already outstanding prior to January 1, 1995, must pay to depositories all principal and income payments on such issues in same-day funds on payment date within the time schedule established by each depository. Recognizing that paying agents for certain issues may need to modify their current business arrangements to account for this change, depositories will continue to compensate paying agents with the same rate they now realize as a result of the agents' paying municipal interest, and municipal

---

[12] DTC and NSCC "Same Day Funds Settlement (SDFS) System Conversion," July 29,1994.

and corporate redemption payments to depositories in same-day funds on payment date.

Once the securities industry converts to same-day funds settlement for all securities transactions, depositories will not have funds available for investment to pay these rebates to paying agents, since depositories intend to pay their participants all payments due on payment date in same-day funds. Recognizing that depository participants will realize the benefit of receiving all their expected payments in same-day funds on payment date, depositories will charge their participants, proportionate to each participant's holding in each issue for which a rebate applies, the funds needed to pay the rebate. Effective for payments made on or after August 1, 1996, these rebate payments to paying agents will end.

This recommendation does not apply to existing payments of corporate interest, dividend, and reorganization payments where the paying agent already pays depositories in same-date funds on payment date. Such payments are not subject to interest earning rebates. This recommendation does, however, require that 100% of corporate interest, dividend, and reorganization payments be paid to depositories on the payment date in same-day funds.

3. Effective for payments made on and after January 1, 1995, paying agents must make same-day funds payments to depositories on payment date within the time schedule established by each depository. Each depository will pay its participants all payments due on payment date in same-day funds. To do so, each depository must receive all payments due from paying agents prior to the depository's cut-off time for allocation of such payments.

4. Paying agents must make arrangements with each depository to provide, prior to or on the morning of payment date, CUSIP number identification of each issue for which payment is being sent, as well as the respective dollar amount of payment for each issue. Notifications of payment details are to be made using automated communication unless a paying agent, for a particular payment date, is making payments for 10 issues or fewer. This recommendation would commence with payments made on or after January 1, 1995.

DTC anticipates broad compliance with the Task Force recommendations, and has embarked upon an education campaign to notify participants of procedural and systems changes affecting them.

T+3 SETTLEMENT CONVERSION SCHEDULE

National Securities Clearing Corporation (NSCC) has scheduled the conversion to a three-day (T+3) settlement for June 9-12, 1995.[13] NSCC arrived at this particular schedule by working with an industry "T+3 Advisory Committee." This schedule is believed to be necessary as part of the acceleration of today's T+5 settlement process to T+3, so that one day's trades will not settle before a prior day's trades. According to NSCC, the conversion will involve two double-day settlements. The first double-day settlement scheduled for Friday, June 9, will incorporate trades from Friday June 2 (the last five-day settlement day), and Monday, June 5 (four-day settlement). The second double-day settlement on Monday, June 12, will include trades from Tuesday, June 6 (four-day settlement), and Wednesday, June 7 (the first three-day settlement).

T+3 CONVERSION SCHEDULE - JUNE 1995

Trade Date	Settlement Cycle	Settlement Date
June 2 Friday	5 Day	June 9 Friday
June 5 Monday	4 Day	June 9 Friday
June 6 Tuesday	4 Day	June 12 Monday
June 7 Wednesday	3 Day	June 12 Monday

IMPACT OF RULE CHANGE ON SECURITIES PROCESSING

The rule change will have a very significant impact on the operations, systems, sales, regulatory, and finance departments of securities firms. Let's take a look at these departments and some of the steps that are necessary to prepare for the implementation of the new rule.

---

[13] Readers should contact NSCC to be certain there are no changes to this schedule since the publication of this book.

OPERATIONS

T+3 settlement requires significant changes to operations practices and procedures prior to implementation of the rule. Operations departments should review at least the following areas and maintain contact with clearing corporations, depositories, and self-regulatory organizations to assure that necessary changes to procedures are implemented within regulated timeframes:

1. Review and revise procedures for NSCC's T+1 Comparison changes and the depositories' Depository Eligibility rules and institutional delivery procedures.

2. Review and revise procedures to accommodate exchange floor operations changes for intra-day comparison.

3. Notify all transfer agents of the need to accelerate the transfer process and measure progress.

4. Revise procedures to accelerate the correction process for order entry changes, e.g., account number, name and address, money errors, security description, buy versus sell, quantity, and security number.

5. Revise all operations control "street-side" reports to add new standards and monitor progress and business changes.

6. Revise all operations customer information reports to add new standards and monitor progress and business changes.

7. Revise all operations control regulatory capital charge reports to add new standards and monitor progress and business changes.

8. Revise all rule 15c3-3 possession and control processing procedures.

9. Revise all affected branch office procedures for processing and compliance.

10. Review all changes to procedures with legal department and self-regulatory organizations.

INFORMATION SYSTEMS

The Information Systems departments in firms have a very difficult task to prepare for T+3 settlement. They must begin taking the following steps as soon as possible in order to re-write the major systems that are impacted by T+3 settlement:

1. Develop a work plan by asking all users to identify internal and external business functions and tasks impacted by the T+3 settlement rule changes.

2. Identify all jobs for all systems that derive a settlement date or reference/use "trade date plus" or a "settlement date minus" computation or date.

3. Build a dictionary using automated search utilities to include (a) all T+3 file field names for trade and settlement date, (b) all T+3 copy book labels for trade and settlement date, and (c) all internal program labels for trade and settlement date.

4. Identify, using automated tools, by program, all lines of code that reference trade or settlement dates and trade or settlement date calculations.

5. Develop initial estimates for modifying and testing impacted programs; e.g., start date, end date, number of man days required.

6. Develop scripts and test plans to modify systems used for internal processing for trade entry, figuration, comparison, cancellation/correction, and commission billing.

7. Develop scripts and test plans to modify systems used for internal processing for trade settlement; e.g., continuous net settlement, depository eligible securities, and physical securities processing.

8. Develop scripts and test plans to modify systems used for internal processing for general ledger updating.

9. Develop scripts and test plans to modify all systems used to interface with exchanges, clearing corporations, depositories, and other external feeds.

10. Modify all programs, test all modifications, review results of tests with internal audit and finally, move programs into production.

SALES

The sales and trading areas of firms have the most direct interaction with retail and institutional customers. These areas must prepare to review current practices and procedures related to customer behavior, and educate the internal workforce and their customers as to the reason for the rule and changes that will be coming that impact customer behavior. Here are some of the steps that the sales and trading areas should take:

1. Review and analyze customer purchase, sales and payment practices and related firm procedures to determine how to better meet customer needs in a shortened settlement timeframe.

2. Develop incentives for targeted accounts to make payments sooner.

3. Develop incentives for the sales force to have customers pay sooner.

4. Review potential confirmation processing alternatives, such as centralized production versus decentralized production, and implement systems changes necessary to produce and send confirmations sooner than is the case today.

5. Review the use of vendors other than the U.S. mail to deliver confirmations to clients.

6. Revise automated systems to generate "payment due" information on-line to notify customers immediately after trade execution.

7. Consider the introduction of new technology for payment processing; e.g., ACH transfers, electronic fund transfers, home banking by computer and telephone, automated billing systems, electronic mail, and pre-authorized checks.

8. Develop education plans for retail customers, institutional customers, and any internal sales support staff.

9. Provide a special "help desk" for information for firm personnel and customers.

10. Review all procedures to coordinate with the firm's marketing plans.

REGULATORY AND COMPLIANCE

The Securities and Exchange Commission, the Federal Reserve, the Municipal Securities Rulemaking Board and various self-regulatory organizations have changed and/or may change certain regulations or review procedures to be effective with the implementation of rule 15c6-1. The regulatory and compliance area of the firm should take the following steps to prepare for the new rule:

1. Review all operations changes with various SROs to ensure compliance with regulations.

2. Review all information systems department changes to assure compliance with regulations related to the new rule.

3. Review all sales and trading department changes to assure compliance with the new rule.

4. Review all branch office procedures and customer account forms to assure compliance with the new rule.

5. Review proposed regulatory monitoring procedures by enforcement agencies.

FINANCE AND ACCOUNTING

The impact of shortened settlement could have an adverse impact on interest expense and market or credit risk of firms. The Finance and Accounting areas of firms should take the following steps to prepare for T+3 implementation:

1. Determine and minimize potential interest expense by reviewing customer payment trends, securities sales practices, and revising appropriate procedures and policies to avoid potential interest and expense.

2. Determine and minimize the impact on cash debits by reviewing retail and institutional customers' purchase practices, and implementing new procedures to accelerate payment from customers.

3. Minimize risk and exposure by developing procedures to monitor firm exposure in a T+3 settlement environment, and implement procedures to limit exposure.

4. Review and revise all procedures impacting rule 15c3-3 (possession and control requirements and reserve formula calculation) and rule 15c3-1 (net capital calculations).

5. Assure that all procedures are reviewed with appropriate self-regulatory organizations.

REGULATORY ISSUES POTENTIALLY IMPACTED BY RULE 15c6-1

The Securities and Exchange Commission (SEC), the Municipal Securities Rulemaking Board (MSRB), and various self-regulatory organization (SROs) have extensive regulations that govern securities processing in the U.S. These regulations have been issued for the protection of U.S. investors and to maintain the financial integrity of U.S. capital markets. Implementation of SEC rule 15c6-1 and the equivalent MSRB rule may require amendment or reinterpretation of some of these regulations.

A number of the more important regulations that industry participants are reviewing, a brief description of the regulations, the issues presented relative to SEC and MSRB T+3 settlement rules, and some possible alternatives are presented in Figure 24-1.

RULE	DESCRIPTION	ISSUES	POSSIBLE ALTERNATIVES
SEC 15c3-3 (processing)	15c3-3(d) – Requirement to Reduce Securities to Possession or Control. **SEC Release 34-9922, January 2, 1973 states:** The time at which instructions must be issued to the cashiering section to acquire possession or control or the time at which such instructions may be released to the cashiering section are as follows: (1) In the case of purchases of securities by customers; on or before the business day following settlement date or the business day following actual date of receipt of payment whichever is later. (2) In the case of sales of securities by customers; not earlier than the close of business on the third business day before settlement date, which is deemed to allow adequate time for processing securities for pending deliveries.	Changing the time frames will mean a reprogramming effort by most firms but this is an expected effort with the mandate of T+3. Shortening the time frame may be restrictive for some firms who will continue to need time to gather securities for settlement.	1) Leave existing regulation the way it is. 2) Shorten the amount of time a broker/dealer can take to gather securities.
SEC 15c3-3 (m)	Requires close-out of a customer sale transaction for securities that have not been received within ten business days.	SEC states no change is contemplated.	1) Leave existing rule the way it is.
SEC 15c3-3 (e)	The formula prescribed by Rule 15c3-3(e) is driven primarily by settlement date money and securities' balances.	T+3 change may increase debit balances which would result in: 1) Increased capital requirement for those firms on the alternative method. 2) Increased reserve deposit.	1) Leave existing rule the way it is. 2) Provide capital relief.
SEC 15c3-1	Net Capital Requirements for Broker or Dealers. A broker/dealer must have a consistent policy of reflecting all transactions either on a trade date or a settlement date basis and must compute its net capital on the same basis as it uses in recording its transactions. However, if settlement date accounting is used and there is a "material difference" between trade date accounting, the net capital computation must reflect the trade date position for proprietary positions.	Change should have no impact on proprietary aspects of rule, but time periods for taking proprietary charges are likely to increase capital requirements.	Extend time period for taking proprietary capital charges by two business days.

FIGURE 24-1. SEC Regulations

RULE	DESCRIPTION	ISSUES	POSSIBLE ALTERNATIVES
SEC 15c3-1 (c)(2)(iv)(B)	Certain Unsecured and Partly Secured Receivables.	It is anticipated that customer debits may rise. Thus, deductions related to these accounts may also rise. Since certain of these deductions are determined by compliance with Regulation T, any changes to Regulation T could impact these deductions.	1) Leave existing rule the way it is. 2) Recommend change to rule and/or Regulation T to provide relief.
Federal Reserve Regulation T – Section 220.4 (c)(3)	Time Periods on Margin Accounts. Margin call must be satisfied within 7 business days after the margin deficiency was created or increased; "may be extended" upon application unless SRO believes creditor is not acting in good faith or has not adequately determined that exceptional circumstances warrant such action.	Should the time period be reduced? SEC staff is instructed to request Fed to consider requiring payment from customers within 2 business days after settlement date.	1) This is a trade date based requirement. Since creditors will have an exposure from T+3 instead of from T+5, the creditors' risk should be compressed by two business days. 2) No change. Customers need to have time to send in their margin payment. Firms should have the flexibility to control the situation with their clients. Firms would still be free to sell clients out. Requiring margin by T+5 will only result in more extension requests.
Regulation T Section 220.8 (b) (1)	Time Periods on Cash Accounts. Full cash payment is required within 7 business days "any non-exempt security was purchased" or when unissued or undistributed securities are made available for delivery.	Should the time period be reduced to T+5?	1) This is a trade date based requirement. Since creditors will have an exposure from T+3 instead of from T+5, the creditors' risk should be compressed by two business days. 2) No change. Customers need to have time to send in their payment. Firms should have the flexibility to control the situation with their clients. Firms would still be free to sell clients out. Requiring margin by T+5 will only result in more extension requests.
Regulation T Section 220.5 and 220.8	Extension Procedures.	Should firms be allowed to extend these deadlines?	Allow creditors the ability to grant extensions in-house for 30 days. Possible alternative: 10 days.
Regulation T Section 220.3 (e)	Payment Method – Permissible forms of payment include cash, check, draft or order payable upon presentation.	Should pair-offs be permitted in a cash account with DVP/RVP accounts? Should payment forms be expanded to include wire transfers (e.g. ACH)?	Allow payment forms to be expanded.
Rule 431 (f)(6)	Creditors must obtain required margin or mark-to-market within 15 business days from date *deficiency occurs.*	Should this period be reduced?	1) Reduce to 13 business days. 2) No change.
SEC 10b-10	Customer confirmation rule – requires broker/dealer to send to a customer a written trade confirmation.	Shortening of settlement period will make it less likely that mailed confirmations arrive prior to settlement date. Use of alternative confirmation media, such as fax, telex, computer-to-computer or other electronic means will facilitate more timely trade confirmation.	1) Do nothing and rely on informal advice from the Division of Market Regulation that fax, telex and computer-to-computer are acceptable confirmation media. 2) Ask for explicit recognition of the acceptability of such media in the rule.

FIGURE 24-1. (*Continued*)

RULE	DESCRIPTION	ISSUES	POSSIBLE ALTERNATIVES
MSRB G-12 (b)(ii)(B)	Definition of settlement date.	Clean-Up.	Change from T+5 to T+3.
MSRB G-12 (b)(ii)(C)	Definition of settlement date for when, as and if issued transactions.	Should when issued settlement periods conform to other settlement periods or do when issued trades inherently need more time?	1) Leave at T+5. 2) Change to T+3.
MSRB G-12 (c)(iii)	Dealer confirmation rule for when issued trades of municipal securities.	Confirmations should be accelerated since settlement have been accelerated.	1) Leave at T+2. 2) Move to T+1.
MSRB G-12 (c)(i)	General dealer confirmation rule for municipal securities – currently T+1.	Confirmations should be accelerated since settlement have been accelerated. Enhanced systems might be needed to confirm on trade date.	1) Leave at T+1. 2) Move to trade date.
MSRB G-12 (d)	Broker comparisons – currently most notices between brokers are required to be sent by the next business day following discovery of a discrepancy.	Accelerated settlement might warrant accelerated notification of comparison discrepancies, etc. Enhanced systems might be needed to achieve same-day notifications.	1) Leave at one business day. 2) Change to same day.
MSRB G-12 (d)(iii)	In event broker doesn't receive confirm by T+4 (or T+6 in case of when issued trades) broker should seek to ascertain whether trade had occurred.	Clean-Up.	Move to T+2 and T+? for when issued days.
MSRB G-12 (h)	Close-out rule.	Should five day periods be shortened?	1) Leave as is. 2) Shorten to ? days.
MSRB G-15 (b)(ii)(B)	Definition of settlement date.	Clean-Up.	Change from T+5 to T+3
MSRB G-15 (c)(xii)(A)	Requires securities to be registered in customer's name or as customer directs.	Transfer in the case of physical securities might take longer than 3 business days to complete.	1) Leave rule as is.
MSRB G-15 (d)(C)(D)	Sets time frames for deliveries and confirmations in DVP and RVP transactions when a customer agent is involved.		
	(d)(C) – customer confirmation must be sent by end of T+1	In a T+3 environment, customers may need more time to contact their agent. But it would require enhanced systems to achieve same-day confirmations of trades.	1) Change rule to end of trade date from T+1. 2) Leave rule as is.
	(d)(D)(a),(b) – agent must receive instructions from customer by T+4.	Clean-Up.	1) Move instruction requirement from T+4 to T+2 or T+1.
Securities Act of 1933 – Section 2(10) and Section 5	The Securities Act appears to preclude separate mailings of confirmations and prospectuses.	Timely delivery of a final prospectus with confirmation for new issues has been a problem even under T+5. T+3 will make it more difficult to comply with current law in most cases.	1) Exempt IPOs from T+3. 2) Seek SEC rule to allow prospectus to be sent under cover. 3) Seek legislation to allow prospectus to follow confirmation under separate cover.
Securities Act of 1933 – Section 5	Prospectus Disclosure.	SEC staff directed to propose a disclosure requirement as to depository eligibility.	N/A

FIGURE 24-1. (*Continued*)

RULE	DESCRIPTION	ISSUES	POSSIBLE ALTERNATIVES
SEC Rule 15c6-1	Foreign Securities.	The Rule would require contractual settlement of all securities except those enumerated. No provision for foreign securities settling regular substantially longer than T+3.	1) Exempt foreign securities by order, consistent with Reg T Section 220.8(b)(i)(ii).
SEC Rule 15c6-1	New issues in fixed price underwritings are exempt.	This may cause secondary market fails of trades done on T+1.	1) Rescind exemption. 2) Clarify effect of when issued trading on T+1 and T+2.
SEC 17Ad-2	Guidelines for Transfer Agent turnaround, processing and forwarding of items. Every registered transfer agent (except when acting as an outside registrar) shall **turnaround within three business days of receipt at least 90% of all routine items** received for transfer during a month. Every registered transfer agent acting as an outside registrar shall **process at least 90% of all items received** during a month (1) by the opening of business on the next business day, in the case of items received at or before noon on a business day, and (2) by noon of the next business day, in the case of items received after noon on a business day.	Does turnaround time need to be changed under T+3?	1) Leave rule as is. 2) Strengthen rule.

FIGURE 24-1. (*Continued*)

CHAPTER 25

Same-Day Funds Settlement System and How It Will Work

The Report of the Bachmann Task Force on Clearance and Settlement Reform in the U.S. Securities Markets recommended that all transactions among financial intermediaries, and between financial intermediaries and their institutional clients, be settled in book-entry form only and paid for in same day-funds. At this time, the various regulators have passed appropriate rules to require settlement of all transactions among financial intermediaries and between financial intermediaries and their institutional clients in book-entry form only. The industry is now preparing to develop procedures to pay for them in same-day funds. The Depository Trust Company and the National Securities Clearing Corporation have undertaken a project to convert to a system to have all related payments made in same-day funds, and it is expected that implementation will occur in late 1995, or early 1996.

SAME-DAY FUNDS SETTLEMENT SYSTEM CONVERSION PLAN

The same-day funds conversion project, which is being undertaken jointly by DTC and NSCC, is intended to provide two major benefits: standardization of the form in which funds are settled and risk reduction.

Most participants have agreed that moving current next-day funds activity to same-day funds would be beneficial. It would simplify the cash management practices of firms that process both same-day and next-day funds settling securities, as well as reduce existing overnight exposure. More importantly, the proposed system will have significant risk management controls incorporated in its design.

DTC now processes securities deliveries for many different issue types through two different settlement systems, one that settles in same-day funds (SDFS), and the other in next-day funds (NDFS). DTC's NDFS system primarily services equities and corporate and municipal debt issues; its SDFS system primarily services commercial paper and other money market-like instruments. DTC will combine its NDFS and SDFS systems into a single SDFS system, using its current SDFS system as the base design. This approach should facilitate the conversion, since more than 300 DTC participants already use DTC's SDFS system.

NSCC currently operates a single next-day funds settlement system in which (with limited exceptions) the money settlement obligations of NSCC's participants are the net results of all NSCC activity. This includes primarily post-trade processing operations for transactions in equities, corporate and municipal bonds, and unit investment trusts, but also includes other operations, such as processing mutual fund purchase and redemption orders (Fund/SERV) among other services. NSCC will convert its settlement system in its entirety to a single same-day funds settlement system.

DTC's and NSCC's next-day funds settlement systems and operations are intertwined, reflecting the complementary nature of the functions each organization provides. As the nation's largest depository for corporate and municipal securities, DTC operations include the Institutional Delivery (ID) system, which enables financial institutions to communicate with their agent banks, directing them to receive and deliver securities on their behalf through DTC or elsewhere. NSCC, in addition to its other services, operates the industry's largest trade clearance and settlement system (its Continuous Net Settlement, or CNS, system), which serves as the primary clearing mechanism for, among other marketplaces, the New York Stock Exchange, the American Stock Exchange, and the National Association of Securities Dealers' NASDAQ system.

In the proposed system, DTC and NSCC will employ a mandatory netting procedure (which, with rare exceptions, is already in place in the form of mandatory cross-endorsement). Under this procedure, a participant's net debit at one organization will be netted against the amount of its net credit, if any, at the other organization. All end-of-day net debits and credits will be rolled up into one amount per participant for this purpose, regardless of the number of separate accounts the participant may have at NSCC or DTC.[1] Participants will continue to settle remaining obligations separately with DTC and NSCC.

Money settlement for DTC will follow the same procedures employed in DTC's current SDFS system; participants will either remit or receive Fedwire payments. Participants without direct access to the Fedwire system will employ settling banks. Settlement will occur through DTC's account at the Federal Reserve Bank of New York.

NSCC will expand its regional bank network to create a settling bank system. Each settling bank will settle with NSCC, on a net basis, on behalf of the participants using that bank. NSCC will consider, on a case-by-case basis, permitting individual participants to settle with NSCC outside of its settling bank system. NSCC expects, however, that with the exception of participants engaging solely in certain specialized activity (for instance, mutual fund distributors), virtually all participants will use the settling bank system. Payments to or from NSCC will be made via Fedwire through NSCC's account at a Federal Reserve member bank.

Both DTC's and NSCC's proposed SDFS systems are designed to address guidelines concerning credit risk and liquidity set forth in the Federal Reserve Board's 1992 Policy Statement on Payments System Risk. Accordingly, each would employ a number of risk management tools.

DTC will continue to employ a net debit cap applicable to each participant's net DTC debit to help ensure that it has sufficient liquidity to complete settlement in the event a participant fails to settle, due to temporary operational reasons or a late-day insolvency.[2]

---

[1]   Certain mutual fund activity may be excepted from this roll-up.

[2]   A participant's net credit at NSCC will not be used intra-day to offset, for net debit cap purposes, a net debit it might have at DTC.

DTC had previously proposed that net debit caps would range as high as $750 million, with each participant's individual net debit cap based on its actual net debit experience. Since that time, DTC's regulators have urged that the proposed liquidity controls take into account the possibility that certain net credits in a participant's account could be eliminated, if an issuer of Money Market Instruments (including commercial paper) became insolvent prior to settlement, and DTC reversed that day's MMI transactions pertaining to the issuer. In discussions with the industry on this topic, it was decided that DTC should limit a participant's largest possible net debit, via net debit caps that would reflect the provisional nature of the MMI credits. DTC had previously planned on modifying its net debit cap control some time after the SDFS conversion to address these concerns. DTC will now include the changes in the SDFS conversion.

DTC hopes that its liquidity needs will not rise above the previous projection of $1 billion, but the effect of the new net debit cap methodology has not been quantified and cannot be accurately estimated, without either conducting sophisticated studies, or actually constructing parts of the system. As soon as possible, DTC will study this issue in detail. At the present time, we believe it may be possible that $1 billion in total liquidity could support net debit caps that would exceed $750 million, possibly up to $900 million. If $1 billion in total liquidity suffices, DTC plans to secure it by requiring participants to contribute $400 million (in cash) to its Participants Fund (up from $350 million in previous proposals), while DTC obtains a $600 million line of credit (down from $650 million in previous proposals).

DTC also proposes to maintain its current SDFS control that requires a participant to maintain collateral in its account at least equal to its net settlement debit at all times until daily settlement is completed. DTC's collateralization controls will also be modified to acknowledge the possibility of MMI issuer failure reversals eliminating net credits in participants' accounts. DTC will guard against fluctuations in the value of collateral in its system with a schedule of haircuts on securities prices at the preceding business day's close: 10% for equities, 5% for corporate and municipal debt, 2%–5% for Money Market Instruments.[3]

---

[3] These are general guidelines. Variations will exist as described later in this document.

The proposed interface between DTC's system and NSCC's CNS system is of particular importance in regard to collateralization. NSCC's CNS system, which is currently available only for DTC-eligible securities, continually nets all trades due to settle the next day against each other, and against prior days' unsettled long and short positions in the same securities. As part of NSCC's guarantee of settlement of marketplace transactions in CNS-eligible securities, NSCC becomes the contra-party to each CNS transaction. NSCC participants obligated to deliver securities will deliver them to NSCC as free book-entry movements at DTC (sometimes referred to as "short covers"). Likewise, NSCC participants obligated to receive securities receive them from NSCC, also as free book-entry movements at DTC (sometimes referred to as "long allocations").

At the time DTC and NSCC released the July 1993 paper, there was concern that collateralizaiton controls could block a receive versus payment (RVP) in DTC, even when there existed an offsetting redelivery to CNS. DTC and NSCC had agreed to two measures to solve this problem: First, NSCC would provide a guarantee to DTC for these "turnaround" transactions, based upon the closing price of the securities three days earlier (assuming T+3 settlement for regular way trades had been implemented prior to the SDFS conversion); second, DTC would regard this guarantee as collateral substitute as necessary to allow the RVP to complete. DTC had originally planned to build a systemic procedure to link an RVP that could not complete due to collateralization controls to an existing CNS short cover. Based on studies conducted over the last few months, DTC believes that such a procedure would allow only 2-4 transactions each day to complete that otherwise would have been blocked. Given the modest benefit and substantial cost involved, DTC will defer such development and reanalyze the need for this procedure after implementation. In addition, DTC's studies indicate that participants do not appear to have "turnaround" deliveries blocked, even if NSCC's guarantee to DTC is based on the prior day's market value instead of three (or five) day-old values. Hence, NSCC's guarantees to DTC with respect to RVPs being turned around into CNS will be equal to the prior day's closing value for the issue (as opposed to their value based upon the three day old closing price). DTC and NSCC will continue to monitor the adequacy of this approach once the system is implemented. NSCC's guarantee to DTC with respect to other CNS deliveries (for instance, those made from a participant's start of day position at DTC) will remain as originally proposed, i.e., the prior day's closing value less an applicable haircut.

With respect to CNS long allocations, DTC will guarantee either to return the securities to NSCC, or to compensate NSCC for the loss of this collateral, if the receiving participant redelivers the securities. In such cases, DTC will guarantee NSCC the prior day's closing market value less an applicable haircut.

The DTC/NSCC cross-guarantees described above will eliminate NSCC's potential principal risk with respect to CNS long allocations—i.e., that the securities allocated might not be available to NSCC for close-out purposes, thus causing NSCC to lose the entire value of the securities, not just the difference between their market value and the related CNS debits. Because NSCC becomes the contra-party to each CNS transaction, however, NSCC will retain market risk with respect to CNS transactions. This market risk will continue to be covered, as it is today, by NSCC's Clearing Fund. NSCC is currently reviewing its method of taking CNS market risk into account for Clearing Fund purposes, and may propose changes to its Clearing Fund formula as a result of this review. Any such changes will be implemented independently of the same-day funds conversion.

CNS operations also give rise to the bulk of NSCC's potential short-term funding needs. As part of NSCC's guarantee to complete all CNS transactions of an insolvent participant, NSCC must receive and pay for all deliveries into the CNS system that correspond to the insolvent participant's guaranteed CNS receive obligations. NSCC's need to finance this activity will exist on the day of insolvency, and additional financing will be needed after the day of insolvency, to the extent that additional deliveries are made into CNS corresponding either to guaranteed CNS receive obligations that were scheduled to settle after the day of insolvency, or to open fail positions. The need for short-term funding would be reduced on the day of insolvency, to the extent that the insolvent participant has satisfied its CNS deliver obligations. After the day of insolvency, NSCC can expect to achieve similar reductions, to the extent that securities necessary to satisfy the insolvent participant's deliver obligations were made available to NSCC.

NSCC believes that its current committed liquidity resources should be sufficient to cover short-term funding needs in its new same-day funds settlement system in the event of the insolvency of a major participant. These resources consist primarily of Clearing Fund cash of approximately $200 million currently, and a $300 million committed line of credit secured by other Clearing Fund assets, and by deliveries into the CNS system that would otherwise have been allocated to the insolvent participant (or that had been allocated but were returned to NSCC). NSCC recognizes, however, that these resources may not be sufficient in the extreme case. Therefore, NSCC announced in July, 1993, that it intended to create an additional funding source by taking advantage of its ability to pledge, on an uncommitted basis, deliveries into the CNS system that remain available for pledge after the committed line of credit has been fully drawn down. In addition, NSCC will be authorized to seek financing from its broker/dealer participants on a voluntary basis. As a last resort contingency, NSCC will also be able, after the day of insolvency, to require participants who deliver in securities that would have been allocated to the insolvent, to temporarily take them back and finance them on behalf of NSCC until settlement of the offsetting close-out transactions. NSCC believes that it is extraordinarily unlikely that mandatory participant financing will ever be needed.

DTC's Participants Fund will be set at a level that, in most cases, would provide liquidity resources to complete settlement, without having to draw down lines of credit when a participant fails to settle for any reason. At this time, we expect that each participant will be required to deposit a minimum of $10,000. While some participants will need to deposit only $10,000, most will have to deposit additional amounts, based on the size of their net debits in the system weighted against other participants' net debits. This allocation apportions Fund deposits among participants in proportion to the liquidity requirements they generate for the system. Interest will be paid on Fund deposits, which will be invested overnight in repurchase agreements. Based on current activity levels, a $400 million cash Fund will provide liquidity to cover 98 out of 100 participants' final net settlement debits, without recourse to lines of credit. Greater activity levels could require a larger Fund.

DTC will maintain the Receiver-Authorized Delivery (RAD) control in a substantially modified form, giving receivers protection against improper high-valued deliveries to their accounts. RAD will apply to deliveries valued at or above $15 million; it will not apply to ID deliveries or CNS deliveries, which are based, respectively, on acknowledged and compared trades. Reclamations (returns of deliveries) will be subject to risk management controls, only if they equal or exceed $15 million.

DTC's securities processing system will be largely "closed" in that all securities received versus payment, including CNS deliveries by NSCC (long allocations), will not be permitted to be withdrawn, segregated or freely redelivered in the system (other than as free pledges)[4] until paid for at settlement. Free deliveries and withdrawals during the day could be completed, either after settlement, or from securities positions in participants' accounts that had neither been received versus payment that day nor received from CNS, e.g., start-of-day positions. Closing the system to that extent reduces credit risk to DTC in the event that a sharp market break leads to an insolvency. In addition, it reduces the risk of loss to DTC participants that did not conduct any business with a participant that becomes insolvent, focusing the market risk instead on those participants that made deliveries to the failing participant. Due to participants' financing needs, however, DTC will allow any participant to freely pledge into the system, prior to settlement, securities received versus payment that day, but only if the pledged securities are not otherwise needed to collateralize the participant's net debit at DTC.

DTC plans to employ a single processing schedule for all issue types, with a 3 P.M. (ET) cutoff for deliveries followed by a half-hour period for reclamations. This processing schedule will have an impact on the securities lending business, because it eliminates specific "stock lending" periods that exist in the NDFS system. It should be recognized that conversion to same-day funds settlement itself will have an impact on stock lending, since there will be less time to invest cash collateral. Many industry experts believe that the practices used in securities lending of DTC-eligible issues will come to

---

[4] MMI issues that are received versus payment will not be freely pledgeable until after settlement.

resemble those for the lending of government securities. In addition, based on participants' requests, DTC has also added a late delivery period that is similar to that employed in the current NDFS system. Deliveries entered after 3 p.m. will be accepted until 3:20 p.m., but will require receiver review and approval.

Since the July 1993 document, an industry committee, the Same-Day Funds Payment Task Force, commonly called the P&I Task Force, was formed to take up the issues surrounding the treatment of principal and income payments in an SDFS environment. Contained in this document is a reiteration of their recommendations. Participants and paying agents should be aware that the first phase of the "P&I Recommendations" will become effective January 1, 1995. At that time, all payments made to DTC by paying agents must be made in same-day funds by 2:30 p.m. on payment date. To promulgate this major aspect of the SDFS conversion, DTC has launched an extensive educational campaign. While all payment must be made to DTC in same-day funds beginning January 1, 1995, DTC will *not* allocate *all* payments to participants in same-day funds at that time. DTC will continue to allocate payments in the same manner as is done currently through its SDFS and NDFS systems until all issues are converted to SDFS in either late 1995, or early 1996. Once all issues are converted to SDFS, DTC plans to allow participants to withdraw P&I payments that have been credited to their settlement accounts intra-day, subject to application of the system's risk management controls.

Significant concern has arisen regarding underwriting procedures and DTC's previously proposed recycle (pend) methodology. Some underwriters expressed concern that they could lose control over the order of their deliveries, and that syndicate member deliveries could become blocked due to DTC's risk management controls. While this outcome may not always be avoidable, DTC has modified its proposal regarding recycle methodologies to give participants the ability to choose the procedure which best fits their business practice.

On the NSCC side, in addition to the market risk and liquidity issues discussed above, NSCC will need to address several other issues when it converts to same-day funds settlement. Primary among these are issues relating to NSCC's envelope settlement services, particularly its Envelope Settlement Service (ESS) and its Funds Only Settlement Service (FOSS). Currently, neither of these systems processes high-dollar transactions. However, industry response to the original same-day funds settlement proposal indicated that, in a same-day funds environment, participants might deliver physical money market instruments through the ESS system. In addition, participants could use FOSS to fold current high-dollar same-day funds charges into NSCC's overall net settlement. NSCC would view either of these developments as inappropriate, and will take steps to prohibit them.

CHAPTER 26

Future Changes in U.S. Clearance and Settlement Practices

Securities processing in the United States is undergoing dramatic change. In the previous chapters on implementation of T+3 settlement and Same Day Funds Settlement systems, I discussed a number of those major changes. Industry participants, however, are also considering other significant changes related to clearance and settlement, such as, an industry-wide glossary, development of automated procedures for retail registration alternatives, and cross-margining or cross-collateralization procedures.

INDUSTRY-WIDE GLOSSARY

Demands for more comprehensive information about securities have accelerated in recent years due to rapid product innovation, escalating competition and regulation, and an investing public interested in increasingly sophisticated instruments. From a processing perspective, concerns about risk reduction are shrinking timeframes for completing securities transactions, making the provision of accurate information about securities more time-critical than ever.

The securities environment is characterized by tens of thousands of issuers offering millions of instruments world-wide, without counting the explosion in secondary products derived from these instruments. Cross-border activity has accelerated greatly, with increasing interest in emerging capital markets and in the instruments of issuers in emerging economies. Instruments vary widely in type, properties, processing requirements, and regulatory constraints. Issuers and underwriters are demonstrating increasing creativity in defining instruments with novel properties. Characteristics traditionally associated with only one type of product are now appearing regularly with other product types.

The securities information environment is characterized by a large number of commercial vendors supplying overlapping, and often inconsistent, data in diverse non-standard formats. The vendors themselves have not always been able to meet their customers' demands for more detailed, more accurate, and more timely information about an ever-broadening range of securities. As a result, the industry has experienced a proliferation of narrow information products and specialized information vendors offering inconsistent, and sometimes contradictory, information. Information about significant parts of the market remains sparse, unreliable, or too costly. Some data is unobtainable in electronic form at any price.

Organizations in the financial services sector gather the data they need to process securities transactions into an electronic master file, or glossary. Glossary support staffs in each financial services organization research securities from electronic, published, and human sources. They map, merge, edit, and scrub the available data to meet their systems' needs for format and content. Staffs range from part-time functions in the smallest organizations, to dedicated teams numbering dozens of people in large retail brokerage firms. To minimize storage costs and per-security vendor fees, most organizations regularly purge inactive securities from their glossaries. An organization may research and add 150,000 securities each year, and during the same period, delete 100,000 that are inactive.

Since these glossaries are accessed each day by virtually all processing systems, the impact of error or omission is great. Yet, traditional data sources—and many of the best, newest products—are geared to interpretation by securities professionals rather than computers. Much information is not available in machine-readable form, and must be researched, interpreted, and encoded into glossaries by hand. Complete, reliable information may not be available from real-time sources, increasing risk to any financial services organization involved with the security.

Even if all the data now available to securities professionals were adapted for real-time use by computers, problems would persist. An investing public, less knowledgeable than securities professionals, requires different forms of information and greater levels of explanation. Despite their importance for customer and street-side processing, few organizations' glossaries are capable of maintaining all kinds of information about all kinds of investments, leading to inconsistencies and inaccuracies even within a single organization. Few organizations' staffs and systems are able to access the entire body of available information about all types of securities. Viewed across the industry as a whole, these constraints and deficiencies magnify into a serious information problem that is impacting all financial services organizations.

Industry participants are now proposing the development of an Industry-wide Glossary to focus on information needed by operational processes, including all data needed to process any event occurring in the life of a security, from confirming the first trade in the security, to recording its redemption, expiration, or other event terminating activity in the security. All issues in the Glossary must have a standard reference number, a standard product classification based on the actual features and processing characteristics of the instrument, and a standard description that satisfies all regulatory requirements for customer disclosure of the security. Announcement services, history, and schedule information about dividends, interest, calls, puts, amortization, optional redemptions, and corporate actions must also be provided. The Glossary must track worthless issues, and provide regulatory and compliance data. Agent information must also be included. The Glossary should not be purged of inactive or defunct securities.

The benefits of such a Glossary to the industry are numerous. All information would be available real-time, in machine-readable form. Securities would be defined and described by their innate characteristics. New types of securities, unable to fit any existing description, would be identified when the security is defined to the Glossary, and new classifications based on unique combinations of data elements would be defined immediately to the Glossary, for use by all subscribers. In addition to improving the availability and timeliness of information, an Industry-Standard Glossary for industry-wide use would simplify users' glossary support operations and improve productivity, by centralizing most research and coding efforts into an industry-owned, and industry-controlled, utility function. Users' computer systems could also be simplified, since many of the changes to meet new regulations or to accommodate new types of securities could be undertaken once through the Glossary, relieving subscribers of the need to make changes individually.

AUTOMATED RETAIL REGISTRATION ALTERNATIVES

Registered securities require transfer services to protect the owner in whose name the securities are registered, and to protect the corporation which issued only a specific quantity of securities. When a client of a securities firm purchases registered securities, the client has the option of allowing the shares to remain in the account with the securities firm for safekeeping, or to take delivery of the securities. Generally, if the securities firm retains the customer's certificates, they are stored in the firm's vault or at a depository, and registered in the firm's name. This is commonly referred to as being registered in "street name." If the client wished to receive the registered securities and to have them registered in their name, registration and delivery instructions must be given by the client to the securities firm. The securities firm generally then advises the transfer agent via a transfer instruction, which indicates how the shares are to be registered.

Industry participants are now reviewing an electronic system to provide additional alternatives to retail investors for registration. Advances in technology now permit electronic communication between broker/dealers, transfer agents, and depositories to facilitate a system that might have the following components:

1. Customers and/or broker/dealers could be allowed to request a certificate electronically or otherwise at the time of initial purchase.

2. Electronic acknowledgment that shares have been registered in book-entry form could be provided, with a record of ownership forwarded to the customer. Electronic communication between issuer/transfer agents and depositories would be standardized.

3. Investors could be able to notify issuers to move shares from the books of the issuer to the books of the investor's broker/dealer (who may not be the same broker/dealer who initially purchased the shares on behalf of the customer).

CROSS-MARGINING/CROSS COLLATERALIZATION

After the market breaks of 1987 and 1989, industry participants began reviewing the potential benefits of establishing cross-margining arrangements and cross-collateralization arrangements between clearing entities, to reduce member collateral requirements and to mitigate risk of loss to clearing entities. These efforts are continuing, and the author expects continued growth of cross-collateralization and cross-margining efforts throughout the industry.

CROSS-COLLATERALIZATION

Cross-collateralization is the ability of dual members of two or more clearing entities to have excess collateral at one clearing entity be able to meet collateral obligations at another clearing entity.

CROSS-MARGINING

Cross-margining takes the form of, for example, options and futures clearing houses sharing position information for common clearing members, and calculating an overall margin requirement based on the combined position. It provides financing relief and enhances risk management to the options and futures markets.

There are over twenty different clearing corporations in the United States today for securities and futures, and the author believes that cross-margining and/or cross-collateralization efforts by the industry will be a significant benefit to maintaining the financial integrity of the U.S. marketplace.

INDEX